Public Communication and Behavior

VOLUME 2

Public Communication and Behavior

VOLUME 2

Edited by

GEORGE COMSTOCK
School of Public Communications
Syracuse University
Syracuse, New York

ACADEMIC PRESS, INC.
Harcourt Brace Jovanovich, Publishers
San Diego   New York   Berkeley   Boston
London   Sydney   Tokyo   Toronto

COPYRIGHT © 1989 BY ACADEMIC PRESS, INC.
ALL RIGHTS RESERVED.
NO PART OF THIS PUBLICATION MAY BE REPRODUCED OR
TRANSMITTED IN ANY FORM OR BY ANY MEANS, ELECTRONIC
OR MECHANICAL, INCLUDING PHOTOCOPY, RECORDING, OR
ANY INFORMATION STORAGE AND RETRIEVAL SYSTEM, WITHOUT
PERMISSION IN WRITING FROM THE PUBLISHER.

ACADEMIC PRESS, INC.
San Diego, California 92101

United Kingdom Edition published by
ACADEMIC PRESS LIMITED
24-28 Oval Road, London NW1 7DX

ISBN 0-12-543202-X (alk. paper)
ISSN 0887-932X
This publication is not a periodical and is not
subject to copying under CONTU guidelines.

PRINTED IN THE UNITED STATES OF AMERICA
89 90 91 92   9 8 7 6 5 4 3 2 1

Contents

Contributors ix
Preface xi
Contents of Previous Volume xiii

Exposure to Television as a Cause of Violence
BRANDON S. CENTERWALL

    I. Television and Homicide in South Africa, Canada, and the United States, 1945–1974 1
   II. Testing Falsifiable Hypotheses 24
  III. Natural Exposure to Television as a Cause of Aggression: A Review of the Literature 48
        References 53

Newsflow and Democratic Society in an Age of Electronic Media
DENNIS K. DAVIS AND JOHN P. ROBINSON

      I. Introduction 60
     II. Journalism in the Information Age 63
    III. Toward a Theory of News and Newsflow: Three Theories of News 66
    IV. A Reexamination of Early Newsflow Research 75
     V. Current Research on News 77
    VI. Our News Comprehension Research 83
   VII. Toward "User Friendly" Journalism 95
 VIII. Recommendations for Future Research 99
        References 100

The Forms of Television and the Child Viewer
ALETHA C. HUSTON AND JOHN C. WRIGHT

I.	Introduction	103
II.	An Attribute of the Medium: Television Forms	106
III.	The Child as an Active Viewer	111
IV.	Cognitive Processing: The Match between the Child and the Television Material	116
V.	Television Forms and Social Behavior	147
VI.	Conclusion	151
	References	153

Sexually Violent Media, Thought Patterns, and Antisocial Behavior
NEIL M. MALAMUTH

I.	Introduction	160
II.	Theorized Effects	163
III.	Media Characteristics and Diffusion	167
IV.	Sexually Violent Media and Arousal	169
V.	Media Exposure, Thought Patterns, and Antisocial Behavior	180
VI.	Other Relevant Data	194
VII.	Summary and Conclusions	197
	References	198

Parallel Content Analysis: Old Paradigms and New Proposals
W. RUSSELL NEUMAN

I.	Introduction: Weber, Lasswell, Lazarsfeld, and Hovland	205
II.	The Strategy of Parallel Content Analysis	209
III.	Rethinking the Communications Effects Paradigm	213
IV.	Emerging Models for Communications Research	235
V.	Parallel Content Analysis	253
	References	280

Nuclear War on Television: The Impact of *The Day After*

STUART OSKAMP

I.	Introduction	292
II.	The Variety of Research Studies	297
III.	The Early Instant-Analysis Reports	301
IV.	The More Comprehensive Studies	307
V.	Findings of the Comprehensive Studies	309
VI.	Discussion	343
	References	348

Index 353

Contributors

Numbers in parentheses indicate the pages on which the authors' contributions begin.

BRANDON S. CENTERWALL (1), Departments of Epidemiology and Psychiatry, University of Washington, Seattle, Washington 98195

DENNIS K. DAVIS (59), Department of Speech Communication, Southern Illinois University, Carbondale, Illinois 62901

ALETHA C. HUSTON (103), Center for Research on the Influence of Television on Children (CRITC), Department of Human Development, University of Kansas, Lawrence, Kansas 66045

NEIL M. MALAMUTH (159), Communications Studies, University of California, Los Angeles, Los Angeles, California 90024

W. RUSSELL NEUMAN (205), Massachusetts Institute of Technology, Cambridge, Massachusetts 02139

STUART OSKAMP (291), Faculty in Psychology, Claremont Graduate School, Claremont, California 91711

JOHN P. ROBINSON (59), Survey Research Center, Department of Sociology, University of Maryland, College Park, Maryland 20742

JOHN C. WRIGHT (103), Center for Research on the Influence of Television on Children (CRITC), Department of Human Development, University of Kansas, Lawrence, Kansas 66045

Preface

In the first volume of this series, the editor made explicit his debt to Leonard Berkowitz's *Advances in Experimental Social Psychology* as a model for the present undertaking. That series, begun almost three decades ago, has now reached Volume 22; its contributions to theory and empirical inquiry, by stating what can be said currently about a shifting array of topics, have been an important part of the continuing education of its readers. The present series has the same ambition, but because this is only Volume 2, we offer it as a goal and a hope, with achievement very much yet in the future. As did Berkowitz in his Volume 2 (in 1965), however, it is the proper time to comment on what the contents so far tell us about the field purportedly covered.

That field was defined in Volume 1 as "the study of communicatory behavior that has a public or social character." More concretely, it encompasses research and theory designated as "within a range of disciplines and fields—advertising, child development, education, journalism, political science, sociology, and wherever else such scholarly activity occurs including, of course, social psychology." The contents of the first two volumes attest to the appropriateness of (or at least to the ability of the editor to search out) such a varied representation. So, too, do the contributions underway for inclusion in future volumes. This is a vigorous, lively field, if one that life often seems to outpace in its orderly cataloguing and precise distinctions. It will be interesting to see how much help in this latter respect comes from the forthcoming four-volume *The International Encyclopedia of Communications*, edited by Erik Barnouw; certainly it will attest to the liveliness that makes such niceties a problem. It is absolutely amazing that only three decades ago there appeared in *Public Opinion Quarterly* a set of essays which, on the whole (with the notable exception of a contribution by the late Wilbur Schramm), saw "communications research," the predecessor of much current activity, as withering away, depending on the point of view, from having done all that could be done or from not having done enough to establish itself as a worthwhile endeavor. If this be so, the present series, the *Encyclopedia*, and the work they describe should not exist. Obviously, something was overlooked—perhaps everything: the ability of scholars to reformulate theories to revivify failures, the readiness of social scientists to reexamine questions using new methods or concepts, the ability of old questions to lure newcomers into seeking new answers, and, above all, the enormous and rapid communications technology changes that have refused to allow most questions to appear settled for long. Thus, "null effects," "only reinforcement," and the "obstinate audience" have become transformed into important outcomes amenable to—arguably demanding—continuing research.

In his Volume 2, Berkowitz made similar comments about the diversity and health of social psychology. He saw it as having strong roots in psychology in general, with experimentation (hence his title) as its preferred means of investigation. The study of communicatory behavior, public or social in character, has roots in both psychology in general and social psychology in particular. In the present volume, the former is represented by the work of Huston and Wright and the latter by that of Malamuth. However, it also has a much wider and more mixed parentage. These are exemplified by the synthesis of earlier trends in sociological inquiry with the current agenda for communications research by Neuman and the application of empirical data to the construction of theory in behalf of more effective news reporting—a communications topic if there ever was one—by Davis and Robinson. The experiment similarly has no status as a preferred means of investigation, and this is made clear here by the contributions of Oskamp and Centerwall. The former draws together a large number of studies of a singular media event, the made-for-TV film *The Day After*, and attempts to draw from this array an empirically based picture of what transpired when this controversial broadcast occurred. It could be thought of as a literature review; but because many of these studies would be lost to attention without the intensive search in advance of any publication, it should be thought of as one of those innovation efforts to create a literature, a form of activity which this series hopes to encourage. The latter forcefully attests to the readiness to use methods other than the experiment. Topically, Centerwall thinks "the unthinkable" in giving serious consideration to the possibility that on a widespread basis the mass media have increased violent behavior. The most intriguing aspect, however, is his application of an epidemiological model to a communications issue; that is the kind of boundary crossing for which this series stands.

In short, this volume proceeds with the original ambition of the series intact. Along with Volume 1, it amounts to some evidence that it may be achievable. In any case, none of it has been boring for the editor, and he hopes the same can be said for the contributors and (and here he obviously speaks for them as well) for the readers.

George Comstock

Contents of Previous Volume

Volume 1

An Evaluation of the Models Used to Evaluate Television Series
Thomas D. Cook and Thomas R. Curtin

A Synthesis of 1043 Effects of Television on Social Behavior
Susan Hearold

More Than Meets the Eye: TV News, Priming, and Public Evaluations of the President
Shanto Iyengar and Donald R. Kinder

The Myth of Massive Media Impact: Savagings and Salvagings
William J. McGuire

The Found Experiment: A New Technique for Assessing the Impact of Mass Media Violence on Real-World Aggressive Behavior
David P. Phillips

Index

Contents of Previous Volume

Volume 1
An Evaluation of the Models Used to Evaluate Television Series
  Thomas D. Cook and Thomas R. Curtin
A Synthesis of 1043 Effects of Television on Social Behavior
  Susan Hearold
More Than Meets the Eye: TV News, Priming, and Public Evaluations of the President
  Shanto Iyengar and Donald R. Kinder
The Myth of Massive Media Impact: Savagings and Salvagings
  William J. McGuire
The Found Experiment: A New Technique for Assessing the Impact of Mass Media Violence on Real-World Aggressive Behavior
  David P. Phillips
Index

Exposure to Television as a Cause of Violence

BRANDON S. CENTERWALL
Departments of Epidemiology and Psychiatry
University of Washington
Seattle, Washington 98195

I. Television and Homicide in South Africa, Canada,
   and the United States, 1945–1974 1
   A. Introduction 1
   B. Methods 3
   C. Results 5
   D. Discussion 15
II. Testing Falsifiable Hypotheses 24
   A. Introduction 24
   B. Methods 25
   C. Results 29
   D. Discussion 44
III. Natural Exposure to Television as a Cause
   of Aggression: A Review of the Literature 48
   References 53

I. TELEVISION AND HOMICIDE IN SOUTH AFRICA, CANADA, AND THE UNITED STATES, 1945–1974

A. Introduction

Whether exposing children to television increases their physical aggressiveness has been a source of ongoing concern to physicians and public health practitioners (Feinbloom, 1976; Feingold & Johnson, 1977; Holroyd, 1985; Ingelfinger, 1976; Liebert, 1986; Rothenberg, 1975; Singer, 1985; Somers, 1976a,b; Zuckerman & Zuckerman, 1985). Rothenberg (1975) first brought the issue of television violence, and its effect on children's behavior and mental well-being, to the attention of the medical community. Somers (1976a,b) and

Ingelfinger (1976) soon raised the possibility that the imprint of television violence may not be limited to childhood—that it may lead to increased rates of later violence such as assault, rape, robbery, and homicide.

The effect of natural exposure to television upon children's physical aggressiveness, as compared to no exposure, has been recently elucidated by Joy, Kimball, and Zabrack (1986). In 1973, a small Canadian town ("Notel") acquired television for the first time. The acquisition of television at such a late date was due to problems with signal reception rather than any hostility toward television. Joy, Kimball, and Zabrack studied the effect of the introduction of television into this virgin community upon rates of physical aggression among Notel children. The control groups were two otherwise similar communities that already had television ("Unitel" and "Multitel").

Prior to the introduction of television into Notel, 60 first and second graders (20 in Notel; 40 in Unitel and Multitel) were observed at random intervals in the school playgrounds for rates of predetermined measures of noxious physical aggression (e.g., hitting, shoving, and biting). Two years after the introduction of television into Notel, 45 of the original cohort (16 in Notel; 29 in Unitel and Multitel) were followed up and observed again for rates of physical aggression, using the same definitions as before. A new set of first and second graders was also observed. Children and observers were blind to the hypothesis being tested, and a new set of observers was used in the follow-up.

Rates of physical aggression did not change significantly over the 2-year span for children followed longitudinally in Unitel and Multitel. Rates of physical aggression among children followed longitudinally in Notel increased 160% ($p < .001$). At the time of follow-up, first and second graders in Unitel and Multitel did not differ significantly in rates of physical aggression from first and second graders 2 years previously. In contrast, at the time of follow-up, first and second graders in Notel had rates of physical aggression 51% greater than first and second graders 2 years previously ($p < .05$).

Unable to randomize Notel children to television exposure versus nonexposure, the researchers used two external control groups (the children of Unitel and Multitel) to assess whether exposure to television increases physical aggression in children. Although the possibility of a confounding third variable cannot be absolutely excluded, the double-blind, prospective study design permits a strong inference of causality (Bailar, Louis, Lavori, & Polansky, 1984). The present study uses a similar research design to assess whether exposure of populations to television increases rates of homicide in adults.

The South African government did not permit television broadcasting prior to 1975, even though South African whites were a prosperous, industrialized Western society (Tartter, 1981). Amidst the hostile tensions between the Afrikaner and English white communities, it was generally conceded that any South African television broadcasting industry would have to rely on British and American imports to fill out its programming schedule. Afrikaner leaders felt this would provide an unacceptable cultural advantage to the English-speaking South Africans. Rather than negotiate a complicated compromise, the Afrikaner-controlled government chose to finesse the issue by forbidding television broadcasting entirely. Thus, an entire population of two million whites—rich and poor, urban and rural, educated and uneducated—was nonselectively and absolutely excluded from exposure to television for a quarter century after the medium was introduced into other Western nations.

The South African government sought to prevent any social changes that might occur secondary to the introduction of television (Tartter, 1981). Whether the intervention was (inadvertently) successful with respect to homicide rates is assessed in a case-control study of white homicide rates in South Africa prior to 1975, with the white population of the United States and the entire population of Canada [97% white in 1951 (Leacy, 1983)] serving as external control groups. Other potentially causal variables are also examined.

B. Methods

1. Study Design

The population intervention study design compares a case population with external control groups to determine the effect of interventions upon the real world (Morgenstern, 1982). The design requires comparable case and control populations, a reliable index of effect, baseline rates for both case and control populations, and empirical data gathered prospectively, independent of the hypothesis in question.

As with population intervention studies in general, issues of aggregation bias and ecological fallacy are rendered moot (Centerwall, 1989; Morgenstern, 1982). What are desired are not inferences about individuals but about groups—in this case, the effect of collective television ownership, and its prohibition, upon collective homicide rates.

2. Data Sources

a. Changes in Homicide Rates. Data on homicide victimization rates are from the vital statistics registries of South Africa [Bureau of Census and Statistics (BCS), 1960; Bureau of Statistics (BS), 1964, 1965, 1968; Department of Statistics (DS), 1970, 1972, 1974, 1976], Canada [Dominion Bureau of Statistics (DBS), annual volumes; World Health Organization (WHO), annual volumes], and the United States [Grove & Hetzel, 1968; National Center for Health Statistics (NCHS), annual volumes]. The data are for homicide deaths among whites in South Africa and the United States, and for total homicide deaths in Canada. To smooth out the data, the temporal trends in annual homicide rates are graphed as a 3-year moving average from 1945 to 1973. Data on white homicide rates in South Africa for 1943–1948 are presented as a 6-year average because this is how the data are presented in the vital statistics tables (BCS, 1960). Annual rates of court convictions for murder among South African whites are from the South African police statistics (BCS, 1960; BS, 1964, 1965, 1968; DS, 1970).

b. Changes in Television Ownership. Data on the percentage of Canadian households owning television sets in 1951, 1961, and 1971 are from the Dominion Bureau of Statistics (DBS, 1953, 1963); Industry and Merchandising Division (IMD, 1953) and Statistics Canada (SC, 1973). Data on the percentage of U.S. households owning television sets, 1945–1974, are from the Television Bureau of Advertising (TBA, 1982) and the U.S. Bureau of the Census (USBC, annual volumes). Television broadcasting was not permitted in South Africa prior to 1975 (Tartter, 1981).

c. Changes in Age Distribution. Data on changes in age distribution of the white populations of South Africa (BS, 1964; DS, 1974) and the United States (USBC, 1975), and of the entire population of Canada (Leacy, 1983), are from the respective national censuses.

d. Changes in Urbanization. Data on changes in urbanization of the white populations of South Africa (BS, 1964; DS, 1974) and the United States (USBC, 1975), and of the entire population of Canada (Leacy, 1983) are from the respective national censuses. To assess the direct effect of urbanization upon rates of homicide in the United States between 1960 and 1970, city-population-specific rates of criminal homicide from 1975 [U.S. Federal Bureau of Investigation (USFBI), annual volumes] are applied to the observed distributions of the U.S. population by city population in the 1960 and 1970 censuses (USBC, 1975). Because the same city-population-specific rates are applied to both census years, any change in the projected rate of criminal homicide between 1960 and 1970 is solely due to the effect of urbanization per se. This method permits a quantitative measure of the effect of urbanization independent of other factors; it replicates a statistical approach developed for the National Commission on the Causes and Prevention of Violence to investigate the effect of urbanization upon homicide rates in the United States between the years 1950 and 1965 (Mulvihill, Tumin, & Curtis, 1969). Criminal homicides are a subset of all homicides, excluding legally justifiable homicides (USFBI, annual volumes).

e. Changes in Economic Conditions. Data on changes in annual real per capita product in South Africa (DS, 1976), Canada (Leacy, 1983), and the United States (USBC, annual volumes) are from the respective statistical summaries. These are expressed as real per capita gross domestic product (1963 Rands) for South Africa, real per capita gross national product (1971 Canadian dollars) for Canada, and real per capita gross national product (1958 U.S. dollars) for the United States. Data on changes in real per capita product are not specific by race, but it is assumed that in all three countries the benefits from improved real per capita product accrue principally to whites.

f. Changes in Alcohol Consumption. Data on changes in annual per capita consumption of ethanol, 1960–1972, in South Africa, Canada, and the United States are from the Finnish Foundation for Alcohol Studies (FFAS) and the WHO Regional Office for Europe (1977). Because these data are not specific by race, they may misstate alcohol consumption trends among whites, especially in South Africa, where whites made up only 17% of the population in the 1970 census (DS, 1976). To provide an index of trends in alcohol abuse among whites, data are obtained from the respective vital statistics registries regarding trends in mortality from cirrhosis of the liver, 1960–1972, for the white populations of South Africa (BCS, 1960; DS, 1976) and the United States (NCHS, annual volumes), and for the entire population of Canada (WHO, annual volumes). It has been observed empirically that temporal trends in death rates from cirrhosis of the liver are closely correlated with temporal trends in per capita alcohol consumption in both Canada and the United States (Terris, 1967). For populations in excess of one million, per capita alcohol consumption statistics and death rates from cirrhosis of the liver provide equally stable measures of alcohol abuse (Furst & Beckman, 1981).

g. Changes in Capital Punishment. Data on capital punishment in South Africa are from Omond (1985). Data on capital punishment in Canada and the United States are from the respective statistical summaries (Leacy, 1983; USBC, annual volumes). Data on assault, rape, and robbery in Canada are from the Justice Statistics Division of Statistics Canada (1976). Data on assault, rape, and robbery in the United States are from the Uniform Crime Reports (USFBI, annual volumes).

h. Changes in the Availability of Firearms. The results of national random-sample household surveys on rates of household ownership of handguns in the United States are from the Gallup Poll, as provided by the Roper Center, University of Connecticut. Canadian annual rates of criminal homicide, by weapon, are from the Canadian Centre for Justice Statistics (Scarff, 1983). U.S. annual rates of criminal homicide and aggravated assault, by weapon, are from the Uniform Crime Reports (USFBI, annual volumes). Aggravated assault is assault with intent to kill or inflict severe bodily injury.

C. Results

1. Television and Homicide in South Africa, Canada, and the United States

There was no ownership of television sets in South Africa through 1974 (Tartter, 1981). In contrast, by the 1971 Canadian census, 95.3% of Canadian households had acquired at least one television set (SC, 1973) (see Fig. 1).

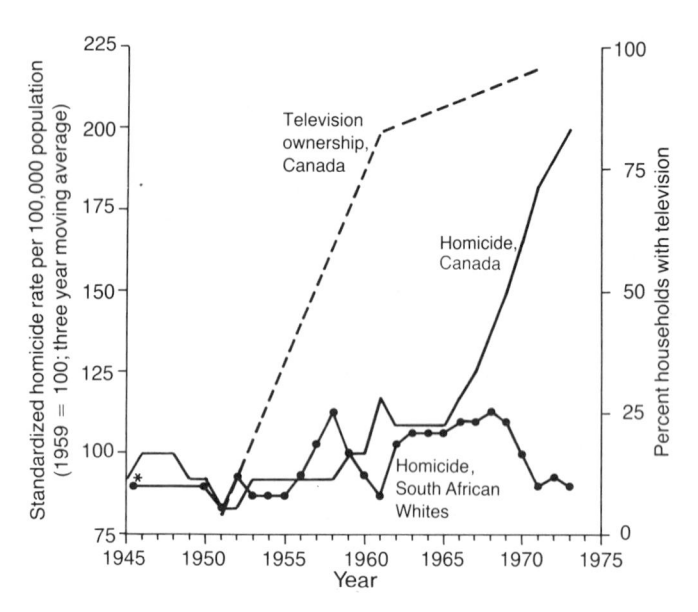

Fig. 1. Television ownership and homicide rates: Canadians and white South Africans, 1945-1973. Asterisk denotes 6-year average. Note that television broadcasting was not permitted in South Africa prior to 1975. Sources of television data: Dominion Bureau of Statistics (1953, 1963), Industry Merchandising Division (1953), and Statistics Canada (1973). Sources of homicide data: Dominion Bureau of Statistics (annual volumes), Bureau of Census and Statistics (1960), Bureau of Statistics (1964, 1965, 1968), and Department of Statistics (1970, 1972, 1974, 1976).

As in Canada, by 1971, 95.5% of U.S. households had acquired at least one television set (TBA, 1982) (see Fig. 2).

In South Africa for the years 1943-1948, there were an average of 63 white homicide deaths annually—2.7 per 100,000 population (BCS, 1960); in 1974, there were 105 white homicide deaths—2.5 per 100,000 (DS, 1976). In Canada in 1945, there were 152 homicide deaths—1.3 per 100,000 (DBS, annual volumes); in 1974, there were 551 homicide deaths—2.5 per 100,000 (WHO, annual volumes). In the United States in 1945, there were 3494 white homicide deaths—3.0 per 100,000; in 1974, there were 10,648 white homicide deaths—5.8 per 100,000 (NCHS, annual volumes).

Between 1943-1948 and 1974, white homicide rates declined 7% in South Africa. Between 1945 and 1974, homicide rates rose 92% in Canada, and white homicide rates rose 93% in the United States. If measured from 1955, when white homicide rates were at their lowest in the United States (2.3 per 100,000; NCHS, annual volumes), the U.S. white homicide rate rose 152% between 1955 and 1974; likewise, homicide rates in Canada rose 127% between 1955 (1.1 per 100,000) and 1974 (2.5 per 100,000) (DBS, annual volumes; WHO,

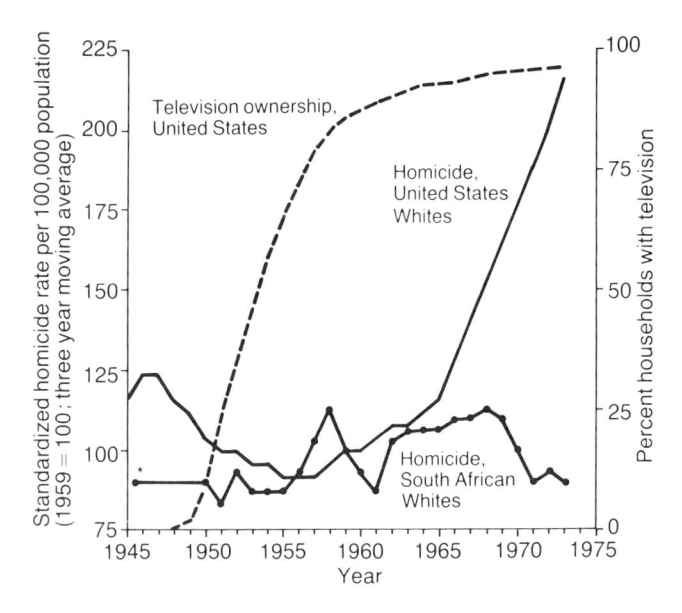

Fig. 2. Television ownership and white homicide rates: United States and South Africa, 1945–1973. Asterisk denotes 6-year average. Note that television broadcasting was not permitted in South Africa prior to 1975. Source of television data: Television Bureau of Advertising (1982). Sources of homicide data: National Center for Health Statistics (annual volumes), Bureau of Census and Statistics (1960), Bureau of Statistics (1964, 1965, 1968), and Department of Statistics (1970, 1972, 1974, 1976).

annual volumes); South African white homicide rates rose 9% between 1955 (2.3 per 100,000) and 1974 (2.5 per 100,000; BCS, 1960; DS, 1976). The rate at which South African whites have received court convictions for murder has remained stable over time at 1 per 100,000 white population (age 7 years and over) (BCS, 1960; BS, 1964, 1965, 1968; DS, 1970).

Following the introduction of television into Canada and the United States—and its exclusion from South Africa—white homicide rates remained stable in South Africa, whereas homicide rates in Canada and white homicide rates in the United States doubled. There is an observed 10- to 15-year lag between the introduction of television and the subsequent doubling of the homicide rate (see Figs. 1 and 2).

The vital and police statistics of the respective countries agree as to the number of homicide deaths to within 10% of one another. For July 1971 through June 1972, the Commissioner of the South African Police reported 118 white victims of criminal homicide (Midgley, 1974), as compared to 101 white homicide victims reported in the 1971 South African vital statistics and 108 white homicide victims reported in the 1972 South African vital statistics (DS,

1974, 1976). In Canada, in 1972, police forces reported 520 criminal homicide deaths (Leacy, 1983), as compared to 513 homicide deaths reported in the 1972 Canadian vital statistics (WHO, annual volumes). In 1972, the USFBI reported 18,520 criminal homicide deaths (USFBI, annual volumes), as compared to 19,638 homicide deaths reported in the 1972 U.S. vital statistics (NCHS, annual volumes).

2. An Evaluation of Alternative Hypotheses

It is necessary to examine alternative hypotheses that might explain the difference between white homicide trends in South Africa versus homicide trends in Canada and white homicide trends in the United States (i.e., changes in age distribution, urbanization, economic conditions, alcohol consumption, capital punishment, civil unrest, and the availability of firearms).

a. Changes in Age Distribution. Persons ages 15–34 years are more likely to commit homicide than are other age groups (USFBI, annual volumes). Therefore, a shift in the age distribution toward persons ages 15–34 may increase the overall homicide rate. Among South African whites, the percentage of the population ages 15–34 increased from 30.7% in 1951 to 32.2% in 1970 (BS, 1964; DS, 1972). Among Canadians, the percentage of the population ages 15–34 increased from 30.8% in 1951 to 32.0% in 1970 (Leacy, 1983). Among U.S. whites, the percentage of the population ages 15–34 decreased from 30.2% in 1950 to 29.5% in 1970 (USBC, annual volumes). Changes in age distribution do not appear to account for a stable white homicide rate in South Africa versus a doubling of the Canadian homicide rate and of the U.S. white homicide rate.

b. Changes in Urbanization. Homicide rates are higher in metropolitan centers than elsewhere (USFBI, annual volumes). Therefore, a shift in the urban-rural distribution of the population toward urbanization may increase the homicide rate. Among South African whites, 1951–1970, the proportion living in urban populations increased 10.7%—from 0.784 in 1951 to 0.868 in 1970 (BS, 1964; DS, 1974). Among Canadians, 1951–1971, the proportion living in urban populations increased 15.3%—from 0.567 in 1951 to 0.654 in 1971 (Leacy, 1983). Among U.S. whites, 1950–1970, the proportion living in urban populations increased by 14.3%—from 0.643 in 1950 to 0.735 in 1970 (USBC, 1975).

All three populations became increasingly urbanized, with upward shifts of approximately equal magnitude. However, these indices are too crude to assess the effect of urbanization on homicide rates. Because large cities have higher homicide rates than small towns (USFBI, annual volumes), the effect of urbanization on homicide rates varies, depending on whether the population distribution is shifting from rural areas primarily into large cities or into small towns.

A more quantitative analysis can be made of the effect of urbanization upon U.S. homicide rates (Table I). The USFBI (annual volumes) has calculated the criminal homicide rates for U.S. populations of varying degrees of urbanization. In 1975, these ranged from 3.9 homicides per 100,000 population in towns of fewer than 10,000 inhabitants to 24.6 homicides per 100,000 population in cities with more than one million inhabitants [Table I, column (b)]. If these 1975 homicide rates had been in effect in 1960, there would have been 17,565 homicides in the United States in that year [Table I, column (c)], or 10.4 homicides per 100,000 population [Table I, column (b)]. If the 1975 homicide rates had been in effect in 1970, there would have been 19,154 homicides in the United States in that year [Table I, column (f)], or 10.2 homicides per 100,000 population [Table I, column (e)]. By using standardized homicide rates for both the 1960 and the 1970 U.S. population [Table I, columns (b) and (e)], any change in the total standardized homicide rate reflects changes in the urbanization distribution of the U.S. population across city-size categories. Changes in U.S. urbanization between 1960 and 1970 did not cause any increase in national homicide rates.

The true U.S. homicide rate rose from 4.7 homicides per 100,000 in 1960 to 8.3 per 100,000 in 1970 (NCHS, annual volumes)—a 77% increase. Changes in urbanization contributed not at all to this increase. This is because the shift in the U.S. population distribution was from rural areas with relatively high homicide rates to smaller cities and towns. The proportion of the U.S. population living in large cities did not change. In 1960, 15.9% of the U.S. population lived in cities with 500,000 inhabitants or more (USBC, 1975). In 1970, 15.6% of the U.S. population lived in cities with 500,000 inhabitants or more (USBC, 1975). The doubling of U.S. homicide rates cannot be attributed even in part to trends in urbanization.

c. Changes in Economic Conditions. Between 1946 and 1974, real per capita South African gross domestic product (expressed in 1963 Rands) rose 86%—from 232 Rands per capita in 1946 to 431 Rands per capita in 1974 (DS, 1976). Real per capita Canadian gross national product (expressed in 1971 Canadian dollars) rose 124%—from $2264 per capita in 1946 to $5072 per capita in 1974 (Leacy, 1983). Real per capita U.S. gross national product (expressed in 1958 U.S. dollars) rose 75%—from $2211 per capita in 1946 to $3875 per capita in 1974 (USBC, annual volumes, 1975).

Economic conditions improved roughly proportionately in the three countries, with Canada showing a greater degree of improvement than South Africa and the United States. If changes in homicide rates, or lack thereof, are attributed either to economic stagnation or to economic growth, no model can account for the observed differences in homicide trends in South Africa versus Canada and the United States (see Figs. 1 and 2). None of the three countries' economies were stagnating; all three were growing.

TABLE I

Changes in the Homicide Rate Attributable to Changes in the Urban Distribution of the Population Alone: United States, 1960 and 1970[a]

Population of city	1960 Population (a)	1960 Homicide rate (1975) (homicides/100,000 population) (b)	1960 Projected homicides [(c) = (a × b)/100,000]	1970 Population (d)	1970 Homicide rate (1975) (homicides/100,000 population) (e)	1970 Projected homicides [(f) = (d × e)/100,000]
≥1,000,000	17,484,000	24.6	4301	18,769,000	24.6	4617
500,000–999,999	11,111,000	20.1	2233	12,967,000	20.1	2606
250,000–499,999	10,766,000	17.6	1895	10,442,000	17.6	1838
100,000–249,999	11,652,000	10.9	1270	14,286,000	10.9	1557
50,000–99,999	13,836,000	7.2	996	16,724,000	7.2	1204
25,000–49,999	14,951,000	5.7	852	17,848,000	5.7	1017
10,000–24,999	17,568,000	4.4	773	21,415,000	4.4	942
<10,000	18,050,000	3.9	704	21,689,000	3.9	846
Rural	54,054,000	8.4	4541	53,887,000	8.4	4527
Total	169,472,000[b]	10.4	17,565	188,026,000[b]	10.2	19,154

[a] Sources of homicide data, FBI Uniform Crime Reports, 1975 (U.S. Federal Bureau of Investigation, annual volumes); source of population data, U.S. Bureau of the Census (1975).

[b] Does not include category "Other urban territory": 9,851,000 in 1960 and 15,186,000 in 1970.

d. Changes in Alcohol Consumption. Alcohol is involved in a majority of criminal homicides (Collins, 1981). Therefore, increasing rates of alcohol use and abuse may lead to an increase in homicide rates. Between 1960 and 1972, annual per capita consumption of ethanol in South Africa rose 61%—from 1.8 liters per capita in 1960 to 2.9 liters per capita in 1972 (FFAS & the WHO Regional Office for Europe, 1977). Annual per capita consumption of ethanol in Canada rose 58%—from 4.8 liters per capita in 1960 to 7.6 liters per capita in 1972. Annual per capita consumption of ethanol in the United States rose 42%—from 4.8 liters per capita in 1960 to 6.8 liters per capita in 1972 (FFAS & the WHO Regional Office for Europe, 1977).

To more specifically assess trends in alcohol abuse among the case and control populations, temporal trends are measured for mortality rates from cirrhosis of the liver. Between 1960 and 1972, white South African mortality from cirrhosis of the liver increased 50%—from 6.2 deaths per 100,000 in 1960 to 9.3 deaths per 100,000 in 1972 (BS, 1964, 1965, 1968; DS, 1970, 1972, 1974, 1976). Canadian mortality from cirrhosis of the liver increased 65%—from 6.2 deaths per 100,000 in 1960 to 10.2 deaths per 100,000 in 1972 (WHO, annual volumes). White U.S. mortality from cirrhosis of the liver increased 30%—from 11.5 deaths per 100,000 in 1960 to 14.9 deaths per 100,000 in 1972 (NCHS, annual volumes).

The three populations exhibit closely similar temporal trends in per capita ethanol consumption and in mortality from cirrhosis of the liver. The particularly close match between South Africa and Canada renders unlikely the hypothesis that the differences in homicide trends between the case and control populations are due to differences in temporal trends in alcohol abuse.

e. Changes in Capital Punishment. It has been theorized that capital punishment deters would-be murderers and, conversely, that the absence of capital punishment encourages homicide. South Africa, with a stable white homicide rate through 1974, has maintained the highest annual number of officially sanctioned executions in the world, averaging 62 executions annually from 1969 through 1974 (Omond, 1985). Canada's last executions took place in 1962 (Leacy, 1983) and the United States had no executions in the years 1968 through 1976 (U.S. Bureau of the Census, annual volumes); both countries experienced major increases in homicide rates during these periods without executions (Figs. 1 and 2).

In 1976, the Canadian Parliament formally abolished the death penalty (Leacy, 1983). In contrast, in the United States, the execution of prisoners resumed in 1977 (USBC, annual volumes). If the threat of capital punishment has anything to do with homicide rates, these diametrically opposite developments should have led to conspicuously different results. In Canada, the homicide rate has remained stable, the homicide rate in 1975 (2.7 per 100,000) being not notably different from the homicide rate in 1983 (2.4 per

100,000) (WHO, annual volumes). In the United States, the white homicide rate has likewise remained stable, the white homicide rate in 1975 (5.9 per 100,000) being not notably different from the white homicide rate in 1983 (5.6 per 100,000) (NCHS, annual volumes). The abolishment of capital punishment in Canada and the resumption of executions in the United States appear to have had the same effect upon homicide rates (i.e., no effect at all). The failure of high rates of executions to deter homicides in South Africa has been discussed by van Niekerk (1970). As pointed out by Kahn (1981), even in South Africa, "a suspected murder results in capital punishment in only two cases out of a hundred."

The doubling of the homicide rate in Canada and the United States was part of a more general doubling of rates of violence in both countries [USFBI, annual volumes; Justice Statistics Division (JSD), 1976]. Because capital punishment was not applied to robbery, assault, and rape in the 1960s in Canada and the United States, the effective abolition of capital punishment in both countries at that time could have no bearing on a doubling in rates of robbery, assault, and rape. If the absence of capital punishment has no role in the doubling of violence rates in general in Canada and the United States, it is unlikely to have a role in the doubling of homicide rates in particular.

f. Changes in Civil Unrest. Despite ongoing tensions between the English and the Afrikaners, since World War II, South African whites have supported their political and cultural institutions without notable exceptions (McLaughlin, 1981). Canadians and U.S. whites have likewise generally supported their institutions. A major exception occurred in Canada in 1969-1970 when the Quebec separatist movement entered into open conflict with Canadian political institutions, resulting in two kidnappings of government officials, general unrest, and, in the climax, the temporary imposition of martial law (accompanied by mass arrests) in Quebec during the October Crisis of 1970 (Bothwell, Drummond, & English, 1981). Likewise, in the United States, from the mid-1960s to the early 1970s, a vocal and highly visible minority of whites were in open conflict with their leadership, especially over the conduct of the Vietnam War. Although the actual number of extralegal dissidents in Canada and the United States were too few to directly explain any increase in homicide rates, it is theoretically possible that they created an atmosphere of turbulence and instability that caused homicide rates to rise.

This theory founders on the observed trends in homicide rates (Figs. 1 and 2). In both Canada and the United States, homicide rates were rising for 5 or more years prior to any substantial civil unrest. Though civil order was restored in Canada by 1971, the homicide rate in 1983 (2.4 per 100,000) was 20% higher than in 1970 (2.0 per 100,000) (WHO, annual volumes). Likewise, although white civil unrest in the United States effectively came to an end in 1972 with the end of U.S. military involvement in the Vietnam War, the white homicide rate in 1983 (5.6 per 100,000) was 14% higher than in 1972 (4.9 per 100,000) (NCHS, annual volumes). It is unlikely that civil unrest in Canada and or white civil unrest in the United States altered the existing trends in homicide rates.

g. *Changes in Availability of Firearms.* With respect to firearms, South African whites may be the most heavily armed private citizenry on earth, perhaps exceeding even whites in the United States (Frye, 1968; Lelyveld, 1985). There are no temporal trend data on firearms availability to whites in South Africa, but the failure of white South African homicide rates to rise prior to 1975 cannot reasonably be attributed to any absolute unavailability of firearms.

The increase in U.S. homicide rates has been attributed to an increase in the availability of firearms (Block, 1975; Constantino, Kuller, Perper, & Cypess, 1977; Farley, 1980; Munford, Kazer, Feldman, & Stivers, 1976; Newton & Zimring, 1970; Ruben & Leeper, 1981; Rushforth, Ford, Hirsch, Rushforth, & Adelson, 1977). For 1965-1975, the annual number of handguns manufactured or imported for sale in the United States increased 128%—from 1,013,300 in 1965 (Newton & Zimring, 1970) to 2,312,262 in 1975 [Bureau of Alcohol, Tobacco, and Firearms (BATF), annual volumes]. This corresponded to an increase in the percentage of U.S. households possessing handguns from 14.5% in 1965 to 18.9% in 1975.

Apart from an increase in the availability of firearms, an increase in the rate of homicides committed with firearms could be due to an increase in the underlying aggressiveness of the U.S. population, such as might occur with exposure of the general population to television. If Americans have become more aggressive, the rate of homicides committed with firearms would increase independent of any change in the availability of firearms.

The underlying aggressiveness of Americans can be estimated by examining the rate at which aggravated assaults and criminal homicides are being committed without any weapons at all (i.e., by beating, kicking, choking, etc.). Because the availability of hands and feet for attacking others is constant over time, changes in the rate of strong-arm attacks can be used as a population index of assaultive aggressiveness independent of weapons availability.

For 1965-1975, the U.S. rate of strong-arm criminal homicides increased by 80%—from 0.5 per 100,000 in 1965 to 0.9 per 100,000 in 1975; the rate of weapon-related criminal homicides increased by 89%—from 4.6 per 100,000 in 1965 to 8.7 per 100,000 in 1975 (Fig. 3) (USFBI, annual volumes). For 1965-1975, the rate of strong-arm aggravated assaults increased by 126%—from 27 per 100,000 in 1965 to 61 per 100,000 in 1975; the rate of weapon-related aggravated assaults increased by 108%—from 80 per 100,000 in 1965 to 166 per 100,000 in 1975 (Fig. 4) (USFBI, annual volumes).

It can be seen from Figs. 3 and 4 that the rate of weapon-related serious

1965

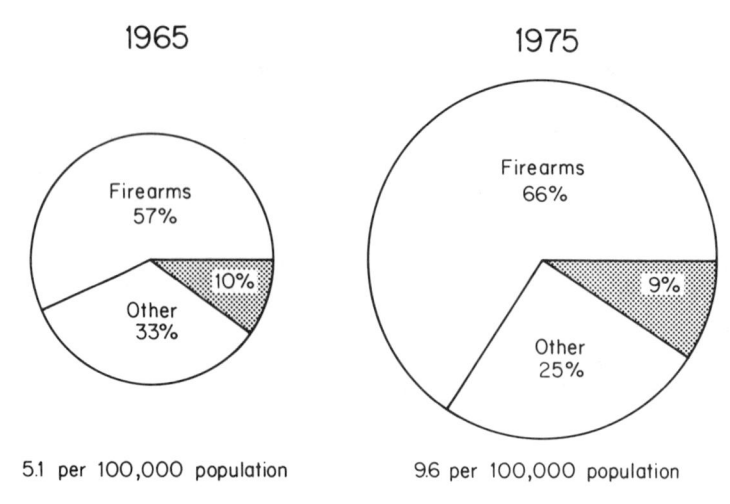

- Firearms 57%
- Other 33%
- 10%

5.1 per 100,000 population

1975

- Firearms 66%
- Other 25%
- 9%

9.6 per 100,000 population

Fig. 3. Rates of criminal homicide: United States, 1965, 1975. The white area represents criminal homicides committed with weapons. The shaded area represents criminal homicides committed by strong-arm attacks (hands, feet, etc.). Source of data: U.S. Federal Bureau of Investigation (annual volumes).

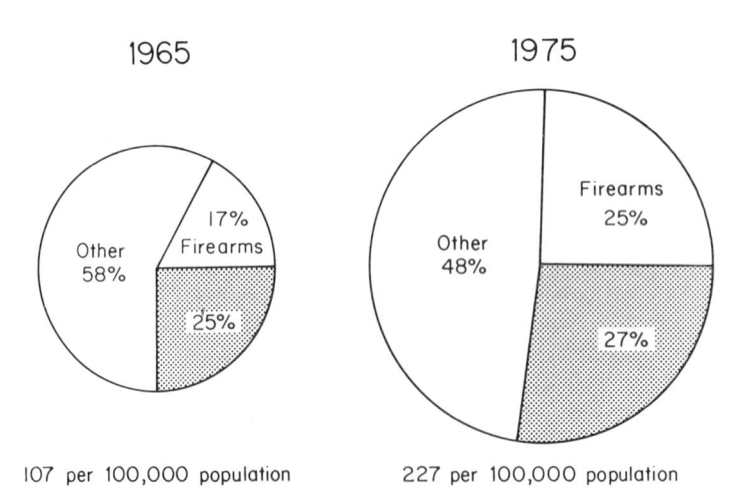

1965

- Other 58%
- Firearms 17%
- 25%

107 per 100,000 population

1975

- Firearms 25%
- Other 48%
- 27%

227 per 100,000 population

Fig. 4. Rates of aggravated assault: United States, 1965, 1975. The white area represents aggravated assaults committed with weapons. The shaded area represents aggravated assaults committed by strong-arm attacks (hands, feet, etc.). Source of data: U.S. Federal Bureau of Investigation (annual volumes).

assaults, both lethal and nonlethal, rose in direct proportion to the rising rate of underlying aggressiveness in the U.S. population, as measured by rates of strong-arm serious assaults. There is no excess of weapon-related offenses that must be attributed to an increase in the availability of weapons.

A similar analysis can be performed for Canadian murders (Fig. 5). For 1965-1975, the Canadian rate of nonfirearm murders increased by 131%—from 0.7 per 100,000 in 1965 to 1.5 per 100,000 in 1975; the rate of firearm murders increased by 122%—from 0.6 per 100,000 in 1965 to 1.3 per 100,000 in 1975 (Scarff, 1983).

An increase in the availability of firearms in the United States appears to have resulted in a shift in the choice of weapon in weapon-related assaults and homicides, but it has not had any discernible effect on total rates of criminal homicide and aggravated assault independent of underlying upward trends in the aggressiveness of the U.S. population (Figs. 3 and 4). In Canada, the proportion of murders committed with firearms did not change notably between 1965 and 1975 (Fig. 5). Therefore, the doubling of the homicide rate in Canada and the United States is not attributable to changes in the availability of firearms.

D. Discussion

1. *Summary of Findings*

Following an intervention in South Africa to prevent the introduction of television technology, white homicide rates remained stable. In two control populations, Canadian and U.S. white homicide rates doubled following the introduction of television (Figs. 1 and 2). An array of other factors—age distribution, urbanization, economic conditions, alcohol consumption, capital punishment, civil unrest, and firearms availability—were examined to determine whether they could explain the findings. None were found to be explanatory. This does not absolutely rule out the possibility of an unmeasured third variable being responsible for increases in the homicide rate in Canada and the United States (or the lack thereof in South Africa). However, because the examined variables cover the major alternative hypotheses, the most parsimonious interpretation of the data is that they are consistent with the introduction of television causing a subsequent doubling of homicide rates. The 10- to 15-year lag between the introduction of television and changes in the homicide rate (Figs. 1 and 2) imply that the behavioral effects of exposure to television are primarily exerted upon children. Given that homicide is an adult activity, the initial generation of children exposed to television would have to age 10-15 years before they could be expected to influence rates of homicide. Consistent with these observations, Hennigan and associates (1982)

1965

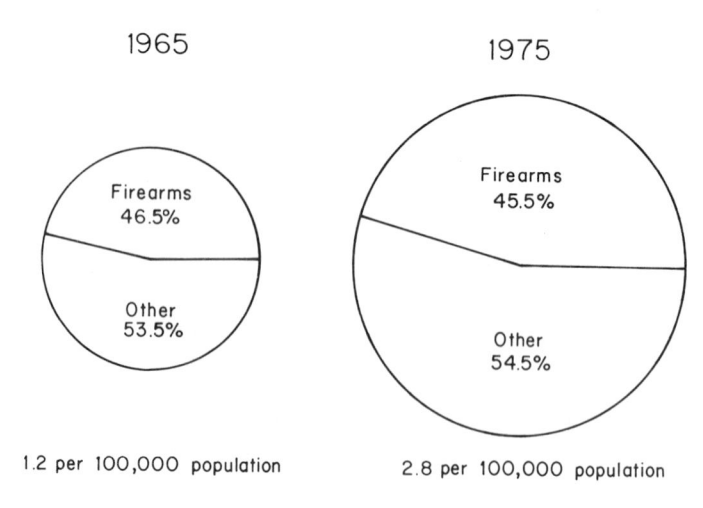

Firearms 46.5%

Other 53.5%

1.2 per 100,000 population

1975

Firearms 45.5%

Other 54.5%

2.8 per 100,000 population

Fig. 5. Rates of murder: Canada, 1965, 1975. From Scarff (1983).

have demonstrated that the introduction of television into the United States had no significant effect upon rates of criminal homicide and assault among adults not previously exposed to television.

2. An Evaluation of the Premises Underlying the Study Design

These conclusions are based on certain premises underlying the study design, regarding the appropriateness of the case and control populations, the reliability of the data, and whether exposure to television can cause a doubling of the homicide rate. These are now addressed in more detail.

a. Is South Africa an Appropriate Case Population? Some cultures are inherently incompatible with television. For example, the Amish in the United States form a sectarian enclave that, on principle, declines ownership of television sets and other household electrical appliances (Hostetler, 1980). Indeed, any Amishman daring openly to own a television set would be likely excommunicated ("shunned"). However, even if not under the observation of other Amish, a true Amishman would not choose to possess a television set under any circumstances. It would be invalid to propose the Amish as a case population for studying the effects of television and its absence because the cultural mores that lead them to reject television in the first instance are radically different from almost any conceivable external control group that possesses television sets.

Unlike the Amish, white South Africans did not choose to be excluded from exposure to television. As in Canada and the United States, the degree to which the average white South African citizen controls policy formation in the central government approaches zero. For almost all practical purposes, central government policy is an external phenomenon, like the weather. A white South African living outside South Africa prior to 1975 (e.g., in the United States) would have felt under no compulsion—moral, cultural, or political—to avoid exposure to television. When television was finally introduced into South Africa in 1975, the initial rush to acquire television sets turned into a stampede (" 'Unbelievable' scramble," 1976). By 1979, 84% of the white population had access to television broadcasts (Tartter, 1981). Far from being culturally incompatible, television has proven to be "enormously popular" among white South Africans; many of the most popular programs are imported from the United States (Tartter, 1981).

The South African whites' enthusiastic embrace of television makes it clear that their prior exclusion from the medium was not due to self-selection. The central government decision to ban television broadcasting was based on particular historical circumstances; had the circumstances been otherwise, there would have been no decision to ban television. Television technology would have been introduced into South Africa if (1) it had come to maturity 10 years earlier when the English South African government was still in power; (2) it had come to maturity 10 years later when the Afrikaner South African government would have felt sufficiently secure to permit its development; or (3) there had been only one white ethnic group in South Africa; and so on.

Although excluded from television broadcasting prior to 1975, white South Africa had well-developed book, newspaper, radio, and cinema industries (Kaplan *et al.*, 1971). Therefore, in comparing South African whites to external control populations, the effect of television can be isolated from that of other media.

b. Canada and the United States As External Control Populations. The countries chosen to be external controls must match South Africa on pertinent historical factors. South Africa, Canada, and the United States all began as frontier colonies initially settled in the seventeenth century by whites from Western Europe. All three eventually came to be dominated by British cultural forces. All three developed lasting schisms between two competing white ethnic groups of distinguishable language and culture—English versus Afrikaner in South Africa, English versus French in Canada, North versus South in the United States. In the period immediately preceding the introduction of television into Canada and the United States, all three countries were involved in World War II as allies against the Axis forces; as measured by combat fatalities per thousand population, the intensity of military involvement in World War II was approximately the same for the three countries (Elting, 1983). All three emerged from the war with their economic infrastructures intact and with industries expanded and invigorated by the war effort

(McLaughlin, 1981). All three were multiparty, representative, federal democracies. Christian religious influences were strong in all three countries (Bothwell *et al.*, 1981; McLaughlin, 1981). For all practical purposes, people of nonwhite races were excluded from real political power in all three countries.

At the dawn of the television era, the United States was a closer match to South Africa than was Canada in several respects. Unlike Canada, South Africa and the United States had extensive histories of frontier violence, especially of violent clashes between white settlers and indigenous populations (McLaughlin, 1981). Unlike Canada, strains between competing white ethnic groups in South Africa and the United States culminated in full-scale civil wars with lasting bitterness thereafter. These disparities in histories of violence are reflected in the homicide rates: In 1949-1951, the average white homicide rate in South Africa and the United States was 2.7 and 2.6 per 100,000, respectively (BCS, 1960; Grove & Hetzel, 1968), whereas the average Canadian homicide rate was only 1.1 per 100,000 (DBS, annual volumes). Unlike Canada, the South African and U.S. economies were partially based on exploitation of black labor, reinforced by formally sanctioned racial segregation and other racially discriminatory practices.

Unlike the United States, both Canada and South Africa had remained part of the British empire. Both were still in the British Commonwealth when television first came to maturity. Therefore, Canadian and South African cultures had a "British" quality in common that was largely absent from U.S. culture.

No other countries provide as good a match with South Africa as do Canada and the United States. Including both Canada and the United States as external control groups permits a replication of findings, so there can be assurance that comparison of South Africa to a single external control group does not yield erroneous conclusions. For example, a comparison of South Africa with only the United States (Fig. 2) could easily lead to the hypothesis that U.S. involvement in the Vietnam War, or the turbulence of the civil rights movement, was responsible for increases in white homicide rates in the United States. The inclusion of Canada as a control group disposes of these hypotheses because Canadians likewise experienced a doubling of homicide rates (Fig. 1) without involvement in the Vietnam War and without the turbulence of the U.S. civil rights movement.

It should be noted that television programming has been similar for the two control populations. In a 1976 study of the 109 most popular television programs shown in Canada, 83 (76%) had been produced in the United States (Williams, Zabrack, & Joy, 1982). Exposure of Canadian and U.S. populations to television has been roughly equivalent, both in percentage of households exposed (Figs. 1 and 2) and in content of television programming.

c. Who Is Killing Whom? Trends in rates of homicide victimization have been compared between the South African whites versus the whites in the

United States and all Canadians (Figs. 1 and 2). However, it is the homicide offender rate, by race, that is of most direct interest in measuring the effect of exposure to television. Rates of homicide victimization are used because they are more complete and accurate (in a proportion of homicides the offender is never identified).

Police statistics in Canada and the United States demonstrate that homicide in those countries is primarily an intraracial phenomenon (Jayewardene, 1980; USFBI, annual volumes). Thus, in Canada (1961-1970), 94% of white victims were killed by other whites, and 83% of Canadian native victims (Canadian Indian and Eskimo) were killed by other Canadian natives (Jayewardene, 1980). Likewise, in the United States (1976-1978), in single-offender-single-victim killings, 89% of white victims were killed by other whites, and 96% of black victims were killed by other blacks (USFBI, annual volumes).

Unlike Canada and the United States, interracial homicides make up a major proportion of murders in South Africa. Of whites murdered in South Africa (1953-1962), 44% were murdered by nonwhites; conversely, of persons murdered by white South Africans, 47% were nonwhites (Welsh, 1969).

The intraracial nature of U.S. and Canadian homicides implies that the trends in homicide victimization rates in Canada and the United States closely parallel the trends in homicide offender rates, with respect to the race of offender and victim. The same cannot be presumed for South Africa; stable white homicide victimization rates (Figs. 1 and 2) may conceal major changes in the racial composition of the offenders. Therefore, the assumption that stable white homicide victimization rates reflect stable white homicide offender rates needs to be verified. And, indeed, it is observed that the annual rate of murder convictions among South African whites has remained stable over time at one per 100,000 white population (age 7 years and over) (BCS, 1960; BS, 1964, 1965, 1968; DS, 1970).

d. How Reliable Is the Diagnosis of Homicide? Due to the social and legal repercussions, putative homicide deaths are subjected to intense scrutiny. Thus, for example, in 1974, 89% of U.S. homicide deaths were autopsied, as compared to 18% of deaths in general (NCHS, annual volumes). This should lead to high reliability in diagnosis, in which *reliability* is the probability that two different observers will agree on the diagnosis.

The reliability of the diagnosis of homicide can be tested directly by comparing medical and police records. Over time, in both Canada and the United States, police record enumerations of homicide deaths have differed from death certificate enumerations by about 5% (Cantor & Cohen, 1980; DBS, annual volumes; Leacy, 1983; WHO, annual volumes). To make a judgment about reliability, it is necessary to know whether these two enumerations are referring to the same deaths. In a case-by-case comparison of police records and medical examiner records in seven cities across the United States, Zahn and Riedel (1983) found that of 1332 deaths described as a homicide in either the police or medical examiner records, 1248 (94%) were described as a homicide in both record systems. The discrepancies revolved around whether deaths due to certain types of manslaughter (e.g., arson) should be called homicides. When considering those homicide deaths so reported by both police and medical examiner systems, agreement as to the race of the victim (white vs. nonwhite) was virtually 100%; agreement as to the category of weapon used was greater than 90%.

It is therefore concluded that homicide deaths are reported with high reliability with respect to their occurrence and also as to the race of the victim and the weapon used. Therefore, the changes in homicide rates observed in the United States and Canada are real and are not the result of statistical artifacts. Time trends for police statistics on homicide in South Africa are not available for comparison with the South African vital statistics registry data. A point comparison in 1971-1972 reveals that at that time South African vital records on homicide deaths were approximately as reliable as in Canada and the United States (DS, 1972, 1974; Midgley, 1974). For the real white South African homicide rate to have doubled between the 1940s and the 1970s, as in Canada and the United States, it is necessary to assume that 1940s death certificates in South Africa were recording twice as many white homicide deaths as were actually occurring. Given the severe repercussions of a falsely positive declaration of homicide, an assumption of overreporting in the 1940s is improbable. It is concluded that the absence of an increase in white homicide rates in South Africa is likewise real and not the result of a statistical artifact.

Because the data in the vital statistics and police registries were gathered prospectively and without regard for the hypothesis being entertained in this study, the data are unbiased with respect to the hypothesis that exposure to television causes increases in rates of violence.

e. Can Exposure to Television Cause a Doubling of the Homicide Rate? Field studies have documented that exposure of children to television increases their average level of physical aggressiveness (Cook, Kendzierski, & Thomas, 1983; Eron, Lefkowitz, Huesmann, & Walder, 1972; Huesmann & Eron, 1986a; Huesmann, Lagerspetz, & Eron, 1984; Singer, Singer, & Rapaczynski, 1984). Typically, however, the relationship between television viewing and subsequent changes in average level of physical aggressiveness is quite mild, usually explaining less than 10% of the observed variance. This would appear to create a problem. It has been argued that such a weak relationship, even if real and causal, is too weak to account for major increases in rates of violence (Cook *et al.*, 1983; Freedman, 1984; McGuire, 1986; Tan, 1986; Wilson & Herrnstein, 1985). Can exposure of the general population to television plausibly account for a doubling of the homicide rate in Canada and the United States (Figs. 1 and 2)?

Homicide is an extreme manifestation of aggression—so extreme that only

1 person out of 20,000 (approximately) committed homicide annually in the United States in the mid-1950s (USFBI, annual volumes). If the aggressiveness of all U.S. citizens could be plotted on a Gaussian normal distribution, from the least aggressive to the most aggressive, homicide offenders were manifesting levels of physical aggressiveness 3.9 standard deviations (σ) or greater above the mean (Fig. 6). If exposure of the entire population to television causes an upward shift in the average level of aggression of 0.2σ, then the proportion of the population falling above the homicide threshold will double (Fig. 6); the doubling in the tail of the curve is an unavoidable intrinsic mathematical property of the Gaussian normal distribution. An increase in mean levels of aggression of 0.2σ is equivalent to 8% of the population shifting from a below-average to an above-average level of aggression. This is comparable to the moderate increases in mean level of physical aggression observed in studies of natural populations exposed to television (Cook *et al.*, 1983; Eron *et al.*, 1972; Huesmann *et al.*, 1984; Huesmann & Eron, 1986a; Singer *et al.*, 1984). Thus, the results of observational television studies are consistent with, and predictive of, a major increase in the homicide rate (a similar point has been made by Rosenthal, 1986).

If this is so, it is expected that those observational television studies that focus on extreme levels of aggression (rather than on average levels of aggression) will show major effects. In the Notel study, 2 years of natural exposure to television caused a 160% increase in the absolute rate of extreme physical aggression (hitting, choking, biting, etc.) in previously unexposed elementary school children ($p < .001$) (Joy *et al.*, 1986). In a case-control study of 1565 adolescent boys (ages 12-17), boys with an above-average lifetime exposure

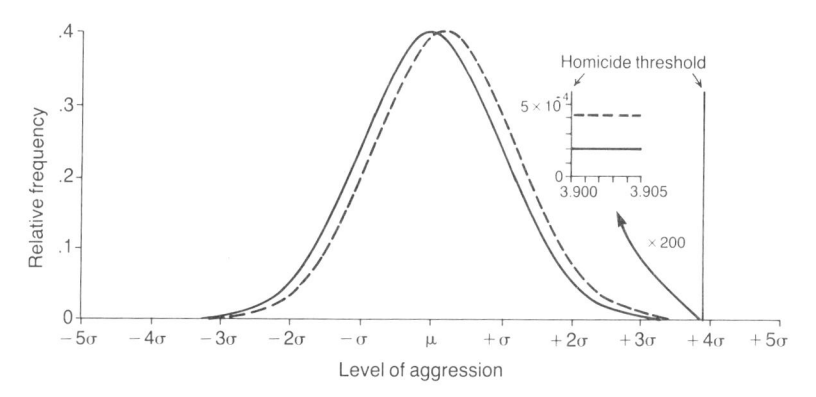

Fig. 6. Relationships between television, aggression, and homicide in the general population: a model. Population distribution of aggression: solid line, without television; broken line, with television.

to television violence had a 49% higher rate of seriously violent acts (i.e., assault, rape, major vandalism, and abuse of animals) than did matched boys with a below-average lifetime exposure to television violence ($p = .02$) (Belson, 1978). In a long-term prospective study of a complete age cohort in a rural county ($N = 875$), it was observed that the frequency of television viewing at age 8 years predicted the seriousness of criminal acts committed by age 30 [the "seriousness" of a criminal act was weighted to reflect the severity of violence involved, using a standardized scale (Rossi, Waite, Bose, & Berk, 1974)]; children who were watching television frequently at age 8 years on the average were convicted by age 30 of criminal acts several times more serious than the criminal acts of adults who had been infrequent viewers of television at age 8 years (Fig. 7); this held true for both men ($p < .001$) and women ($p < .05$) (Eron & Huesmann, 1984). These studies are in accord with the present study's conclusion that the introduction of television into Canada and the United States caused a major increase in rates of homicide.

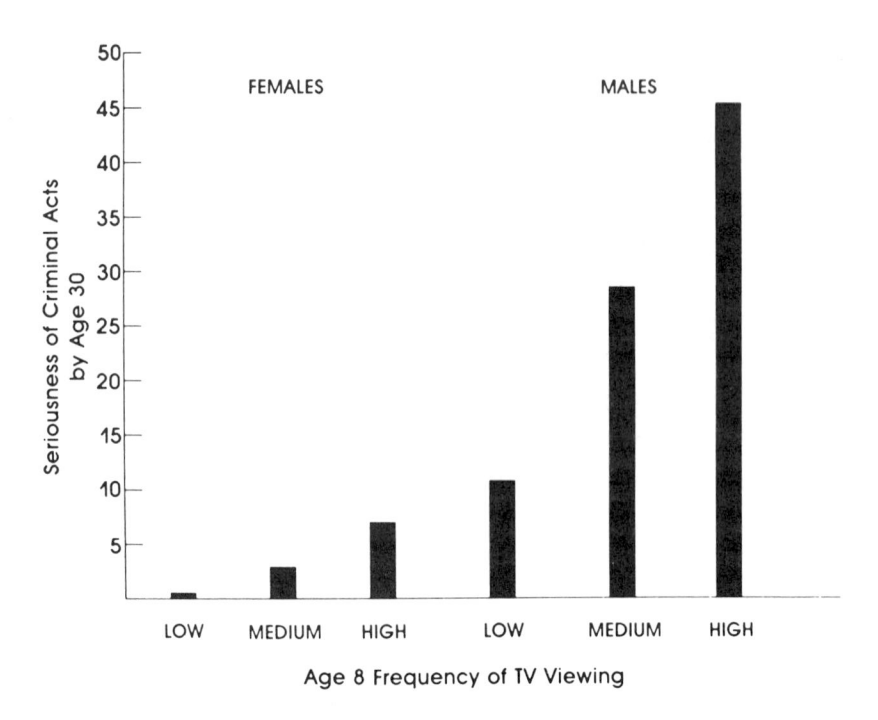

Fig. 7. Relation of TV viewing frequency at age 8 to seriousness of crimes committed by age 30: Columbia County Cohort Study, 1960–1981. From Eron & Huesmann (1984). Reprinted by permission.

3. Television and Homicide after 1974

There was a 10- to 15-year lag between the introduction of television into Canada and the United States and subsequent increases in the homicide rate (Figs. 1 and 2). This corresponds to the time required for preadolescent children exposed to television to become old enough to affect prevailing homicide rates. As measured by percentage of households with television sets, Canadian and U.S. populations became saturated with television sets by the early 1960s (Figs. 1 and 2); therefore, the effect of exposure to television upon subsequent homicide rates should likewise reach a saturation point 10-15 years later (i.e., by the mid-1970s). Thereafter, there should be no major changes in homicide rates except under the influence of factors other than television. This is what is actually observed. Canadian homicide rates doubled from 1.3 per 100,000 in 1945 to 2.5 per 100,000 in 1974; in 1983, Canadian homicide rates were still 2.4 per 100,000 (WHO, annual volumes). U.S. white homicide rates doubled from 3.0 per 100,000 in 1945 to 5.8 per 100,000 in 1974; in 1983, U.S. white homicide rates were still 5.6 per 100,000 (NCHS, annual volumes).

Due to the long time lag between exposure to television and subsequent changes in the homicide rate, it is expected that white homicide rates in South Africa will not increase immediately after the introduction of television in 1975. This predicted absence of an immediate increase in white homicide rates also is observed. South African white homicide rates remained stable from 1943-1948 [2.7 per 100,000 (BCS, 1960)] through 1974 [2.5 per 100,000 (DS, 1976)]. In 1983, the South African white homicide rate was 3.9 per 100,000 [Central Statistical Service (CSS), 1986], up from 3.1 per 100,000 in 1979 (CSS, 1982). Whether this is the beginning of an upward shift in white homicide rates remains to be seen. It is predicted that South African white homicide rates will double in the 1980s or, at the latest, by the early 1990s.

4. The Need To Test Falsifiable Hypotheses

The data indicate that the introduction of television into Canada and the United States caused a doubling of homicide rates. Competing theories have been examined—changes in age distribution, urbanization, economic conditions, alcohol consumption, capital punishment, civil unrest, availability of firearms; none has provided a viable alternative explanation of the findings.

Even so, as in the Notel study (Joy *et al.*, 1986), these data alone do not absolutely exclude the possibility that an unknown confounding variable is creating a spurious temporal association between television and homicide in Canada and the United States. Perhaps a different specification of the examined variables, or some multivariate combination of them, would reveal a confounding process that would render the present analysis invalid.

It is not possible within these data to exclude the possibility of confounding because, no matter how complete or well specified the data, one can always postulate the existence of an invisible confounding variable. Therefore, as with any scientific theory, the ultimate test of the present conclusion's validity is whether it can generate falsifiable hypotheses. If the hypotheses are tested and the results conform with the theory that exposure of populations to television causes major increases in rates of violence, then the theory is validated. If the hypotheses are tested and the results do not conform with the theory, then the theory is invalidated. The second part of this study generates and tests falsifiable hypotheses from the theory that exposure of populations to television causes major increases in rates of violence.

II. TESTING FALSIFIABLE HYPOTHESES

A. Introduction

In the first part of this study, it was demonstrated that homicide rates in Canada and the United States doubled following the introduction of television, whereas in South Africa, where television broadcasting was banned prior to 1975, white homicide rates remained stable over the same time period. There was an observed time lag of 10-15 years between the introduction of television and the subsequent doubling of the homicide rate. This indicates that exposure to television has little or no immediate effect on levels of homicidal violence in adolescents and adults not previously exposed to television, an observation consistent with the findings of Hennigan and associates (1982). Rather, the data suggest that exposure to television increases the physical aggressiveness of preadolescent children, who must then grow into late adolescence and adulthood before their increased aggressiveness will affect prevailing rates of serious violence. Consistent with this inference, research in natural settings has established that chronic, natural exposure of children to television does increase their average levels of physical aggressiveness. The literature examining natural exposure to television as a cause of aggression is reviewed in Section III.

If these inferences are valid, several falsifiable hypotheses logically follow that predict the relationships that will be observed between exposure of populations to television and patterns of violence. As mentioned, if the hypotheses are tested and the results conform with the theory that exposure of populations to television causes major increases in rates of violence, then the theory is validated. If the hypotheses are tested and the results do not conform with the theory that television causes violence, then the theory is invalidated.

B. Methods

There are three major hypotheses:

Hypothesis A: In populations in which causality has been inferred at the level of the individual, exposure to television is followed by a major percentage increase in rates of violence.

The hypothesis is limited to populations in which causality has been inferred at the level of the individual because it is known that not all cultures necessarily respond to television violence (Bachrach, 1986; Sheehan, 1986; Wiegman, Kuttschreuter, & Baarda, 1986). To take into account differing baseline rates of violence, changes are measured by the percentage of increase rather than by the absolute increase in rates of violence. Although a few laboratory studies suggest that exposure of individuals to audiovisual violence can create aggression de novo (Walters & Thomas, 1963; Walters, Thomas, & Acker, 1962), most have found that exposure to audiovisual violence augments preexisting levels of aggression rather than creating it as such (Berkowitz, 1965, 1974; Berkowitz & Alioto, 1973; Berkowitz, Corwin, & Heironimus, 1963; Berkowitz & Geen, 1966, 1967; Berkowitz & Rawlings, 1963; Donnerstein & Berkowitz, 1981; Doob & Climie, 1972; Geen, 1978, 1981; Geen & Berkowitz, 1966, 1967; Geen & O'Neal, 1969; Meyer, 1972; Worchel, Hardy, & Hurley, 1976; Zillmann, 1971).

Hypothesis B: Across populations exposed to television, the timing of the population's acquisition of television predicts the timing of the subsequent increase in rates of violence.

Population ownership of television sets in 1955 is used as an index of when television was acquired. Those populations with a higher rate of television set ownership in 1955 acquired television sets earlier (USBC, annual volumes). The timing of the increase in rates of violence (e.g., homicide) is measured by two methods (Fig. 8). For increases in the homicide rate (HR) between 1955 and 1975, the timing of the increase is measured as either 1965 HR/1955 HR (Method I) or (1965 HR − 1955 HR)/(1975 HR − 1955 HR) (Method II). With either Method I or II, the greater the ratio, the earlier was the increase in the homicide rate. In this study, both methods are used, each serving as a cross-check for the other. It is predicted that rates of television set ownership in 1955 are positively correlated with the timing of the increase in homicide rates.

Hypothesis C: Following the introduction of television, increases in rates of committing acts of violence occur first in the youngest age group, then later in successively older age groups.

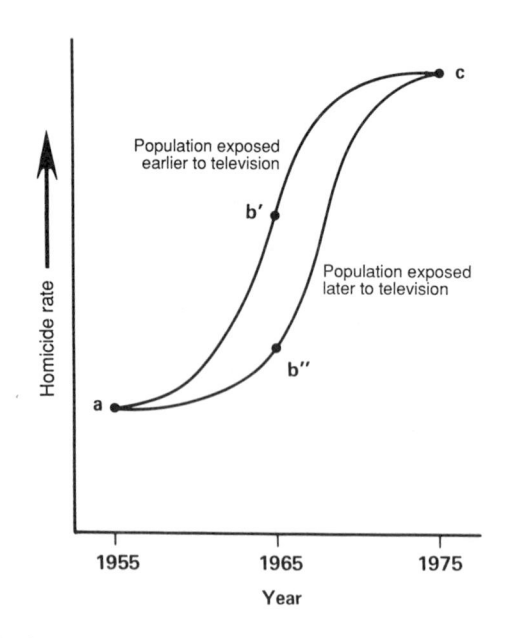

Fig. 8. Hypothesized effect of television on homicide rates in exposed populations.

It is observed in Canada and the United States that there was a lag of 10–15 years between the introduction of television and the subsequent doubling of the homicide rate (Figs. 1 and 2). This implies that if exposure to television caused a doubling of the homicide rate, the effect occurred primarily in preadolescent children: the initial television-watching generation cohort had to age 10–15 years before their increased propensity for violence could begin to affect national homicide rates. If this theory is correct, the effect of the "television generation" upon rates of violence will first be observed in the youngest age group, then later in successively older age groups. Evidence is sought for a "television generation" effect, using age-specific U.S. urban arrest rates for violent crimes (i.e., criminal homicide, aggravated assault, forcible rape, and robbery) from 1958 to 1972 [U.S. Office of Management and Budget (USOMB), 1973].

Hypotheses A and B are elaborated into a set of more specific hypotheses with respect to particular populations:

Hypothesis 1A: In countries where exposure to television can be inferred to increase levels of aggression in individuals, the introduction of television is followed by a major percentage increase in the homicide rate.

Hypothesis 1B: Across such countries, the timing of the population's acquisition of television sets predicts the timing of the subsequent increase in the homicide rate.

Hypothesis 1A is limited to countries in which one or more studies of natural exposure to television permit the inference that exposure to television increases individual levels of aggressiveness [i.e., Canada (Granzberg, 1980b; Joy et al., 1986), England (Belson, 1978), Finland (Lagerspetz & Viemerö, 1986), Israel (Bachrach, 1986), Poland (Fraczek, 1986), and the United States (Cook et al., 1983; Eron & Huesmann, 1984; Eron et al., 1972; Huesmann & Eron, 1986b; Kruttschnitt, Heath, & Ward, 1986; Milavsky, Kessler, Stipp, & Rubens, 1982)]. The index of population television set acquisition is the number of television sets per capita in 1955 (USBC, annual volumes). Israel is not included in the analysis testing of Hypothesis 1B because television broadcasting did not begin in Israel until 1968 (Bachrach, 1986); Poland is not included because Polish homicide rates are not available for the mid-1950s (WHO, 1958). Annual homicide rates, by country, are from the WHO (1958, annual volumes). To control for variation due to small numbers of homicides, national rates are presented as 3-year averages.

Hypothesis 2A: For the nine census regions of the United States, the introduction of television is followed by a major percentage increase in the homicide rate.

Hypothesis 2B: Across the nine census regions, the timing of a region's acquisition of television sets predicts the timing of the subsequent increase in the homicide rate.

The index of regional television set acquisition is the percentage of households possessing television sets in 1955; television data for 1955, by region, are from CBS Television Research [Broadcasting Telecasting (BT), 1956]. U.S. homicide rates, by region, are from the U.S. vital statistics (NCHS, annual volumes); regional homicide rates are presented as 3-year averages. Alaska and Hawaii are not included in the regional analysis because they were not states in 1955, the reference year chosen for comparing homicide rates and rates of television set ownership in the United States.

Hypothesis 3A: The introduction of television into the United States was followed by major percentage increases in average rates of criminal homicide in cities and towns of all population sizes.

Hypothesis 3B: Across U.S. cities and towns with populations of different sizes, the timing of the population acquisition of television sets predicts the timing of the subsequent increase in average rates of criminal homicide.

In 1955, the percentage of U.S. households owning television sets ranged from 52% in towns of fewer than 10,000 inhabitants to 82% in cities of more than 1,000,000 inhabitants (USBC, annual volumes). Detailed data are lacking for rates of television set ownership by size of city population. It is assumed that in the 1950s, when television stations and set ownership centered around major urban centers, the percentage of households owning television sets was positively correlated with city population. Therefore, city population is used as an index measure of percentage of households owning sets. Because city populations ranged over several orders of magnitude, this variable is expressed as the log of city population. This minimizes biases inherent in comparing changes in homicide rates to an otherwise highly skewed variable.

Data on criminal homicide rates in the United States are from the Uniform Crime Reports (USFBI, annual volumes). Criminal homicides are a subset of all homicides, excluding from all homicides those that are considered to be legally justifiable. Homicide rates and criminal homicide rates in the United States usually do not differ by more than 5% (Cantor & Cohen, 1980). The Uniform Crime Reports data collection system was revised in 1957 and again in 1976 (USFBI, annual volumes); therefore, analysis of these data was confined to the years 1958 through 1975. For cities and towns aggregated by size population, the log of population in 1958 is compared with the timing of the subsequent increase in the average criminal homicide rate (CHR). It is hypothesized that the log of city population (an index of television set ownership rates) predicts the timing of the subsequent increase in the criminal homicide rate, whether the latter is measured as 1965CHR / 1958CHR (Method I) or (1965CHR − 1958CHR) / (1975CHR − 1958CHR) (Method II).

The annual number of U.S. homicides in metropolitan and nonmetropolitan counties is from the vital statistics (NCHS, annual volumes). Population estimates for the metropolitan and nonmetropolitan counties are from periodic estimates by the USBC (annual volumes), with straight-line extrapolation for years between estimates.

Hypothesis 4A: For the United States, the acquisition of television sets was followed by a major percentage increase in the homicide rate among both whites and nonwhites.

Hypothesis 4B: Because U.S. whites acquired television sets sooner (on the average) than nonwhites, the homicide rate began to increase among whites sooner than among nonwhites.

Homicide rates, by race of victim, are from the vital statistics (NCHS, annual volumes). Although the homicide data do not specify the race of the offender, homicide in the United States is primarily an intraracial phenomenon. Thus, in U.S. single-offender–single-victim criminal homicides (1976–1978), 89% of white victims were killed by whites and 96% of black victims were killed by blacks (USFBI, annual volumes). Therefore, homicide rates by race of victim will closely parallel homicide rates by race of offender.

Hypothesis 5A: The introduction of television into the United States has been followed by a major percentage increase in the rate of committing acts of violence by both men and women.

Hypothesis 5B: Because U.S. boys and girls had equal onset of exposure to television, the subsequent increase in the rate of committing acts of violence occurred at the same time for men and women.

Exposure to television has been documented to have an aggression-enhancing effect on both boys and girls in the United States (Cook *et al.*, 1983; Eron & Huesmann, 1984; Huesmann & Eron, 1986b; Milavsky *et al.*, 1982). Therefore, a major percentage of increase in the rate of committing violence is expected for both men and women. Data on urban arrest rates for violent crimes (i.e., criminal homicide, aggravated assault, forcible rape, and robbery), by sex of offender, are from the Uniform Crime Reports (USOMB, 1973).

The test of statistical significance is a *p* value less than .05 in a one-tailed test. The test is one-tailed because the theory specifically predicts that the relationship between population exposure to television and changes in rates of violence is positive, not negative.

C. Results

Hypothesis 1A: In countries where exposure to television can be inferred to increase levels of aggression in individuals, the introduction of television is followed by a major percentage increase in the homicide rate.

Studies of natural exposure to television permit the inference that exposure to television increases individual levels of aggressiveness in Canada (Granzberg, 1980b; Joy *et al.*, 1986), England (Belson, 1978), Finland (Lagerspetz & Viemerö, 1986), Israel (Bachrach, 1986), Poland (Fraczek, 1986), and the United States (Cook *et al.*, 1983; Eron & Huesmann, 1984; Eron *et al.*, 1972; Huesmann & Eron, 1986b; Kruttschnitt *et al.*, 1986; Milavsky *et al.*, 1982).

Television was introduced into England, Canada, and the United States in the late 1940s (UNESCO, annual volumes). Between 1954–1956 and 1974–1976, the average annual homicide rate in England increased from 0.6 homicides per 100,000 population to 1.0 homicides per 100,000—an 80% increase (WHO, 1958, annual volumes). The average annual homicide rate in Canada increased from 1.2 to 2.5 homicides per 100,000—a 108% increase (WHO, 1958, annual volumes). The average annual homicide rate in the United States increased from 4.6 to 9.8 homicides per 100,000—a 113% increase (WHO, 1958, annual volumes). Television was introduced into Finland in 1955 (Lagerspetz & Viemerö,

1986). Between 1964–1966 and 1974–1976, the average annual homicide rate in Finland increased from 2.1 to 3.2 homicides per 100,000—a 52% increase (WHO, annual volumes). Television was introduced into Poland in 1955 (Fraczek, 1986). Between 1963–1964 and 1983–1984, the average annual homicide rate in Poland increased from 1.0 to 1.6 homicides per 100,000—a 60% increase (WHO, annual volumes). Television was introduced into Israel in 1968 (Bachrach, 1986). Between 1971–1973 and 1981–1983, the average annual homicide rate in Israel increased from 1.0 to 1.9 homicides per 100,000—a 90% increase (WHO, annual volumes).

Hypothesis 1B: Across such countries, the timing of the population's acquisition of television sets predicts the timing of the subsequent increase in the homicide rate.

In 1955, the number of television sets per capita ranged from 0.00 television sets per capita in Finland to 0.22 television sets per capita in the United States (see Table II) (USBC, annual volumes). U.S. homicide rates began to increase in 1959 (NCHS, annual volumes), whereas Finnish homicide rates did not begin increasing until 1969 (WHO, annual volumes). When the timing of the increase in the homicide rate is measured by (b) / (a) (Method I; see Fig. 8), the correlation between television sets per capita in 1955 and the timing of the subsequent increase in the homicide rate is 0.98 ($p = .01$; Table II; Fig. 9). When the timing of the increase in the homicide rate is measured by (b − a) / (c − a) (Method II; see Fig. 8), the correlation between television sets per capita in 1955 and the timing of the subsequent increase in the homicide rate is 0.84 ($p = .08$; Table II; Fig. 10). Populations that acquired television sets earlier had an earlier increase in their homicide rates; populations that acquired television sets later showed a later increase in their homicide rates.

Hypothesis 2A: For the nine census regions of the United States, the introduction of television is followed by a major percentage increase in the homicide rate.

Between 1954–1956 and 1974–1976, all census regions of the United States experienced major percentages of increase in rates of homicide, ranging from a 38% increase in the East South Central region to a 228% increase in the Middle Atlantic region (Table III).

Hypothesis 2B: Across the nine census regions, the timing of a region's acquisition of television sets predicts the timing of the subsequent increase in the homicide rate.

In 1955, the percentage of U.S. households with television sets ranged from 45% in the East South Central region to 80% in the Middle Atlantic Region

TABLE II
Television Sets per Capita (1955) and Homicide Rates (1955–1975): Canada, England, Finland, and the United States[a]

Country	Homicide rate[b] (homicides/100,000 population) 1955 (a)	1965 (b)	1975 (c)	Timing of the homicide rate increase[c] (Method I) (b)/(a)	Timing of the homicide rate increase[c] (Method II) (b − a)/(c − a)	Television sets per capita (1955)
Canada	1.2	1.3	2.5	1.08	0.08	0.13
England and Wales	0.6	0.6	1.0	1.00	0.00	0.09[d]
Finland	2.8	2.1	3.2	0.75	−1.75	0.00
United States	4.6	5.5	9.8	1.20	0.17	0.22

[a] Source of homicide data, World Health Organization (annual volumes); source of television data, Statistical Abstract of the United States (U.S. Bureau of the Census, annual volumes).
[b] Three-year bracketed average.
[c] See Fig. 8.
[d] United Kingdom.

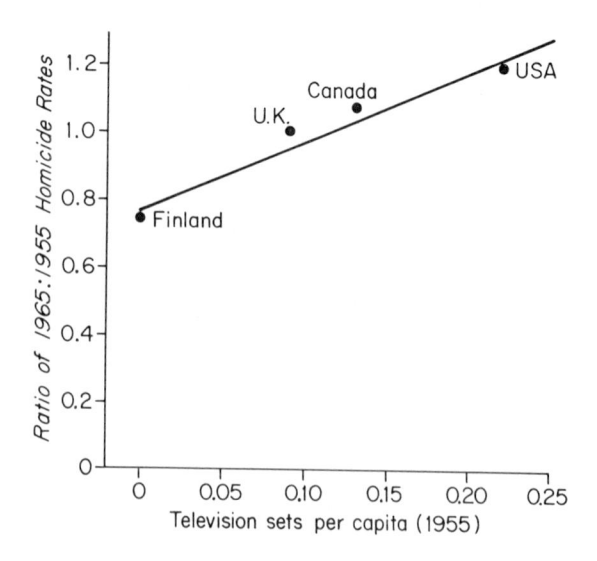

Fig. 9. Correlation between television sets per capita (1955) and subsequent changes in the homicide rate (1955–1975) by country (Method I): Canada, United Kingdom, Finland, and the United States. $r = 0.98$; $p = 0.01$; $y = 0.78 + 2.04x$. Source of homicide rates: World Health Organization (annual volumes). Source of television data: U.S. Bureau of the Census (annual volumes).

(Table III) (BT, 1956). Middle Atlantic homicide rates began to increase in 1958, whereas West South Central homicide rates did not begin increasing until 1964; homicide rates in other census regions began to increase in intermediate years (NCHS, annual volumes). When the timing of the increase in the homicide rate is measured by (b) / (a) (Method I; see Fig. 8), the correlation between the percentage of households with television sets in 1955 and the timing of the subsequent increase in the homicide rate is 0.82 ($p = .003$; Table III; Fig. 11). When the timing of the increase in the homicide rate is measured by (b − a) / (c − a) (Method II; see Fig. 8), the correlation between percentage of households with television sets in 1955 and the timing of the subsequent increase in the homicide rate is 0.80 ($p = .005$; Table III; Fig. 12). Regions that acquired television sets earlier had an earlier increase in their homicide rates; regions that acquired television sets later had a later increase in their homicide rates.

Hypothesis 3A: The introduction of television into the United States was followed by major percentage increases in average rates of criminal homicide in cities and towns of all population sizes.

Between 1955 and 1975, homicide rates in U.S. nonmetropolitan counties rose from 4.5 to 7.2 homicides per 100,000 population—a 60% increase;

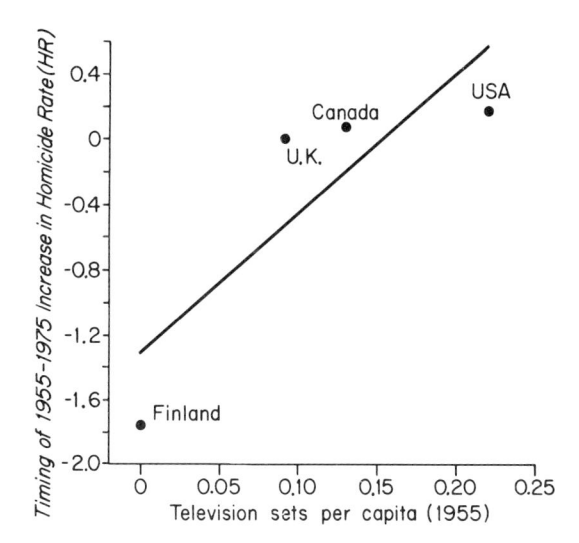

Fig. 10. Correlation between television sets per capita (1955) and subsequent changes in the homicide rate (1955-1975) by country (Method II): Canada, United Kingdom, Finland, and the United States. $r = 0.84$; $p = 0.08$; $y = -1.31 + 8.51x$. The timing of the increase in the homicide rate was measured by (1965 HR − 1955 HR) / (1975 HR − 1955 HR). A larger number is equivalent to an earlier timing. Source of homicide rates: World Health Organization (annual volumes). Source of television data: U.S. Bureau of the Census (annual volumes).

homicide rates in U.S. metropolitan counties rose from 4.7 to 11.5 homicides per 100,000—a 145% increase (Fig. 13) (USBC, annual volumes; NCHS, annual volumes). Between 1958 and 1975, rates of criminal homicide rose in cities and towns of all population sizes, ranging from an average increase of 63% in towns of fewer than 10,000 inhabitants to an average increase of 332% in cities of more than 1,000,000 inhabitants (Table IV).

Hypothesis 3B: Across U.S. cities and towns with populations of different sizes, the timing of the population acquisition of television sets predicts the timing of the subsequent increase in average rates of criminal homicide.

In 1955, 50% of households in U.S. nonmetropolitan counties possessed television sets, as compared to 78% of households in metropolitan counties (USBC, annual volumes). Although metropolitan and nonmetropolitan counties had the same homicide rate in 1950, the homicide rate increased earlier in the metropolitan counties than in the nonmetropolitan counties (Fig. 13).

In 1955, the percentage of U.S. households owning television sets ranged from 52% in towns of fewer than 10,000 inhabitants to 82% in cities of more than 1,000,000 inhabitants—a 1.58-fold range (i.e., 82% / 52% = 1.58; USBC,

TABLE III
Television Ownership (1955) and Homicide Rates (1955–1975) by Geographic Region: United States[a]

Region	Homicide rate[b] (homicides/100,000 population) 1955 (a)	1965 (b)	1975 (c)	Timing of the homicide rate increase[c] (Method I) (b) / (a)	Timing of the homicide rate increase[c] (Method II) (b − a) / (c − a)	Percentage of households with television (1955)
New England	1.2	2.0	3.7	1.67	0.32	78
Middle Atlantic	2.6	5.1	8.5	1.96	0.42	80
East North Central	3.4	4.2	9.2	1.24	0.14	77
West North Central	2.6	3.2	5.4	1.23	0.21	61
South Atlantic	8.7	9.4	13.7	1.08	0.14	58
East South Central	9.5	9.2	13.1	0.97	−0.08	45
West South Central	7.4	8.2	13.2	1.11	0.14	53
Mountain	4.2	4.6	7.9	1.10	0.11	46
Pacific	3.5	4.5	9.2	1.29	0.18	67

[a] Source of homicide data, National Center for Health Statistics (annual volumes); source of television data, CBS-TV Research (Broadcasting Telecasting, 1956).
[b] Three-year bracketed average.
[c] See Fig. 8.

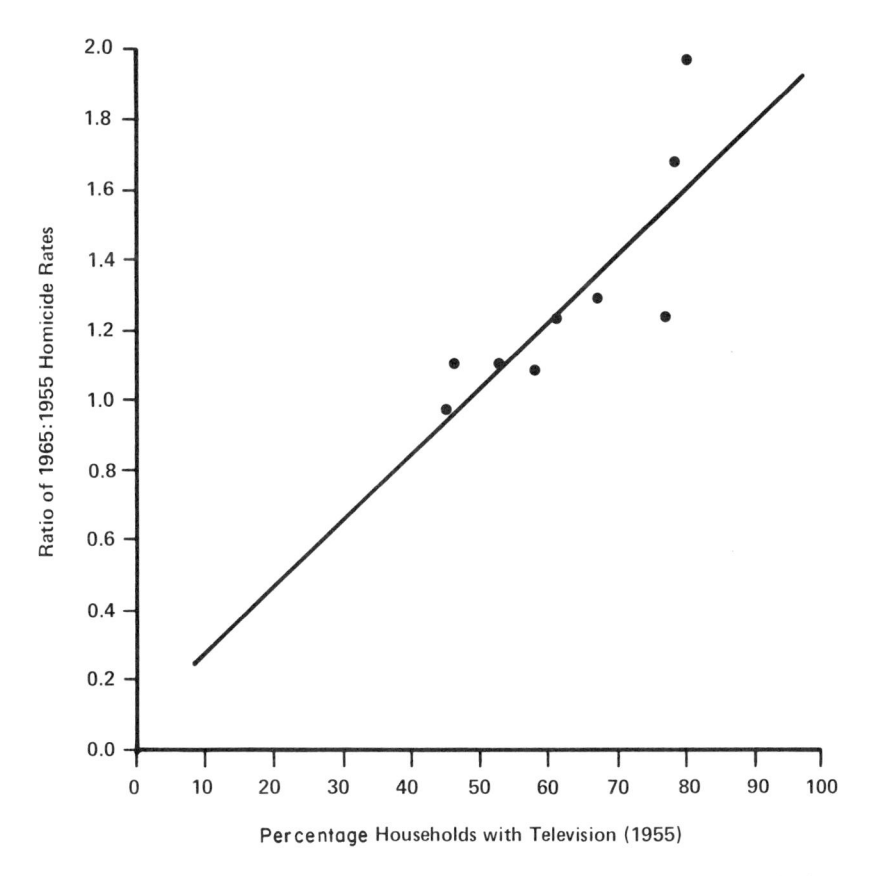

Fig. 11. Correlation between percentage of households owning television sets (1955) and subsequent changes in the homicide rate by region (Method I): United States, 1955–1975. $r = 0.82$; $p = 0.003$; $y = 0.081 + 0.019x$. Source of homicide rates: National Center for Health Statistics (annual volumes). Source of television ownership data: CBS-TV Research (Broadcasting Telecasting, 1956).

annual volumes). For cities and towns aggregated by population size, in 1958, the log of city population ranged from 3.74 for towns of fewer than 10,000 inhabitants to 6.55 for cities of more than 1,000,000 inhabitants (Table IV)— a 1.75-fold range (i.e., 6.55 / 3.74 = 1.75) (USFBI, annual volumes). Using the log of city population in 1958 as an index of rates of household ownership of television sets provides a range of values closely similar to the range of observed rates of household ownership of television sets in 1955; using the log avoids a skewing bias.

For cities with more than 250,000 inhabitants, the average criminal homicide rate began to increase in 1956, whereas for towns with fewer than 10,000

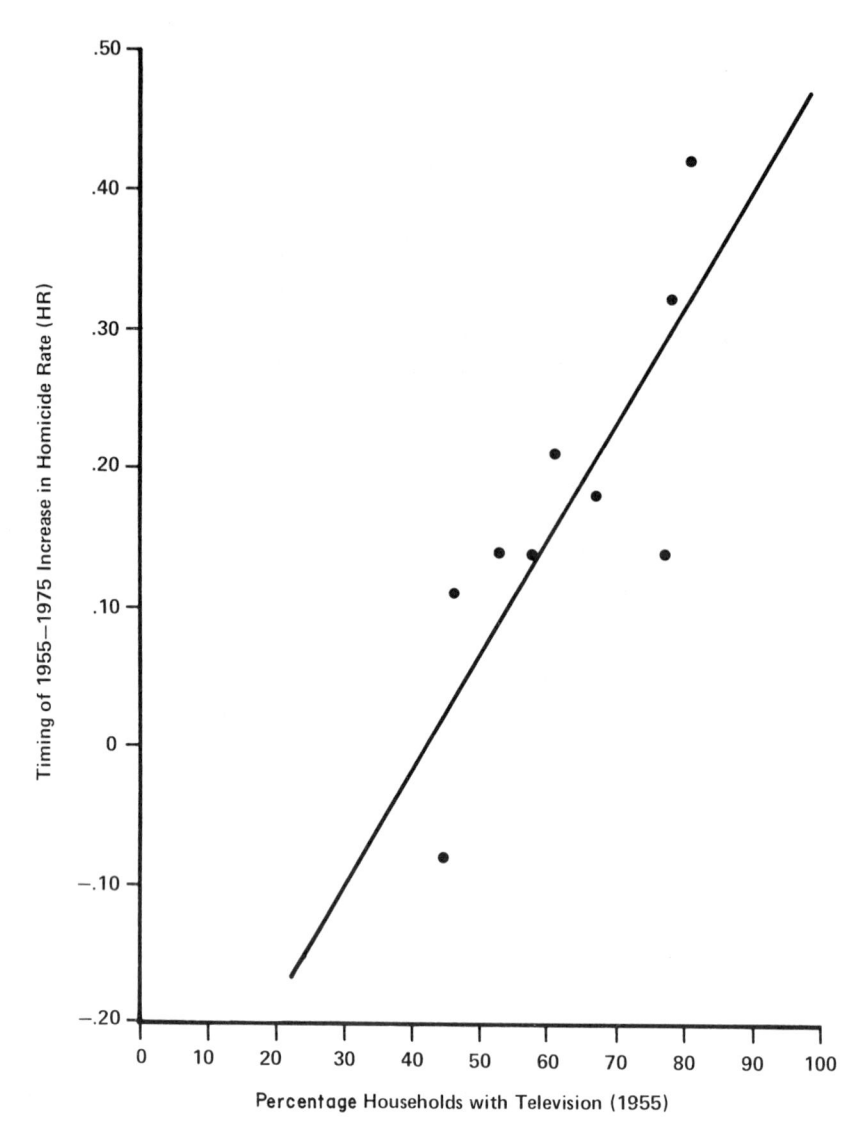

Fig. 12. Correlation between percentage of households owning television sets (1955) and subsequent changes in the homicide rate by region (Method II): United States, 1955–1975. The timing of the increase in the homicide rate was measured by (1965 HR − 1955 HR) / (1975 HR − 1955 HR). A larger number is equivalent to an earlier timing. $r = 0.80$; $p = .005$; $y = -0.339 + 0.008x$. Source of homicide rates: National Center for Health Statistics (annual volumes). Source of television ownership data: CBS-TV Research (Broadcasting Telecasting, 1956).

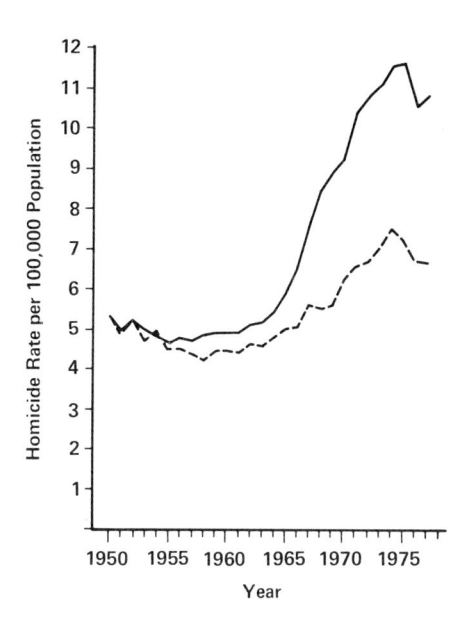

Fig. 13. Homicide rates in standard metropolitan statistical areas (SMSAs) (solid line) and in non-SMSAs (broken line): United States, 1955–1977. Source of homicide data: National Center for Health Statistics (annual volumes). Source of population data: U.S. Bureau of the Census (annual volumes).

inhabitants the average criminal homicide rate did not begin increasing until 1964; populations living in cities of intermediate population size began to experience increases in criminal homicide rates in intermediate years (USFBI, annual volumes). Using the log of city population in 1958 as an index of rates of television set ownership (Table IV), the correlation was examined between the log of city population in 1958 and the timing of the subsequent increase in the average rate of criminal homicide. When the timing of the increase in the criminal homicide rate is measured as (b) / (a) (Method I; see Fig. 8), the correlation is 0.89 ($p = .002$; Table IV; Fig. 14). When the timing of the increase in the criminal homicide rate is measured as (b − a) / (c − a) (Method II; see Fig. 8), the correlation is .74 ($p = .02$; Table IV; Fig. 15). City populations acquiring television sets earlier had an earlier increase in their criminal homicide rates; city populations acquiring television sets later had a later increase in their criminal homicide rates.

Hypothesis 4A: For the United States, the acquisition of television sets was followed by a major percentage increase in the homicide rate among both whites and nonwhites.

TABLE IV
Criminal Homicide Rates by Population of City: United States, 1958-1975[a]

Population of city	Number of cities in sample 1958	Mean population of cities 1958	Log of mean population of cities 1958	Criminal homicide rate (homicides/100,000 population) 1958 (a)	1965 (b)	1975 (c)	Timing of the homicide rate increase[b] (Method I) (b) / (a)	Timing of the homicide rate increase[b] (Method II) (b − a) / (c − a)
≥1,000,000	5	3,581,991	6.55	5.7	9.6	24.6	1.68	0.21
500,000–999,999	17	710,487	5.85	7.1	10.4	20.1	1.46	0.25
250,000–499,999	23	370,836	5.57	6.5	7.2	17.6	1.11	0.06
100,000–249,999	85	148,862	5.17	5.2	6.4	10.9	1.23	0.21
50,000–99,999	173	68,266	4.83	3.6	3.5	7.2	0.97	−0.03
25,000–49,999	361	34,914	4.54	2.8	3.1	5.7	1.11	0.10
10,000–24,999	820	15,774	4.20	2.1	2.3	4.4	1.10	0.09
<10,000	1,792	5,468	3.74	2.4	2.0	3.9	0.83	−0.27

[a] Source: Population and criminal homicide data, FBI Uniform Crime Reports (U.S. Federal Bureau of Investigation, annual volumes).
[b] See Fig. 8.

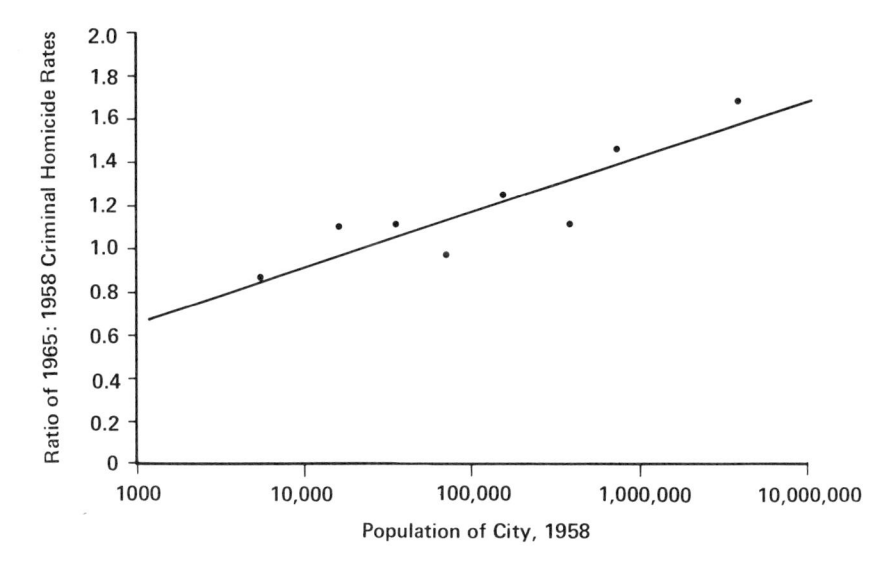

Fig. 14. Correlation between log of city population (1958) and subsequent changes in average criminal homicide rate by size population of cities (Method I): United States, 1958-1975. $r = 0.89$; $p = .002$; $y = -0.14 + 0.26 \log x$. Source of criminal homicide rates: U.S. Federal Bureau of Investigation (annual volumes).

Between 1955 and 1975, homicide rates among U.S. nonwhite groups rose from 22.8 to 37.1 homicides per 100,000 population —a 63% increase; white homicide rates rose from 2.3 to 5.9 homicides per 100,000—a 157% increase (NCHS, annual volumes).

Hypothesis 4B: Because U.S. whites acquired television sets sooner (on the average) than nonwhites, the homicide rate began to increase among whites sooner than among nonwhites.

On the average, white populations in the United States acquired their first television sets before blacks and other nonwhite populations. As late as 1960, 73% of nonwhite households owned television sets as compared to 89% of white households (USBC, 1963). For the total U.S. population, it took 5 years for the percentage of households with television sets to increase from 72% to 89% (TBA, 1982). Assuming that the time curve for acquiring television sets was the same for whites and nonwhites, the 1960 data indicate that blacks and other nonwhite households acquired their first television sets an average of 5 years later than white households. White homicide rates began increasing in 1958, whereas homicide rates among blacks and other nonwhite populations did not begin increasing until 1962—a difference of 4 years (Fig. 16).

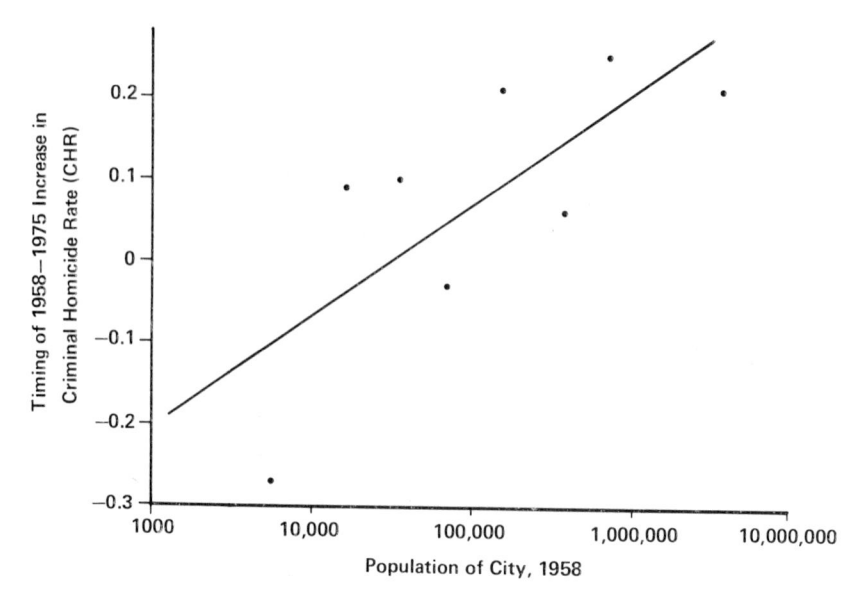

Fig. 15. Correlation between log of city population (1958) and subsequent changes in criminal homicide rate by size population of cities (Method II): United States, 1958-1975. The timing of the increase in the criminal homicide rate (CHR) was measured by (1965 CHR − 1958 CHR) / (1975 CHR − 1958 CHR). A larger number is equivalent to an earlier timing. $r = 0.74$; $p = .02$; $y = -0.61 + 0.14 \log x$. Source of criminal homicide rates: U.S. Federal Bureau of Investigation (annual volumes).

Hypothesis 5A: The introduction of television into the United States has been followed by a major percentage increase in the rate of committing acts of violence by both men and women.

In U.S. studies, exposure to television increases levels of aggression in boys and girls (Cook *et al.*, 1983; Eron & Huesmann, 1984; Huesmann & Eron, 1986b; Milavsky *et al.*, 1982). In a prospective 22-year study of a U.S. birth cohort, the frequency of watching television at age 8 years significantly predicted the seriousness of criminal offenses committed by age 30 for both men ($p < .001$) and women ($p < .05$) (Eron & Huesmann, 1984). For U.S. men, annual urban arrest rates for violent crimes (i.e., criminal homicide, aggravated assault, forcible rape, and robbery) rose from 206.5 arrests per 100,000 population (age 10 years and over) in 1958 to 492.5 arrests per 100,000 (age 10 and over) in 1972—a 138% increase (Fig. 17) (USOMB, 1973). For U.S. women, annual urban arrest rates for violent crimes rose from 24.9 arrests per 100,000 (age 10 and over) in 1958 to 53.3 arrests per 100,000 (age 10 and over) in 1972—a 114% increase (Fig. 17) (USOMB, 1973).

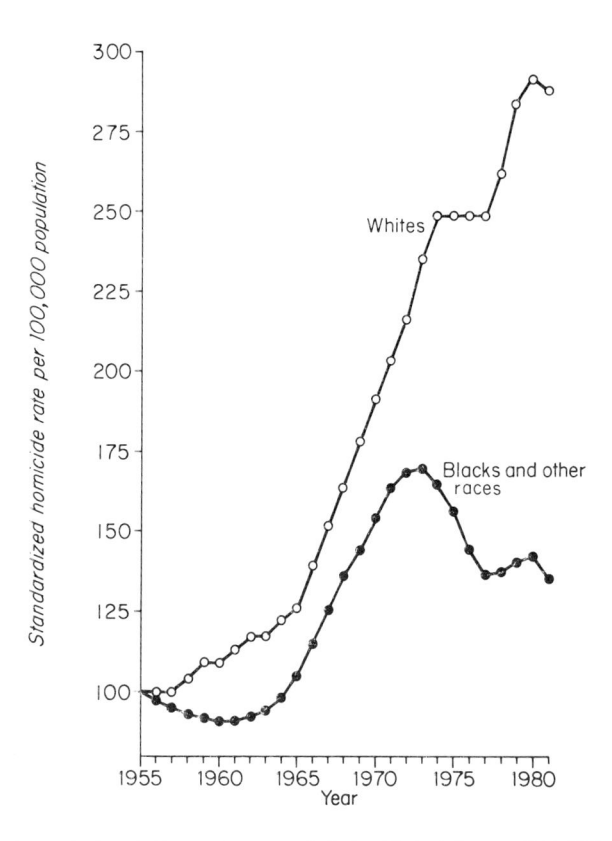

Fig. 16. Change in homicide rate by race of victim: United States, 1955-1981 (1955 = 100; 3-year moving average). Source of data: National Center for Health Statistics (annual volumes).

Hypothesis 5B: Because U.S. boys and girls had equal onset of exposure to television, the subsequent increase in the rate of committing acts of violence occurred at the same time for men and women.

Onset of change in U.S. urban arrest rates for violent crimes occurred at the same time for men and women (Fig. 17).

Hypothesis C: Following the introduction of television, increases in rates of committing acts of violence occur first in the youngest age group, then later in successively older age groups.

Between 1958 and 1967, U.S. urban arrest rates for violent crimes rose 41% for adults ages 25 and older, 45% for young adults ages 18-24, 102% for adolescents ages 15-17, and 222% for children ages 10-14 (Fig. 18).

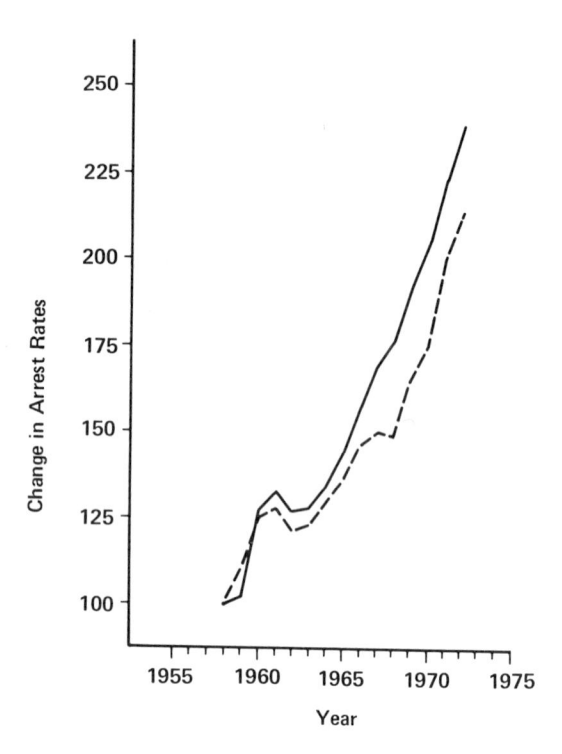

Fig. 17. Change in urban arrest rates for violent crimes (murder, aggravated assault, forcible rape, and robbery) by gender of offender: United States 1958-1972 (1958 = 100). Solid line, males; broken line, females. Source of data: U.S. Office of Management and Budget (1973).

Children ages 10-14 exhibited changes in arrest rates for violent crimes that paralleled those of older individuals until 1960, at which time they began to rise disproportionately (Fig. 18). Half of all American households had acquired television sets by 1954 (TBA, 1982). If 1954 is taken as the median year in which television exerted its initial influence upon American children, this implies a 6-year lag before the effect of television on children in 1954 manifested itself as increased rates of violence among children ages 10-14. The data are internally consistent; children ages 10-14 in 1960 would have been 4-8 years old in 1954.

Adolescents ages 15-17 exhibited changes in arrest rates for violent crimes that paralleled those of older individuals until 1965, at which time they began to rise disproportionately (Fig. 18). This implies an 11-year lag before the effect of television on American children in 1954 manifested itself as increased rates

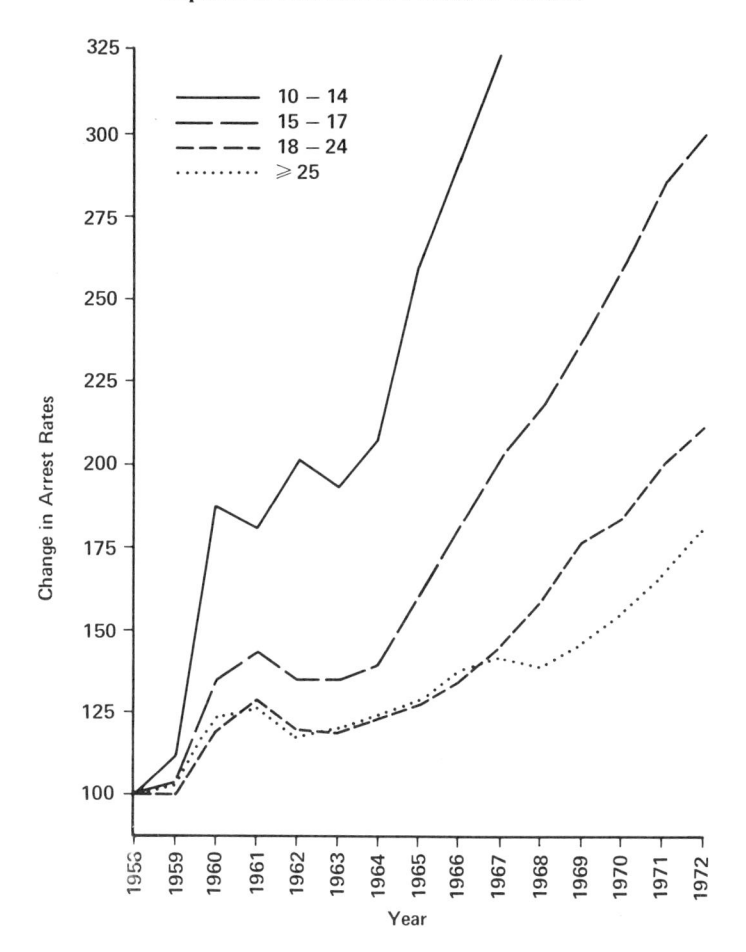

Fig. 18. Change in urban arrest rates for violent crimes (murder, aggravated assault, forcible rape, and robbery) by age of offender: United States, 1958–1972 (1958 = 100). Data for children ages 10–14 are limited to 1958–1967. Source of data: U.S. Office of Management and Budget (1973).

of violence among adolescents ages 15–17. The data are internally consistent; adolescents ages 15–17 in 1965 would have been 4–6 years old in 1954.

Young adults ages 18–24 exhibited changes in arrest rates for violent crimes that paralleled those of older individuals until 1968, at which time they began to rise disproportionately (Fig. 18). This implies a 14-year lag before the effect of television on American children in 1954 manifested itself as increased rates of violence among young adults ages 18–24. The data are internally consistent; young adults ages 18–24 in 1968 would have been 4–10 years old in 1954.

D. Discussion

Comparisons of South Africa with Canada and the United States indicated that the introduction of television into Canada and the United States caused a subsequent doubling of their respective homicide rates (see Section I). The more general theory—that exposure of susceptible populations to television causes a major percentage increase in rates of violence—has been tested here against 11 falsifiable hypotheses. All 11 hypotheses have been empirically validated, supporting the theory of a causal relationship between exposure of populations to television and a major percentage increase in rates of serious violence. Of six statistical tests of the causal association, five reach statistical significance (Figs. 9, 11, 12, 14, and 15) and the sixth approaches statistical significance (Fig. 10). Variations in the time of population acquisition of television sets account for 55-96% of the variance in the timing of subsequent increases in homicide rates (Figs. 9-12 and 14-15). A birth-cohort effect is demonstrated, with major increases in rates of committing acts of violence occurring first in the youngest age group and then in successively older age groups, as the "television generation" comes of age (Fig. 18).

Barnett, Kleitman, and Larson (1975) observed that rates of criminal homicide increased in every major U.S. city between 1963 and 1972. From their statistical analysis, they found that the pattern of increases in homicide rate by city could be almost entirely explained as variations around a common national trend (i.e., increases in the rate of criminal homicide for a given city could be better explained in terms of a national phenomenon than in terms of the unique political and historical determinants of that city). They further observed that the increase in the national criminal homicide rate was mathematically best described by a saturation curve (Fig. 8 contains examples of saturation curves). As to what national phenomenon was saturating the nation, that question was left unanswered.

As with other studies without internal controls, it is important that the data testing a falsifiable hypothesis be examined *after* the hypothesis has been formulated (Bailar *et al.*, 1984). It was not possible to meet this criterion in all respects in the present study. I already knew from prior research that there had been major increases in homicide rates among both whites and nonwhites in the United States (Centerwall, 1984) and that homicide rates had increased in all regions of the United States. And, of course, I already knew that national homicide rates had increased in Canada and the United States (see Section I). Therefore, data necessary for testing two of the hypotheses (Hypotheses 2A and 4A) were known prior to the analysis, as well as part of the data for testing a third hypothesis (Hypothesis 1A). The remainder of the data were examined and analyzed after the hypotheses were formulated.

In the present study the issue of the ecological fallacy is rendered moot.

The ecological fallacy occurs whenever there is an attempt to use aggregated data to infer causality at the level of the individual (Robinson, 1950). Because a causal relationship between exposure to television and subsequent increases in physical aggression has already been established at the level of the individual (Bachrach, 1986; Belson, 1978; Cook *et al.*, 1983; Eron & Huesmann, 1984; Eron *et al.*, 1972; Fraczek, 1986; Huesmann & Eron, 1986b; Joy *et al.*, 1986; Kruttschnitt *et al.*, 1986; Lagerspetz & Viemerö, 1986; Milavsky *et al.*, 1982; Singer *et al.*, 1984), there is no further need in this study for inferences to be made regarding the nature of causality at the level of the individual. The issue addressed in this study is whether certain hypotheses, regarding the effect of aggregate exposures to television upon aggregate rates of violence, are correct or not—hypotheses that can only be tested through the use of aggregated data (Centerwall, 1989).

All the hypotheses examined the relationship between population patterns of television set acquisition and subsequent changes in rates of violence. It is trivially obvious that later patterns of violence cannot cause earlier patterns of television set acquisition. Therefore, either earlier patterns of television set acquisition caused later patterns of violence or some third variable created a spurious association between earlier patterns of television set acquisition and later patterns of violence. Such a third variable would have to be more closely correlated with both television and violence than television and violence are with each other. Because earlier exposure to television and later changes in homicide rates are already closely related ($r = .74-.98$; Figs. 9-12 and 14-15), any presumptive third variable would have to be very closely correlated indeed with both television and violence in order to explain away the observed association between the latter two.

Because television sets are a luxury commodity, it is amusing to speculate whether the key variable might not be some luxury commodity other than television (backyard barbecue grills? four-slice toasters?). Because ownership of these other luxury items would be correlated with the ownership of television sets, it is a priori likely that they would also correlate with subsequent changes in rates of violence. Such speculation must necessarily ignore the large body of empirical knowledge relating exposure to television and audio-visual violence with subsequent aggression (see Section III) (Bachrach, 1986; Belson, 1978; Berkowitz, 1965, 1974; Berkowitz & Alioto, 1973; Berkowitz *et al.*, 1963; Berkowitz & Geen, 1966, 1967; Berkowitz & Rawlings, 1963; Comstock, Chaffee, Katzman, McCombs, & Roberts, 1978; Cook *et al.*, 1983; Donnerstein & Berkowitz, 1981; Doob & Climie, 1972; Eron & Huesmann, 1984; Eron *et al.*, 1972; Fraczek, 1986; Geen, 1978, 1981; Geen & Berkowitz, 1966, 1967; Geen & O'Neal, 1969; Huesmann & Eron, 1986b; Joy *et al.*, 1986; Kruttschnitt *et al.*, 1986; Lagerspetz & Viemerö, 1986; Meyer, 1972; Milavsky *et al.*, 1982; Pearl, Bouthilet, & Lazar, 1982; Singer *et al.*, 1984; Walters & Thomas, 1963;

Walters *et al.*, 1962; Worchel *et al.*, 1976; Zillmann, 1971), and must also pass over the absence of any credible rationale for how the ownership of backyard barbecue grills and four-slice toasters leads to higher rates of violence. Moreover, since it is only the observed relationship between television and violence which leads to speculations regarding the relationships between barbecue grills (or toasters) and violence, the latter hypotheses have no independent predictive value. Gathering the data and working out the correlations would add nothing to what is already known.

More seriously, the ownership of television sets is a sign of economic well-being, and rates of violence in the United States increased during a period of economic growth and prosperity. Therefore, it may be economic prosperity itself that is causing both the patterns of television set acquisition and the patterns of increased rates of violence. This theory would be consistent with the data observed in this analysis.

If the economic theory is correct, it would follow that those populations that made greater economic gains should have had greater percentages of increase in rates of violence. Between 1955 and 1975, the per capita income for U.S. nonwhites, expressed in constant dollars (USBC, 1979), rose 84%, as compared to 51% for whites (Darity, 1980). According to the economic theory, there should have been a greater percentage of increase in homicide rates among nonwhites as compared to whites. However, between 1955 and 1975, homicide rates among blacks and other nonwhites increased by only 63% as compared to a 157% increase among whites (Fig. 16).

Between 1959 and 1974, rates of poverty declined by 57% in U.S. nonmetropolitan areas, as compared to a 37% decline in metropolitan areas (USBC, 1981). According to the economic theory, there should have been a greater percentage of increase in homicide rates in nonmetropolitan areas as compared to metropolitan areas. However, between 1959 and 1974, homicide rates in nonmetropolitan areas increased by only 70% as compared to a 135% increase in metropolitan areas (Fig. 13).

Between 1959 and 1974, rates of poverty in the U.S. South decreased by 56%, as compared to a 43% decrease elsewhere (USBC, 1981). According to the economic theory, there should have been a greater percentage of increase in homicide rates in the South as compared to elsewhere. However, between 1959 and 1974, homicide rates in the South increased by only 79% as compared to a 165% increase in other regions of the United States (NCHS, annual volumes).

In each instance of testing the economic theory, the results are in the direction opposite from what was predicted. Rather than increasing homicide rates, it appears that improving economic status actually ameliorates the increase in the homicide rate, making it less than it otherwise would be. But if improving economic status serves to ameliorate the increase in homicide rates, then something else must be causing the homicide rates to go up in the first place. Exposure to television is associated with economic prosperity, but the former increases rates of violence whereas the latter ameliorates that increase.

Any alternative explanation will need to account for an array of findings: (1) why homicide rates increased among Canadians and U.S. whites but not among South African whites; (2) why homicide rates increased among U.S. whites prior to increasing among U.S. nonwhites; (3) why homicide rates increased among more urban U.S. populations prior to increasing among less urban populations; (4) why homicide rates increased in some regions of the United States prior to others; (5) why rates of committing acts of violence have increased proportionately for both men and women in the United States; and (6) why rates of committing acts of violence increased first in the youngest age group followed by increases in successively older age groups. The constraints these findings place upon any possible alternative explanation are so severe that the a priori probability of such an alternative explanation being found is quite low.

The theory of a causal relationship between exposure to television and subsequent violence has been tested successfully against falsifiable hypotheses. The available information meet the epidemiological criteria for causality (Rothman, 1982): The observed relationship is consistent across diverse populations. The timing of the acquisition of television predicts the timing of the subsequent increase in rates of violence. The observed relationship is consistent with the results of numerous controlled experiments and observational studies. And there is a biologically plausible explanation for how exposure to television can cause increases in rates of violence (Comstock *et al.*, 1978; Huesmann, 1986; Pearl *et al.*, 1982; Tan, 1986).

What has been the effect of exposure to television upon rates of violence in the United States? Following the introduction of television in the 1950s, homicide rates doubled (see Fig. 2). A doubling of the homicide rate after everyone is exposed to television implies that the relative risk of homicide after prolonged exposure to television, as compared to no exposure, is approximately 2:1. A 2:1 relative risk indicates that exposure to television is not a strong risk factor for homicide. It is only by virtue of being ubiquitous that it exerts an effect on general rates of violence. If the doubling of the homicide rate is primarily attributable to the introduction of television, then the population attributable risk is approximately 50%. In other words, the evidence presented in this study indicates that, of the approximately 20,000 homicides occurring annually in the United States (NCHS, annual volumes), 50%—or approximately 10,000 homicides annually—are caused in part by exposure of the U.S. population to television. As previously noted (Section I.D.2.e.), exposure of the U.S. population to television need only increase mean levels of physical aggressiveness by 0.2σ—a minor effect—to cause a doubling of the homicide rate (Fig. 6). Although the data are not as well-developed for other forms of violence, it appears plausible that exposure to television is also causally related to a major proportion—perhaps half—of rapes, assaults, robberies, and other forms of interpersonal violence in the United States (Figs. 17 and 18).

III. NATURAL EXPOSURE TO TELEVISION AS A CAUSE OF AGGRESSION: A REVIEW OF THE LITERATURE

Studies at the individual level have investigated whether natural exposure to television increases levels of physical aggressiveness in individual viewers. For prospective studies of naturally exposed individuals, the research paradigm now accepted for assessing causality was developed by Milavsky and associates in the National Broadcasting Company (NBC) Panel Study (Milavsky et al., 1982):

The basic model of this approach, expressed here in linear terms, is the following equation for respondent$_i$:

$$A_t = a + b_1 A_{(t-1)} + b_2 TV_{(t-1)} + u_i \qquad (1)$$

In the equation, the lagged influences of violent television exposure (TV) and aggression (A) at time $t - 1$ are studied, with the individual's prediction error indicated by u_i. The outcome of interest is aggression measured at time t.

Note that the lagged aggression measure, $A_{(t-1)}$, is included as a predictor along with the lagged exposure measure, $TV_{(t-1)}$. As a result, this model effectively rules out any influence on the television effect caused by the initial correlation between earlier television and aggression, and, hence, also the influences of the causal forces that created the initial correlation. This model also ensures that any observed television–aggression association cannot be due to an influence from a tendency of previously aggressive children to self-select violent programs. Any such effect will be part of the initial correlation and thus will be controlled out. In the absence of any other causes of aggression that are related to $TV_{(t-1)}$, the coefficient b_2 thus yields an unbiased estimate of television's lagged causal influence on aggression. (Milavsky et al., 1982, pp. 115–116)

Because controlling for aggression at time $t - 1$ factors out all influences which determine aggression at time $t - 1$, it also factors out any influence television exerted on the individual's level of aggression over a lifetime of exposure through time $t - 1$. Thus, this model measures only the causal influence television exerts upon aggression between times $t - 1$ and t, above and beyond the causal influence exerted prior to time $t - 1$. It follows that, although the model permits a strong test of causality, the measured effect of exposure to television between times $t - 1$ and t will substantially underestimate the total effect of a lifetime's exposure to television. The longer the observed time span between $t - 1$ and t, the greater will be the observed cumulative effect of exposure to television. Conversely, as the time span between $t - 1$ and t approaches zero, the observed effect b_2 also approaches zero [when the time span is zero (i.e., time t = time $t - 1$), then $A_t = A_{(t-1)}$ and $b_2 = 0$; see Equation (1)]. Milavsky and associates have documented empirically that for preadolescent children, the observed partial coefficient b_2 for the effect of exposure to television violence upon children's level of aggressiveness is, on the average, greatest when the observational time span is 2 years or more (Milavsky et al., 1982, pp. 130, 238). The observed relationship between length of observational time span and b_2 is not to be expected unless exposure to television actually does cause changes in levels of aggressiveness. Based on the observations of Milavsky and associates, the present review of the literature is limited to studies in which the observational time span is 2 years or more.

In a cross national study (completed in 1983) utilizing the NBC Panel Study model, investigators in five countries prospectively observed cohorts of first and third graders for 2 years to determine the effect of exposure to television violence upon levels of physical aggression (Bachrach, 1986; Fraczek, 1986; Huesmann & Eron, 1986b; Lagerspetz & Viemerö, 1986; Sheehan, 1986). In a cohort of 221 American girls, levels of viewing television violence over the 2 years significantly predicted levels of physical aggressiveness on follow-up ($p < .01$; standardized $b_2 = 0.14$) (Huesmann & Eron, 1986b). For a cohort of 191 American boys, levels of viewing television violence over the 2 years—combined multiplicatively with the boys' degree of identification with aggressive television characters—significantly predicted levels of physical aggressiveness on follow-up ($p < .01$; standardized $b_2 = 0.15$) (Huesmann & Eron, 1986b). The same multiplicative measure applied to a cohort of 80 Finnish boys also significantly predicted levels of physical aggressiveness on 2-year follow-up ($p < .01$; standardized $b_2 = 0.20$) (Lagerspetz & Viemerö, 1986). Levels of physical aggressiveness in a cohort of 85 Finnish girls were not significantly influenced by the television violence they watched (Lagerspetz & Viemerö, 1986). In a cohort of 85 Israeli city children, levels of viewing television violence over the 2 years significantly predicted levels of physical aggressiveness in both boys ($p < .05$; standardized $b_2 = 0.29$) and girls ($p < .01$; standardized $b_2 = 0.52$); levels of physical aggressiveness in a cohort of 73 Israeli kibbutz children were not significantly influenced by the television violence they watched (Bachrach, 1986). In a cohort of 95 Polish boys, preferences for violent television over the 2 years significantly predicted levels of physical aggressiveness ($p < .05$; standardized $b_2 = 0.14$); levels of physical aggressiveness in a cohort of 84 Polish girls were not significantly influenced by the television violence they watched (Fraczek, 1986). Australian schoolchildren, whether boys or girls, were not significantly influenced by the television violence they watched (Sheehan, 1986).

In this metastudy of five countries and six populations (counting Israeli city and kibbutz children as distinct populations), there were 12 independent tests of the theory that exposure to television violence causes increased levels of aggressiveness (counting boys and girls separately in each population). Of these 12 tests, 6 yielded statistically significant confirmations of the theory (and 4 of these 6 were significant at $p < .01$). The appearance of this many statistically significant confirmations among 12 tests is far in excess of what would be maximally expected to occur by chance alone (England, 1975).

In a similarly designed study, investigators in the Netherlands prospectively observed cohorts of first and third graders for 2 years to determine the effect of exposure to television violence upon levels of physical aggressiveness (Wiegman et al., 1986). After controlling for baseline levels of aggressiveness, there was no evidence that Dutch schoolchildren, whether boys or girls, were significantly influenced by the television violence they watched.

Singer, Singer, and Rapaczynski (1984) prospectively observed 63 American 7-year-old children for 2 years. It was found that, after controlling for levels of physical aggressiveness at age 7, levels of physical aggressiveness at age 9 were significantly predicted by levels of exposure to television action-adventure drama at age 7 ($p < .05$; standardized $b_2 = 0.23$).

Joy, Kimball, and Zabrack (1986) prospectively investigated the effect of the introduction of television into a previously unexposed community ("Notel"), using as control groups two demographically similar communities that already had television ("Unitel" and "Multitel"). A cohort of 45 first and second graders (16 in Notel; 29 in Unitel and Multitel) were observed prospectively over 2 years for objective rates of physical aggression (e.g., hitting, shoving, and biting). Rates of physical aggression did not change significantly for children followed longitudinally in Unitel and Multitel. Two years after the introduction of television, rates of physical aggression among children followed longitudinally in Notel had increased by 160% ($p < .001$).

Granzberg (1980a) prospectively investigated the effect of the introduction of television into a previously unexposed community of Cree Indians in northern Manitoba (Norway House), using as a control group another northern Manitoba Cree community that continued to be unexposed to television (Oxford House). A cohort of 49 third-, fourth-, and fifth-grade boys (33 in Norway House; 16 in Oxford House) were studied prospectively over 4 years for expressed willingness to use physical aggression [as measured by their responses to standardized questions (e.g., 'What would you do if someone called you a name?")]. On the average, the professed willingness of boys to engage in physical aggression increased at Norway House over the 4 years of exposure to television, whereas it decreased among the boys who continued unexposed to television at Oxford House, the difference approaching statistical significance ($p < .10$). These findings might appear somewhat removed from the issue at hand—whether natural exposure to television causes physical aggression—were it not observed by Granzberg and others that acts of violence by Cree children increased following the introduction of television into Norway House (Granzberg, 1980b, 1982):

> After television was introduced, children fought more, used more dangerous weapons, and did more damage to each other (for example, the number of eyes lost in fights increased greatly). (Granzberg, 1982)
>
> According to many, children's proneness to copy television has produced an increase in the level of violence in their behavior. For example, after an episode of Happy Days was broadcast in which Fonzie's "All American" friends got into trouble with a leather jacket gang called the "Red Devils," gangs of kids appeared at school the next day calling themselves red devils, blue devils, green devils, etc. The fighting that took place under these banners disrupted school activities for several days. (Granzberg, 1980b)

Because traditional Cree Indian culture emphasizes nonviolent approaches to conflict resolution (Granzberg, 1980a), the effect of television upon Cree children's physical aggressiveness was all the more evident.

Milavsky and associates (1982) prospectively observed several hundred American schoolchildren (ages 7-12) for 2-3 years. Five prospective studies were made of the effect of viewing television violence upon subsequent levels of physical aggressiveness, controlling for initial levels of physical aggressiveness. For boys judged to be giving valid responses, all five results were in the direction consistent with a causal relationship ($p < .05$; average standardized $b_2 = 0.08$). For girls judged to be giving valid responses, only three of the five results were in the predicted direction; however, when the female sample was made more homogeneous by including only white, middle-class girls (approximately 70% of the original sample), all five results were in the direction consistent with a causal relationship ($p < .05$; average standardized $b_2 = 0.12$) (Cook *et al.*, 1983).

Eron and associates (1972) prospectively observed a cohort of 211 boys for 10 years, from ages 8 until 18 years. Controlling for initial levels of aggression at age 8, preferences for watching violent television at age 8 significantly predicted levels of aggressiveness at age 18 ($p < .01$; coefficient $b_2 = 0.25$). No such relationship was observed for a cohort of 216 girls followed prospectively from ages 8 until 18.

In a retrospective, case-control study, Belson (1978) examined the relationship between current violent behavior in adolescent boys and their prior, lifetime exposure to television violence. The subject population was a stratified, random population sample of 1565 London males, ages 12-17. For each boy, data were gathered on serious violent behavior (i.e., assault, rape, major vandalism, and abuse of animals) committed within the prior 6 months and on lifetime exposure to television violence from 1959 to 1972—the time of the interview. Data were also gathered from each subject on 100 potentially confounding variables. Stratifying for confounding variables, adolescent males who had watched above-average quantities of television violence during their lives were currently engaged in rates of serious violence 49% higher than that of adolescent males who had watched below-average quantities of television violence ($p = .02$). No support was found for the alternative hypothesis (i.e., that inherently violent males will choose to watch more violent television). Modifying the parameters of the analysis did not markedly alter the findings.

Milavsky and associates (1982) prospectively observed several hundred adolescent boys (ages 12-16) for 2-3 years, looking for the effect of viewing television violence upon the occurrence of seriously violent delinquent acts (i.e., participation in muggings, knifings, and gang fights). No significant causal relationship was observed between television violence viewing and violent delinquent acts.

It should be noted that of the three studies examining the effect of television violence upon adolescent aggression (Belson, 1978; Eron *et al.*, 1972; Milavsky *et al.*, 1982), the negative study of Milavsky and associates (1982) examined the effect of *adolescent* exposure to television violence upon adolescent aggression, whereas the positive studies of Belson (1978) and Eron and associates (1972) were examining the effect of earlier, *childhood* exposure to television violence upon subsequent adolescent aggressiveness.

Kruttschnitt *et al.* (1986) examined the relationship between adult criminal violence and childhood exposure to television violence. One hundred male felons, ages 18-25, imprisoned for violent crimes (e.g., murder, assault, and rape), were compared to 65 men without a history of violent offences, matching for age, race, and census tract of residence at ages 10-14 years. The violent offenders reported watching, from ages 8 to 12, 15% more violent television programs per week than did the matched controls. After controlling for school performance, exposure to parental violence, and baseline level of criminal aggressiveness, the relationship between adult criminal violence and childhood exposure to television violence approached statistical significance ($p < .10$; standardized $b_2 = 0.12$).

As mentioned previously, Eron and Huesmann (1984) prospectively observed a population cohort of several hundred boys for 22 years, from ages 8 until 30. After controlling for the boys' aggressiveness, intelligence, and socioeconomic status at age 8, the boys' viewing of television violence at age 8 significantly predicted the average seriousness of the crimes for which he was convicted by age 30 ($p < .05$; coefficient $b_2 = 0.18$) (Huesmann, 1986). The "seriousness" of a crime was measured using a standardized scale, "seriousness" being weighted by the degree of violence associated with the crime (Rossi *et al.*, 1974).

To summarize: Studies at the level of the individual indicate that exposure to television increases individual levels of physical aggressiveness (Bachrach,

1986; Belson, 1978; Cook *et al.*, 1983; Eron & Huesmann, 1984; Eron *et al.*, 1972; Fraczek, 1986; Granzberg, 1980b; Huesmann & Eron, 1986b; Joy *et al.*, 1986; Kruttschnitt *et al.*, 1986; Lagerspetz & Viemerö, 1986; Milavsky *et al.*, 1982; Singer *et al.*, 1984), but not in all cultures (Bachrach, 1986; Sheehan, 1986; Wiegman *et al.*, 1986), nor necessarily in both genders within a culture (Fraczek, 1986; Lagerspetz & Viemerö, 1986). The critical period of exposure appears to be during preadolescent childhood (Bachrach, 1986; Belson, 1978; Cook *et al.*, 1983; Eron & Huesmann, 1984; Eron *et al.*, 1972; Fraczek, 1986; Granzberg, 1980b; Huesmann & Eron, 1986b; Joy *et al.*, 1986; Kruttschnittt *et al.*, 1986; Lagerspetz & Viemerö, 1986; Milavsky *et al.*, 1982; Singer *et al.*, 1984). Later variations in exposure to television, in adolescence (Milavsky *et al.*, 1982) and adulthood (Hennigan *et al.*, 1982), do not appear to exert any additional effect. However, the aggression-enhancing effect of exposure to television during preadolescent childhood is chronic, extending into adolescence (Belson, 1978; Eron *et al.*, 1972) and adulthood (Eron & Huesmann, 1984; Huesmann, 1986; Kruttschnitt *et al.*, 1986).

REFERENCES

Bachrach, R. S. (1986). The differential effect of observation of violence on kibbutz and city children in Israel. In L. R. Huesmann & L. D. Eron (Eds.), *Television and the aggressive child: A cross-national comparison* (pp. 201-238). Hillsdale, NJ: Erlbaum.

Bailar, J. C., III, Louis, T. A., Lavori, P. W., & Polansky, M. (1984). Studies without internal controls. *New England Journal of Medicine*, **311**, 156-162.

Barnett, A., Kleitman, D. J., & Larson, R. C. (1975). On urban homicide: A statistical analysis. *Journal of Criminal Justice*, **3**, 85-110.

Belson, W. A. (1978). *Television violence and the adolescent boy.* Westmead, England: Saxon House.

Berkowitz, L. (1965). Some aspects of observed aggression. *Journal of Personality and Social Psychology*, **2**, 359-369.

Berkowitz, L. (1974). Some determinants of impulsive aggression: Role of mediated associations with reinforcements for aggression. *Psychological Review*, **81**, 165-176.

Berkowitz, L., & Alioto, J. T. (1973). The meaning of an observed event as a determinant of its aggressive consequences. *Journal of Personality and Social Psychology*, **28**, 206-217.

Berkowitz, L., Corwin, R., & Heironimus, M. (1963). Film violence and subsequent aggressive tendencies. *Public Opinion Quarterly*, **27**, 217-229.

Berkowitz, L., & Geen, R. G. (1966). Film violence and the cue properties of available targets. *Journal of Personality and Social Psychology*, **3**, 525-530.

Berkowitz, L., & Geen, R. G. (1967). Stimulus qualities of the target of aggression: A further study. *Journal of Personality and Social Psychology*, **5**, 364-368.

Berkowitz, L., & Rawlings, E. (1963). Effects of film violence on inhibitions against subsequent aggression. *Journal of Abnormal and Social Psychology*, **66**, 405-412.

Block, R. (1975). Homicide in Chicago: A nine-year study (1965-1973). *Journal of Criminal Law and Criminology*, **66**, 496-510.

Bothwell, R., Drummond, I., & English, J. (1981). *Canada since 1945.* Toronto, Ontario: University of Toronto Press.

Broadcasting Telecasting. (1956). *1956–1957 telecasting yearbook–marketbook*. Washington, DC: Broadcasting Publications, Inc.

Bureau of Alcohol, Tobacco, and Firearms. (annual volumes). *Alcohol, tobacco and firearms summary statistics*. Washington, DC: U.S. Government Printing Office.

Bureau of Census and Statistics. (1960). *Union statistics for fifty years, 1910–1960 jubilee issue*. Pretoria, South Africa: Government Printer.

Bureau of Statistics. (1964). *Statistical year book, 1964*. Pretoria, South Africa: Government Printer.

Bureau of Statistics. (1965). *Statistical year book, 1965*. Pretoria, South Africa: Government Printer.

Bureau of Statistics. (1968). *South African statistics, 1968*. Pretoria, South Africa: Government Printer.

Cantor, D., & Cohen, L. E. (1980). Comparing measures of homicide trends: Methodological and substantive differences in the Vital Statistics and Uniform Crime Reports time series (1933–1975). *Social Science Research*, **9**, 121–145.

Centerwall, B. S. (1984). Race, socioeconomic status, and domestic homicide, Atlanta, 1971–72. *American Journal of Public Health*, **74**, 813–815.

Centerwall, B. S. (1989). Exposure to television as a risk factor for violence. *American Journal of Epidemiology*, **129**(4).

Central Statistical Service. (1982). *South African statistics, 1982*. Pretoria, South Africa: Government Printer.

Central Statistical Service. (1986). *South African statistics, 1986*. Pretoria, South Africa: Government Printer.

Collins, J. K. (Ed.). (1981). *Drinking and crime: Perspectives on the relationship between alcohol consumption and criminal behavior*. New York: Guilford Press.

Comstock, G., Chaffee, S., Katzman, N., McCombs, M., & Roberts, D. (1978). *Television and human behavior*. New York: Columbia University Press.

Constantino, J. P., Kuller, L. H., Perper, J. A., & Cypess, R. H. (1977). An epidemiologic study of homicides in Allegheny County, Pennsylvania. *American Journal of Epidemiology*, **106**, 314–324.

Cook, T. D., Kendzierski, D. A., & Thomas, S. V. (1983). The implicit assumptions of television research: An analysis of the NIMH report on *Television and behavior*. *Public Opinion Quarterly*, **47**, 161–201.

Darity, W. A., Jr. (1980). Illusions of black economic progress. *Review of Black Political Economy*, **10**, 153–168.

Department of Statistics. (1970). *South African statistics, 1970*. Pretoria, South Africa: Government Printer.

Department of Statistics. (1972). *South African statistics, 1972*. Pretoria, South Africa: Government Printer.

Department of Statistics. (1974). *South African statistics, 1974*. Pretoria, South Africa: Government Printer.

Department of Statistics. (1976). *South African statistics, 1976*. Pretoria, South Africa: Government Printer.

Dominion Bureau of Statistics. (annual volumes). *Vital statistics*. Ottawa, Ontario: Queen's Printer and Controller of Stationery.

Dominion Bureau of Statistics. (1953). *Ninth census of Canada, 1951: Vol. 3. Housing and families*. Ottawa, Ontario: Queen's Printer and Controller of Stationery.

Dominion Bureau of Statistics. (1963). *1961 census of Canada: Vol. 2. Part 2: Households and families*. Ottawa, Ontario: Queen's Printer and Controller of Stationery.

Donnerstein, E., & Berkowitz, L. (1981). Victim reactions in aggressive erotic films as a factor in violence against women. *Journal of Personality and Social Psychology*, **41**, 710–724.

Doob, A. N., & Climie, R. J. (1972). Delay of measurement and the effects of film violence. *Journal of Experimental Social Psychology*, **8**, 136–142.

Elting, J. R. (1983). World War II: Costs, casualties, and other data. In *The encyclopedia Americana* (Vol. 29, pp. 529-531). Danbury, CT: Grolier.

England, J. M. (1975). *Medical research: A statistical and epidemiological approach*. New York: Churchill-Livingstone.

Eron, L. D., & Huesmann, L. R. (1984). The control of aggressive behavior by changes in attitudes, values, and the conditions of learning. In R. J. Blanchard & D. C. Blanchard (Eds.), *Advances in the study of aggression* (Vol. 1, pp. 139-171). New York: Academic Press.

Eron, L. D., Lefkowitz, M. M., Huesmann, L. R., & Walder, L. O. (1972). Does television violence cause aggression? *American Psychologist*, 27, 253-263.

Farley, R. (1980). Homicide trends in the United States. *Demography*, 17, 177-188.

Feinbloom, R. I. (1976). Children and television. *Pediatrics*, 57, 301-303.

Feingold, M., & Johnson, G. T. (1977). Television violence—Reactions from physicians, advertisers and the networks. *New England Journal of Medicine*, 296, 424-427.

Finnish Foundation for Alcohol Studies & the World Health Organization Regional Office for Europe. (1977). International statistics on alcoholic beverages: Production, trade and consumption, 1950-1972. *The Finnish Foundation for Alcohol Studies*, 27, 1-231.

Fraczek, A. (1986). Socio-cultural environment, television viewing, and the development of aggression among children in Poland. In L. R. Huesmann & L. D. Eron (Eds.), *Television and the aggressive child: A cross-national comparison* (pp. 119-159). Hillsdale, NJ: Erlbaum.

Freedman, J. L. (1984). Effect of television violence on aggressiveness. *Psychological Bulletin*, 96, 227-246.

Frye, W. R. (1968). *In whitest Africa: The dynamics of apartheid*. Englewood Cliffs, NJ: Prentice-Hall.

Furst, C. J., & Beckman, L. J. (1981). Alcohol-related mortality and alcohol consumption statistics: Stability of estimates for small areas. *Journal of Studies of Alcohol*, 42, 57-63.

Geen, R. G. (1978). Some effects of observing violence upon the behavior of the observer. In B. Maher (Ed.), *Progress in experimental personality research* (Vol. 8, pp. 49-92). New York: Academic Press.

Geen, R. G. (1981). Behavioral and physiological reactions to observed violence: Effects of prior exposure to aggressive stimuli. *Journal of Personality and Social Psychology*, 40, 868-875.

Geen, R. G., & Berkowitz, L. (1966). Name-mediated aggressive cue properties. *Journal of Personality*, 34, 456-465.

Geen, R. G., & Berkowitz, L. (1967). Some conditions facilitating the occurrence of aggression after the observation of violence. *Journal of Personality*, 35, 666-676.

Geen, R. G., & O'Neal, E. C. (1969). Activation of cue-elicited aggression by general arousal. *Journal of Personality and Social Psychology*, 11, 289-292.

Granzberg, G. (1980a). The psychological impact of television among Algonkians of central Canada. In G. Granzberg & J. Steinbring (Eds.), *Television and the Canadian Indian: Impact and meaning among Algonkians of central Canada* (pp. 321-359). Winnipeg, Manitoba: University of Winnipeg.

Granzberg, G. (1980b). The introduction of television into a northern Manitoba Cree community: A study of meanings, uses and effects. In G. Granzberg & J. Steinbring (Eds.), *Television and the Canadian Indian: Impact and meaning among Algonkians of central Canada* (pp. 77-181). Winnipeg, Manitoba: University of Winnipeg.

Granzberg, G. (1982). Television as storyteller: The Algonkian Indians of central Canada. *Journal of Communication*, 32(1), 43-52.

Grove, R. D., & Hetzel, A. M. (1968). *Vital statistics rates in the United States, 1940-1960*. Washington, DC: U.S. Government Printing Office.

Hennigan, K. M., Del Rosario, M. L., Heath, L., Cook, T. D., Wharton, J. D., & Calder, B. J. (1982). Impact of the introduction of television on crime in the United States: Empirical findings and theoretical implications. *Journal of Personality and Social Psychology*, 42, 461-477.

Holroyd, H. J. (1985). Children, adolescents, and television. *American Journal of Diseases of Children,* **139,** 549-550.

Hostetler, J. A. (1980). *Amish society* (3rd ed.). Baltimore, MD: The Johns Hopkins University Press.

Huesmann, L. R. (1986). Psychological processes promoting the relation between exposure to media violence and aggressive behavior by the viewer. *Journal of Social Issues,* **42**(3), 125-139.

Huesmann, L. R., & Eron, L. D. (Eds.). (1986a). *Television and the aggressive child: A cross-national comparison.* Hillsdale, NJ: Erlbaum.

Huesmann, L. R., & Eron, L. D. (1986b). The development of aggression in American children as a consequence of television violence viewing. In L. R. Huesmann & L. D. Eron (Eds.), *Television and the aggressive child: A cross-national comparison* (pp. 45-80). Hillsdale, NJ: Erlbaum.

Huesmann, L. R., Lagerspetz, K., & Eron, L. D. (1984). Intervening variables in the TV violence-aggression relation: Evidence from two countries. *Developmental Psychology,* **20,** 746-775.

Industry and Merchandising Division. (1953). *Radio and television receiving sets, December, 1952.* Ottawa, Ontario: Dominion Bureau of Statistics.

Ingelfinger, F. J. (1976). Violence on TV: An unchecked environmental hazard. *New England Journal of Medicine,* **294,** 837-838.

Jayewardene, C. H. S. (1980). The nature of homicide: Canada 1961-1970. In R. A. Silverman & J. J. Teevan, Jr. (Eds.), *Crime in Canadian society* (2nd ed., pp. 267-289). Toronto, Ontario: Butterworth.

Joy, L. A., Kimball, M. M., & Zabrack, M. L. (1986). Television and children's aggressive behavior. In T. M. Williams (Ed.), *The impact of television: A natural experiment in three communities* (pp. 303-360). New York: Academic Press.

Justice Statistics Division. (1976). *Homicide in Canada: A statistical synopsis.* Ottawa, Ontario: Statistics Canada.

Kahn, E. (1981). What is happening to the death penalty? *South African Law Journal,* **98,** 103-105.

Kaplan, I., McLaughlin, J. L., Marvin, B. J., Nelson, H. D., Rowland, E. E., & Whitaker, D. P. (1971). *Area handbook for the Republic of South Africa.* Washington, DC: U.S. Government Printing Office.

Kruttschnitt, C., Heath, L., & Ward, D. A. (1986). Family violence, television viewing habits, and other adolescent experiences related to violent criminal behavior. *Criminology,* **24,** 235-267.

Lagerspetz, K., & Viemerö, V. (1986). Television and aggressive behavior among Finnish children. In L. R. Huesmann & L. D. Eron (Eds.), *Television and the aggressive child: A cross-national comparison* (pp. 81-117). Hillsdale, NJ: Erlbaum.

Leacy, F. H. (Ed.). (1983). *Historical statistics of Canada* (2nd ed.). Ottawa, Ontario: Statistics Canada.

Lelyveld, J. (1985). *Move your shadow: South Africa, black and white.* New York: Times Books.

Liebert, R. M. (1986). Effects of television on children and adolescents. *Journal of Developmental and Behavioral Pediatrics,* **7,** 43-48.

McGuire, W. J. (1986). The myth of massive media impact: Savagings and salvagings. In G. Comstock (Ed.), *Public communication and behavior* (Vol. 1, pp. 173-257). New York: Academic Press.

McLaughlin, J. L. (1981). Historical setting. In H. D. Nelson (Ed.), *South Africa: A country study* (pp. 1-61). Washington, DC: U.S. Government Printing Office.

Meyer, T. P. (1972). The effects of sexually arousing and violent films on aggressive behaviors. *Journal of Sex Research,* **8,** 324-331.

Midgley, J. (1974). Public opinion and the death penalty in South Africa. *British Journal of Criminology,* **14,** 345-358.

Milavsky, J. R., Kessler, R. C., Stipp, H. H., & Rubens, W. S. (1982). *Television and aggression: A panel study.* New York: Academic Press.

Morgenstern, H. (1982). Uses of ecologic analysis in epidemiologic research. *American Journal of Public Health,* 72, 1336-1344.

Mulvihill, D. J., Tumin, M. M., & Curtis, L. A. (1969). *Crimes of violence: Vol. 11. A staff report submitted to the National Commission on the Causes and Prevention of Violence.* Washington, DC: U.S. Government Printing Office.

Munford, R. S., Kazer, R. S., Feldman, R. A., & Stivers, R. R. (1976). Homicide trends in Atlanta. *Criminology,* 14, 213- 232.

National Center for Health Statistics. (annual volumes). *Vital statistics of the United States.* Hyattsville, MD: U.S. Department of Health and Human Services.

Newton, G. D., & Zimring, F. E. (1970). *Firearms and violence in American life: A report to the National Commission on the Causes and Prevention of Violence.* Washington, DC: U.S. Government Printing Office.

Omond, R. (1985). *The apartheid handbook.* New York: Viking Penguin.

Pearl, D., Bouthilet, L., & Lazar, J. (Eds.). (1982). *Television and behavior: Ten years of scientific progress and implications for the Eighties: Vol. 2. Technical reviews.* Rockville, MD: National Institute of Mental Health.

Robinson, W. S. (1950). Ecological correlations and the behavior of individuals. *American Sociological Review,* 15, 351-357.

Rosenthal, R. (1986). Media violence, antisocial behavior, and the social consequences of small effects. *Journal of Social Issues,* 42(3), 141-154.

Rossi, P. H., Waite, E., Bose, C. E., & Berk, R. E. (1974). The seriousness of crimes: Normative structure and individual differences. *American Sociological Review,* 39, 224-237.

Rothenberg, M. B. (1975). Effect of television violence on children and youth. *Journal of the American Medical Association,* 234, 1043-1046.

Rothman, K. J. (1982). Causation and causal inferences. In D. Schottenfeld & J. F. Fraumeni (Eds.), *Cancer epidemiology and prevention* (pp. 15-22). Philadelphia, PA: W. B. Saunders Company.

Ruben, E. R., & Leeper, J. D. (1981). Homicide in five Southern states: A firearms phenomenon. *Southern Medical Journal,* 74, 272-277.

Rushforth, N. B., Ford, A. B., Hirsch, C. S., Rushforth, N. M., & Adelson, L. (1977). Violent death in a metropolitan county: Changing patterns in homicide (1958-1974). *New England Journal of Medicine,* 297, 531-538.

Scarff, E. (1983). *Evaluation of the Canadian gun control legislation: Final report.* Ottawa, Ontario: Ministry of the Soliciter General.

Sheehan, P. W. (1986). Television viewing and its relation to aggression among children in Australia. In L. R. Huesmann & L. D. Eron (Eds.), *Television and the aggressive child: A cross-national comparison* (pp. 161-199). Hillsdale, NJ: Erlbaum.

Singer, D. G. (1985). Does violent television produce aggressive children? *Pediatric Annals,* 14, 804, 807-810.

Singer, J. L., Singer, D. G., & Rapaczynski, W. S. (1984). Family patterns and television viewing as predictors of children's beliefs and aggression. *Journal of Communication,* 34(2), 73-89.

Somers, A. R. (1976a). Violence, television and the health of American youth. *New England Journal of Medicine,* 294, 811-817.

Somers, A. R. (1976b). Health policy 1976: Violence, television, and American youth. *Annals of Internal Medicine,* 84, 743-745.

Statistics Canada. (1973). *1971 census of Canada: Housing* (Vol. 2, Part 4). Ottawa, Ontario: Information Canada.

Tan, A. S. (1986). Social learning of aggression from television. In J. Bryant & D. Zillmann (Eds.), *Perspectives on media effects* (pp. 41–55). Hillsdale, NJ: Erlbaum.

Tartter, J. R. (1981). Government and politics. In H. D. Nelson (Ed.), *South Africa: A country study* (pp. 219–292). Washington, DC: U.S. Government Printing Office.

Television Bureau of Advertising. (1982). *Trends in television: 1950 to date.* New York: Author.

Terris, M. (1967). Epidemiology of cirrhosis of the liver: National mortality data. *American Journal of Public Health,* **57,** 2076–2088.

"Unbelievable" scramble for TV sets. (1976, January 6). *The Cape Times,* p. 1.

UNESCO. (annual volumes). *Statistical yearbook.* Paris, France: UNESCO Press.

U.S. Bureau of the Census (annual volumes). *Statistical abstract of the United States.* Washington, DC: U.S. Government Printing Office.

U.S. Bureau of the Census. (1963). *U.S. census of housing, 1960: Vol. 1. States and small areas. Part 1: United States summary.* Washington, DC: U.S. Government Printing Office.

U.S. Bureau of the Census. (1975). *Historical statistics of the United States: Colonial times to 1970.* Washington, DC: U.S. Government Printing Office.

U.S. Bureau of the Census. (1979). Consumer income: Money income in 1977 of families and persons in the United States. *Current Population Reports* (Series P-60, No. 118). Washington, DC: U.S. Government Printing Office.

U.S. Bureau of the Census. (1981). Characteristics of the population below the poverty level: 1979. *Current Population Reports* (Series P-60, No. 130). Washington, DC: U.S. Government Printing Office.

U.S. Federal Bureau of Investigation. (annual volumes). *Uniform crime reports for the United States.* Washington, DC: U.S. Government Printing Office.

U.S. Office of Management and Budget. (1973). *Social indicators,* 1973 (pp. 69–70). Washington, DC: U.S. Government Printing Office.

van Niekerk, B. v. D. (1970). . . . Hanged by the neck until you are dead. *South African Law Journal,* **87,** 60–75.

Walters, R. H., & Thomas, E. L. (1963). Enhancement of punitiveness by visual and audio-visual displays. *Canadian Journal of Psychology,* **17,** 244–255.

Walters, R. H., Thomas, E. L., & Acker, C. W. (1962). Enhancement of punitive behavior by audio-visual displays. *Science,* **136,** 872–873.

Welsh, D. (1969). Capital punishment in South Africa. In A. Milner (Ed.), *African penal systems* (pp. 395–427). London: Routledge & Kegan Paul.

Wiegman, O., Kuttschreuter, M., & Baarda, B. (1986). *Television viewing related to aggressive and prosocial behavior.* The Hague, Netherlands: SVO.

Williams, T. M., Zabrack, M. L., & Joy, L. A. (1982). The portrayal of aggression on North American television. *Journal of Applied Social Psychology,* **12,** 360–380.

Wilson, J. Q., & Herrnstein, R. J. (1985). *Crime and human nature.* New York: Simon and Schuster.

Worchel, S., Hardy, T. W., & Hurley, R. (1976). The effects of commercial interruption of violent films on viewers' subsequent aggression. *Journal of Experimental Social Psychology,* **12,** 220–232.

World Health Organization. (annual volumes). *World health statistics annual.* Geneva, Switzerland: Author.

World Health Organization. (1958). *Epidemiological and vital statistics report, 1958.* Geneva, Switzerland: Author.

Zahn, M. A., & Riedel, M. (1983). National versus local data sources in the study of homicide: Do they agree? In G. P. Waldo (Ed.), *Measurement issues in criminal justice* (pp. 103–120). Newbury Park, CA: Sage.

Zillmann, D. (1971). Excitation transfer in communication-mediated aggressive behavior. *Journal of Experimental Social Psychology,* **7,** 419–434.

Zuckerman, D. M., & Zuckerman, B. S. (1985). Television's impact on children. *Pediatrics,* **75,** 233–240.

Newsflow and Democratic Society in an Age of Electronic Media

DENNIS K. DAVIS
Department of Speech Communication
Southern Illinois University
Carbondale, Illinois 62901

JOHN P. ROBINSON
Survey Research Center
Department of Sociology
University of Maryland
College Park, Maryland 20742

I. Introduction	60
II. Journalism in the Information Age	63
A. Research on News Organizations	63
B. Constraints on News Story Production	65
III. Toward a Theory of News and Newsflow: Three Theories of News	66
A. Theory of the Social Construction of Reality	66
B. Narrative or Dramatist Theory	69
C. Information-Processing Theory	71
IV. A Reexamination of Early Newsflow Research	75
A. Interpreting Newsflow Research	75
B. The Early Research on Newsflow	76
C. Conclusions from the Early Newsflow Research	77
V. Current Research on News	77
A. The Knowledge Gap Hypothesis	77
B. Agenda Setting	78
C. The Spiral of Silence	79
D. The Lang Model of Opinion Formation	80
E. Uses and Gratifications Research	82
VI. Our News Comprehension Research	83
A. Research Design and Data Collection	83
B. The News Comprehension Variable	86
C. Story Factors and News Story Recall	86
D. Story Themes and Learning	87

VII. Toward "User Friendly" Journalism 95
   A. Beyond Libertarianism and the Profit Motive 95
   B. The Responsibility to Inform the Public 95
   C. Recommendations for Story Structure 96
VIII. Recommendations for Future Research 99
   A. Design of Future News Research 99
   B. Utility of Research on Schemas 99
   C. Applications for News Research 100
   References 100

I. INTRODUCTION

Ours is an age of information, an era in which the definition, production, and distribution of information continues to be radically transformed by the development of new technology. A generation ago, the rapid expansion of television made attractively packaged news and information content easily accessible to most Americans. Now, it is personal computer technology that promises to revolutionize the way we gain access to specialized information. In just a few years, many Americans will be gaining entry to vast libraries of information from the comfort of their living room.

The prospects for significant increases in public knowledge and understanding of the social environment, then, seem never to have been better. But although the changes that technology permits in accessibility of information are not difficult to trace, the consequences of these changes for information use by average persons may prove to be highly problematic. There is mounting evidence of ineffective consumer utilization of older "new technologies." Quite apart from the bureaucratic and economic constraints on information production and distribution are the problems encountered by most persons as they routinely process information. Based on our analysis of the shortcomings of television as a medium for news information (Robinson & Levy, 1986; Robinson, Sahin, & Davis, 1982), we suspect that comprehension and utilization of information will inevitably lag far behind access.

Cheap and easy access to attractive new forms of information via television does not appear to have produced sharp increases in public knowledge about the social and political environment. Though television has expanded the audience for news, it has hardly realized its promise as a medium that might equalize the flow of information to every American. Today, after three decades of easy access to television and after unparalleled increases in the level of public education, public knowledge about the political and economic system may not be much better than it was in the 1950s. The poor performance of television as an information medium implies that personal computers, laser disk technology, and information banks will not guarantee increases in public knowledge. A mere change in the technology used to deliver information may do little to change present patterns of knowledge distribution.

However, the distribution of public knowledge does have increasingly important implications for the type of social and political order that we develop. In the American political system, decision making at all levels is strongly influenced by levels of public knowledge about institutions, issues, and events. As knowledge about institutions and issues becomes widespread, the potential grows that individuals can be activated to work for political changes. Conversely, public ignorance can lead to an acquiescence to official action, which gives political elites too much freedom to act in their own self-interest.

It is not overly idealistic to view public knowledge about the social environment, then, as a key element in our political system. Politicians can be quite sensitive to changes in public knowledge that signal increasing public concern. They watch for evidence that individuals are being mobilized in support of specific policies. Scandal and counterproductive policy seem inevitably to occur in areas where public ignorance and apathy are widespread.

The challenge faced by successive generations of Americans has been to renew and expand participation in democratic government so that the long-term ideals of the Founding Fathers might be realized. One very practical strategy or first step for expanding participation could be to increase public learning. But we have learned that the problem of producing such increases in learning is not an easy one to solve.

In previous eras, the quality and quantity of information available was necessarily much more limited. Partisan news and propaganda could produce widespread misunderstanding and alienation. The persistence of high levels of ignorance and apathy during those periods can now be understood as in part a consequence of an irregular flow of complicated, biased information.

Although many of the technical barriers to the flow of useful information are being removed and access to better quality information has been sharply increased, we continue to be embarrassed by the failure of this information to raise the levels of public knowledge even in those areas where the flow of information is greatest.

Why has technology failed to solve the problem of public ignorance? Why is ignorance and apathy still widespread even as the flow of information has risen geometrically? Could technology be used more effectively to communicate information? Have social, psychological, and other barriers to the flow of information gone unnoticed that should be identified and removed? Are the present levels of public ignorance inevitable, or could they be ameliorated by changes in journalistic practice?

We have sought answers to these difficult questions in a review of research on newsflow and audience learning. We identify a variety of barriers to information flow and use that have been revealed by social research. These barriers fall into two general categories: *source* barriers and *receiver* barriers. Source barriers involve economic and organizational constraints found in the news industries that lead to the production of news that is too often "beyond comprehension" by average audience members. Receiver barriers include inadequately developed decoding skills and difficulty in ascertaining the personal relevancy of news stories.

The existence of these barriers between journalists and audiences makes it hardly surprising that public learning has lagged behind information access. We suggest several specific steps that could be taken to improve the flow and use of information, some of which will be easier to achieve than others. Improvements in technology may make it practical to implement certain changes without great difficulty or cost. However, we see the major barriers as arising from the lack of societal and organizational commitments to improve public knowledge.

Though sharply critical of the status quo, we do not view the existence of these barriers as proof that the flow of information is being managed and manipulated in the interest of a particular ideology or class. Neither do we accept the inevitability of public ignorance and apathy. We view the removal of these barriers to public learning as viable and logical steps toward realization of democratic government. Removing barriers to the flow of information can thus be seen as analogous to enfranchisement of segments of the public in the seventeenth and eighteenth centuries. How effective can participation in self-government or how meaningful can the right to vote be without an adequately informed public?

We believe that a major source of the problem of news communication, however, is inherent in the profound gap between journalists and their audiences in terms of skills needed to communicate with each other. Almost all journalists are college graduates, and many of them have had graduate education as well. That is the case for less than 20% of the ordinary citizens, or potential news consumers. Journalists also differ, from even this educated group of news consumers, in terms of their familiarity, interest, and involvement in news events. These are two serious gaps that are rarely and explicitly recognized in the preparation of news stories.

The ignorance of the American public, even in the face of improved educational levels and sophisticated news media, is legendary. Most journalists have either heard about or prepared poll stories detailing how only minorities of the public know who their Congressperson is, which countries are involved in a conflict or where they are located, or what such basic political terms as liberal or conservative mean. But such findings have had virtually no impact on how journalists develop their stories. In our own research, we have found that journalists in general show a level of knowledge about current news stories well above the top 5% of the news audience. Trying to bridge that gap, or even addressing that gap, would (and we feel should) require a thorough restructuring of current journalistic practices. How do you explain blockage of a bill by Congress to a citizenry that does not completely understand the difference between the House of Representatives and the Senate? How do you explain the implications of a new two-China policy to an audience that is largely unaware of the existence of two distinct Chinese governments?

These are not problems for which journalists are to blame, but they are problems that journalists need to address. As we show in this chapter, news research does show that journalism can convey certain information to less-educated audiences, but it is done on a fragmentary basis that has little hope of eventual enlightenment of the public. It is that larger goal to which we address ourselves.

We begin our assessment of the barriers to information flow with an examination of the segment of the news industry that many believe serves as a primary source of information for most adults—namely, television news. We first review the philosophical, economic, and practical constraints on the gathering, packaging, and distribution of news. We then turn our attention to the manner in which news audiences make use of TV news. A review of three decades of newsflow studies suggests several primary barriers to newsflow. We conclude with recommendations for altering production, distribution, and use of information based on findings of news comprehension research.

II. JOURNALISM IN THE INFORMATION AGE

A. Research on News Organizations

During the 1970s, a series of studies of news organizations assessed modern journalistic practice (Epstein, 1973; Fishman, 1980; Gans, 1979; Tuchman, 1978). This research found many contradictions between professed norms and values and routine journalistic practices. Procedures used to define, gather, write, and edit news stories were found to be based largely on pragmatic considerations. Practices developed and persisted because they permitted efficient production of an attractive, salable product. Idealistic norms of objectivity and public service were used to legitimate specific practices but did not guide most work.

Gans (1979) reports a widespread commitment to libertarian ideals that is difficult to translate into practices that will guarantee financial survival in competitive markets. News broadcasters face the challenging task of competing to deliver news in a form that will routinely attract the largest audiences while meeting certain minimal public service standards (Epstein, 1973). In the ratings game, ideal goals of public service give way to strategies that promise to boost the market share (Turow, 1983).

Other research has argued that existing professional practices are poorly conceptualized and tradition bound. Though they are said to serve the public interest, they more often serve to make the job of journalists easier to perform or to make news more acceptable to mass audiences. Schiller (1981) and Schudson (1978) examined a variety of historical evidence and concluded that the journalistic norm of objectivity emerged as part of an overall marketing strategy to broaden the appeal and reduce costs of large urban newspapers as they competed for culturally diverse audiences of urban readers. Objective news was less likely to offend members of specific groups or to attract lawsuits. With the development of wire services, objective news packaged in Chicago by the Associated Press (AP) could be printed with little revision anywhere in the nation. Schudson and Schiller point out that objective news is necessarily selective because some criteria must be used to determine what is newsworthy and what is not. To argue that some criteria are more objective than others is simply to ignore the values inherent in the criteria that are favored. But journalists have been quite reluctant to make such assessments and have been highly critical of those offered by academics. An insightful discussion of implicit values offered by Gans (1979) has been largely rejected by news practitioners.

Other field research has provided evidence that values are implicit in professional practices routinely used to gather news and structure news stories. Tuchman (1972) concluded that the print and TV journalists used "strategic rituals" to gather information that permitted the easy construction of simple, descriptive stories. In such stories, the details of actual events were often obscured or distorted in order to create an attractive, standardized product that fits narrow criteria of what they call "objective news." Reporters routinely sought out conflicting sources in order to produce "balanced" stories. They distorted trivial details to provide colorful angles on otherwise mundane events, and they searched for facts that would fit stereotypes while ignoring contradictory facts.

Tuchman found little evidence that journalists are effectively guided by broadly conceived norms of public service. Rather, they are bound by tradition and ritual to seek out certain categories of facts in order to produce news that editors will find acceptable and appealing for audiences. They act with little awareness of the limitations of their practices or the potential for misinforming the public. She concludes that so-called objective news criteria contain an inherent bias toward the status quo. Innovative events or groups tend to be contrasted in unfavorable ways with the views of leaders of more traditional organizations. When status quo leaders or organizations are criticized, no credible alternatives are presented. By implication, the only reasonable approach to dealing with social problems is what Gans (1979) has called "moderatism"—a middle-of-the-road position that assumes that most social problems are being routinely solved through minor reform of the status quo. When reform is necessary, journalists expect it to be led by the more enlightened members of the existing elite.

Fishman (1980) reports similar limitations in news production practices. He presents evidence that what was called a "crime wave" by New York newspapers was actually the result of skillful manipulation by government and police officials. His research indicates how promotional communicators can manage the release of information so that journalists will find it useful in creating news stories. Though reliance on official sources facilitates the production of news that meets the traditional standards of objectivity, such news typically serves the interests of its sources and not the public. The occasional, expensive investigative report is drowned in a flood of superficially edited promotional communication. The large newshole of big city monopoly newspapers can most profitably be filled by reporters who increase their productivity by relying on sources to do much of their work for them. Similarly, it is difficult for TV journalists to avoid coverage of dramatic, visually attractive pseudoevents staged for their cameras by elites with large budgets for promotional expenses.

B. Constraints on News Story Production

A common problem identified by news organization research is a lack of time for reflection or self-analysis. Most journalists report that deadline pressures allow them little free time to evaluate their work. Reporters assume that editors will catch errors or warn them of bad practices. Reporters are rewarded for production of standardized news stories, not for conscientiousness in the pursuit of facts or for innovation in story structure or substance. Editors are rewarded for efficiently managing the work of reporters, not for experimenting with innovative reporting practices that might better serve the high ideals they profess. Attempts to develop such practices by reporters and editors would prove costly and would result in the production of news that did not fit current standards of objectivity.

Past research on news organizations reports little evidence that the press operates with any well-developed theory of professional practice. This situation exists even though there has been a growing recognition among academics and practitioners that communication freedom cannot exist apart from social responsibility (Siebert, Peterson, & Schramm, 1956). The report of the Commission on the Freedom of the Press (1947) represented an impressive effort to consider the range of services that media technology could and should provide for a pluralistic social order. But its recommendation that media should begin to develop specific services for various cultural and ethnic minority groups has been ignored. Thus, despite widespread consensus that mass communication practitioners owe responsibilities to the public, there is little agreement over what those responsibilities are and how they should be discharged. There is much discussion of the public's right to know, but little consensus concerning what the public should know or how much effort should be made to make certain that specific information is known.

III. TOWARD A THEORY OF NEWS AND NEWSFLOW: THREE THEORIES OF NEWS

It is increasingly apparent that existing standards for news production are inadequate to guide responsible professional practice. These standards are grounded in a naive and quite simplistic view of the role informational communication can and should play in a modern pluralistic social order. It simply is not possible for journalists to create objective and impartial reports of all significant social events. Care should be given to the development of professional practices that will serve a greater variety of public needs and interests. Given the heterogeneity of news viewers, it is impossible to structure stories that will be useful to them without more precise understanding of what they already know and what they want to know.

We consider three relatively innovative theories (summarized in Table I), that offer insight into news and its social role, and we discuss how these theories might be integrated into a broad approach that would guide future research and possibly professional practice. We then use these theories as a basis for reviewing past research on newsflow, permitting us to derive conclusions that indicate how professional practices might be changed.

A. Theory of the Social Construction of Reality

The theory of the social construction of reality has roots in symbolic interactionism and in the sociology of knowledge. It is grounded on the notion that every individual constructs numerous orientations toward the social world that are more or less useful (Berger & Luckmann, 1966). To the extent that these orientations are useful in achieving socially defined objectives and the actions they structure are accepted by others, the orientations are experienced by the individual as being "real."

Some symbolic interactionists have argued that our experience of an "objective reality" may actually be quite fragile and maintained through constant revision of our orientations toward the social world. Erving Goffman (1974)

TABLE I
Three Theories for Interpretation of News and Prediction of News Comprehension

	Theory of the social construction of reality	Narrative theory	Information-processing theory
Source of the theory	Sociology of knowledge Phenomenology Symbolic interactionism Neo-Marxism	Literary and rhetorical analysis Hermeneutics Dramatist theory Symbolic interactionism	Learning theory Artificial intelligence theory Psycholinguistics
Central concepts	Social world Reality Institutions Situational definitions Social roles	Narrative structure Script Theme Characters Setting/stage	Cognitive structure/schema Content cues Processing of information Decoding Short- and long-term memory
Assumptions	Individual experience of reality is a function of participation in society Social world is made up of multiple realities that are promulgated by various social institutions Each reality consists of sets of interrelated situational definitions and social roles	An understanding of narrative structure is acquired through routine exposure to stories Once learned, narrative structure is relied on to interpret both stories and everyday life in the world	Preexisting schemas guide decoding of most new information In the absence of relevant schemas, decoding will be influenced by content structure and cues Learning can be predicted based on schemas and content factors
Application to news research	News tends to promote realities associated with dominant social institutions and to ignore or denigrate alternatives	News can be structured by and can reinforce existing narratives, or it can create new ones; new narratives are necessary for social change to occur	News is typically decoded by activating existing schemas; news that does not fit such schemas is difficult to decode, process, and remember

has argued that news stories may play an important role in routinely redefining how the world is interpreted. Many news stories describe good and bad deviation from normality. They trace the origin and consequences of important forms of deviation. They imply which actions will be sanctioned or rewarded. In an increasingly ambiguous social world, they offer insight into widely accepted standards for action in specific situations.

Social construction of reality theory has been applied in several relatively recent studies of news content. This research has focused on the definitions and labels routinely used for specific objects, persons, and actions (Adoni & Cohen, 1978; Adoni, Cohen, & Mane, 1984; Adoni & Mane, 1984). The research has sought to assess whether certain views of the social world are gaining or losing prominence and/or acceptance. Changes in the use of definitions or labels are interpreted as evidence that the perspectives associated with them are accepted to a greater or lesser degree.

Superficially, such research has some similarities to past studies of news bias. But bias research was grounded in the notion that there was a single "true" perspective on social reality, which could and should be used by journalists to describe events. Any deviation from this true perspective was defined as bias. Social construction of reality theory states that every social event can be viewed from many perspectives, none of which has precedence over the others. Each perspective is experienced as real or true by those who have learned it. This means that bias research was itself biased in its assumption that truth could be assessed.

Social construction of reality theorists view news stories as potentially complex representations of events. A single news story may contain elements and definitions that support several quite different or even contradictory perspectives. Although several perspectives may be expressed, one may be subtly favored over the others. Such stories may be quite functional in a pluralistic society because they appear to recognize the legitimacy of differing viewpoints and cultures.

Some social construction of reality theorists assume that ideologies exist that provide broad, consistent orientations to the social world. News content is said to promulgate certain ideologies whereas alternative perspectives are either ignored or their legitimacy questioned. Specific ideologies are found to routinely structure stories, guiding choice of these and other story elements. For example, researchers at the University of Glasgow (Glasgow University Media Group, 1976, 1980) have concluded that capitalist ideology guides construction of BBC coverage of labor disputes in Britain. Such ideological bias could be so subtle that journalists are unaware of it.

Other reality construction theorists have argued that because the social world itself is fundamentally ambiguous and open to many conflicting interpretations, there is inevitable disagreement over which definitions are best.

In pluralistic societies, this ambiguity may provide a continuing source of social change and conflict as new definitions gain acceptance while others become rejected. It may be unlikely that broad ideologies are or can be promoted by news media. Rather, media act as brokers in an ongoing effort to construct more or less useful views of events. Stories are not constructed in social isolation. Event participants and expert analysts are looked to by journalists for themes. They are asked to identify important story elements. Because most story sources are members of elites who share certain orientations, the themes they suggest will inevitably reflect an elite bias. Routine news practices that give prominence to themes and story elements suggested by elite sources serve to maintain the status quo (Tuchman, 1978). By studying story themes and other elements as well as routine news production practices, it may be possible to gauge such bias and draw conclusions about social stability and social change.

Although social construction of reality theory has advantages over earlier notions of political bias, it also has its own limitations. The most important of these is that the theory tells us very little about the process by which audience members learn orientations and definitions from news content. The theory does not tell us enough about the structure of orientations toward reality. On the basis of the theory, it is not possible to predict what forms of content will be especially effective in communicating orientations. It reveals nothing about the use that news consumers will make of individual stories. Answers to some of these questions can be found by integrating reality construction theory with narrative theory.

B. Narrative or Dramatist Theory

Narrative theory originated in literary analysis and rhetorical theory. One of its early proponents, Kenneth Burke (1945, 1950), became noted for the links that he drew between the structure of everyday communication and theatrical productions. Narrative theory assumes that humans routinely use their practical knowledge of narrative or dramatic structure to interpret information they receive from an ambiguous social world.

Our skill in interpreting the world increases as we learn specific narratives and learn how to apply them. Knowledge of narratives enables us to anticipate actions and predict short- and long-term consequences of actions. Persons can be interpreted as characters in narratives, possessing all the attributes associated with certain roles. Once the narrative structure of a story has been determined, its elements can be anticipated and routinely interpreted. Thus, messages having a clear and easily determined narrative structure can serve as an effective medium for communicating information because the structure can guide interpretation and facilitate recall. Conversely, stories lacking narrative structure (or containing several structures) are more difficult to interpret and remember. Simply structured, visually attractive, and interesting stories should serve as very effective vehicles for transmission of information.

Narrative structure can be briefly summarized as having the following interrelated elements:

1. A plot or action sequence that has a dramatic form (i.e., rising and falling levels of action, conflict, melodrama, etc.).

2. Characters who possess certain personal attributes, play specific social roles (i.e., enact expected action sequences), possess motives for action, and seek to achieve meaningful objectives through their actions.

3. A setting or stage that serves to frame the action, placing it at a particular time and place, as well as fixing its social context (i.e., social status, culture, etc.).

4. Objects or props used by characters as they perform especially significant actions—such objects often take on symbolic meaning, providing important clues/cues for the interpretation of actions.

5. Short- and long-term action consequences that imply that everything that has gone before leads to specific conclusions—characters who play particular roles and engage in specific actions in a given setting will achieve (or suffer) certain consequences.

All human societies have created a stock of narratives that are used to construct stories. By learning the roles and action sequences included in common narratives, the attributes and motives of typical characters, and other common narrative elements, individuals can orient themselves toward action in their culture. They can learn to conduct themselves as persons who are easily labeled and understood by others. Narratives provide an extremely flexible means of communicating cultural norms and values. They enable essentially arbitrary ways of ordering the social world to be experienced as having meaning or significance. When such narratives are known and accepted by entire communities, they define social reality for those groups.

Bennett and Edelman (1985) have discussed how narrative theory might be applied to the analysis of news. They categorize stories as one of several "situation defining forms," which include metaphors, theories, and ideologies. They differentiate between constructive stories, which provide new and useful insights into social life, and recurring or stereotypical stories, which "elicit powerful responses of belief or disbelief in distant audiences without bringing those audiences any closer to practical solutions for the problems that occasioned the stories in the first place" (p. 156). Their concern is that mass media contain too few constructive stories and too many stereotypical stories. They argue that it is in the interest of elites to disseminate stereotypical stories that present little new information or insight. Although such stories may address important social problems, they do not offer alternative solutions.

Instead, they imply that current elites are doing the best they can to cope with a problem that has no apparent solution. The stories simply serve to promote acquiescence to the status quo and reinforce existing views of social reality.

Although narrative theory provides a potentially useful focus for the analysis of news content, it fails to provide a sufficiently detailed examination of the process that underlies learning from stories. Why do stereotypical stories result in little useful learning? How could failure to learn be empirically measured? When will a constructive story effectively communicate its insights and when will it simply be ignored? It may be possible to find answers to these questions in information-processing theory.

C. Information-Processing Theory

Information-processing theorists have conceptualized learning as a complex, multistage process in which new information must be attended to, briefly stored in short-term memory, fitted into preexisting interpretive schemas, and finally transferred to long-term memory. The outcome of each of these stages can be influenced by a variety of personal, social, and message factors. When what is learned is strongly influenced by cues in message content, it is said to be "bottom-up" learning. Such learning tends to be passive and is not structured by factors unique to the learner. Learning can also be "top-down," dominated by such factors as existing knowledge and motivation.

These two basic types of learning are especially relevant to news research (Woodall, Davis, & Sahin, 1983). Salomon (1979) has argued that television messages are experienced by most viewers as providing very concrete and easy-to-interpret descriptions of events. The same routinized skills that are used to make sense of everyday life events seem applicable to processing television content because it appears to represent reality so directly. But watching a television depiction of an event does not make one an eyewitness. Viewers who assume that they are seeing the news as it happens are likely to passively process content and rely heavily on content cues to guide their interpretation (bottom-up processing). As a result, the learning that occurs may be quite superficial and discrete—focused around recall of trivial but vivid visual details or colorful, dramatized verbal descriptions. Such learning is likely to fade quickly from memory because the crucial transfer from short- to long-term memory does not take place. The transfer to long-term memory is also made more difficult by the short length of most stories and the fast pace of news programs. Viewers do not have time to engage in the reflection necessary to learn story content.

Several conceptualizations have been created to explain how long-term memory is structured so that it can guide routine interpretation of new information. One concept that has been developed is that of a semantic network

(Woodall *et al.*, 1983). This theory focuses on the *representation* of knowledge in long-term memory. It assumes that learners *activate* networks of past knowledge and use these to decode or interpret new information.

Semantic network researchers have studied the *deep processing*, which they believe must occur if new information is to be assimilated into an existing semantic network and stored in long-term memory. Their research has identified various factors that appear to induce deep processing. Assimilation is more likely to occur if individuals either are already knowledgeable or are highly motivated to learn. Specific emotional states such as excitement or fear can affect or interfere with assimilation. Learning is enhanced if individuals are induced to reflect on specific stories. For example, conversations with others or repeated exposure to the same story in different media can force an individual to think through story details and form interpretations of it.

Another concept that can be used to explain the role of existing knowledge is the schema (Anderson, 1980). Schemas are defined as "large, complex units of knowledge that organize much of what we know about general categories of objects, classes of events, and types of people." Schema theory has been concerned with identifying the sets of concepts that are activated and used in *initial* decoding of new information. Thus, it has been especially concerned with explaining short-term learning rather than with deep processing. A schema might consist of a particular portion of a larger semantic network, which is activated and used to process new information.

Schrank and Abelson (1977) have studied and developed computer simulations of one type of schema—scripts. They argue that each of us has learned many scripts for action in common social situations. These scripts enable us to quickly orient ourselves in such situations, form expectations for action by others, and structure our own actions so that desired outcomes are reached. For example, most of us have learned a restaurant script that guides our perceptions and actions in restaurants. Research indicates that when people read stories that deviate in minor ways from standardized scripts, their perception of the stories tends to be distorted to make them consistent with the script. Details missing from stories will often be filled in with expected events, objects, or attributes. Persons, actions, and objects that are not part of a script will tend to be ignored or forgotten.

Semantic network and schema theories can be combined with the arguments of Bennett and Edelman to produce some useful predictions about learning from news. A stereotypical story is likely to be structured by a familiar script. It contains cues that lead to the activation of that script in the semantic network. The information in the story is then quickly and routinely decoded by viewers and placed in short-term memory. It is not likely that deep processing of this information will occur. Perhaps, if there are quite important deviations from the script, the viewer might reflect upon these inconsistencies. Or, a brief conversation with someone else might trigger further processing. Thus, though the information from such stories may be successfully decoded, it has little long-term importance.

It is likely that there are frequently very significant gaps between the raw information that people receive from news, the information that they actually decode, and the information that is finally integrated into long-term memory. Woodall (1986) has emphasized the necessity for research to differentiate between these different forms of processing. He argues for careful differentiation of two categories of learning variables: *remembering* and *comprehension*. Remembering involves successful decoding of information and short-term learning. Comprehension involves "deep processing" of information and integration of that information into a semantic network for long-term learning.

If the semantic network and schema theories are valid, they would predict that the constructive stories that Bennett and Edelman prize might also have little impact, but for reasons very different from those that impede comprehension of stereotypical stories. By definition, constructive stories do not follow a widely known script and much of the information that they contain will be innovative. Such stories will be difficult to decode, so unless there are factors present that assist decoding, the information in such stories will not be placed in long-term memory. Factors that might assist in decoding would include repetition of key points or the presence of visual images that are congruent with verbal information. Viewers who are alerted to the decoding problem might then be motivated to make an extra effort to make sense of the information.

Experience may teach journalists that innovative stories present serious decoding problems for average news consumers. Few persons are likely to be confused or complain when stereotypical schemas are used to report events. On the other hand, production of constructive stories would run the risk of alienating viewers. Such stories could even begin to raise doubts in the minds of viewers about the credibility of the news coverage. When widely known scripts can be relied on by consumers to interpret stereotypical stories, these stories will tend to be experienced as realistic and objective. Constructive stories may present viewers with serious interpretation problems. Viewers may resolve these problems by changing existing schemas so that the new information can be learned or by rejecting the information. In the latter case, they may also question the credibility of the source of the information.

Research by Vallone, Ross, and Lepper (1985) provides additional evidence of linkage between schemas and perceptions of objectivity. They found that political partisans were more likely to perceive two-sided coverage of events as biased against their position. Pro-Arab and pro-Israeli subjects were shown the same television news coverage of the Beirut massacre. Subjects saw the coverage as more favorable toward the position they opposed and less favorable toward their own. They remembered more references unfavorable toward their position, and they described program editors as holding views contrary to their own. These effects were found to be strongest for those persons who knew the most about the massacre and for those who were most emotionally involved in and concerned about their cause.

The findings of Vallone and colleagues are consistent with information-processing theory. Political partisans, and especially those who are already knowledgeable, should have developed complex schemas to guide their processing of new information. They will be likely to notice and remember information that contradicts their schemas while consistent information will be quickly processed and forgotten. The investigators point out that the effects they observe may be limited to persons who are both intellectually and emotionally involved in the events and issues they are viewing; they could not find similar effects for political party supporters who viewed standard campaign coverage. If our interpretation is correct, content structure and substance should also be important. The most effective content would be ambiguous, not relying upon stereotypical story formulas that might implicitly communicate a point of view. Content would show contradictory information and then fail to resolve the contradictions.

Doris Graber (1984) has used information-processing theory to conceptualize and interpret data gathered from a sample of 21 voters over a 12-month period during an election campaign. She reports that most respondents relied on very simple schemas that focused their recall on unusual, dramatic, or especially vivid details of events. But these details were rarely stored in long-term memory. Within a few weeks, most of the information was forgotten. Learning of important information such as the positions of candidates on issues was rare. When it occurred, it was the more knowledgeable and politically interested respondents who learned such information. Such persons would have been more likely to have developed semantic networks and schemas that facilitated decoding and then enabled long-term storage of information. Their preexisting interest in politics may have prompted the reflection that led to deep processing.

A set of elaborate experiments has been used by Iyengar and Kinder (1986) to explore hypotheses derived from information-processing theory. They argue that TV news may have the power to "prime" viewers to focus on certain areas of presidential performance while neglecting others. Given the range of presidential activity, voters could choose to evaluate performance based on success or failure in many different areas, such as defense, inflation, and terrorism. Iyengar and Kinder present evidence that when TV news focuses on specific areas, it can induce persons to perceive those areas as more important in evaluating presidential performance. This priming effect is strongest if individuals are exposed to coverage over a period of days and if presidential responsibility is explicitly discussed in the stories.

The Iyengar and Kinder research suggests that the influence of TV news may be quite subtle. Shifts in coverage patterns and in the way the president is described can apparently have significant consequences for public opinion. Perhaps alterations in coverage lead to activation of different schemas. These schemas are then more likely to be used in processing other information or to structure personal reflection about events and political actors. Iyengar and Kinder point out that personal reflection about politics is unlikely to be based on long and careful consideration of even the information that has already been learned. Rather, most persons will tend to develop opinions by using knowledge that is most easily accessible (e.g., recently learned). We would add that this knowledge is likely to be framed or interpreted using the most accessible schemas (e.g., those recently activated).

IV. A REEXAMINATION OF EARLY NEWSFLOW RESEARCH

A. Interpreting Newsflow Research

These three theories provide a comprehensive framework for the analysis of newsflow through electronic media. They indicate how news could be a rather central means by which orientations toward the social world are communicated, especially the social world that lies beyond the personal experience of a news consumer. That world may be defined by schemas learned by the news itself. Such schemas may serve to define a rather static political world that is more or less controlled by an active, colorful, and normally benevolent elite. It may be a world in which minor reforms are constantly being implemented and elites are depicted as seeking new ways to serve the public more effectively. Widely held values such as freedom, individualism, and pluralism are respected. Social movements that seek to implement radical social changes are presented as deviating in significant ways from the scripts and stereotypes that define the "good society"; such movements represent problems to be solved by elites rather than by mechanisms that offer solutions to problems created by elites.

Next, the perspective derived from these three theories has been used to reinterpret the newsflow research that has been conducted over the past three decades. This reinterpretation permits further development of the perspective and provides some initial evidence of its utility.

B. The Early Research on Newsflow

Beginning in the mid-1940s, a series of studies was conducted that assessed the sources, speed, and extent of learning about persons and events reported in news stories in various media. A number of factors that impeded or accelerated the flow of news to the public were identified. Variables such as social position (as indexed by demographic measures), group membership and involvement, and psychological attitudes such as interest in news topics were studied in relation to learning from the news. Mediating variables such as time of day when news events occurred, routine use of media for news, and the structure of event reports were also considered.

Early newsflow research found that although the public generally became informed about events of some significance such as the health of a President or a major disaster, most routinely covered events did not become widely known. Even when learning did occur, it tended to be quickly forgotten (Funkhouser & McCombs, 1971). Important events became widely known in part because interpersonal conversation was initiated. People told each other about such events and then everyone turned to the mass media for further information. The best documentation of this pattern of newsflow is found in a set of studies conducted following the Kennedy assassination (Greenberg, 1964a, 1964b; Greenberg & Parker, 1965).

In a series of information flow studies summarized by De Fleur and Larsen (1958), the authors report that it proved difficult to accurately transmit information. They conducted a series of field experiments in which civil defense leaflets were dropped on small towns. Awareness of information contained in the leaflets was found to be a direct function of the number of leaflets dropped. Word-of-mouth communication of the information was found to be important in increasing diffusion of message content, but it resulted in less-accurate recall. Greatest accuracy was achieved when large numbers of leaflets were dropped. In another experiment in which free coffee was distributed to persons who learned a short slogan, even higher levels of word-of-mouth communication were stimulated. Again, accurate recall of the slogan was uncommon; most persons had shortened it, confused it with similar slogans, or remembered only a few key words.

News diffusion studies during the 1960s have isolated several consumer factors that are consistently linked to learning about news content. These include preexisting knowledge, interest level in story topic, level of education, level of communication with members of social groups, and position in social groups. These studies indicate that the persons who are most likely to find out about news events soon after they occur are those who are interested in the events, already know something about the events, are well-educated, are active in groups, and occupy central positions in groups.

C. Conclusions from the Early Newsflow Research

The early newsflow research suggests that formal education and group participation may be crucial in the development of semantic networks necessary for deep processing of news. Although many persons may learn the simple schemas necessary for routinely decoding stereotypical news stories, most are not sufficiently motivated to remember content for even short periods of time. Persons who are prominent members of social groups would be more likely to possess such motivation because they would anticipate discussing news with others and the necessity of answering questions about news events. Persons may gain prominence in social groups in part because they have developed semantic networks and learned schemas that facilitate remembering and comprehension. Group participation should tend to provoke reflection and analysis of news, which would result in long-term learning.

V. CURRENT RESEARCH ON NEWS

A. The Knowledge Gap Hypothesis

Tichenor, Donohue, and Olien (1970, 1980) have conducted a series of studies that extend the early newsflow research. They identify factors associated with learning from news and raise concern about the learning differences they have identified. Their research has focused on three variables: (1) level of education, (2) level of preexisting knowledge, and (3) level of interest. Consistent with the early newsflow research, they found that persons who are better educated, with high levels of interest in and knowledge about the topic areas, tend to learn more correct information from reading news stories and also become aware of events sooner (Robinson, 1972).

They formulated the knowledge gap hypothesis to summarize their findings. Because better educated and informed persons will routinely learn more about events and issues in the news, a gap in knowledge will normally widen between such persons and those who are poorly educated and ill informed. This hypothesis has since been supported by a series of studies (Tichenor *et al.*, 1980) and has been replicated in Sweden (Nowak, 1977). Knowledge gaps have been found to be greatest for complex, abstract topics that are of interest to only a few persons.

Tichenor and his colleagues (1980) have found that knowledge gaps may be narrowed when social conflicts arise that stimulate widespread public discussion of specific topics. Gaps narrowed the most when conflict levels were high and the communities in which the conflicts occurred were homogeneous. These findings imply that widespread ignorance or apathy are not permanent social conditions but can fluctuate as social conditions change.

If prominent and dramatic news stories articulate demands for resources or services, even normally apathetic segments of the public may be stirred to pay attention and learn about issues. Interpersonal communication may play an important role in providing repeated exposure to new information and forcing reflection on it.

The three theories reviewed earlier are consistent with the knowledge gap findings. To the extent that news is structured by schemas that are of relatively low utility to average consumers, knowledge gaps should be commonplace, especially for complex or abstract topics. Knowledge gaps will be narrowed only when schemas are learned by persons who were previously ill informed. But before such learning occurs, some changes in social conditions must occur that will motivate and facilitate the learning of schemas. For example, escalating social conflict over an issue in a community may lead to widespread discussion. Effective participation in this discussion may necessitate learning of schemas, which in turn facilitates learning from news. In some cases, learning of new schemas may be promoted by group leaders.

B. Agenda Setting

The newsflow research suggests that social factors beyond the control of journalists may strongly constrain learning, but other research has investigated the possibility that journalists can exercise some direct control over learning. McCombs and Shaw (1972; McCombs, 1981) have developed the *agenda-setting hypothesis*, which states that the media may not have the power to change "what people think" but can influence "what people think about." Media can call public attention to specific people, events, and issues. By extending coverage over days or weeks, media can imply that these people, events, and issues are more important than those that are not covered. Information-processing theory would predict that if news coverage patterns can induce increased public interest in a topic, then learning should increase as new schemas are learned.

McCombs and Shaw (1977) have found that there are strong statistical correlations between the amount of newspaper coverage that issues receive during a political campaign and the ranking of those issues by voters, but such effects have been harder to find for television news. Other researchers have reported mixed results when studying the power of the media to influence agendas during noncampaign periods. McLeod, Becker, and Byrnes (1974) found little evidence that high levels of media coverage of certain issues or events had any consistent influence on the amount of public discussion of those events. Thus, news coverage patterns may have little impact on talking about issues. Perhaps, it is the coverage of only certain types of events (i.e., those involving controversy or conflict) that provokes discussion and influences learning.

C. The Spiral of Silence

Noelle-Neumann (1974, 1984) has argued that media coverage has the ability to bring about rapid shifts in public opinion through coverage, which implies that certain opinions are becoming less popular. She argues that people are less willing to talk about opinions that media reports label as "unpopular," thereby creating a self-fulfilling prophecy. As people talk less about certain positions, opposing positions tend to gain prominence. She has labeled this phenomenon the "spiral of silence."

Empirical support for this hypothesis has been mixed, but some consistent findings have emerged. Media labeling of opinion positions appears to have the greatest influence for those positions that are not strongly held and that are based on relatively little knowledge. On the other hand, when individuals have strong interest in certain issues and have developed well-founded issue positions, media coverage is likely to have little impact on their willingness to discuss a position. In some cases, such coverage may even inspire individuals to talk more about their position in an effort to win back public acceptance.

These findings are consistent with information processing theory. Persons who have schemas that enable them to process information efficiently should also have well-developed interests and viewpoints. They may be quite skeptical of media reports stating that their views are losing popularity, and they could react by seeking out additional information or by seeking to persuade others of the merits of their views.

Both the agenda-setting and spiral-of-silence hypotheses suggest that under certain conditions, the media can have a direct influence on news audiences. During political campaigns in which public attention to political news is stimulated, the amount of coverage given issues may alter perception of the importance of those issues. Issue positions that are said to be losing favor will be less likely to be discussed if their supporters are not strongly committed to them. In both cases, social factors may constrain media influence in important ways. Participation in group activities could serve to reverse the effects of either agenda setting or the spiral of silence.

Neither of these hypotheses has been concerned with the power of the media to affect schemas, yet the findings they describe may be attributable to such effects. Continuing coverage of certain issues may prompt interest in certain topics and learning of schemas necessary to decode and interpret coverage. Similarly, coverage that rejects certain issue positions may discredit schemas associated with these positions. To the extent that such schemas are neither well developed nor of great social utility, they may tend to be replaced by schemas linked to other positions.

D. The Lang Model of Opinion Formation

Agenda setting and spiral of silence effects may prove to be quite superficial if they are not linked to the learning of new schemas. In a book that reviews the Watergate crisis, the Langs (1983) have traced a complex opinion-formation process involving news coverage, opinion change, knowledge, and discussion. They have argued that news coverage may have triggered an opinion-formation process that ultimately led to profound changes in how the public viewed the Nixon Presidency. Their discussion suggests that it will be necessary to develop more complex conceptualizations of the interrelationships among various social factors, news coverage, and newsflow. According to the Langs, routine reporting practices may have initially retarded learning about Watergate. During the 1972 campaign, journalists consciously balanced McGovern's Watergate-related accusations with denials from the White House. This led to creation of stereotypical news stories, which implied that Watergate was strictly a partisan issue. Opinion polls revealed that public knowledge about Watergate remained quite low throughout the campaign despite frequent coverage in campaign stories. The burglary itself was remote from most persons' lives, and information about it came from partisan sources.

After the election, the structure of Watergate news coverage changed radically, especially in prestigious papers such as the *Washington Post* and the *New York Times*. The trial of the Watergate burglars and the Senate hearings were given prominent coverage. Almost every day brought new revelations about the involvement of the Nixon administration. Knowledge of Watergate rose, and gradual changes in public opinion occurred. Following "the Saturday Night Massacre," in which the Special Prosecutor, Archibald Cox, was fired, the view that Nixon was personally involved began to gain favor. Eventually, the public accepted the unprecedented resignation of a president as legitimate, even necessary.

The Langs (1983) refer to the perspective as "agenda building" and describe it as follows:

> Media attention was necessary before Watergate could be considered a problem. Yet, in publicizing a high-threshold issue like Watergate, the media do more than direct attention to a problem; they influence how people will think about it. They supply the context that, by making the problem politically relevant, gives people reasons for taking sides and converts the problem into a serious political issue. In this sense the public agenda is not so much set by the media as built up through a cycle of media activity that transforms an elite issue into a public controversy. (p. 58)

The theories we have reviewed would suggest that, initially, news coverage was structured using stereotypical narratives. These narratives focused on the political conflict between Nixon and McGovern. McGovern's Watergate charges were easily interpreted as a routine campaign strategy designed to win votes away from a popular president. Because each charge was countered by plausible explanations, voters had no basis for ascertaining who was right. Graber (1984) has found that when voters encounter such conflicting messages, they tend to ignore them or quickly forget them.

After the election, changes in reporting practices and the narrative structure of news coverage may have played an important role in stimulating learning. Thus, the trial of the Watergate burglars may have captured public interest primarily because of the way in which journalists chose to structure their stories. Highly dramatized narratives were created in which John Sirica was portrayed as a heroic figure who acted to defend goodness in defiance of a sitting president. In these stories, Sirica's charges were not "balanced" by White House rebuttals. Similarly, the Senate Watergate hearings also provided ideal material for the construction of narratives depicting a classic confrontation between good and evil. Such narratives stimulated public interest in Watergate and convinced most Americans that Watergate-related events were important. Increases occurred in attention to Watergate news and public knowledge and discussion of it. Gradually, public opinion began to turn against Nixon, with important long-term political consequences.

Figure 1 diagrams this agenda-building process and identifies media coverage as a critical variable affecting agenda building. Routinely covered events induce superficial learning and no significant change in public knowledge or opinion. Nonroutine coverage can initiate a cycle of rising public

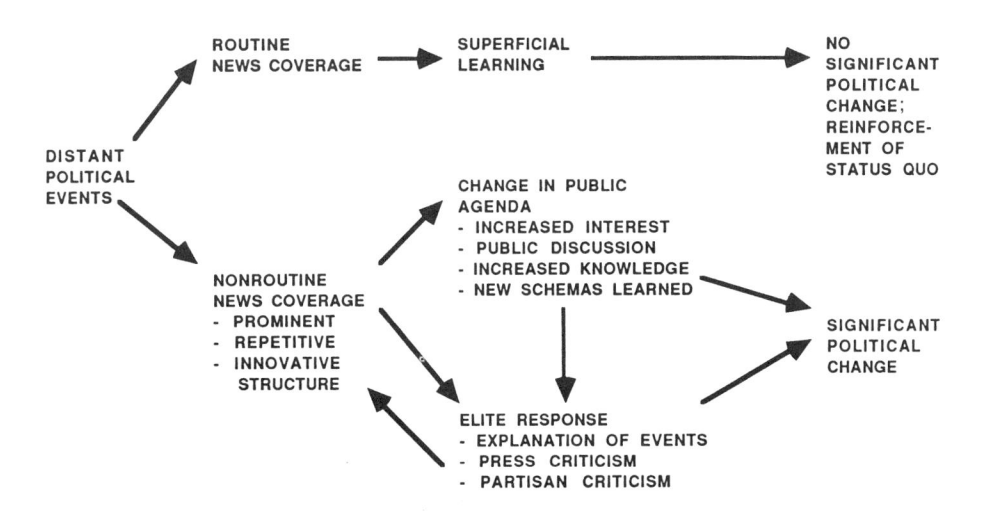

Fig. 1. Agenda-building model.

concern and discussion (and build a new agenda), which in turn affects ongoing media coverage and also impacts political elites, forcing changes in their actions designed to avert a growing crisis. Elite response also affects media coverage. Agenda building could be "short-circuited" by an effective elite response that either (1) induces journalists to adopt more routine reporting practices or (2) successfully explains old events in terms of news themes and schemas.

The recent Iran-Contra affair would appear to fit this model quite well. Initially, events occurred that were so remote from public concern that even routine coverage did not occur. Perhaps to avoid charges of political partisanship, journalists for major newspapers avoided coverage of events about which they were aware until after the November, 1986 election. Not coincidentally, the first significant coverage of the affair began on election day. But even if this coverage had preceded the election, the outcome would most likely not have been affected. Most Republican and independent voters would likely have viewed the stories originating in Tehran as lies fabricated by a hostile regime to embarrass the president. Postelection coverage has been structured by themes and schemas that are both innovative and damaging to the Reagan administration. Reagan is depicted as a naive, ignorant figurehead atop a disorganized White House. He is said to have failed to control subordinates who pursued desired ends through illegal means even though he was aware of their actions.

The Reagan administration response to such coverage has been defensive and ineffective. Efforts were made to shield the president from involvement and to pressure journalists to ease up on coverage. Administration spokesmen, like Patrick Buchanan, accused journalists of pursuing a vendetta. Little was done to usefully reframe the original events. Instead, clumsy explanations were constructed, which have since been exposed as lies. As a result, the earlier mistakes were compounded. The crisis continues, with changes in public opinion that might affect a future election campaign and its outcome, perhaps as dramatically as Watergate affected the 1976 campaign.

E. Uses and Gratifications Research

Another body of research that has probed learning from television news has linked such learning to the conscious forms of media content. The approach in its current form was pioneered by Jay Blumler in a series of studies (Blumler & Katz, 1974; Blumler & McQuail, 1969). Blumler and McQuail found modest correlations between the uses of media that audience members reported and the types of learning that took place. Voters who were categorized as "strongly motivated to follow the campaign on TV" tended to learn more about candidates and issues. Motivation to use TV was not correlated with changes in political attitudes; however, some evidence was found that motivated voters were *less* likely to shift toward the British Labour party. Blumler and McQuail concluded that the competing political arguments and campaign propaganda that characterize British electoral TV may largely serve to reinforce partisan positions.

The effects described by uses and gratifications theorists can be accounted for by the aforementioned three theories. Uses and gratifications theory serves to differentiate among three types of news-consumer roles, based on patterns of usage (Gurevitch & Blumler, 1977): the spectator role, the informed voter role, and the partisan role. Each news consumer type would be likely to use different sets of schemas to decode and interpret news. Each might seek out different types of stories and be likely to learn different things from these stories. It is likely that most of the campaign news stories would be stereotyped, and therefore these stories would be easily decoded by news consumers, using their preferred schemas. The stories' content is not likely to be of sufficient novelty or interest to warrant the reflection necessary for storage in long-term memory. If there is not widespread public discussion of campaign events, learning is likely to be minimal, and voting will be routine, even among those choosing the informed voter role.

The uses and gratifications approach has emphasized the notion that media users actively seek out content and the effects that result from content use. But such active seeking of content is likely to be strongly influenced by the social environment and the structure of media coverage. Much of the use that normally occurs may be highly routinized and passive, resulting in little long-term change in schemas, knowledge, or opinions. Truly active seeking of information may not occur until after the public agenda is altered by nonroutine coverage of events.

The foregoing findings from research on newsflow are summarized in Table II.

VI. OUR NEWS COMPREHENSION RESEARCH

A. Research Design and Data Collection

In 1978 and 1979, we conducted two news audience surveys, one in Great Britain and one in the United States, that permitted us to make an exploratory assessment of what is learned by viewers while watching typical news broadcasts (Robinson & Levy, 1986). The British survey interviewed a national sample of 489 adults and was conducted on four evenings in June, 1978, by interviewers from the Audience Research Department of the British Broadcasting Corporation (BBC). The U.S. survey interviewed 447 persons and was

TABLE II
Summary of Research Findings on Newsflow

Source	Quotation
Funkhouser & McCombs (1971)[a]	Except for Nixon's announcement concerning the draft, the events we traced followed a consistent pattern: the higher the audience interest, the higher the proportion of knowers in the population and the less the amount of "dip" in the diffusion curve early in the evening. The event of lowest audience interest, the Ohio prison riot, not only had the largest early-evening dip of all the events except the Nixon announcement, but, as previously noted, actually experienced an overall decline in the percentage of knowers over the course of the evening.... The results of this study indicate that the higher the audience interest in a news event, the larger the proportion of the audience that will be aware of it at any given time during its diffusion. Also, the less susceptible its diffusion will be to forgetting or to competition from other news events. (pp. 112–113)
De Fleur & Larsen (1958)	What circumstances appeared related to the accurate transmission of the message? In general, our data showed that stimulus intensity, age, sex and family size were not significantly related to the degree to which the message knowers recalled the content. However, accuracy of recall was significantly related to the channel through which the knowers first contacted the message. When the population saw a leaflet, either from direct physical diffusion or from social pass-on diffusion, their level of accuracy was significantly greater than when their initial contact with the message was via social oral diffusion. (pp. 202–203)
McCombs & Shaw (1977)[b]	To sum up, there are two distinct phases in election year agenda-setting. In the summer and early fall the prime mover is the newspaper alone. Newspapers perform more of an initiating role in public opinion than does television.... But as we move into the fall campaign period, this influence of the press built up across time is shared with television. Since there are major stylistic as well as technological dissimilarities between newspapers and television, this later phase in agenda-setting is sharing rather than reinforcement. (p. 155)
Noelle-Neumann (1985)	The spiral of silence simply represents one link in the chain; the hypothesis applies to certain situations in the process of public opinion and hence should be seen as part of a more inclusive theory. A spiral of silence will only develop where there is public debate, particularly where there is a change in attitudes about emotionally charged topics, and especially when the moral dimension of "good" and "bad" is included. Where other topics are concerned, there is no threat of isolation and hence there is no spiral of silence either. (p. 92)

Tichenor, Donohue, & Olien (1980)[c]	Among the conditions that may lead to greater equalization of knowledge within a social system is social conflict of the type associated with community issues of basic concern to the population generally. As an issue becomes more intense, an increasing amount of newspaper publicity is generated and attention to that publicity increases. The conflict stimulates discussion among different persons, so that the joint result is a narrowing (but not necessarily an elimination) of knowledge gaps on the issue. (p. 200)
Blumler & McQuail (1969)[d]	There was no indication that responsibility for the increasingly pro-Labour mood of our respondents could be traced to any single source of political comment or propaganda.... It is not that campaign exposure helped to produce favourable attitudes to the Labour party.... Instead, the effect of high campaign exposure can be visualized as a braking action on the attitudes of the strongly motivated voters—checking the extent of their pro-Labour swing. (pp. 207–209)
Graber (1984)[e]	Most of our panelists absorbed sufficient information to be aware of a large number of important political and nonpolitical current issues. The ability to retain stories and retrieve them varied widely. Interest in news appeared to be the chief factor explaining above average memory capabilities in general and for remembering particular stories. But, at best, memory for news stories was quite limited when it came to retention of detail. For the most part, recall was hazy and incomplete.... Our findings about the casualness of the news selection process and the defects of memory are thus no grounds for pessimism about people's capabilities and inclinations to keep informed about current affairs. Rather, the findings indicate that people know how to cope with information overload, that they balance a healthy respect for their own pleasures with moderate willingness to perform their civic duties, and that they have learned to extract essential kernels of information from news stories while discarding much of the chaff. (p. 97)

[a] Reprinted with permission from Funkhouser & McCombs (1971). *Public Opinion Quarterly*, **50**, 107–113. Chicago: University of Chicago Press.
[b] Reprinted by permission from *The Emergence of American Political Issues: The Agenda Setting Function of the Press* by M. E. McCombs and D. Shaw; Copyright © 1977 by West Publishing Company, Pg. 155. All rights reserved.
[c] From P. J. Tichenor, G. A. Donohue, and C. N. Olien, p. 200 in *Community Conflict and the Press*. Copyright © 1980. Reprinted by permission of Sage Publications, Inc.
[d] Reprinted with permission from Blumler & McQuail (1969). *Television in politics: Its uses and influence*. Chicago: University of Chicago Press.
[e] From *Processing the News: How People Tame the Information Tide* by Doris A. Graber. Copyright © 1984 by Longman Inc. All rights reserved.

conducted in nine American cities on three evenings in June of 1979. The combined study covered broadcasts on seven evenings, with a total of 89 separate news stories.

The findings of these surveys have already been described in detail elsewhere (Davis & Vincent, 1986; Davis, Vincent, & Woodall, 1985; Robinson & Levy, 1986; Robinson et al., 1982). Our purpose in reviewing these findings here is to discuss them in relation to the three theories. We have given particular attention to findings derived from content analyses of both news stories and viewer reports of story content. These findings indicate that news story structure and content do influence viewer learning.

B. The News Comprehension Variable

A central objective of our research was to be able to identify specific news stories that had been well or poorly remembered. Only respondents who had viewed specific broadcasts were interviewed. They were asked what they could recall about individual news stories. Brief verbal cues were used to aid recall. Responses were recorded verbatim by interviewers. These responses were later coded by our research team. Initially, a 7-point scale was devised to code this data. Each story was identified as containing one or more main elements. Viewers who correctly reported those elements scored 4 points. Scores up to "7" were assigned, based upon the amount of additional information given by the viewer. If main elements were incorrectly reported or if only vague details were given, scores of fewer than 4 points were assigned. In this way, comprehension scores ranging from 0 to 7 were obtained for each story.

In later analyses, respondent story descriptions were coded in more detail. Viewers' usage of certain keywords which implied that viewers were using concepts derived from stories to structure their recall was noted. Stories were content analyzed to locate themes, and the respondents' descriptions were examined for evidence that these themes had been learned by viewers.

C. Story Factors and News Story Recall

In the initial analysis, a content analysis of the 89 stories from both nations was performed and more than 20 story attributes were coded. Attributes were chosen based on previous research, which had identified certain attributes as being linked to viewer learning. We were able to identify a set of attributes that frequently occurred in the same news story and were most consistently linked to recall of story content: (1) personalization, (2) human interest, (3) overall excitement, (4) strength of emotional content, (5) amount of visual information, (6) uniqueness of visual information, and (7) vividness of visual information. All were positively related to recall, except for vividness of visual information, which appeared to impede rather than enhance recall.

Ten stories possessed all of these attributes at rather high levels. Five dealt with the Pope's trip to Poland; others dealt with the aftermath of a DC-10 crash in Chicago, the death of actor Jack Haley, a freighter fire, the collapse of a Kansas City arena, and a race between robot mice. All of these stories were well remembered. Though these findings imply that the story attributes aid recall, the learning induced by such stories may not persist. In general, these stories were easy to decode because they had simple, very straightforward narrative structures. Main elements were visually shown as well as verbally described. But, in general, there was little in these stories to provoke reflection or conversation. Deep processing of story information was unlikely.

The links found between story attributes and recall led to the conclusion that visual factors were quite essential to viewer decoding of information. Attractive, unique pictures that arouse positive emotions and are congruent with verbal content may greatly increase the probability that short-term learning will be induced. On the other hand, quite vivid or routine pictures or those that arouse negative emotions or are incongruent with verbal content may impede decoding, perhaps because they distract viewers from attending to verbal information crucial for making sense of story content. The findings suggest that viewers may approach decoding of TV news content quite passively and rely on pictures to assist them.

D. Story Themes and Learning

Narrative theory suggests that longer stories with narrative structure should have a greater long-term influence on news viewer learning. We investigated this by conducting a content analysis of the themes contained in story content and then compared these themes to what was reported to us by viewers (Davis et al., 1985). We were fortunate in having available a content analysis of story themes prepared independently by Nimmo and Combs (1985). Their analysis of news coverage of disasters included the DC-10 crash in Chicago that our survey also covered. Nimmo and Combs assessed themes presented over a period of several weeks following the crash. Our survey began 4 days after the crash and covered a 3-day period.

1. Themes Used to Structure Air Crash Stories

CBS avoided early identification of a single cause of the crash. Instead, coverage focused on the investigation process, often showing "experts" using sophisticated testing equipment and computers. Nimmo and Combs label this theme the *high-tech search*. By contrast, ABC quickly identified *a sheared off bolt as the cause* of the crash but later was forced to alter this explanation. NBC chose a rather different approach, telling a complex story of *human frailty and endurance*. The crash had no single cause. It resulted from many different mistakes, bad policies, and lax enforcement of regulations, but people survived the tragedy and went on.

Each network had secondary themes. CBS focused on the *problems of the airline industry*. The DC-10 crash was seen as the latest in a series of crises to hit the industry. Airlines were being forced to cope with problems that were threatening to overwhelm them. ABC chose to voice direct and rather severe criticisms of the Federal Aviation Administration (FAA), arguing that every step of the investigation had been bungled and that the FAA put the welfare of the airline industry ahead of the public interest. This *muckraking theme* was complemented by a focus on the *troubles of "little people"* at airports. NBC covered an unfolding drama of *competing interest groups and the FAA* locked in a struggle to decide whether or not DC-10s should be grounded.

Visually, there was little to distinguish the coverage of the networks. NBC showed more "talking heads" as they concentrated on competing interest groups. CBS showed undramatic visual footage of aircraft and people in airports along with more interesting pictures of investigators at work. ABC tended to feature their own reporters on camera offering interpretations of FAA action (or inaction). All three networks showed numerous pictures of the crash. All featured many pictures of airport activity.

We judged NBC coverage to be both ambitious and complicated. It made regular use of multiple "on-camera" sources and often did not resolve stories, in favor of awaiting future developments. ABC coverage initially had the advantage of focusing on a single cause that could be visually represented; however, by the time of our survey, ABC was forced to retract this simple story in favor of reporting a complex sequence of events that might have led to the crash. The "little people" theme should have had human interest appeal.

CBS coverage had the greatest simplicity and consistency over time. The high-tech search theme was repeated, as was the industry problems theme over a period of several days. In most stories, the narration was controlled by the reporter, who rarely permitted other sources to interrupt description of points.

2. *Viewer Descriptions of Story Content*

We coded viewer responses to determine the frequency with which the various themes were evident. CBS viewers were twice as likely to refer to the recent developments in the ongoing crash investigation. Thirty-two percent of all CBS story recall contained such references, versus 12% and 17% for NBC and ABC, respectively. NBC viewers were more than four times as likely to refer to dramatic conflict between interest groups (37%, versus 1% for CBS and 8% for ABC).

To some extent, the themes of the plight of the airlines and problems of "little people" are complementary. The same information can be used to develop each. Lines of waiting passengers can be seen as a problem that troubled airlines must solve, or they can be seen as individuals suffering through a personal crisis of inconvenience. In its coverage, CBS chose the first theme, whereas ABC chose the second. The consequences of this difference in focus were apparent in the responses: 28% of CBS viewers mentioned the problems of the airlines, whereas only 7% referred to problems experienced by passengers. On the other hand, only 4% of ABC viewers spoke of airline problems, whereas 8% mentioned the problems experienced by passengers. Only 2% of NBC viewers mentioned airline problems, and none mentioned passenger problems.

We were also able to link the way that respondents described the actors (i.e., airlines, government agencies and officials, Airline Passengers Association, etc.) in stories to the themes used by the networks to structure the stories. NBC was the only network that regularly referred by name to many different actors. NBC respondents were much more likely to mention actors (77%, compared to 55% for CBS and 43% for ABC). Forty-nine percent of NBC viewers used specific nouns (i.e., named a specific airline or official) rather than vague pronouns (i.e., the government, they, someone). Only 18% of CBS viewers and 9% of ABC viewers used specific pronouns.

But while the NBC approach succeeded in communicating the identity of various actors, it also resulted in miscomprehension. The NBC story reported that after a court hearing to determine whether DC-10s should be grounded, the judge granted an FAA request to delay his decision for 1 day. Fully one third of all NBC respondents who could recall this story thought that DC-10s had been grounded. The story structure may have made it difficult for many respondents to decode it accurately. The story began with an ambiguous headline and established its main point in a brief closing statement. The story presented several arguments in favor of grounding the DC-10s, and the FAA position was very briefly stated. Some viewers may have been left with the impression that the planes were grounded because the arguments were weighted so heavily in favor of grounding.

The ABC theme, which emphasized the bolt as the cause of the crash, appeared clearly to influence viewer recall. Out of 143 ABC viewers, 40 specifically mentioned the bolt, compared to 3 CBS viewers and 4 NBC viewers. The main point of the ABC story on the day we did our survey was that the bolt was *not* the cause of the crash. But of the 40 persons who mentioned the bolt, 20 still referred to it as the cause of the crash. For the other 20, the bolt still remained a point of orientation.

We coded the favorability of respondent references to the FAA and the airlines. If the ABC muckraking theme had influenced viewers, it should have resulted in an increase in the number of unfavorable comments. But only 7% of ABC respondents referred to either the FAA or the airlines, and only 3% of comments were negative. There were no unfavorable references made by CBS viewers, but 5% of NBC viewers made negative remarks. NBC viewers heard critical comments from both the Airline Passengers Association and the Airline Stewardesses Association. Overall, negative references were far outweighed by neutral comments.

Thus, criticism in news stories does not ensure viewer recall. It will be important for future research to ascertain whether viewers can recall criticisms made in news stories by sources or by reporters. It is possible that the scripts that viewers use to decode stories lead them to ignore critical statements. For example, a simple conflict script might have been used to decode the NBC courtroom conflict story. Such a script might have focused viewer learning on the details of the conflict and the actors involved, but it might not have encouraged them to pass judgment on the merits of the arguments presented. Even more importantly, it led them to think that the most frequently argued position was successful when it was not.

These findings suggest that the themes used to structure continuing news stories may influence audience decoding. Themes may serve to activate scripts that emphasize certain aspects of stories and ignore others. In general, viewers did not offer spontaneous critical comments. This may mean that the themes prompted viewers to adopt a more or less objective stance toward events and encouraged them to suspend judgement. Or, this lack of critical comment could be a methodological artifact; viewers may not readily volunteer critical comments but might offer them if they were asked.

3. *Analysis of Viewer Recall of Political News*

We also conducted an analysis of viewer responses to political news stories (Davis & Vincent, 1986). A set of 14 stories broadcast by the 3 U.S. networks during the 3 days of our survey were considered. We found the story structure and audience recall of 5 of these stories to be especially noteworthy. Most were relatively long stories (over 1 minute) and had a definite structure. Next, we discuss each of these stories and interpret the audience response to each. This analysis indicates how the aforementioned theories can be used to explain audience learning.

a. The President and Zimbabwe-Rhodesia. One story covered the announcement of a decision by President Carter not to lift economic sanctions in Zimbabwe-Rhodesia because elections held there had not been "free and fair." This was the lead story on the night on which it was broadcast. It was structured with a conflict theme, which emphasized that Carter was taking a position that was opposed by the Senate. The story opened with the White House reporter, moved to Carter speaking to the press, and then moved to the anchor reading a quote from the Zimbabwe-Rhodesia leader, President Musarewa, who declared that Carter's action was not that of a Christian. The scene then shifted to a reporter at the Senate who stated that there was strong opposition to Carter in the Senate, but two senators who were interviewed made comments that were noncommittal.

This story clearly uses a conflict theme to structure the content. Carter's policy decision is set against a background of ongoing and, by implication, unsuccessful confrontation with Congress. This theme is maintained even though little direct evidence is offered for it in the story. In fact, the comments of the senators who are interviewed on camera appear to contradict the theme. One Carter critic states, "I believe the President, under the reasons he has given us, is entitled to have people like myself very carefully review his reasons, which are weighty and critical to the national interest of the United States and then take a mature decision and be able to answer his reasons if we don't agree and on the other hand if we do agree, to fight for him."

The conflict theme was explicitly mentioned by 34 persons, or 44%, of the 78 respondents who could recall anything about this story. Several stated that the president and Congress were disagreeing again. The conflict theme apparently was a familiar one to some news viewers. This story may be a good example of what Bennett and Edelman (1985) have labeled "stereotypical" stories. It provided almost half the viewers with an easy-to-use perspective on the event and facilitated their decoding of story information, but it is unlikely that this story structure would have prompted reflection or encouraged any innovative learning.

Viewer reports about this story tended to be rather fragmentary. Twenty-eight persons referred to economic sanctions, whereas 31 mentioned the election that had been held. None offered direct criticisms of either the president or Congress. None offered any favorable or unfavorable comments on the Carter decision.

b. Truck Drivers' Strike. Though coverage of the truck drivers' strike was quite minimal, viewer recall was the highest recorded for any political story. A brief, 45-word story was read by the anchor, with a graphic of a truck in the background. Several factors may account for the high recall: The strike had great potential to directly affect the lives of persons traveling on interstate highways that were being blockaded, and the main points of the story were simple and concrete.

There was some evidence that news story content may have influenced recall in certain ways. The story used the phrase "diesel fuel prices and supply" in referring to the reasons for the truckers protest. Forty-three of the 106 respondents who recalled this story (41%) used the term "diesel fuel" in their descriptions, nine persons used the term "diesel," 13 persons said "gas," and one said "diesel gas." If diesel gas had been used in the story, these figures might well have been reversed. The story used the term "blockade" in referring to strike activity, and 27 respondents used this term in their descriptions. These two examples illustrate the potential ability that news may have in attaching labels to these events.

A more potentially important example of this labeling power was found. The story used the term "protest" twice in referring to the strike, and 25 persons (24%) used the term "protest" to label it. Interestingly, 9 of these 25 persons became confused and explicitly stated that the protest had taken place in Washington, DC. This miscomprehension could be a result of a script being used to decode the story information. Viewers may have learned a "protest or demonstration" script, which always involves activity in Washington, DC. The use of the term "protest" in the story may have induced viewers to activate this script and use it to decode the story. Because activity in Washington is part of the script, it was erroneously recalled. Thus, activation of this schema aids recall but leads to inevitable confusion on the part of some viewers.

c. Union Meeting. This was a relatively long story about a speech by President Carter before a newly formed union of food and commercial workers. The speech announced that he would not impose wage and price controls even if it meant he would not be reelected in 1980. The speech was explicitly labeled by the news anchor as both political and presidential, and the point regarding wage and price controls was repeated in the story. After a brief voice-over, Carter was permitted to make an impassioned statement about his willingness to "safe-guard the future of our country" even if it will "cost me some political support.... I will never fight inflation by deliberately throwing millions of Americans out of work, as has been done in the past." The story concluded with commentary to the effect that Carter was seeking to regain union support and avoid defections to Ted Kennedy.

Evaluation of viewer response to this story was complicated by the fact that the label "union meeting" prompted only 61 of the 148 viewers to describe the Carter speech. But, the story that followed this one dealt with wage and price *guidelines*. The verbal cue "wage and price guidelines" induced an additional 24 viewers to remember the wage and price *controls* theme of the Carter speech. Few respondents appeared to grasp the distinction between guidelines, which were then in effect, and controls, which were being threatened. Of the 85 respondents who recalled this story, 35 (41%) correctly remembered that Carter promised not to impose controls. Two persons thought he would impose controls. Of those who remembered Carter's promise, six mentioned that he would not impose controls even if it jeopardized his election chances. Nine mentioned that Carter did not want to throw people out of work. Three persons offered explicit critical comments about Carter, referring to his speech as "bunk," courting the unions, and soft-soaping the unions. Eight persons noted that the new union would support Carter. Five persons explicitly referred to Ted Kennedy.

Viewer recall of this story seems to have been aided by repetition of its main point concerning wage and price controls. Secondary story points dealing with Carter's motives or the political context for his actions were not learned with any consistency. The three critical comments voiced by viewers about Carter were atypical. Recall for most stories contained no explicit criticisms. By explicitly labeling this as a political speech, journalists may have induced some viewers to activate partisan schemas. Also, the references to Kennedy may have activated such schemas. Activation of partisan schemas may have led to a more negative evaluation of Carter's remarks than would otherwise have occurred. However, to the extent that emotional responses were prompted by the story, deeper processing of story content may also have been prompted. This would increase the likelihood of long-term learning.

d. Nicaragua. Viewer recall of this story was interesting, given the continuing importance of Nicaragua in the U.S. news. Story content dealt with the decision by Somoza to declare a state of siege in order to cope with a 3-day-old general strike declared by the Sandinistas. In opening the story, the anchor noted that Somoza's order meant that persons could be arrested by the military without warrants and that the government could restrict news media. A reporter in Managua was shown on camera. He provided a voice-over for a film showing the conditions in the city. The story focused on concrete consequences of the general strike and the imposition of martial law. Visual coverage showed closed shops, an empty Sears parking lot, and lines at gas stations and at the central market kept open by government soldiers. People were shown hurrying home with their purchases.

Though half of the viewers could recall some details from this story, much of the recall was fragmentary. Of the 76 persons who gave descriptions of the story, only 9 mentioned the state of siege. Use of this term by the reporter seemed especially unfortunate because it probably was not understood by most viewers. The things most frequently mentioned were fighting (20 persons), closed stores or shops (19 persons), guerrillas (12 persons), people afraid or fearful (10 persons), and the strike (10 persons). Much of the recall involved visual details, in contrast to most of the recall from other stories, which focused on verbal information. The two points made by the anchor in his opening statement concerning arrests and censorship of the news media did little to guide learning. Only 4 persons referred to arrests, and no one mentioned news media restrictions.

Recall from this story illustrates the importance of repeating main points in the body of a story and avoiding the use of technical terms that viewers may not understand. The story apparently failed to activate any useful schemas for most viewers, and much of the learning that was induced seemed to involve recall of visual imagery. It is not likely that such learning will be useful or long-lasting.

e. Jews and Arabs. A long feature story dealt with conflicts between Arabs and Jews in the West Bank district. After a brief introduction by the anchor, the story shifted to the reporter on the scene. The camera showed scenes from an Arab village while the voice-over explained that children were building a barricade to play a game called demonstration. During an interview with an Arab family, the parents, who were university professors, described how children throw sticks and stones to protest Israeli occupation. They accused the Israelis of answering with gunfire. The scene shifted to an Israeli settlement, and an Israeli professor—an immigrant from Canada—was interviewed. He defended the occupation and admitted to using a gun in self-defense against Arab protesters. The story closed by summarizing the conflict and repeating the sticks-and-stones versus guns theme.

Recall of this story was relatively low considering its length and the repetition of its main point. Fifty-seven percent of viewers could recall some details from the story, and most of these made some reference to fighting due to a dispute over land. Fifteen persons explicitly mentioned fighting, 16 referred to rocks or stones, and 8 mentioned guns. Two viewers objected to what they considered the pro-Arab slant of the story, and one of them made the following comment:

> It was some kind of fake news story. They rigged some little Palestinian kid playing "riot." The whole thing was staged. It appeared to be an Israeli concentration camp for Arabs where the Israelis were permitted to shoot them if they even threw a rock at a Jew. They interviewed a Palestinian couple and a Jewish man. I tuned out after two minutes of it.

Of all the stories in the newscasts that we studied, this story may come the closest to fitting the Bennett and Edelman (1985) category of "constructive" stories. For some viewers, it may offer a relatively innovative angle by looking at the Arab–Israeli conflict from the viewpoint of respectable, middle-class West Bank Arabs. As we argued previously, constructive stories may confuse or alienate because viewers do not have schemas that can guide their decoding. In this case, though, a familiar script is used (the underdog battling strong opposition). Respectable Arabs are unexpectedly cast in the underdog roles. Because most Americans probably have learned to view the Israelis as underdogs in previous wars with disreputable Arabs, the role reversal may have proven problematic for them. This was well-illustrated by the comments of the viewer who felt it was a "fake" story. Apparently, the story so deviated from acceptable schemas that he found it necessary to reject its authenticity.

The story clearly offers criticism of the Israeli occupation, but little of this criticism appears to have been understood and learned by viewers. Most simply had their vague conceptions of the Arab–Israeli situation reinforced by the story. They learned that the fighting was still going on and that things were not getting any better. Thus, although the story clearly contains innovative information and uses a familiar schema to structure it, little of this information appears to have been effectively communicated. The sticks-and-stones versus guns theme may not have assisted decoding. Rather, for the viewers who bothered to pay attention to the story script, it seems to have resulted in misunderstanding or confusion.

VII. TOWARD "USER FRIENDLY" JOURNALISM

A. Beyond Libertarianism and the Profit Motive

U.S. journalists often legitimize their craft by invoking ideas drawn from libertarian theory. In the ideal world envisioned by libertarianism, public-spirited citizens routinely use news media to inform themselves so that their public actions are wise and effective. In this world, corrupt politicians are voted out of office based on investigative reports by hardworking independent journalists who have little concern for making profits from the sale of news. Communication freedom enables a dynamic and ever-improving political order to be maintained.

Existing social research provides little support for this conception of the social world. Journalism is a business that has developed professional practices designed to make profits. Considerable time and money has been spent to develop program formats and content formulas aimed at increasing readership or audience size, but learning from news has been ignored. There is growing evidence that news generally and TV news in particular is failing to systematically inform the public about important issues and events. As we have noted, the current structure of TV news programs is biased against understanding. Hodgepodge, fast-paced coverage of a myriad of discrete events challenges the sense-making ability of even the most educated and well-informed viewers.

B. The Responsibility to Inform the Public

We believe it is time for journalists to take seriously their responsibility to inform the public. This will not be an easy task. They will need to give more careful consideration to the perspectives implicit in their news stories and accept the responsibility for communicating certain points of view while ignoring others. They will also need to design news that is tailored to the backgrounds and interests of audience members. Such news would be constructed with an understanding of the limited knowledge and interest of most news consumers. It would seek to overcome these limitations by developing program and story formats that assist rather than challenge viewers. Content should be designed implicitly to say to the audience "You can understand this." It must do this delicate task without being or appearing to be paternalistic or condescending.

Our recommendations assume that most routine processing of news will be relatively passive and casual, and that the principle of "least or minimum effort" will be operating. Except in situations of crisis or disaster, processing of news will not and probably should not be a central activity in most individuals' lives, but it can be a casual activity that leads to gradual increases in both interest and knowledge about important issues and events. Misunderstanding and misinformation can be avoided and corrected. News can serve to create a vital social resource: a basic level of public awareness and knowledge about the social world, upon which our nation can draw when circumstances demand widespread, informed public action.

C. Recommendations for Story Structure

The following recommendations are particularly relevant for the design and production of television news. However, with minor editing, most could be applied to news in other media. Our recommendations are not completely innovative; most can be recognized as basic principles of effective communication, whatever the medium, subject, or purpose.

1. Stress a Single, Clear Theme

Stories should minimize abstract or complex verbal content and repeat a well-developed and clearly articulated theme.

The utility of this principle is rather obvious but it is one that is difficult to put into practice. Again and again in our research we have encountered cases where use of technical terms or the seemingly random recitation of facts have impeded interpretation of themes. For example, terms such as "economic sanctions," "state of siege," and "wage and price controls" may not have been widely understood.

We recognize that some stories are not easily capsulized into a simple theme. Capsulization may be impossible without assuming a particular point of view on an event. Considerable creative talent and editorial ability will be required. However, given the fast pace and fragmentation of current news programs, a focus on simple, explicitly developed themes is a necessary condition for long-term learning.

2. Whenever Practical, All Stories of Any Significance Should Be Tightly Constructed around an Explicitly Verbalized Theme

All story elements should be consistent with and, whenever possible, should serve to reinforce the theme. Useful categories for labeling and summarizing content should be offered. Visual content should ideally show *why* an event has occurred and not only *who* was involved or *where* it occurred. Ambiguous visual content that is not closely linked to the theme should be avoided, especially if the content is visually attractive and interesting.

The utility of this recommendation was clearly demonstrated by the research we reviewed. When themes were explicitly repeated, they were generally learned, especially if secondary points were closely related and pictures were congruent with verbal content. The most effective stories were tightly structured, and the least effective stories were not. In general, most visuals were only marginally related to story themes. This common problem may prove quite difficult to resolve. News production teams are trained to look for "good" pictures—attractive, interesting visuals that are largely irrelevant to story themes. It will be difficult for them to subordinate the art of locating and capturing powerful visual images to the craft of story construction. Often, themes cannot be visually reinforced. We can only look at pictures of the places where events have occurred. Photographs cannot show us secret negotiations or rising deficits.

Ideally, category labels should assist viewers by inducing them to activate and apply relevant schemas. We noted how the use of the term "protest" in relation to the truckers' strike may have led to confusion about protest activity in Washington. It is likely that labels can often have such ability to induce processing that leads to inaccurate or distorted learning. Clearly, the use of categories needs to be done carefully. In our view, it can only be done responsibly if it is based on careful research, to determine the likely consequences of the use of certain labels or categories.

3. When Necessary, Contrasting or Conflicting Theme(s) Should Be Introduced Carefully

In longer news stories, it is possible to use complex story structures in which two or more themes are contrasted or compared. Research suggests that when such structures are carefully developed, significant learning can occur. One of the most commonly used story formulas involves "balanced" presentation of two opposing viewpoints. Too often, such stories imply that the experts are in disagreement over things that are too complex for average persons to understand. Neither position is adequately explained, nor are the reasons for holding a position explored. It is not surprising that such stories do not facilitate learning.

The most important news stories will require the development of more than one theme, especially stories about ambiguous events or reports about the causes and consequences of conflicts or controversies. If such stories are handled with a single theme, public confusion or misunderstanding may result. For example, when a simple theme was used to explain the crash of the DC-10 in Chicago, most viewers learned that the bolt caused the crash. However, later, when new evidence forced revision of this theme, confusion resulted, and many persons persisted in their belief that the bolt was the cause. A more useful story construction strategy was to contrast several explanations for the crash while emphasizing that the search for the cause was still in progress. Visual images effectively reinforced this "high-tech search" theme.

4. *Main and Contrasting Themes Should Be Clearly Separated*

Such separation is necessary if viewers are to clearly differentiate elements of each. Too often when several themes are included in a story, they are intermixed. In these stories, we first see a proponent for one point of view, and we then see an opponent. Then both positions are analyzed by the reporter. Viewers can easily become confused about who said what. If visual content is included, the potential for confusion rises exponentially. The potential for confusing viewers should never be underestimated, given the minimum effort being expended by viewers as they attend to and process program content.

5. *Similar Stories Should Be Separated*

Close grouping of similar stories makes it difficult for viewers accurately to separate out the details of each story. One of the guiding principles of news programming is to group together similar stories. This can create difficulties for viewers, resulting in confusion of story details. Sometimes this confusion is unimportant, as when the location of trivial events is confused, but some confusion may be more serious.

In other cases, grouping of similar stories may be functional, as when a story about a recent disaster or accident precedes a discussion of safety recommendations. We found instances where viewers appeared to be likely to learn information because the preceding stories had alerted them to a given topic, perhaps mobilizing their interest and activating relevant schemas. For example, viewers may have been more likely to note that Carter and Schmidt discussed energy problems because this story was preceded by a story on energy. On the other hand, the story on wage and price guidelines may have been forgotten or found to be confusing because it was preceded by Carter's speech dealing with wage and price controls. Grouping of stories must be done with a careful evaluation of the possible consequences of learning.

6. Clearly Explain Why Each News Story Is Important and for Whom It Is Relevant

Given the current structure of news broadcasts, viewers cannot be expected to grasp the relevance of stories for themselves or others. Journalists often assume that the relevance of a story is obvious. They forget that viewers observing a rapid succession of stories will not bother to consider the relevance of individual stories. Statements about relevance may be quite important in alerting viewers to important stories. Such statements can increase interest and lead to the activation of relevant schemas. Viewers should be more likely to reflect upon stories that include convincing statements of relevance.

7. Exercise Caution When Including Human Interest or Conflict Stories

Though such themes are frequently used to embellish stories and increase their attractiveness for viewers, they can easily distract viewers from important information or lead to serious misinterpretations. Though dramatization of news stories can enhance viewer comprehension, it can also distract from story themes by focusing on trivial or superficial details. As a general rule, dramatization need not be avoided but it must be subordinated to the communication of substantive themes. The potential for distraction and misunderstanding must be assessed before a "good" storyline is introduced. Drama can be used to facilitate learning about issues; it should not be the focus of news stories. The "news" should have precedence over the "story" in news stories.

VIII. RECOMMENDATIONS FOR FUTURE RESEARCH

A. Design of Future News Research

Implementation of our recommendations will be impossible without ongoing social research to guide story construction and evaluate audience learning. Our recent work provides an illustration of how this research might be designed. Public knowledge about institutions and issues could be regularly monitored, along with the flow of news and the story structures being used to communicate news. Gaps in public understanding could be identified. The ability of innovative story structures to communicate information might be tested, using field study or experimental methods. Such research could improve the practice of journalism while advancing theory development.

B. Utility of Research on Schemas

One area in which research might be especially useful involves schemas. As noted, schemas are semantic networks or sets of interrelated concepts that are held in long-term memory and can serve to guide decoding and storage of new information. Persons who are already knowledgeable on a topic have probably developed one or more schemas to guide their learning. When new information is encountered, the individual has only to activate a particular schema and then use it to quickly and routinely decode the information and determine which specific items of information are to be learned. Without such relevant schemas to guide the decoding of new information, less relevant schemas may be activated. New information is likely to be ignored as confusing or irrelevant.

If this theory of news processing is correct, then learning from news is strongly linked to the activation of relevant schemas. Well-structured news items can assist viewers by activating appropriate schemas while minimizing the activation of less-relevant or inappropriate schemas. If it is known that relatively few viewers have developed appropriate schemas, then an effort could be made to systematically develop such schemas. In this way, television journalists could play an important role in assisting the development of public knowledge about specific topics.

C. Applications for News Research

Well-designed information-processing research could be used to assess the schemas used by audience members to guide their interpretation of important, continuing news topics such as nuclear arms negotiations, public health threats such as AIDS, and political turmoil in Central America. This research could evaluate the nature and content of existing schemas and offer insights to guide news construction. Journalism could take a much more active role in promoting public learning. As new electronic media are developed, their potential for informing the public could be more effectively exploited. In time, public communication could become a more vital and omnipresent force in the political system. Increased public learning from news may be a necessary precondition for increased public interest and participation in politics.

ACKNOWLEDGMENTS

This article received the 1987 Donald McGannon award for social and ethical responsibility in communication policy research, from the McGannon Research Center at Fordham University. Data collection was made possible by a grant from the John and Mary R. Markle Foundation.

REFERENCES

Adoni, H., & Cohen, A. A. (1978). Television economic news and the social construction of economic reality. *Journal of Communication,* 28(4), 61–70.
Adoni, H., Cohen, A. A., & Mane, S. (1984). Social reality and television news: Perceptual dimensions of social conflicts in selected life areas. *Journal of Broadcasting,* 28(1), 33–49.

Adoni, H., & Mane, S. (1984). Media and the social construction of reality: Toward an integration of theory and research. *Communication Research*, **11**(3), 323-340.
Anderson, J. R. (1980). *Cognitive psychology and its implications.* San Francisco: Freeman.
Bennett, L., & Edelman, M. (1985). Toward a new political narrative. *Journal of Communication*, **35**(4), 156-171.
Berger, P., & Luckmann, T. (1966). *The social construction of reality.* Garden City: Doubleday.
Blumler, J. G., & Katz, E. (Eds.). (1974). *The uses of mass communication: Current perspectives on gratifications research.* Newbury Park, CA: Sage.
Blumler, J. G., & McQuail, D. (1969). *Television in politics: Its uses and influence.* Chicago: University of Chicago Press.
Burke, K. (1945). *A grammar of motives.* New York: Prentice-Hall.
Burke, K. (1950). *A rhetoric of motives.* New York: Prentice-Hall.
Commission on Freedom of the Press. (1947). *A free and responsible press.* Chicago: University of Chicago Press.
Davis, D. K., & Vincent, R. (1986, August). *Making sense of political news on TV: What people learn from dramatized political events.* Paper presented at the roundtable session of the American Political Science Association, Washington, DC.
Davis, D. K., Vincent, R., & Woodall, G. (1985, November). *Making sense of air disaster news: Viewer perceptions and story content.* Paper presented at the Mass Communication Division meeting of the Speech Communication Association, Denver, CO.
De Fleur, M. L., & Larsen, O. N. (1958). *The flow of information.* New York: Harper.
Epstein, E. J. (1973). *News from nowhere: Television and the news.* New York: Random House.
Fishman, M. (1980). *Manufacturing the news.* Austin: University of Texas Press.
Funkhouser, G., & McCombs, M. (1971). The rise and fall of news diffusion. *Public Opinion Quarterly*, **50**, 107-113.
Gans, H. (1979). *Deciding what's news.* New York: Pantheon.
Glasgow University Media Group. (Eds.). (1976). *Bad news.* London: Routledge & Kegan Paul.
Glasgow University Media Group. (Eds.). (1980). *More bad news.* London: Routledge & Kegan Paul.
Goffman, E. (1974). *Frame analysis: An essay on the organization of experience.* New York: Harper & Row.
Graber, D. (1984). *Processing the news.* New York: Longman.
Greenberg, B. S. (1964a). Diffusion of news of the Kennedy assassination. *Public Opinion Quarterly*, **28**, 225-232.
Greenberg, B. S. (1964b). Person to person communication in the diffusion of news events. *Journalism Quarterly*, **41**, 489-494.
Greenberg, B. S., & Parker, E. (1965). *The Kennedy assassination and the American public: Social communication in crisis.* Stanford, CA: Stanford University Press.
Gurevitch, M., & Blumler, J. G. (1977). Linkages between the mass media and politics. In J. Curran, M. Gurevitch, & J. Woollacott (Eds.), *Mass communication and society.* London: Edward Arnold.
Iyengar, S., & Kinder, D. R. (1986). More than meets the eye: TV news, priming, and public evaluations of the president. In G. Comstock (Ed.), *Public communication and behavior* (Vol. 1, pp. 135-171). New York: Academic Press.
Lang, K., & Lang, G. E. (1983). *The battle for public opinion: The president, the press, and the polls during Watergate.* New York: Columbia University Press.
McCombs, M. E. (1981). The agenda-setting approach. In D. D. Nimmo & K. R. Sanders (Eds.), *Handbook of political communication* (pp. 121-140). Newbury Park, CA: Sage.
McCombs, M. E., & Shaw, D. (1972). The agenda setting function of the mass media. *Public Opinion Quarterly*, **36**, 176-187.
McCombs, M. E., & Shaw, D. (1977). *The emergence of American political issues: The agenda setting function of the press.* St. Paul, MN: West Publishing.

McLeod, J., Becker, L., & Byrnes, J. E. (1974). Another look at the agenda-setting function of the press. *Communication Research*, **1**, 131-166.

Nimmo, D. D., & Combs, J. (1985). *Nightly horrors*. Knoxville: University of Tennessee Press.

Noelle-Neumann, E. (1974). The spiral of silence: A theory of public opinion. *Journal of Communication*, **24**, 43-51.

Noelle-Neumann, E. (1984). *The spiral of silence: Public opinion—our social skin*. Chicago: University of Chicago Press.

Noelle-Neumann, E. (1985). The spiral of silence: A response. In D. R. Sanders, L. L. Kaid, & D. Nimmo (Eds.), *Communication yearbook 1984*. Carbondale: Southern Illinois University Press.

Nowak, K. (1977). From information gaps to communication potential. In M. Berg et al. (Eds.), *Current theories in Scandinavian mass communication research*. Granaa, Denmark: Forlaget, GMT.

Robinson, J. P. (1972). Mass communication and information diffusion. In F. G. Kline & P. J. Tichenor (Eds.), *Current perspectives on mass communication research*. Newbury Park, CA: Sage.

Robinson, J. P., & Levy, M. (with Davis, D., in association with Goodall, W. G., Gurevitch, M., & Sahin, H.). (1986). *The main source: Learning from television news*. Newbury Park, CA: Sage.

Robinson, J. P., Sahin, H., & Davis, D. K. (1982). Television journalists and their audiences. In J. Ettema & D. C. Whitney (Eds.), *Individuals in mass media organizations: Creativity and constraints*. Newbury Park, CA: Sage.

Salomon, G. (1979). *Interaction of media, cognition and learning*. San Francisco: Jossey-Bass.

Schiller, D. (1981). *Objectivity and the news: The public and the rise of commercial journalism*. Philadelphia: University of Pennsylvania Press.

Schrank, R. C., & Abelson, R. P. (1977). *Scripts, plans, goals and understanding: An inquiry into human knowledge structures*. Hillsdale, NJ: Erlbaum.

Schudson, M. (1978). *Discovering the news: A social history of American newspapers*. New York: Basic Books.

Siebert, F. S., Peterson, T., & Schramm, W. (1956). *Four theories of the press*. Urbana: University of Illinois Press.

Tichenor, P. J., Donohue, G. A., & Olien, C. N. (1970). Mass media flow and differential growth in knowledge. *Public Opinion Quarterly*, **34**, 159-170.

Tichenor, P. J., Donohue, G. A., & Olien, C. N. (1980). *Community conflict and the press*. Newbury Park, CA: Sage.

Tuchman, G. (1972). Objectivity as strategic ritual. *American Journal of Sociology*, **77**, 660-679.

Tuchman, G. (1978). *Making news: A study in the construction of reality*. New York: The Free Press.

Turow, J. (1983). Local television: Producing soft news. *Journal of Communication*, **33**(2), 111-123.

Vallone, R. P., Ross, L., & Lepper, M. R. (1985). The hostile media phenomenon: Biased perception and perceptions of media bias in coverage of the Beirut massacre. *Journal of Personality and Social Psychology*, **49**(3), 577-585.

Woodall, W. G. (1986). Information processing. In J. P. Robinson & M. Levy (with D. K. Davis, in association with W. G. Woodall, M. Gurevitch, & H. Sahin), *The main source: Learning from television news* (pp. 133-158). Newbury Park, CA: Sage.

Woodall, W. G., Davis, D. K., & Sahin, H. (1983). From the boob tube to the black box: Television news comprehension from an information processing perspective. *Journal of Broadcasting*, **27**(1), 1-23.

The Forms of Television and the Child Viewer

ALETHA C. HUSTON and JOHN C. WRIGHT
Center for Research on the Influence of Television
on Children (CRITC)
Department of Human Development
University of Kansas
Lawrence, Kansas 66045

I. Introduction	103
II. An Attribute of the Medium: Television Forms	106
A. Definitions and Measurement	106
B. Comparison of Different Types of Children's Programs	108
C. Language Forms on Children's Television	109
D. Summary	110
III. The Child as an Active Viewer	111
A. Active versus Passive Viewing	111
B. Developmental Changes	114
IV. Cognitive Processing: The Match between the Child and the Television Material	116
A. Information Getting	116
B. Children's Comprehension of Television Form	129
C. Formal Features and Comprehension of Content	141
V. Television Forms and Social Behavior	147
A. Theories Relating Form and Social Behavior	147
B. Experimental Studies of Form and Social Behavior	148
C. Summary of Findings	151
VI. Conclusion	151
References	153

I. INTRODUCTION

When television was introduced in the United States, social scientists and social critics both lauded and decried the new medium. Its visual representations, its "nonlinear" method of presenting information, and its compelling attraction for all ages were topics of discussion and theory. Much of the research in the 1950s was designed to learn how the medium of television per se influenced family life, social relations, and academic achievement, to mention only a few of the major topics (see, e.g., Himmelweit, Oppenheim, & Vince, 1958; Schramm, Lyle, & Parker, 1961).

Before these questions could be resolved beyond a rather rudimentary and descriptive level, however, television research turned to investigations of content, particularly violence. In the 1960s and early 1970s, studies of violence, prosocial behavior, advertising, social stereotypes, and social knowledge were carried out, using television as the stimulus (Friedrich & Stein, 1975). In most cases, however, these studies could in principle have been conducted using any medium; they did little or nothing to take into account the possibility that a televised presentation is different in form than a book, a radio program, or an oral description.

In recent years, there has been a "new wave" of research devoted to exploring how the medium and its attributes are used by and affect developing children. Because the unique qualities of television reside in the structure and forms for presenting information rather than in its content, we and others have undertaken efforts to examine how television forms are related to cognitive processing of the medium and to its social behavioral effects.

Our initial interest in the forms of television resulted partly from the confounds of form and content in existing programming. It seemed possible that formal feature differences might be responsible for some of the behavioral effects that had been attributed to violent or prosocial content in earlier studies (see Stein & Friedrich, 1975, for specific findings of these studies). For example, in cartoons, violence is associated with rapid action, loud music, quick cuts, and other production techniques that could be important for maintaining children's attention and could stimulate active, aggressive behavior. By contrast, the increases in prosocial behavior and task persistence that follow viewing *Mr. Rogers' Neighborhood* could result from the quiet, calm, slow pace of the program as well as from the content messages stressing helping and persistence. It seemed important to disentangle the effects of form and content, not only for more accurate understanding of the processes involved, but also so that television producers might have more precise information about what features of programs are important for maintaining children's attention and communicating social messages.

Our exploration of television forms has been guided throughout by a dual concern for advancing basic theory and for generating socially applicable knowledge. Television is an ideal medium for investigating basic cognitive and social development processes because it provides a common stimulus to a large population. It may be the only widely used medium that can be controlled so precisely for purposes of investigating questions about attention, comprehension, or social behavior. It may also be unique in the combination of precise experimental control and ecologically valid content that it offers to the psychological researcher. At the same time, knowledge generated from such investigations may be useful in designing better television programs for children.

Another impetus for our interest in form was the emergence of a set of critics, ranging from serious theorists to social polemicists, who argued that television was inherently unsuited for active or complex cognitive processing (Lesser, 1977; Postman, 1979; Winn, 1977). Ironically, these analyses were instigated largely by *Sesame Street* and related efforts to use publicly broadcast television for education. These critics argued that television as a medium led to passive, intellectual processing rather than to active forms of learning. They expressed concern that televised instruction would supplant other forms of learning that were more beneficial and create for children a generalized tendency to be passive learners.

Singer (1980) elaborated the view that the perceptually demanding quality of many children's programs leads children to be overwhelmed by the immediate audiovisual experience. He argued that rapid pace leaves no time for children to reflect or consider what they are learning; they process information only at the superficial level of perceptual recognition. Singer does not consider these properties inherent in the medium; he asserts that slow-paced programs with low levels of perceptually demanding forms (such as *Mr. Rogers*) can induce active learning. Hence, his theory leads to the hypothesis that the type of learning resulting from television depends on the forms used to present the content.

We and others (see, e.g., Anderson & Lorch, 1983; Anderson & Smith, 1984; Collins, 1983; Salomon, 1983) dispute the view that learning from television is inherently passive or superficial. We assume that children are active cognitive processors of their experience (Huston & Wright, 1983; Wright & Huston, 1983). They spontaneously select, organize, and rehearse certain aspects of the sights and sounds they encounter on television, just as they do of their real-world experience. They attend selectively to those aspects of programs that they find interesting, entertaining, and comprehensible. That is not to say that children are always at peak levels of mental work when they watch television, but it does mean that they are not zombies being controlled by the perceptual events of television. They can process television at many levels, ranging from superficial enjoyment of sight gags and perceptual tricks to intense concentration on a demonstration of how the special effects of *Star Wars* were created.

Given this assumption, the question is not whether television leads to active or passive processing, but when and how television induces more or less active processing. That is, rather than assuming that children are uniformly active or passive in their encounters with television, we assume that their activity, effort, involvement, and mode of processing can vary from moment to moment or program to program. The determinants of that variability are of major research interest and include both attributes of the medium and characteristics of the developing child.

We first describe the formal features of the medium, particularly those features frequently used in children's programming. We then turn to a description of children's cognitive processing in a developmental framework to set the stage for understanding how televised information is processed. Subsequently, information about children's attention, comprehension, and social behavior is discussed in a framework based on an interaction between the attributes of the medium and the qualities of the developing child.

II. AN ATTRIBUTE OF THE MEDIUM: TELEVISION FORMS

A. Definitions and Measurement

The forms of television are relatively content-free auditory and visual attributes that are the consequences of specific production techniques, including what is done with the camera, postproduction, editing, special effects, and the like. Formal features include visual techniques such as cuts, dissolves, fades, pans, zooms, wipes, visual special effects, and so on. They also include auditory characteristics, such as adult and child male and female speech, peculiar speech (like that of cartoon animal characters), sound effects, background and foreground music, singing, and so on. There are some slightly higher order features: action, the rate of physical motion of characters through space; pace, the rate of scene and character changes; and variability, the number of different scenes and characters.

Form is distinguished from content, in that content is the message or storyline; form is the vehicle in which the message is presented—a vehicle that could, in principle, be used with a wide range of content. There are a few ambiguous cases that are settled by definition. Level of activity or character movement is defined as form; the specific actions of characters (hitting, kissing) is content. The occurrence of dialogue by adults, children, and nonhuman characters is defined as a formal feature; what they say is content.

Program formats are also formal attributes of television; they are the recognizable structures of television programs, such as drama, magazine, quiz, and so on. They are defined by how they are structured, not by their content, so that drama, for example, includes any story. Magazine formats include any program comprising relatively short, independent bits, such as talk shows, variety programs, *Sesame Street*, and the like. The quiz format would include any audience-contestant show. Format is usually stable over all episodes of a series, and it is one of the means by which children classify the show they are watching.

To determine how television forms are used in children's programs, we recorded 137 children's programs on the commercial networks and on the Public Broadcasting System (PBS) during a week in November, 1977 and a week in February, 1978 (Huston *et al.*, 1981). The definition of a children's program was the presence of any of the following attributes: animation, at least one major character who was a child or adolescent, broadcasting during children's prime time (Saturday morning), a host saying that it was for children, or a central character who had supernatural powers. All programs fitting this definition were coded for formal features. Violent content was also coded because of its importance in the children-and-television literature.

Trained scorers coded 23 formal features by making multiple passes through a taped program, using a solid-state event recorder. The recorder generates a record of all features entered by the scorer in real time, and that record is dumped directly into a computer through a terminal and modem. Some of the features are instantaneous, and are thus only entered once, like a cut or a scene change. Others have an onset, offset, and duration, such as dialogue, music, and action (physical movement by characters). Scorer agreement was evaluated by having two scorers code the same program at different times and by having one scorer code it on different occasions. Agreement was defined as the occasion on which both scorers coded the same event with a time discrepancy of less than or equal to .04 minutes. By this definition of agreement, the scoring criterion was 80% agreement.

The features were grouped in two stages on the basis of correlations and cluster analysis of co-occurrence. The final groupings are shown in Table I. With the exception of zooms, features having both frequency and mean duration showed high positive correlations between the two, and so only frequencies were analyzed.

There were three final groupings. *Perceptually salient* features included rapid action, rapid pace, high variability, tempo, noise, music, visual trickery, and visual change. These features were all considered high in sensory demand quality and they matched Berlyne's (1960) collative properties—movement, contrast, change, novelty, intensity—that elicit attention. *Dialogue* by adults, children, and nonhumans was the second grouping. The third group, described as *reflective features*, included singing, long zooms, and moderate action defined as movement through space at less than the equivalent of human running speed. Each of these features appeared to have the potential for rehearsing, repeating, and emphasizing important content.

TABLE I

Formal Features in Children's Programs

Perceptually salient cluster
    Rapid action—movement at a rate faster than walking
    Variability—number of different scenes
    Pace (tempo)—rate of scene and character changes
    Music—foreground and background
    Noise—sound effects and nonspeech vocalizations
    Visual trickery—special effects, dissolves, zooms
    Visual change—cuts and pans
Dialogue
    Nonhuman dialogue
    Child dialogue
    Adult dialogue
Reflection
    Singing
    Long zooms
    Moderate action—movement through space at about the speed of walking

---

B. Comparison of Different Types of Children's Programs

The programs analyzed were grouped by broadcast time: Saturday morning, daytime educational, and prime time. They differ in two important respects. Saturday morning and daytime educational programs are intended primarily for young children; prime-time programs are aimed at older children and families. Saturday morning and prime time are designed primarily for entertainment, whereas daytime educational programs are designed to teach or enhance children's development. The differences among the three program types are illustrated in Fig. 1.

Most Saturday morning programs were animated. All features belonging to the perceptually salient cluster, plus nonhuman dialogue, were more frequent in animated than in "live" children's programs. Conversely, the less salient sets of features we had come to regard as carrying most of the content and plot information were significantly less frequent in animated than in "live" programs. Included in this category were human dialogue (child and adult) and reflection (singing, long zooms, and moderate action). Even the live Saturday morning programs differed significantly from the other program types; they contained more perceptually salient formal features and fewer of the other feature clusters.

Educational daytime programs for children contained high rates of reflective features—singing, long zooms, moderate character action—and more child dialogue. Educational programs used moderate levels of some salient features (variability, visual tricks, nonhuman dialogue, and noise), and low levels of

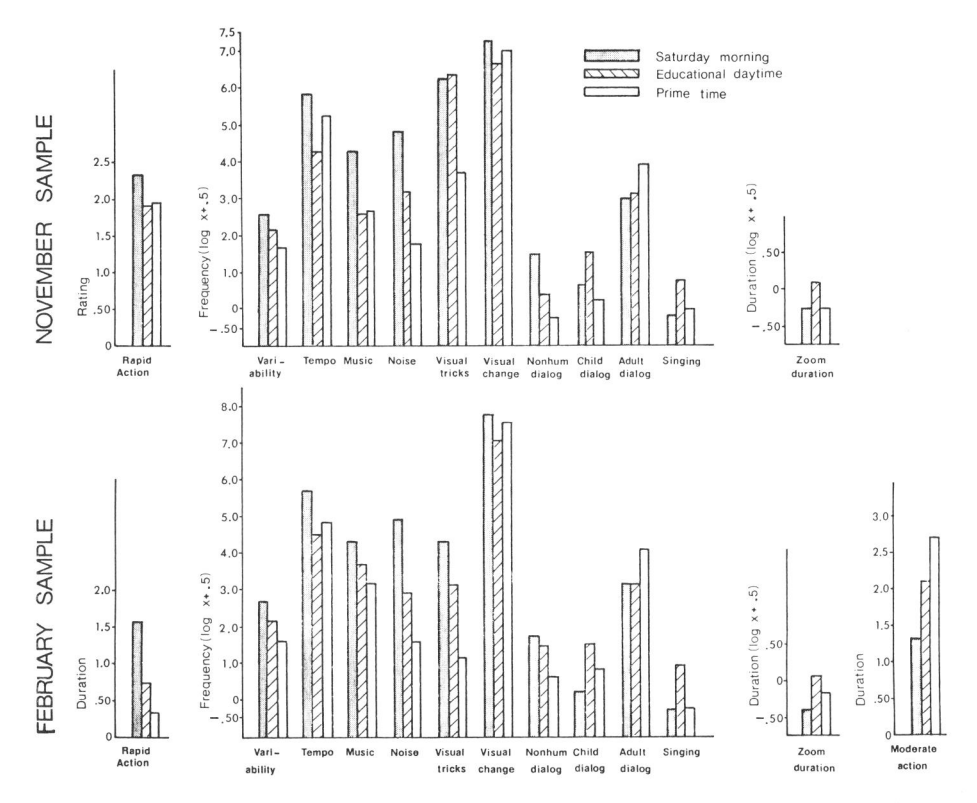

Fig. 1. Mean levels of formal features in three types of children's programs during two 1-week samples. From Huston *et al.*, *Journal of Communication*, 1981, **31**(3), 42. © 1981 *Journal of Communication*. Reprinted by permission.

others (rapid action, music, pace, and visual change). Thus, educational programs contained some of the attention-getting techniques of commercial children's programs, but at a reduced level, and they also used the linguistically informative and other communicative features that promote reflection and recapitulation. The prime-time programs were more adultlike, in that they had high levels of adult dialogue and moderate character action, but they were low on all perceptually salient features except pace and visual change.

C. Language Forms on Children's Television

Some television forms, such as dialogue and narration, are linguistic. Rice (1983, 1984) carried out a detailed analysis of the linguistic features of several children's programs. In one study, six programs were selected from educational and commercial programs aimed at preschool and older children. A second intensive analysis of *Mr. Rogers' Neighborhood* and *Sesame Street* was then performed (Rice & Haight, 1986).

The educational programs used language in ways that are characteristic of mothers' talk to young children and appear well suited to children's linguistic abilities. The rates of speech were slow; words and phrases were repeated; sentences were simplified; speakers used complete sentences and stressed single words; and their words often referred to people, objects, and activities that were simultaneously shown on the screen. *Focusing operations*, defined as verbal sequences that approach an idea from varying perspectives, characterized the language of educational programs more than that of commercial ones.

The language in commercial programs appeared less comprehensible to young children. The rates of speech were rapid; many of the words referred to objects and events that were not present; and there were many nonliteral word uses, such as puns and sarcastic remarks.

D. Summary

The analyses of television form have proceeded from identifying clusters of formal features to an analysis of their potential functions in the process of communicating to children. The cluster of formal features that characterizes commercial programs designed for children consists of perceptually salient visual and auditory production and editing techniques. The limited dialogue they contain is complex and requires considerable sophistication for full understanding. Educational programs contain moderate levels of perceptually salient features, but they also use linguistic and nonlinguistic techniques that appear to promote reflection and to enhance children's comprehension and retention of the content message. Contrary to some critics' assertions, *Sesame Street* and other popular educational programs do not mimic the perceptually salient qualities of cartoons; instead, they contain a judicious mixture of moderate levels of sensory intensity with carefully planned dialogue and accompanying features that can facilitate thoughtful processing of content.

The effects of these various types of formal features on children's attention, comprehension, and social behavior have been investigated in a series of studies. One set of questions concerns how levels and patterns of attention are affected by formal features, rather than content. In some cases, for example, we have attempted to separate the effects of form from the effects of violent content. A second set of questions concerns children's understanding of television forms and the effects of form on their understanding of content. We have been especially concerned with children's comprehension of the syntactic and connotative functions of formal features and their ability to use that understanding to detect content messages. Because television forms may be arousing or may carry some content meaning, they may also have effects on children's social behavior. Those effects are the topic of a third set of investigations.

All of these effects of television forms on children's attention, comprehension, and social behavior are a result of the interaction between those formal features and the individual attributes of the child. In particular, developmental changes in general cognitive processing skills affect how children use and respond to both form and content. We turn now to a conceptualization of children's cognitive processing and some important developmental changes occurring during the early years of children's interactions with television.

III. THE CHILD AS AN ACTIVE VIEWER

A. Active versus Passive Viewing

Critics of the television medium often assert that it lends itself to passive intellectual processing that is superficial and intellectually lazy. This view has been disputed in many recent models of television cognitive processing that assume an active viewer who is selective in the disposition of attention to television rather than being passively manipulated by the medium (Anderson & Lorch, 1983; Collins, 1982; Salomon, 1981; Wright & Watkins, 1978). The view of children as inherently active cognitive processors is consistent with recent trends in the study of cognitive development across a wide range of domains (see, e.g., Brown, Bransford, Ferrara, & Campione, 1983), but different theorists use the terms "active" and "passive" with several meanings that are only partially overlapping and that can usefully be distinguished from one another.

1. Performing Cognitive Operations on Television Material

First, an active processor is one who performs cognitive activities or operations on information received. Active processors select important or interesting aspects of incoming information; they use schemas or cognitive structures to anticipate, organize, and rehearse events; they perform the mental operations necessary for differentiating and integrating, such as discriminating and equating, classifying and combining entities; they perform transformations, such as sequencing in time or seriating along ordinal dimensions; and they elaborate on the information by interconnecting it with other information, schemas, and knowledge.

A central concept in this view is the schema. Schemas are cognitive organizational structures, relating objects and events on the basis of their spatial or temporal contiguity (Mandler, 1979). A child might have a schema for a bedroom that groups together beds, dressers, toys, clothes, fear of the dark, and controversies with parents about picking things up, all sharing a schema because of their spatiotemporal contiguity in the child's experience. A schema can also consist of a sequence of events that usually occur in temporal contiguity, like getting dressed or going to school. At a slightly more abstract level, a schema may be composed of those objects, activities, and attributes that are associated with one category of person. Gender schemas, for example, represent abstractions of the qualities associated with females and males (Martin & Halverson, 1981). Schematic organization is distinguished from categorical or taxonomic structures, in which objects are grouped by common attributes, such as size, shape, function, or abstract similarities (Mandler, 1979, 1983).

Schemas are not only structures derived from experience with the world; once operative, they create expectations about what will occur in future situations. When a schema is well ingrained, the occurrence of an event that actuates it will lead to the expectations and prediction that the other parts of the schema will also be present. This predictive function of schemas is important because it enables the child to fill in gaps in experience by calling upon schematic knowledge. If the child sees a television scene about a child getting out of bed in her pajamas, followed by a scene in which she is dressed (and eating cereal from a bowl), the child will assume that the intervening event of getting dressed has occurred.

Such common event schemas are important in children's understanding of television events. Collins (1982) demonstrated that children's comprehension of televised stories depends partly on the schemas about people and events that they bring to the viewing situation. As children develop schemas for the real world, those schemas will be used to interpret television as well. Conversely, television can serve as a means of learning event schemas that may be applied—some successfully and some not—to the real world (Hawkins & Pingree, 1982).

2. Expenditure of Mental Effort

A second definition of cognitive activity, proposed by Salomon (1981), is the amount of invested mental effort (AIME). Invested mental effort is defined partly by the amount of cognitive elaboration performed (similar to the foregoing definition of cognitive activity), but it also depends on the degree to which such elaborations are nonautomatic. That is, applying schemas to information is more "active" if the same type of information has not been processed before than when it has been processed many times. The amount of mental effort that a viewer invests is determined in part by his or her perception of the difficulty of the material to be processed. Processing routines are established early for the most frequent and invariant scripts one encounters, whether in real life or on television. If it is low-level, homogeneous material, the response will be fairly mechanical and automated. More difficult material either elicits proportionately more processing effort or is ignored.

3. Perceptual versus Conceptual Processing

A third way in which the terms passive and active are sometimes used is to distinguish between sensory-perceptual and abstract conceptual levels of processing. If children respond primarily to the immediate sensory and perceptual events on television, their processing is passive. That is, if they process concrete images and sounds, then their representation in memory is more iconic, more analogical. Correspondingly, if they respond to the abstract and implied content messages, particularly the verbal or linguistic messages, their processing is active (Anderson & Lorch, 1983), and their representations will be more symbolic and digital, more abstract, and more extensively based on inferences about feelings, motives, events, and conditions not actually portrayed (Collins, 1983).

4. Participation and Manipulation of the Stimuli

The degree to which learning is receptive as opposed to participatory is a fourth dimension of passive and active. Television viewing is primarily a receptive activity; the material is organized, sequenced, selected, and presented to the viewer with little or no opportunity for the viewer to manipulate, order, organize, or otherwise influence what is presented (Watkins, Huston-Stein, & Wright, 1981; Wright & Watkins, 1978). Interactive television and computerized learning activities can overcome this limitation in part, but broadcast television remains largely nonparticipatory. The child who is truly acting on the information environment, querying it, repeating and organizing it, is providing structure and thereby adding information to it, and is in that important sense an active participant.

5. Planful, Goal-Directed Cognitive Activity

The degree to which learning is externally controlled by environmental stimuli and events, as opposed to internally controlled by the child's own plans and goals, is the fifth component of the distinction between passive and active (Brown *et al.*, 1983; Flavell, 1985). Internally guided processing is sometimes described as top-down, whereas externally directed processing is bottom-up. That is, when the selection and organization of information is guided from the "top" by a conceptual framework, schema, or goal-directed plan, it is active in the sense that it is guided by the individual. When the individual is primarily responsive to events or stimuli as they occur, then the processing of them is more fragmented and more likely to be guided by external influences.

This distinction forms one basis for two modes of information getting—exploration and search—proposed in the theory guiding much of our research (Wright & Vlietstra, 1975). Exploration is characterized by immediate responding to perceptually salient cues in the environment, lack of connection between responses, and no general guiding plan or strategy. Search is a more active mode, in which cues are selected for their relevance to a goal, and responses are connected or related to one another in a coherent plan or strategy. Exploration is determined bottom-up, whereas search is executed top-down.

In summary, the definition of active as opposed to passive processing has several components that are separable and do not necessarily imply one another. They include (1) applying mental structures and operations, (2) exerting mental effort, (3) using conceptual rather than sensory-motor modes of organizing, (4) being participatory rather than receptive, and (5) being internally controlled by one's goals and plans, rather than being externally controlled by environmental stimuli.

We propose that television viewing can be active or passive on several of these dimensions. There is nothing inherent in the medium that cultivates intellectual passivity. In the United States, the popular image of television as passive may be encouraged by its devotion to mass entertainment and by the fact that most productions rely on redundant and conventional techniques that do not begin to exhaust the possibilities of the medium for varied form and content. Our major questions concern when and how children engage in different modes of cognitively processing television, particularly how the qualities and abilities of the child interact with the form and content of the television material to which that child is exposed.

B. Developmental Changes

Although various local and transient determinants influence levels of activity in these dimensions of cognitive functioning, it is generally the case that, with growth and experience, children's processing becomes increasingly active in most of the aforementioned meanings of the term.

As children develop, the number and complexity of their schemas increases, and the interconnections among schemas become more elaborated and complex. Hence, they can apply available schemas and cognitive operations to increasingly complex and varied sets of information. As children move from the preschool years to middle childhood, their preferences for television programs become more varied. Not only do younger children prefer simpler content, but also they prefer more homogeneous material that repeats the same themes again and again (Ross, Wartella, & Lovelace, 1982).

A second developmental change is a gradual shift from perceptual to conceptual forms of mental representation. On the whole, younger children more often think in iconic images; they represent their experience in pictures and sound images that are similar to their perceptual experiences. As children grow older, symbolic modes of representation, particularly language, become a more important means of mentally representing their experiences (Bruner, Olver, & Greenfield, 1966). Hence, one might expect a gradual shift from interest in the visual and auditory perceptual events in a television program to the abstract, conceptual meanings of the material presented.

A third general change in cognitive functioning is the degree to which the children's thinking is reflexive and self-aware—the degree to which they can plan, guide, and control their own cognitive activities. This increasing cognitive control forms the basis of Wright and Vlietstra's (1975) hypothesis that there is a developmental shift from exploration to search, occurring in two steps. First, there is a shift from perceptual exploration to perceptual search, due primarily to familiarization with an environment during repeated exposures, leading to habituation of attention and interest. The recurrence of the familiar is more interesting to younger children, while novelty becomes more appealing with increasing experience in a setting. A second part of the shift is from perceptual search to logical search, a shift based largely on the maturation of abstract reasoning abilities and the acquisition of generalized executive and control processes, rather than on mere experiential familiarization.

Most theorists propose that these developmental shifts are not solely, or perhaps even primarily, due to ontogenetic or maturational changes in the child, but to the cumulative effects of experience. Moreover, developmental changes in one content area or domain do not necessarily imply generalized changes in other domains. Cognitive developmental theory has shifted away from the assumption that cognitive skills are global and generalized, and it has moved instead toward the notion that most cognitive skills are domain specific (see, e.g., Gelman & Baillargeon, 1983). For example, children are often able to take the perspective of another person in one context, but not in another. One variable accounting for variations in cognitive level is the child's knowledge about and experience with the content area. Children who are familiar with working-class lifestyles can comprehend a television program about working-class families better than middle-class children (Collins, 1983).

The domain specificity of cognitive developmental changes suggests that developmental changes in children's cognitive processing of television will be variable, depending on the content domain assessed, the complexity of the content, the child's previous knowledge about the content and forms used, and the form in which the material is presented. There may be some generalized individual differences in the rate of cognitive development, as assessed by measures of intelligence, but there will also be considerable variability across different types of programming.

IV. COGNITIVE PROCESSING: THE MATCH BETWEEN THE CHILD AND THE TELEVISION MATERIAL

A. Information Getting

In ordinary language, we often use two contrasting idioms to describe a person's acquisition of information and knowledge: *getting meaning from* an event, and *giving meaning to it*. The terms bear an analogy to Piaget's twin mechanisms of accommodation and assimilation, respectively. In the section that follows, we use the term "information getting" to refer to two very general kinds of mental activity: (1) exploring an environment in order to gain a general sense of what it offers while enjoying its novelty and unfamiliarity, and (2) interpreting an environment's structure and content with reference to one's own interests and involvements so that it can be systematically and effectively searched for the content one is seeking.

The former is the process of familiarization, and while active in most of the aforementioned meanings of that word, it is still controlled more by the external events encountered than by the child's informational needs and previous agendas. The latter is clearly a more active process of interpreting and assigning meaning to events and estimating the likelihood that a particular bit of the environment contains or will prove to contain interesting and relevant material.

Both of these processes are involved in the attentional decisions one continually makes while "watching" television. But where the former is governed more by the events of the medium themselves, such as novelty, perceptual salience, and the "gee whiz" excitement that often abounds in children's television programming, the latter is a more complex function of the anticipated informativeness of events and their apparent comprehensibility. Both processes are influenced not only by the viewers' levels of cognitive development and previously acquired skills and knowledge, and not only by the form and content of the particular program, but also, and more especially, by their past experience with the medium and their reasons for viewing it in the present instance. Changes over time in general cognitive development and in experience with television lead to changes in children's modes and levels of processing the television that is available to them.

1. Perceptual and Informative Qualities of Television Forms

Our initial hypotheses about the effects of television forms on attention were based on the exploration–search model (Wright & Vlietstra, 1975). One of the most striking aspects of many children's programs is their perceptually demanding quality, the sheer volume and intensity of sights and sounds that characterize the Saturday morning cartoon. For young and inexperienced viewers, we predicted that the principal mode of information getting from television would be exploration; hence, perceptual salience (i.e., movement, contrast, intensity, novelty, and change) of formal features in children's programs would elicit and maintain attention.

With cumulative exposure to such features, children were expected to become habituated or less responsive to the perceptual qualities of television forms, leaving the way open for attention to be guided by more active search, based on the informative qualities of the form and content of the program. Hence, older and more experienced viewers were expected to use formal features in informative ways to help them understand and appreciate the content messages (Huston & Wright, 1983).

2. General Model of Attention and Interest

Television viewing can be placed within an overall model of attention and interest (Rice, Huston, & Wright, 1982), derived from the discrepancy hypothesis, as applied to curiosity by Hunt (1961). Figure 2 shows the inverted U-shaped function that illustrates interest as a function of a family of

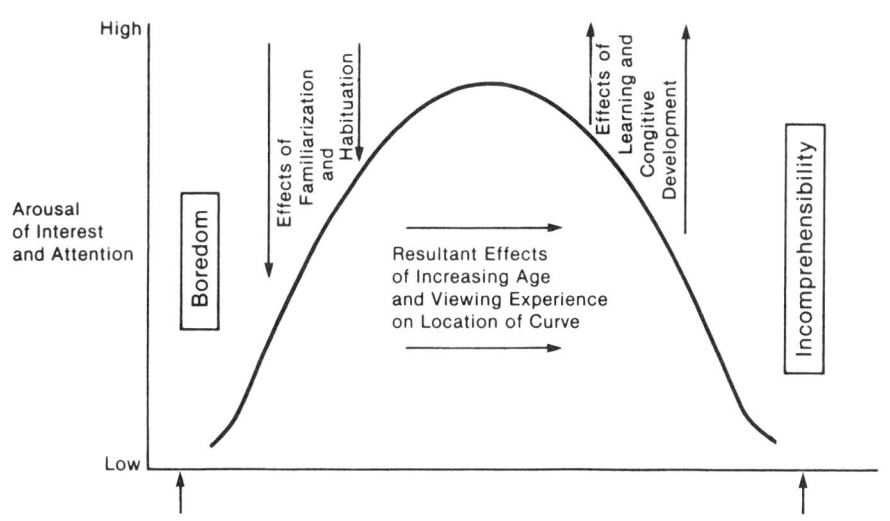

Fig. 2. A model of developmental changes in interest and attention. From Rice, Huston, & Wright (1982).

associated variables describing the adaptation level of the child in relation to a specifiable range of stimuli. The variables along the abscissa serve to identify stimuli either that are uninteresting because they are overly familiar and simple on the left or that are uninteresting because they are overly complex and unfamiliar on the right.

What we have added to the familiar discrepancy model predicting maximum interest in whatever is moderately novel, complex, surprising, etc. is the mechanism of change over time, derived from hypotheses about familiarization with television. Stimuli to the left of center, to the extent that they occur and are at least sometimes attended to, become increasing familiar and begin to habituate, together with other members of the conceptual classes to which they belong (Faulkender, Wright, & Waldron, 1974). But stimuli on the right-hand side of the curve, while not fully comprehended, are being attended to somewhat and are becoming more familiar, and hence more comprehensible over time and successive exposures. Presumably that increasing familiarity generalizes just as does habituation on the left-hand side.

For any one individual in a domain of stimuli in which the curve is manifest, the effect of growing familiarity and comprehension of stimuli is a gradual shift of the curve to the right, which increases the interest value of stimuli on the right and reduces the interest value of stimuli on the left. The region of maximum interest and attention is thus like a lens that moves from simpler, more common, and more redundant stimuli toward more complicated, unpredictable, and rare stimuli. Or put the other way around, stimuli that are initially incomprehensible gradually "move" toward and through the child's focal lens of maximum interest, and then lose attention as they are habituated and become "old hat."

Notice that the model predicts attention will be a joint function of stimulus features, both form and content, and the characteristics of the viewer, such as the history of exposure to stimuli of that type and ability to comprehend their meaning. While the form of the curve and the dynamics of its movement over time are said to be universal, it cannot be specified for a particular set of ordered stimuli until something is known of the history of the individual child's experience with them.

3. *Empirical Tests of the Theory*

a. Formal Features Associated with Visual Attention. The major means of testing theoretical predictions about information getting is direct observations of visual attention to selected television programs. Although visual orientation is not a perfect index of cognitive activity, it is reasonable to assume that variations in visual attention represent variations in some aspects of active processing. When form or content affects visual attention, those media attributes are affecting activity of processing along at least some of the five dimensions of activity described so far.

In laboratory studies, attention usually refers to the percentage of program time during which the child is visually fixating on the television screen. Continuous records of such attention can be made readily, and the agreement between scorers is typically 90% or better (Alwitt, Anderson, Lorch, & Levin, 1980; Wright, Calvert, Huston, & Watkins, 1980).

In "macrolevel" analyses, attention is measured during whole segments or programs selected to represent different levels of form and content. For example, preschool children's attention to television commercials with high versus low levels of perceptually salient formal features, such as action (movement), pace (rate of scene and character changes), and visual features (cuts, pans, and trucks) was observed. Children viewing in pairs, with distracting toys present, looked more at the salient than at the nonsalient commercials (Greer, Potts, Wright, & Huston, 1982). In another study, elementary-school children watched programs that were of high or low pace and either high or low in story continuity (stories vs. magazine formats). Attention was greater for stories than for magazine formats, but pace had relatively little effect on attention (Wright *et al.*, 1984).

The results of these investigations provide strong support for the prediction that children attend to programs with high levels of action, visual and auditory special effects, and many other salient features (Rice *et al.*, 1982). However, pace (rate of scene and character changes) does not strongly affect attention, a finding consistent with other investigations (Anderson, Levin, & Lorch, 1977).

In a "microlevel" analysis, attention is continuously recorded, as are formal features. The percentage of time the child attends while a feature is occurring can be compared to the percentage of looking when the feature is not occurring to determine whether the feature is positively or negatively related to attention. A more refined method is to separate the recruiting and maintaining effects of features. The conditional probability that a child who was not looking begins to look after the onset of a feature constitutes an index of that feature's power to *recruit* attention. Correspondingly, the conditional probability of an ongoing look continuing while a feature is present constitutes an index of that feature's power to *maintain* visual attention. When these indices are corrected to take into account the probability of a look beginning or ending in the absence of that feature, they become useful differential indices for comparing the attention-recruiting and -maintaining potentials of features across programs and viewers.

These kinds of analyses have yielded similar results in several investigations, using a variety of children's programs (Anderson, Alwitt, Lorch, & Levin, 1979; Anderson & Levin, 1976; Calvert, Huston, Watkins, & Wright, 1982; Wright, Calvert, Huston, & Watkins, 1980). Attention was recruited by auditory changes and auditory special effects. Nonverbal vocalizations and peculiar character voices both recruited and maintained attention, as did lively or loud music. Children's and women's voices maintained attention, but adult male voices lost children's attention. Among the visual characteristics, movement and action maintained attention, as did animation. Cuts and pans were weaker, but still positive maintainers of attention, whereas animal photography and long zooms lost attention.

These data provide mixed support for the hypothesis that attention is guided by perceptual salience. Although most salient features recruit and maintain attention, other "nonsalient" features, such as children's speech, also have positive effects on attention. Moreover, there is little evidence of the predicted decline in responsiveness to perceptual salience with age. No age differences in selective attention to salient features were found in studies comparing preschoolers and older children (Anderson & Lorch, 1983; Calvert *et al.*, 1982; Rice *et al.*, 1982; Wright & Huston, 1981; Wright, Calvert, Huston, & Watkins, 1980; Wright *et al.*, 1984). In fact, in the very early years (ages 1 to 4 years), there is an increase in attention to such features (Anderson & Levin, 1976).

b. Formal Features Associated with Audience Size. Another means of testing form and content influences on children is analysis of audience data. In one study (Wright, Huston-Stein, *et al.*, 1980), we analyzed family viewing diaries from 3000 American households for all children's programs broadcast by the commercial networks during two Saturdays in 1977 and 1978, a total of 33 programs that were tape-recorded and scored for their formal features. The viewing audience figures were special age breakdowns calculated by the Arbitron Corporation from representative samples in the greater viewing areas of New York, Chicago, and Los Angeles. While many of the feature correlates of audience size varied from city to city or by gender, the overall age trends indicated a decline with age in the number of salient features that predicted viewership of programs. A similar decline characterized the number of occasions on which violent content was a significant predictor of viewing audience. By contrast, pace, variability of scene and character and human dialogue showed an increase from age 2 years to age 9 in the number of occasions on which they were significant positive predictors of audience size. Hence, these data provide some support for the hypothesized developmental change in the importance of perceptually salient features.

c. Separate Effects of Form and Content. The fact that certain formal features are consistently associated with changes in attention cannot be interpreted as evidence that form per se influences children's attention. Because form and content are often confounded in children's television programs, children could attend to particular forms because of their association with content. In fact, a few years ago, Anderson and Lorch (1983) concluded that "there is as yet no evidence that visual attention to television is determined by formal features separately from content" (p. 26). For example, in our analyses of children's programs, violent content was associated with animation, rapid action, rapid pace, visual special effects, loud music, and noise—that is, with the perceptually salient cluster of formal features. Programs with high rates of dialogue and reflective features, on the other hand, had relatively little violence (Huston et al., 1981).

i. Action versus violence. One method of separating form and content was to select programs representing all possible combinations of high and low levels of salient forms and high and low levels of violent content. Violent content was selected for study because of its social and theoretical importance. Network television producers often equate violence with "action," and they assume that it is an important determinant of children's interest. Three studies were designed to determine the relative importance of salient forms and violent content as influences on children's attention.

In these studies, the formal feature used for program selection was action, but because many other features covary with action, the stimuli differed on pace, noise, visual special effects, auditory effects, and music as well. Violence was defined as physical and object aggression. In the first study (Huston-Stein, Fox, Greer, Watkins, & Whitaker, 1981), three cartoons were selected to represent high-action–high-violence, high-action–low-violence, and low-action–low-violence. Preschool children were more visually attentive to both high-action programs than to the low-action program. Violent content was not related to attention.

In the second study of preschool boys (Potts, Huston, & Wright, 1986), programs representing all four possible combinations of high and low action with high and low violence were included. In each of the four action–violence cells, there were two programs—one animated and one live. Again, the formal features had a strong effect on attention; there was no significant difference as a function of violent content.

A third study of 5- and 7-year-old children did not replicate these findings (Alvarez, Huston, Wright, & Kerkman, 1989). Children saw four animated programs, representing all combinations of high and low action and high and low violence, in one session. Boys' attention did not vary across programs; girls attended more to the low-action than to the high-action programs and more to high violence than to low violence. The differences among studies may be a function of age, gender, and/or methodological variations (viewing in pairs or individually, watching a sequence of programs or one program).

ii. Child and adult forms with equivalent content. A second method of separating form from content was to make television materials in two different forms, but with identical content (Campbell, Wright, & Huston, 1987). Nine pairs of public service announcements were created. The content was held constant in both members of each pair, but the formal features in one member of each pair were those typically used in children's programs, and in the other member of the pair, the features were those typical of adult programs. The child-oriented bits were animated and had children's or peculiar character voices, together with sprightly music. The adult bits, with virtually identical visual shot lists and scripts, had adult male narrators, live photography, and sedate background music. Regardless of content, the adult format bits received less attention from kindergarten children than the child format segments (see Fig. 3). The difference was highly significant. Clearly, attentional decisions were made in part on the basis of form.

The majority of these studies support the proposition that television forms such as animation, action, and sound effects have important influences on preschool children's attention and that those effects are at least partially independent of content. Nonetheless, they raise several questions about age and gender differences in responses to television form and content, as well as questions about the effects of the viewing context.

d. Gender Differences in Attention. Although not predicted by any theory, gender differences in attention occurred in six of nine studies in which both genders were tested. When there were differences, boys were always more attentive than girls. Moreover, boys' attention appeared to vary less than girls' across programs or across variations in form and content. A careful analysis of the programs to which boys attended more than girls suggested that animation and action may account for some of the difference (Alvarez *et al.*, 1989). In camera records of home television viewing, Anderson, Lorch, Field, Collins,

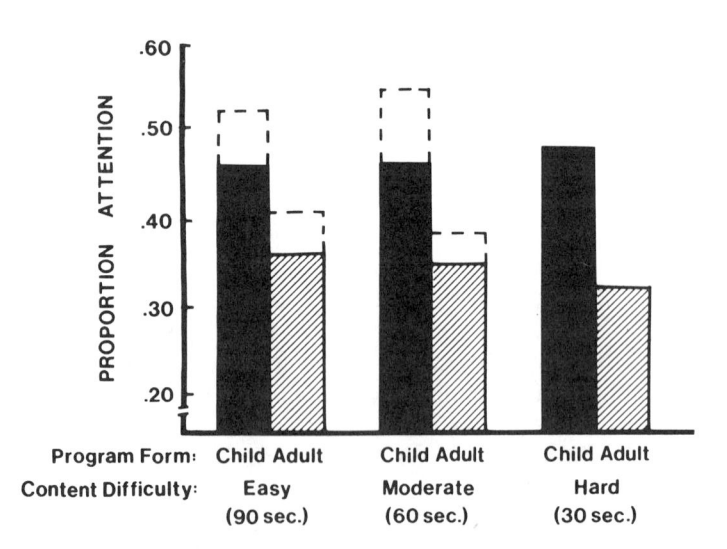

Fig. 3. Percentage of attention to educational television bits made in pairs, using either child or adult formal features, at three levels of difficulty. Dashed line represents mean for first 30 seconds. From Campbell, Wright, & Huston (1987).

and Nathan (1986) found that adult men were more attentive than adult women, but there were no gender differences among children.

e. Summary. Observations of children's visual attention and home viewing patterns both support the prediction that perceptually salient forms such as action, visual and auditory special effects, animation, and loud music recruit and maintain children's attention. These effects appear to be at least partially independent of the content with which the forms are associated. For the most part, however, attention to perceptually salient formal features of television does not typically show generalized habituation with age. It seems likely, therefore, that those features instigate active processing for reasons other than their perceptual qualities.

4. *Informative Qualities of Form and Content*

According to our initial model, children's information getting from television gradually shifts from an exploration mode to a search mode; hence, their attention is increasingly guided by informative formal features that help them to comprehend the content messages. Children's goals in watching television shift from a focus on the sight gags, jingles, and perceptual thrills to an interest in understanding and enjoying the story line or message. Collins (1983) refers to children's efforts to understand and follow television content as "straining for meaning."

Anderson and his associates have articulated a related position, arguing that even young children make attentional decisions based largely on the comprehensibility of content (Anderson & Lorch, 1983; Anderson, Lorch, Field, & Sanders, 1981; Lorch, Anderson, & Levin, 1979). As they view, children evaluate their understanding of the material they are viewing and make implicit predictions about how well they will understand in the immediate future. If they judge the material too difficult or too redundant and easy, attention will be reduced. Hence, attention follows the inverted U-shape function shown in Fig. 1, with content difficulty being the major dimension along the abscissa and the major determinant of developmental movement of the right or leading edge.

Within the framework of different definitions of active processing described earlier, the types of cognitive activity thought to be affected by cognitive comprehensibility are the degree to which the child performs cognitive operations on the content and the degree to which conceptual rather than perceptual modes of processing are used. Maximum cognitive activity will be exerted on content for which the child has applicable schemas that are not quite complete, so that attention to television content involves filling in the gaps in those schemas (Anderson & Lorch, 1983; Anderson & Smith, 1984).

The evidence for this hypothesis is strong at the extreme upper range of incomprehensibility. For example, when Anderson *et al.* (1981) showed 3- and

5-year-old children segments of *Sesame Street* with Greek dialogue or backward speech, visual attention declined sharply. Scrambling of scenes within a segment, however, did not reduce attention. At more moderate levels of comprehensibility, however, the relationship is less clear. Attention declines when language difficulty is increased by presenting words without visual referents (Anderson *et al.*, 1981). However, Campbell *et al.* (1987) found no effects of content difficulty. Wright *et al.* (1984) found that low-pace programs were easier to recall than high-pace programs (i.e., they were more comprehensible), but low pace did not increase attention.

The amount of attention devoted to a program can also determine one's subsequent comprehension (Lorch *et al.*, 1979). Calvert *et al.* (1982) found that attention to informative features, such as child dialogue and moderate character action (movement) predicted comprehension, as did inattention to adult narration and long zooms. In two studies, experimental variations in content and form produced improved comprehension as well as increased attention (Calvert, Huston, & Wright, 1984; Campbell *et al.*, 1987). Regression analyses demonstrated that attention differences accounted for the comprehension differences, suggesting that attention mediated the changes in comprehension.

In sum, children's perceptions of content comprehensibility and their anticipations about subsequent comprehensibility appear to account for differential attention to extremely difficult versus easy material, but less clearly for variations in the more moderate ranges of difficulty. In the moderate ranges, comprehensibility may be a necessary, but not sufficient, condition for active processing.

5. *Feature–Signal Hypothesis*

Formal features may inform the viewer about content by signaling the type of content that is about to be presented. This feature–signal hypothesis, suggested by Lorch *et al.* (1979) and elaborated by Huston and Wright (1983), suggests that many aspects of content associated with viewer interest, including entertainment value, program genre, humor, and comprehensibility, come to be associated with particular formal features because of the customs of production. Other features become associated with unappealing or incomprehensible content. Once the viewer understands these form–content associations, formal features can be used as signals of the attention-worthiness of content, and thus can affect the activity of processing. One dimension of activity that may be affected is the amount of mental effort exerted to process and understand what is presented (Salomon, 1983).

This hypothesis has the advantage of relying on established form–content linkages and the known capacity of the young child to respond to associated cues as if they were the event with which they are associated. So far the evidence on the feature-signal hypothesis is mostly indirect. Recall, for example, that children stop looking with the onset of adult male narration. Presumably, adult male voices signal content that is dull and incomprehensible because they have been associated in children's viewing experiences with verbal messages intended for adult audiences, such as news.

Features also signal what is fun, enjoyable, frightening, interesting, and so on. Animation in U.S. television signals content designed for children that is likely to be funny, full of action, and possibly violent (Huston *et al.*, 1981). A laugh track signals that a program will be funny, even to a child too young to understand the humor (Huston & Wright, 1983). Similarly, formal features signal whether a program is a continuous story or a magazine-format show composed of independent segments, and they can thereby prepare a child for the show's attentional and processing requirements—whether one has to remember and integrate content across scene-change boundaries or not (Wright *et al.*, 1984). Features such as logos and theme music can serve to mark regular segments within a program or a whole program series. As such, they can affect attention to those segments and programs. An example is the music and song, "one of these things is not like the others..." that serves to introduce segments devoted to sorting or oddity problems on *Sesame Street*. If you like them, you attend more carefully; if not, you look away (Palmer, 1978).

6. *A Stimulus-Sampling Model*

Huston and Wright (1983) proposed a stimulus-sampling model to account for serial attentional decisions. Very simply, it states that at critical points in a program, a child makes a series of attentional decisions. If the child is looking, then she or he decides whether to continue or to stop looking at scene-change boundaries, commercial breaks, and other marked transitional moments. If the child is not looking, auditory cues may signal a scene change or other content change that provides the occasion for another attentional decision whether to continue not to look or to start to look again. Note that although the discrimination of such nodes or choice-points may not be self-conscious in younger children, the sharpness of correlated auditory and visual changes at such boundaries probably interrupts attention more at those nodes than elsewhere. The older the child, the more these segmental boundaries become the nodes for attentional decisions (Alwitt *et al.*, 1980).

As can be seen in Table II, the model describes general processing decisions as well as looking decisions. Some examples are "How much effort will be required in order to understand this material?", "Does the program assume (like a soap opera) that I already know a lot about the characters, their motives, and the interpersonal context of the action?", or "Will this program offer jokes, sight gags, special effects, and other perceptually enjoyable content that I will readily understand?"

TABLE II
Roles of Formal Features, Levels of Processing Television, and Criteria of Involvement

Roles played by formal features	Cognitive processing	Motivational criteria
Features as perceptually salient events	Initial orienting and attending	Is it perceptually thrilling, exciting, funny, novel, etc.?
Features as signals of content type, markers of particular programs, indicators of program's difficulty and intended audience, conveyors of connotative meanings	Do I recognize it? Is it comprehensible? Is it for me or people like me? Can it be assimilated to my existing TV schemes and scripts? Is it real-fictional; masculine-feminine; story-magazine format?	Is this one I liked before? Does it fit my goals and reasons for viewing right now? Will it be funny, affectively involving, full of suspense? Will favorite characters appear? Does its reality level, gender type, etc. appeal to me?
Features as representations of cognitive operations, key content, selective emphasis; features that segment and structure the flow of content and provide cues for logical and temporal integration	Can I encode it? Verbally? Iconically? What parts are central-incidental? Is logical-temporal integration needed? Am I getting it? What inferences are needed? How much mental effort will be required to follow it further? Implications for subsequent viewing	Would this be fun to share? Is it memorable? Is it obvious or uncertain how it will come out? Can I anticipate what will happen next? Will the satisfaction be worth the mental effort required?
Program/series identifiers, standard introduction, music, set, characters, logo, etc.	What features are reliable indicators of all other episodes of this program/series?	Do I want to watch this program again?

The model attempts to incorporate the best supported aspects of the hypothesis described earlier. From the salience hypothesis, it takes the notion that perceptual salience is attention worthy and directly enjoyable. From the comprehensibility hypothesis, it takes the notion that children want to know in advance, and not as a result of trial and error, whether they will understand a program before they invest much mental effort in trying to understand it. And from the feature-signal hypothesis, it takes the notion that standardized formal features come to act as signals that can be reacted to quickly without waiting to process the content if they promise disinteresting material to follow, or that can be reacted to with enhanced alertness, careful attention, and increased investment of mental effort if they signal that such efforts will be worthwhile.

The stimulus-sampling model suggests that formal features play a critical role in several dimensions of active processing. They can help the viewer to parse, segment, and sequence the flow of content into chunks that can be evaluated for their attention-worthiness at the nodes that mark their boundaries, and thereby set the occasion of attentional decisions. Moreover, the model takes account of the potential of formal features to signal both the entertainment value of the program and the amount and kind of mental effort that will be necessary to comprehend it. Finally, it suggests that formal features can provide strong hints as to the nature of the content and the audience for whom it was intended, hints that should facilitate the formation of accurate expectations and the accessing of appropriate background world and TV knowledge, as well as the effective deployment of attention. Children's ability to use formal features in any of these ways will depend on developmental changes in control processes, cognitive operations, world knowledge, and other dimensions of active processing discussed earlier, as well as on the familiarity with the specific conventions of the television medium that may result from viewing experience.

7. *Auditory Attention*

Traditionally attention has been assessed in one of three ways. One is the measurement of the involuntary components of the orienting reflex during presentation of controlled stimuli. This procedure has been used very rarely in television research with children, most notably by Watt and Krull (1975), who found that the amount of feature change, unpredictability, and unfamiliarity in a television segment predicted the magnitude of galvanic skin response (GSR), heart rate deceleration, and blood volume changes associated with orienting.

The second method is the one used in most of the television research with children to date, including the studies cited in this section: the recording of visual fixations as on or off screen. It has been well established as a valid and reliably recordable measure, but it has the singular flaw that it does not index the child's attention to the sound track when not looking at the screen. For example, in the foregoing microanalyses, a visual feature cannot logically recruit attention in a child who is not looking—only auditory features can recruit or prevent a look—while both auditory and visual features can maintain or lose visual attention.

The third method is indirect, as it involves inferring what was attended to from an analysis of what is recalled. In television research, recall has been used to index visual and auditory information getting. Several investigators have found a persistent "visual superiority" effect (Hayes & Birnbaum, 1980; Hayes, Chemelski, & Birnbaum, 1981). Similarly, the intermedia comparison literature shows that children recall relatively more visual and less verbal material from televised presentation of stories, as compared with radio and picturebook versions (Meringoff, 1980; Pezdek & Hartman, 1983; Pezdek & Stevens, 1984).

A more direct measure of auditory attention was developed by Rolandelli, Wright, and Huston (1982, 1985). In two studies, at selected moments in programs, they electronically caused a deterioration in the clarity of the sound track by cross-fading it with white noise. The effect resembled the loss of radio reception when a weakening signal is increasingly overridden by static. Children were told that the TV set sometimes had sound trouble, but that they could fix it if they chose by pressing a lever at the edge of their play table. If the child pressed the lever, sound clarity was restored instantly. If not, after 12 seconds, the sound quality restored itself. These outcomes were demonstrated to the child in pretraining so that they were well understood by the start of the stories. The latencies of restore responses (assigning a score of 12 seconds to those degrades that the child never restored) served as a measure of auditory attention (or more properly inattention, as high values indicate low attention). Measures of visual orientation to the television screen were also collected in order to compare patterns of visual and auditory attention.

While auditory attention was not greater during narrated than nonnarrated stories, auditory attention did predict both recall of verbal material that was not interrupted by sound degradation and the making of correct inferences based on both auditory and visual information. Visual attention predicted all kinds of comprehension.

It appears that visual fixation indexed both specifically visual attention and general attentiveness and effort invested in processing. Visual fixation probably implies listening as well, particularly for young children (Field & Anderson, 1985). Therefore, it probably indicates a more intense kind of involvement than does listening only.

But auditory attention also has a dual role. Auditory attention predicted both semantic processing of verbal content and the selectivity of visual attention to the most informative moments of the stories. Auditory attention is obviously necessary for a child to get information from the sound track, of which the most important is usually verbal. But the additional role of auditory attention is the monitoring of the program, which serves as a basis for deciding when to look, or knowing when to decide about looking during periods of nonlooking.

8. *Summary*

The formal features most often associated with high attention to television include character action, visual and auditory special effects, and other perceptually salient features. Some informative features, such as child dialogue and moderate action levels, also hold children's attention. Studies separating form and content indicate that the formal features themselves account for variations in children's attention; their effects are not entirely dependent on associations with content. In particular, animation, high action, and related formal features had more influence on attention than did violent content.

The general developmental model of attention used to conceptualize these processes is based on the notion that stimuli that are moderately familiar and comprehensible will be more interesting than those that are extremely simple and redundant or those that are very unfamiliar and complex. As children grow older and have increasing experience with real-world events and with television, they move toward interest in increasingly complex content.

A set of related hypotheses are proposed to explain the relations of formal features to attention. All of them are based on the assumption that increases in visual or auditory attention in response to formal features indicate increases in active cognitive processing. These hypotheses are integrated in a stimulus-sampling model, according to which children sample bits of television content and make attentional decisions partly on the basis of formal feature cues about the entertainment value, comprehensibility, or interest of the content. Children's ability to make these decisions accurately depends both on general cognitive development and on their acquisition of knowledge about media conventions. Therefore, we turn now to investigations of how and when children learn the syntactic and connotative meanings of television forms.

B. Children's Comprehension of Television Form

1. Syntactic Functions of Television Form

Formal features are the syntax of television; they mark beginnings and endings, time shifts forward and backward, place changes, and other structural aspects of content. Some of the codes are similar to those in the real world (e.g., the fade to black designating a loss of consciousness). Others have no parallel in the real world (e.g., flashbacks, instant replays, rapid shifts in perspectives). A "literate" viewer of television must comprehend its syntax and its representational codes in order to understand the content message presented. Salomon (1979) has demonstrated that children gradually acquire understandings of such codes as quick cuts, shifts in perspective, and close-ups, and that their understanding of those codes in turn can affect their comprehension of the content presented.

Media codes function at different levels of generality: (1) those that are specific to particular programs or genres (e.g., the meaning of a theme song), (2) those that are specific to the medium (e.g., the conventions signaling a commercial break), and (3) those that are generic and apply to the broader world in which the child lives (e.g., the meaning of the words used by an announcer).

a. Children's Comprehension of Television Syntax. Children younger than about age 6 or 7 years understand relatively simple television codes that are similar to real-world perceptual events and that represent content for which they have available schemas. Young children do not appear to have good comprehension of subtle cues or media conventions that violate real-world event sequences. Smith, Anderson, and Fischer (1985) designed brief videotaped stories in which parts of simple event sequences were edited out by cuts to the next scene (e.g., a boy was shown at the top of the stairs, then outdoors playing after asking his mother if he could go out and play). Three- and five-year-old children reproduced the story events equally well after seeing the edited and unedited versions. In the second study, brief video segments were made using more complex film codes, including ellipsis and parallel simultaneous action sequences. Four-year-olds performed moderately well in understanding the spatial and temporal relations portrayed, as well as understanding the perspectives of the characters. And 7-year-olds understood most of the film sequences quite well. These investigators concluded that young children can understand commonly used media codes when the event sequences portrayed are simple and familiar and when children are tested by asking them to reconstruct events rather than simply reporting verbally what they comprehend. Other data suggest that comprehension of syntactic codes in the complexity of real television production is more difficult for young children.

b. Segmental Cues. One of the most basic syntactic functions of formal features is segmentation, or marking beginnings and endings of content units. Fades, dissolves, cuts, and special effects, such as simple or multifaceted wipes of three-dimensional rotations, are often used, along with music or sound cues. Children younger than 6 or 7 years appear to have poor understanding of the conventions marking segment boundaries—scene changes, transitions between program and commercial, and so on. In a pilot study in our laboratory (Mayberry & Wright, 1981), children were shown a televised story. At selected points during the story, they were asked whether the people were in the same place or a different place than they had been before. Half of the probes occurred immediately after a scene change, and half occurred when no scene change had taken place. Young children performed just a little better than chance levels in identifying scene changes.

Attention patterns to rapid- and slow-paced programs also provide indirect evidence that young children do not detect the segmental cues for scene changes (Wright et al., 1984). By definition, the slow-paced programs had longer scenes than the rapid-paced programs. The average duration of children's "looks" at the screen was correspondingly longer during slow-paced programs for 8- to 10-year-old children, suggesting that they were timing their looks in conjunction with the length of scenes. Younger children (5- and 6-year-olds) had the opposite pattern; their looks were shorter during slow-paced than during rapid-paced programs, indicating that they were not being guided by segmental boundary cues.

c. Special Codes of Television—the Instant Replay. One example of a code that is peculiar to television or to a particular genre of television program is the instant replay, used primarily in sports broadcasts. The instant replay is particularly interesting because it violates real-world laws of temporal sequences; in order to understand it, the child must know both that television has special codes and what those codes mean.

Children's understanding of instant replays was investigated in two studies of 4- to 9-year-olds (Rice, Huston, & Wright, 1986). Children saw brief bits of television taken from different types of programs, including sports (a play from a baseball game) and simple stories about everyday events (a person making a phone call). Each bit contained an instant replay. Most of the children detected that a repetition of events had occurred in the bits they saw, but they often thought that the event had really been repeated (e.g., that the batter had hit the ball twice or the person had made two phone calls), even though the discontinuity created by the replay made such repetition unlikely. At about age 6 or 7, children began to recognize that the replay was a media technique, particularly in the sports sequence. Younger children appeared unaware of this media code.

These findings are a good demonstration of active processing, in that children used their existing event schemas to interpret and make sense of a media presentation, even when the jump from the end of a set of actions to the beginning was abrupt. Preschool children have schemas for repeated events in the real-world, but they do not have specialized schemas for media codes that violate real-world temporal sequences. Rather than being bewildered by the instant replay, they interpret it as an entirely ordinary series of actions.

d. Separators and Boundary Markers. In children's television, segments are often separated by specially designed audiovisual markers, containing a variety of visual and auditory special effects, such as a whirling bat accompanied by sound effects in *Batman* cartoons. It has been assumed by producers and psychologists alike that such markers make the task of segmentation easier for the young child. The assumption formed the basis for the requirement adopted in the 1970s in the regulatory guidelines for children's advertising that "separators" be inserted between programs and commercials.

Empirical tests of such markers have uniformly shown that children do not interpret these inserts as segmental markers, even when they consist of highly salient features. Palmer and McDowell (1979) found that the program-commercial separators used by the three major networks did not help 5- and 6-year-old children discriminate programs from commercials. In some cases, the children interpreted the markers as bridges connecting segments. In another investigation using several ways of measuring children's comprehension, standard network separators did not help children from 4 to 8 years old to identify commercials correctly. However, a separator that included a stop sign and the explicit statement that a commercial was coming next did improve children's comprehension (Ballard-Campbell, cited in Dorr, 1985).

Similarly, Mayberry and Wright (1981) inserted a marker consisting of an animated flying horse and a sound effect at some of the probe points in their study of children's detection of scene changes. Children were no more likely to recognize scene changes with these markers than without them. Finally, in the investigations of instant replays, the beginning and ending of some of the replays were marked with an expanding and contracting diamond of the kind often used in sports broadcasts. There was no indication that the marker improved children's comprehension of the replay (Rice *et al.*, 1986).

e. Developmental Differences in Understanding Media Syntax. In most of these investigations, children younger than 6 or 7 years of age appear relatively unskilled in interpreting the syntactical codes of television. They understand simple editing techniques that require them to fill in brief bits of missing content, and they understand film codes presenting simple, brief, and familiar content. They have difficulty with cues for segmenting scenes and programs that require mental crossing of longer time and space gaps. They interpret an instant replay as a real repetition of an action, apparently not understanding that it is a media code depicting time sequences that cannot occur in the real world.

Children's poor understanding of media codes does not necessarily indicate passive cognitive processing. The fact that children interpreted instant replays and perceptually salient inserts in meaningful ways, albeit not as adults intended, demonstrates clearly that they are using their available schematic and conceptual knowledge. Their schemas for temporal sequences and complex story narratives probably limit their ability to understand the syntax of television sequences, regardless of the forms used. What changes over time, therefore, is not so much the activity of their processing as the complexity and richness of the structures and operations that they bring to bear on the task, and the extensiveness of their knowledge base.

2. *Gender Connotations of Television Form*

Although formal features are in principle independent of content, they can carry connotative meaning because of their associations with content in television production. Animation suggests that a program is for children; animation in conjunction with other perceptually salient features connotes humor, violence, and high action. Formal feature connotations also result partly from their similarity to symbols and conventions in the broader world. Children's comprehension of feature connotations have been investigated in two domains: gender appropriateness and fiction versus reality.

Efforts to detect children's comprehension of formal feature connotations have benefited from the distinction between implicit and explicit knowledge articulated by psycholinguists. In language, as in television, the primary focus of the participants is the content of the message. Children's knowledge of the grammar, syntax, and social conventions about the forms of language exists largely at an implicit level—they can use the knowledge in producing or understanding language, but they cannot readily articulate the principles involved. In order to elicit implicit knowledge, the overriding focus on content must be overcome. For example, Edelsky (1977) tested children's understanding of gender-linked language forms (e.g., "I was *just* furious" versus "I was *very* mad"). She found that sixth-graders understood the gender connotations. First-graders did not, partly because they focused on the content of the sentence rather than the form.

a. Content Analysis. Gender connotations of television forms were demonstrated in an analysis of 60 toy commercials broadcast during the fall of 1977, 20 in each of three categories (male oriented, female oriented, and gender-neutral) (Welch, Huston-Stein, Wright, & Plehal, 1979). The categories were defined by the gender(s) of the children in the ad, with neutral ads being those in which males and females were approximately evenly represented. The mean levels of formal features for the three types of advertisements are shown in Table III.

Male ads contained more inanimate action (movement by toys), variability, sound effects, rapid cuts and loud music than neutral or female ads. Female ads contained lower rates of cuts, but more soft background music, fades, and dissolves than the other types. Female characters talked very little in the neutral commercials but a great deal in the female commercial. Unseen adult

TABLE III

Mean Levels of Formal Features for Advertisements with Different Gender Connotations

	Gender connotation[a]		
Feature	Male ad	Neutral ad	Female ad
Action			
Animate	1.97	1.65	1.73
Inanimate*	2.10[b]	1.10[c]	1.02[c]
Pace			
Variability of scenes*	2.80[b]	2.30[b]	2.30[b]
Total	5.35	4.30	4.10
Visual effects			
Cuts**	9.70[b]	8.45[b]	5.40[c]
Fades and dissolves**	.90[b]	2.15[b,c]	3.60[c]
Dialogue and narration			
Child dialogue, male*	4[b]	2[b]	0[c]
Child dialogue, female**	0[b]	2[b]	8[c]
Talking narration, male**	50[b]	50[b]	10[c]
Talking narration, female**	0[b]	4[b]	30[c]
Singing narration, male	24	10	14
Singing narration, female*	4[b]	14[b,c]	26[c]
Nonverbal auditory			
Background music*	64[b]	74[b,c]	86[c]
Foreground music*	20[b]	6[b,c]	2[c]
Noise	26[b]	8[c]	4[c]

[a] Action means are the mean rating per interval. Frequencies represent the number of occurrences per 30-second commercial; durations represent the percentage of time during which the feature occurred. Means in the same row with different superscripts are significantly different at $p < .05$, according to Fisher's L.S.D. tests.

*F for main effect, $p < .05$. **F for main effect, $p < .01$.

narrators were predominantly male in the male and neutral ads; there were more female narrators and singing narrators in the female ads. Male ads were the only ones in which physical and object aggression occurred (Welch et al., 1979).

Clearly, the formal features of television commercials directed toward children mimic many of the cultural symbols of masculinity and femininity. They implicitly teach and reinforce the gender stereotypes that are found more generally in our culture. The association of gender-typed form with gender-typed content may thus provide young children with an early opportunity to learn stereotypes.

b. Children's Comprehension of Gender Connotations. A series of investigations in our laboratory was designed to examine children's understanding of gender connotations of television forms. Several methods were used to select or produce stimuli in which either gender-typed forms were varied while maintaining content that was identical across forms and/or the forms were gender neutral. In the first study (Huston, Greer, Wright, Welch, & Ross, 1984), children from first to sixth grades were presented three types of stimuli: (1) commercially produced advertisements with neutral content and gender-typed formal features, (2) experimentally produced pseudo-commercials with abstract and meaningless content in which feminine versus masculine formal features were systematically varied, and (3) verbal descriptions of the same features. Children were exposed to the stimuli one at a time and were asked to decide whether the stimulus would be more appropriate for advertising a feminine or masculine toy (a toy baby buggy or a toy truck).

Children as young as kindergarten level recognized the gender-typed connotations of the formal features in all three types of stimuli. The means are shown in Fig. 4. For the commercially produced advertisements, however, they responded "correctly" only when they were instructed to consider form rather than content (e.g., to think about the kind of music or camera techniques used). As in the language studies, their knowledge of form connotations

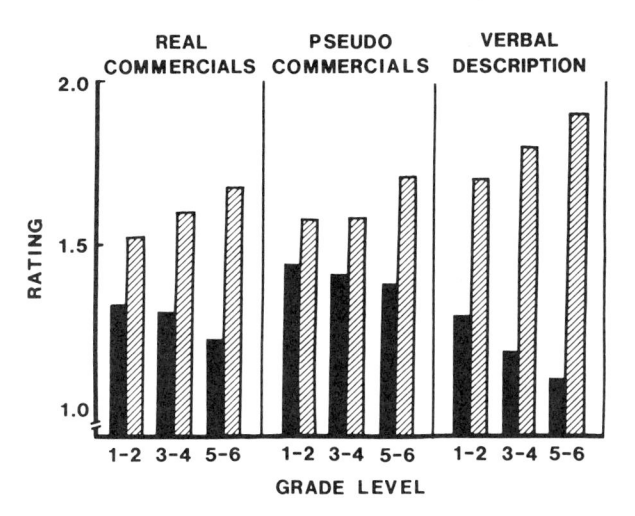

Fig. 4. Children's ratings of television stimuli made with masculine and feminine formal features and neutral content (high rating = feminine; low rating = masculine). Stimuli were real commercials, pseudo commercials, and verbal descriptions. Solid bar, masculine formal features; striped bar, feminine formal features. From Huston, Greer, Wright, Welch, & Ross (1984). Copyright (1984) by the American Psychological Association. Reprinted by permission of the publisher.

appeared to exist at an implicit level and emerged only when content cues were eliminated by instructions or by constructing stimuli with meaningless content.

In a second study (Leary, Huston, & Wright, 1983), the effects of gender-typed connotations on play choices, as well as on comprehension, were measured. Feminine and masculine form versions of advertisements for each of two gender-neutral toys were produced. The content of the advertisements was carefully controlled and was gender-neutral. The toys were modified versions of commercially produced design toys that had been rated by children as equally appropriate for girls and boys. Narration was done by two children (a girl and a boy) whose voices could not be reliably identified as male or female. Only the hands of a child were visible in the advertisement.

Children from kindergarten through fifth grade first saw one advertisement for each toy—a feminine form version for one toy and a masculine form version for the other. They then had an opportunity to play with both toys. There were no effects of formal features on children's stated preferences for the toys or on the amount of time they played with the toys. Subsequently, they saw all four advertisements and were asked whether they thought each ad had been made for girls or for boys. Once again, even the youngest children often understood the gender-typed connotations of the commercials. It appears, therefore, that children know the gender connotations of television forms, but that their behavior is not significantly affected by those connotations.

These two investigations not only demonstrate children's understanding of the gender connotations of formal features, but also suggest some hypotheses about the relations between content and form, or perhaps between explicit and implicit knowledge. Content messages are explicitly recognized by viewers, and those messages predominate in the viewer's interpretation. Formal cues are implicitly understood, but they are often not explicitly recognized by young viewers. The fact that behavior and preference were a function of the attributes of the toy rather than the formal feature cues in the Leary *et al.* (1983) study suggests that the explicitly recognized message was the primary determinant of behavior. Although implicitly understood messages may at times influence behavior, we do not yet have any information about how or when such influences may occur.

3. *Reality versus Fiction Connotations*

It can be argued that formal features are more reliable cues concerning the "reality" of content than are content cues. The classic "War of the Worlds" broadcast by Orson Wells was believed by many people, despite the fantastic nature of the content, largely because its form corresponded to a news broadcast—it followed the forms and formats used for real events.

a. Explicit Understanding of Reality Cues. Formal features differentiate among programs differing in factual reality. Live broadcasts of events as they occur have poorer audio quality, more noise, and less polish than staged and scripted studio productions. They contain unrehearsed speech that is characterized by awkward pauses, talking over another person, and disfluencies. Special wipes, superimposed print, slow and fast motion, freezes, and replays are characteristic of synthetic production or postproduction and editing techniques, but not necessarily of scripted content. These techniques are heavily used in news and documentaries, for instance. Fictional stories have audiovisual quality, accompanying music, and access to private thoughts and conversations.

To the extent that formal feature cues are important for discriminating reality from fiction, children's developing understanding of those cues is critical for their interpretation of the television messages they see and hear. Some theorists have suggested that the social behavioral effects of television violence may be modified by children's perception of the violent events as real or fictional (see, e.g., Feshbach, 1972). Available studies of children's ability to distinguish fiction from reality on television indicate that, by age 5 years or so, children understand that animation, muppets, and pixilation signify "unreality," but they generally define all live productions as "real." During the elementary years, children name formal feature cues as important increasingly often (Dorr, 1983; Morrison, Kelly, & Gardner, 1981). These studies assessed explicit knowledge—they asked children what cues they used to distinguish real from unreal television programs. Other investigations provide information about implicit knowledge of fiction-reality cues.

b. Implicit Understanding of Reality Cues. One example can be found in advertisements that contain techniques that make products and events appear "real," even to reasonably sophisticated viewers. In toy advertisements, for example, a real-life analogue of the toy is shown in conjunction with the toy. The effects of these analogs on children's perceptions were investigated in two studies of advertisements for model race car sets (Ross *et al.*, 1984). Of particular interest here was the comparison of ads showing live action automobile race footage for about one third of the duration of the ad with similar or identical ads showing the model racer in operation. Boys from 8 to 15 years of age who saw the live action footage less often realized that the ad was staged and scripted; instead, they interpreted it as a spontaneous slice of life. They also made exaggerated estimates of the physical properties of the toy, such as its size and speed, suggesting that they perceived the toy as more like a real set of racing equipment.

A second investigation was designed to isolate formal feature cues about reality while holding content as comparable as possible. We chose to focus on two types of real content: live broadcasts of events as they occurred and documentaries about real events (Leary, Wright, & Huston, 1985). Matched pairs of real and fictional television segments with very similar content were assembled. In two pairs, the real version was a live broadcast of an event (the British royal wedding and a space shuttle launch); the fictional version was a story (the movie drama based on the royal wedding and a space ship launch from a children's space story). In the other two pairs a documentary about an event (the *Dr. Who* convention and the making of *The Wizard of Oz*) was matched with a fictional story (scenes from *Dr. Who* and *The Wizard of Oz*).

Segments were shown one at a time to 5- and 7-year-old children. After each, they were asked a series of questions designed to assess their understanding of the type of program and the fictional or real nature of the content. More specifically, four aspects of comprehension were assessed.

1. Factuality ("Was it something that happened in real life or just on TV?", "Was it pretend stuff?")
2. Extent to which the program was scripted and rehearsed ("Did the people practice what they said and did before going on TV?")
3. Program type ("Was it from TV news, or a TV movie, or some other kind of TV show?")
4. Social realism ("Did the people look, talk, or do stuff like people around here?")

Each question was administered in a multiple choice form, with three alternatives arranged in a Likert-type scale. The results are shown in Fig. 5. Despite

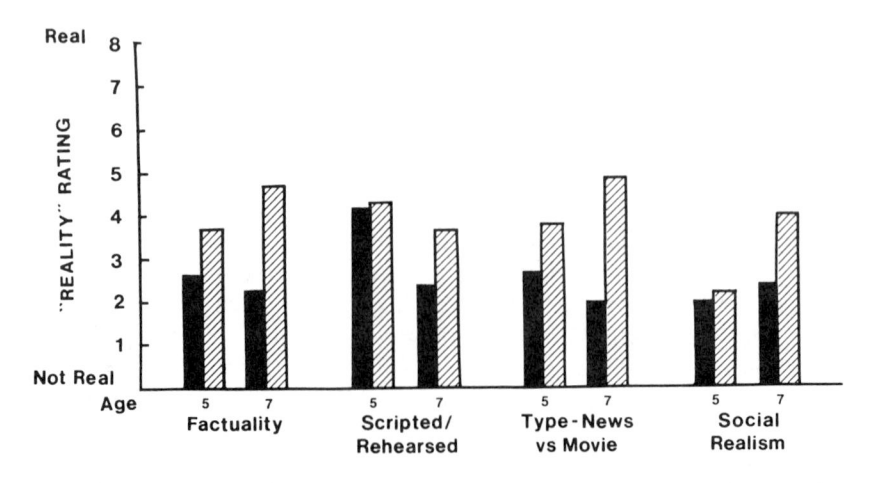

Fig. 5. Children's comprehension of formal feature cues for real and fictional television bits. Solid bar, fictional stimuli; striped bar, real stimuli. From Leary, Wright, & Huston (1985).

the fact that the differences between pairs of segments were often subtle, children did perceive and identify those differences at greater than chance accuracy. Even 5-year-old children could sometimes detect reality connotations of the formal feature cues shown, though their understanding was far from perfect. Children often understood feature signals of reality at an implicit level even though their explicit knowledge of these cues may not be evidenced until a few years later.

4. Developmental Changes and Media Experience

Three groups of variables were proposed as potential contributors to developmental changes in children's comprehension of television form: (1) general cognitive developmental changes, (2) acquisition of domain-specific schemas and concepts, and (3) experience with the television medium.

The importance of general developmental change is indicated by improvements with age in children's comprehension of both gender connotations and cues for fiction and reality. A more precise index of cognitive developmental level was obtained in the study of fiction versus reality by administering the Peabody Picture Vocabulary Test. Within age groups, Peabody scores were positively related to correct identification of fictional and real segments, supporting the hypothesis that children's comprehension of media codes is partly a function of their general level of cognitive development (Huston, Wright, Leary, & Eakins, 1985).

Domain-specific knowledge about gender schemas (sex-role stereotypes) was measured in one of the studies of gender connotations (Huston *et al.*, 1984). There was no relation of gender knowledge to comprehension of gender-typed formal features. The lack of correlation does not necessarily indicate that gender schemas are unimportant, but perhaps that they are virtually universal. Almost any child in American culture has sufficient awareness of gender stereotypes by the age of 5 to provide a basis for comprehending televised symbols about gender (Huston, 1983).

Television viewing experience was measured in several studies, with mixed results. In the investigations of gender connotations, children responded to a checklist survey containing approximately 50 programs broadcast in the previous 3 days. They indicated how often they watched each program. In one study, the reported frequency of viewing children's programs was positively related to comprehension of gender connotations (Huston *et al.*, 1984); in the other study, there was no relation (Leary *et al.*, 1983).

The investigation of fiction–reality comprehension was carried out for a sample of children who were participants in a 2-year longitudinal study of home television viewing. Parents completed 5-week-long viewing diaries at 6-month intervals over the 2-year period before the children were tested. There were virtually no correlations between comprehension of fiction–reality and children's total television viewing or viewing of particular categories of television (Huston et al., 1985).

With one exception, these findings suggest that individual differences in children's television viewing experience were relatively unimportant influences on their comprehension of formal feature connotations. A certain minimum amount of experience with the medium is probably necessary, but most children may exceed that minimum. General cognitive-developmental changes appear to be more important than domain-specific schemas or the amount of viewing experience.

Unlike studies of syntax, in these studies, even children as young as 5 years showed considerable awareness of the connotative meanings of formal features. This difference may be due to the fact that the prerequisite conceptual and schematic knowledge for gender meanings and for fiction–reality are acquired earlier than the knowledge required to understand complex temporal and spatial relationships. Elaborate gender knowledge is well established by age 5 years (Huston, 1983). We know less about the development of children's understanding of fiction and reality, but at least the rudiments of the distinction are learned during the preschool years (Jaglom & Gardner, 1981). By contrast, before age 9 or 10, children have considerable difficulty both with comprehending and reconstructing complex temporal sequences and with inferring implicit plot events (Collins, 1983).

5. Summary

To the extent that the production conventions of the medium follow the culturewide conventions and stereotypes, children's general knowledge is readily applied to their understanding of television. Thus, age and general intelligence predict knowledge of the formal conventions of television better than does viewing experience per se. Television viewing in turn probably tends to strengthen the conventional stereotypes through practice and exposure to programming, which children not only process but also share and discuss with peers as a major source of material on which to practice their growing social knowledge.

We may hazard the conclusion that the more widespread and uniform the cultural convention, the earlier it appears in children's television processing. Stereotypes of masculine and feminine gender, even when conveyed by form and not by content, are readily understood by young viewers. But content is always the first attribute to be consciously and deliberately processed by children, and the effects of content are rarely absent in children's understanding of forms. For example, the instant replay—a synthetic, media-specific feature—is first assumed to be a property of the real world, then understood to be television-specific in the context of its most commonly associated content—sports programming. Only the older children began to understand that it was a formal feature that could be used in the medium for any content.

Specialized media-specific cues that are designed especially for children do not have an impressive track record as contributors to understanding. Scene boundary and program–commercial separators do not appear to function as markers of change points, even though the attentional patterns of older children show that they use these points for making attentional decisions, and they thus must be able to recognize them. Therefore, there are some strong limits to the construction of media-specific features with either syntactic or semantic functions not found in the symbol systems of the culture as a whole. The most general conclusion, then, is that children are functionalists rather than structuralists in their use of media. That is, their understanding is pragmatic, rather than formal, and indeed, the specific, conscious knowledge of television forms and how they are used does not appear independently of general cultural knowledge and television content until middle childhood when other forms of metacognitive understanding begin to appear (Flavell, 1985). Children are in some respects extremely knowledgeable about their favorite medium, but until they are cognitively mature enough to reflect on its formal structures, their understanding is more a product of their general cultural knowledge and familiarity with television content than it is of a knowledge of the symbol system of the medium.

C. Formal Features and Comprehension of Content

1. *Effects of Television Forms*

We now turn to an analysis of the ways in which formal production features influence children's active cognitive processing of the content message. In some respects, television should be easily processed by children because it presents information in pictures and sounds that are familiar from real-world experiences. On the other hand, television presentations are successive, dynamic, and linear. Viewers experience one item or event at a time, at a fixed rate, in a fixed order. The successive mode can be contrasted with a presentation like a picturebook that is simultaneous, static, and spatial, where all items of information are simultaneously available, and viewers may attend to any parts as often as they like, as slowly as they like, and in any order.

The forms used in a television production can enhance or interfere with comprehension of its content messages. The set of investigations described in this section has been concerned with how children use television forms to understand and interpret content. Do formal features and formats guide selective patterns of attention, and do they serve as modes of organizing and representing the content presented? Do forms and formats affect the child's effort and motivation to process content? Can formats be designed to make television viewing more participatory and to activate relevant schemas for processing?

2. Forms as Processing Aids

Active processing of material presented in a successive mode requires the viewer to select, organize, and anticipate information on the basis of partial information about the content. Formal production techniques may affect various aspects of active processing, either by stimulating children to use schemas they already possess or by supplying aids to organization and conceptualization that can be used by those children who lack them. These two functions are similar to the processes of activation and supplantation proposed by Salomon (1979). He demonstrated that media codes can have either function, depending in part on the child's level of mental skill.

a. Stimulating Mental Effort. When formal features signal content that is interesting, comprehensible, funny, and/or relevant to the child's goals, they may lead to an increase in motivation and mental effort. In the investigation by Campbell *et al.* (1987), which compared nutritional messages produced in child-oriented forms with identical messages produced in adult-oriented forms, children not only attended more to the child-form versions, but they *recalled* more of the content from the child-form messages than they did from the adult-form messages. The patterns of recall are shown in Fig. 6. Formal features did more than draw children's eyes to the screen; they stimulated more thorough processing.

This conclusion is supported by comparing these results to a study in which children's visual attention was experimentally manipulated by providing toys during viewing to one group and giving another group no alternative activity

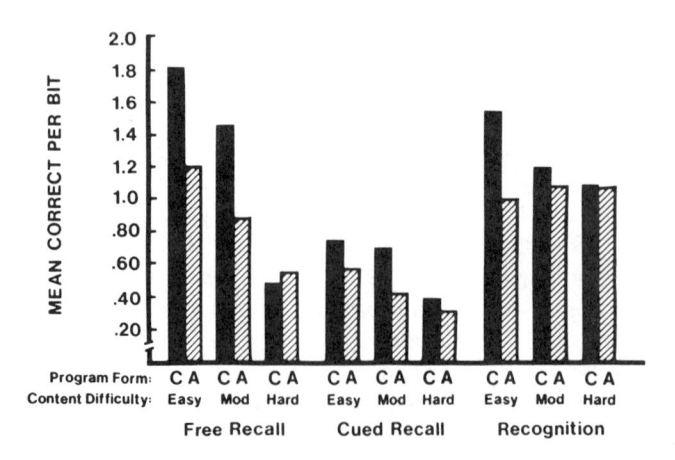

Fig. 6. Mean scores on free recall, cued recall, and recognition of nutritional messages from educational bits made with child- and adult-oriented formal features at three levels of difficulty. Solid bar, child forms; striped bar, adult forms. From Campbell *et al.* (1987).

(Lorch *et al.*, 1979). The time spent looking at the screen was much greater for the group without distractors, but their comprehension of the content did not differ from the group with toys. The manipulation of attention by factors external to the program apparently did not influence children's processing activity; by contrast, variables that are intrinsic to the program and that signal relevant content can influence processing.

Conversely, features that signal dull or very difficult content may reduce efforts to comprehend. One such cue is an adult male voice. In one experimental version of a children's program, a male narrator offered explanatory comments. There was no improvement in children's comprehension (Watkins, Calvert, Huston-Stein, & Wright, 1980). In another investigation of a children's program containing segments of explanation by an adult male, children's attention to these segments was *negatively* related to comprehension (Calvert *et al.*, 1982). His comments may have been difficult to understand, or children may associate male adult voices with difficult content.

The format of an entire program may activate cognitive structures for processing. The investigation comparing story programs with magazine format programs described earlier (Wright *et al.*, 1984) indicated that children could use the temporal continuity provided by a story to organize their recall of events and that they attended more closely to stories than to magazine programs, suggesting that they were processing the stories more carefully.

b. Stimulating Participation. Television permits few opportunities for direct participation by children, but some forms and formats may activate participation and spontaneous rehearsal of content. Two investigations tested the effects of inserting pauses for reflection in televised materials. Simple pauses did not improve comprehension, but a pause accompanied by an instruction to point to the right answer did improve children's acquisition of concepts (Dennis, 1981; Watkins *et al.*, 1980).

c. Aiding in Selection of Central Content. Just as a spotlight guides the gaze of an audience or a musical crescendo signals a plot climax, so television features, such as character action, sound effects, and music, can be used to highlight certain aspects of content, guiding the viewers' attention selectively. If central or important content is highlighted, children's comprehension may be aided; if incidental or misleading content is emphasized, their understanding may be hindered.

In one investigation, targeted items of content of a prosocial children's program were classified as central or incidental to the plot (Calvert *et al.*, 1982). Within each category, events were separated into those presented with salient forms, such as character action, visual special effects, and sound effects, versus those presented without such forms. The latter were usually presented with low-action dialogue. Children recalled central plot information better when it was presented with salient formal features than when it was presented with nonsalient features. Salient formal features were especially helpful to younger children (4–6 years); older children (8–10 years) understood almost equally well regardless of the forms accompanying content. The means are shown in Fig. 7. Comprehension was highest for children who attended selectively to nonverbal auditory cues such as sound effects and nonspeech vocalizations. That is, those children whose attention followed and used the formal feature cues were the most successful in selecting central information for recall.

In a subsequent study, the presence of formal feature cues was varied experimentally (Calvert & Gersh, 1984). Four versions of a story containing a dream sequence were made, varying the presence or absence of a sound effect, and the presence or absence of a content cue (a boy lying in bed sleeping) marking the beginning and end of the dream. The sound effect not only recruited children's attention but also led to improved comprehension of the abstract central content of the story. The formal feature had more clear effects on comprehension than the content cue.

Verbal features may also guide selective attention to central content. In one experiment, children saw two cartoons originally made without dialogue or narration; both contained music and appropriate sound effects (Rolandelli et al., 1985). One group viewed the original; the other saw a version with narration added. Children attended more and recalled more plot information

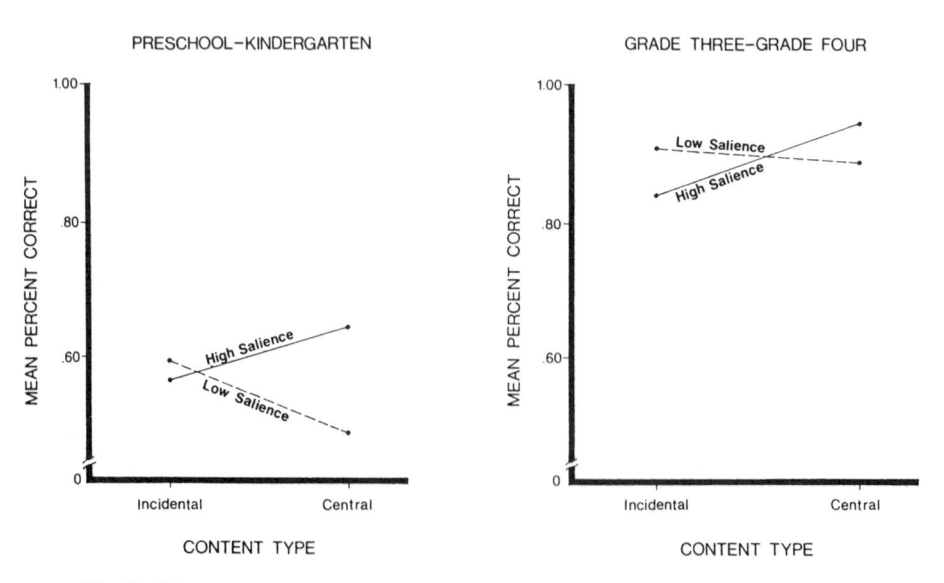

Fig. 7. Mean correct recall of central and incidental story content presented with formal features high or low in perceptual salience. From Calvert, Huston, Watkins, & Wright (1982).

in the narrated version. Narration enhanced recall of information that was presented only in the visual mode, suggesting that it recruited attention at moments when important plot-relevant visual information was presented.

These studies together indicate that children can be aided in selecting central or important content by the judicious placement of form cues (particularly auditory cues) that can recruit attention when a child is looking away. Most of the aforementioned attributes of form that influence attention also influence degree of processing of content, and therefore comprehension and recall.

d. Assisting in Conceptualizing Content. Certain formal features can provide modes of representing and organizing information that children can use for active processing. Because young children readily process information in visual modes, visual representations of central ideas in the form of character actions often aid their comprehension. For example, in an episode of *Fat Albert and the Cosby Kids*, Fat Albert is shown sneaking through the streets and alleys to deliver a box of fudge to the teacher. His intentions and embarrassment are portrayed visually in a mode that children may decode more readily than they would if the same ideas were presented in dialogue. In fact, young children understood the visually presented plot events better than those presented verbally in this program (Watkins *et al.*, 1980).

In another investigation (Calvert *et al.*, 1987), visual portrayals were varied experimentally during "preplays" that presented major plot themes before each segment of a children's story. Children who saw preplays containing visual portrayals recalled the visually presented plot information better than those who saw verbal preplays (narrator's talking head) without visual enactments of story events. Visual content also enhanced children's comprehension in an investigation that compared audiovisual with auditory presentations of story sequences (Gibbons, Anderson, Smith, Field, & Fischer, 1986). Children recalled both the actions and the dialogue of characters better from audiovisual than from auditory presentations.

Just as forms can be used to enhance comprehension, they can also interfere with children's understanding of a content message. Advertisements often contain combinations of visual and verbal forms that readily mislead children because the two are juxtaposed in ways that contradict one another and induce incorrect inferences. In one investigation (Ross, Campbell, Huston-Stein, & Wright, 1981), we compared commercials for cereals and drinks containing fruit with those for similar products made with artificial fruit flavors. Children from first to sixth grade believed the artificial fruit beverages and cereals contained fruit; that impression *increased* when they were asked to look carefully at the advertisements, suggesting that the commercials promoted incorrect inferences. The artificial fruit commercials contained pictures of fruit with the product, and the word "fruit" was embedded in complex verbal messages denying real fruit content (e.g., "real artificial fruit flavor").

Verbal formal features can be a major source of conceptual tools because linguistic codes are more complex and more comprehensive than other representational codes of television. The fact that young children do not spontaneously generate verbal modes of representation means that it may be particularly helpful to supply them. Rice's (1984) analysis of language on television suggests that preschool children benefit most from verbal presentations that are concrete, closely related to visually portrayed events, redundant, and composed of simple sentences.

Verbal features can enhance children's comprehension when the verbal presentation is appropriate to their level of understanding. Children's attention to child dialogue in a prosocial story was positively related to their recall of the content (Calvert et al., 1982). In the investigation described earlier in which narration was added to a children's story (Rolandelli et al., 1985), narration improved children's understanding of inferential content—that is, their ability to infer implied events from the materials in the program. Similarly, in the study of preplays, two types of verbal narration were compared: concrete (the narrator described the actions and events) and inferential (the narrator presented implicit information about character motives and feelings). Comprehension of inferential content was best after inferential narration, but that improvement was greatest for the oldest children (fourth graders). In fact, first graders performed better after the concrete narration, possibly because the inferential narration was too difficult for them to comprehend readily (Calvert et al., 1987).

Adults coviewing with children can supply verbal comments that improve comprehension or involve the child in more active processing. Children show improved comprehension of central and inferential story content when a coviewing adult inserts explanatory comments (Collins, Sobol, & Westby, 1981; Watkins et al., 1980). Coviewing adults can also help children to maximize learning from educational programming (Salomon, 1977). Raeissi and Wright (1983) found that a responsive coviewing adult produced far better generalization of television-trained Piagetian conservation to other tasks and to nontelevised modes of presentation than was found when children viewed with a nonresponsive adult. This adult mediation may be a critical factor if we are to have educational television that can both stretch and stimulate the imagination by transcending real-world experience on the one hand, and yet provide credible and transferable factual knowledge about real-world events on the other.

3. *Summary*

We have seen that children's understanding and recall of television content depends in part on the formal features with which programs are made. Selective attention, motivation and effort, thoroughness of processing, extensiveness of relating content to an existing knowledge base, and making of inferences about content that is implied, but not seen, all depend in part on the child's use of formal features. To the extent that the child cannot do the processing required to understand, some of those logical operations can be carried out for him or her by forms and formats that supplant the logical operation. Salient forms can help the child select the portions of content most worthy of further thought when he or she is not sure which are the most memorable. Responsive coviewers can help children understand implications, contexts, motives of characters, and other less obvious aspects of content.

With age, of course, children come to need these kinds of aids less, and they take some satisfaction in doing their own interpreting. Nevertheless, certain formal features serve as effective stimulators of that processing for the child who knows their significance. Attention does not always serve comprehension—it is necessary, but not sufficient. Other activities, such as querying others, pausing, pointing, and telling also enhance comprehension in those relatively rare instances when the format permits or encourages them. Obviously, the next step is to make learning from television an interactive experience and to make the linear medium a responsive one. But that topic lies beyond our present scope.

V. TELEVISION FORMS AND SOCIAL BEHAVIOR

The effects of television formal features may not end with the child lost in thought. When the content of a program is aggressive, prosocial, or otherwise potentially influential on social behavior, then there are several reasons to expect that formal features might affect social behavior as well as attention and comprehension.

A. Theories Relating Form and Social Behavior

Observational learning theory (Bandura, 1977) has formed the basis for the majority of research on television content and social behavior. In that theory, attention and retention of the behavior observed are important mediators for imitation. Therefore, if formal features induce active processing in the form of attention and memory for program content, the likelihood of imitation would probably be increased.

By the same token, if formal features that recruit and maintain attention constitute potential models of behavior, then children might learn them by observation and imitate them. One formal feature—the level of character action—can be observed and imitated in the form of increased activity level. In fact, in two early experimental studies, children did become more active after observing active, but nonaggressive models (Bandura, Ross, & Ross, 1963; Christy, Gelfand, & Hartmann, 1971). It has also been proposed that rapid pace constitutes a model of frequent changes in activity and might, therefore, lead to short attention spans or reduced levels of task persistence (see, e.g., Singer & Singer, 1983), but experimental comparisons of rapid- and slow-paced programs showed no effects on children's cognitive style or play (Anderson *et al.*, 1977).

Formal features might also affect behavior through a process of generalized arousal (Zillmann, 1982). Arousal, in this theory, is conceptualized as a nonspecific energizer that increases the likelihood of *some* behavior occurring. The particular behavior that results depends largely on environmental cues and individual predispositions. Form and content might either produce arousal directly by intense sensory stimulation or appeal to basic motivational and behavioral systems such as aggression.

One group of investigators (Krull & Watt, 1975; Krull, Watt, & Welty, 1977; Watt & Krull, 1974) have proposed that cognitive complexity and unpredictability of televised stimuli can produce arousal. The television forms they investigated were the rate and variability of scenes and characters. They found some evidence that formal features produced physiological arousal for children and adults. They also reanalyzed the viewing diets of adolescents studied by Chaffee and McLeod (1972), coding the programs for formal complexity as well as violence. Formal complexity predicted aggressive behavior independently of violent content. These findings suggested that formal features could be arousing and that arousal might be translated into behavior, but the processes by which this translation might occur were not clear.

Although observational learning and arousal theories both predict effects of form and content on social behavior, they differ in one important respect. The major premise of observational learning theory is that individuals learn particular behavior patterns by observing them; when they are placed in a situation with relevant cues, they may then imitate those behavior patterns. There is isomorphism between the behavior observed and the behavior performed. Arousal theory does not predict isomorphism between what is observed and the resulting behavior. Because arousal is nonspecific, the direction of the behavior is determined by environmental cues and personal dispositions. Therefore, both form and content might instigate behavior that is quite different from that observed.

B. Experimental Studies of Form and Social Behavior

We have conducted three laboratory experiments with preschool children in order to test the influence of salient forms on social behavior. In one of these studies (Greer *et al.*, 1982), commercials with highly salient features were shown to one group of children, and commercials with low feature salience were shown to another. All children saw the commercials with an episode of *Captain Kangaroo*. Half of each group saw the commercials clustered at the beginning and end of the uninterrupted program; the other half saw them dispersed through the program at the original commercial breaks. Pairs of children were observed playing together before and immediately after viewing. Four types of behavior were coded: aggression, imaginative play, activity level, and positive social interaction.

Children who saw the commercials containing highly salient formal features were more aggressive after viewing than those who saw the commercials with less salient features (see Fig. 8). It appears that the formal features produced general arousal that increased the likelihood of aggression even though there was virtually no aggressive content in the commercials. The arousal interpretation is supported by the fact that aggression was most frequent after seeing the high salience commercials clustered at the end of the program, a condition that would maximize their arousing impact. Because arousal is usually short-lived, its effects should be most obvious when behavior is observed immediately after the arousing stimulus is presented. There were no effects of formal features of the commercials on imaginative play, activity level, or positive social interaction. Arousal should have increased activity level, but it is possible that the small testing room limited variability in children's movement.

In the other two studies, described earlier, both high action (form) and violent content were varied, and children's television programs, rather than

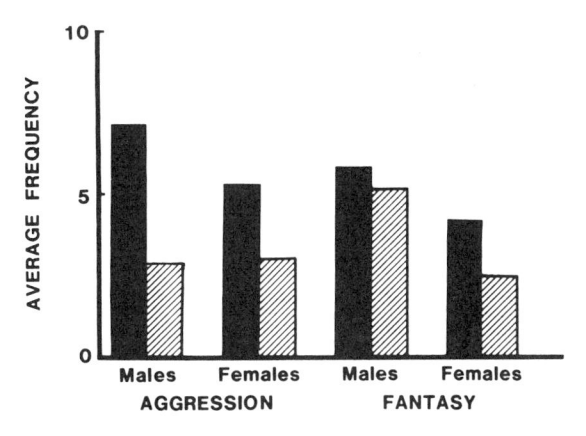

Fig. 8. Mean levels of aggression and imaginative fantasy following exposure to commercials containing formal features either high (solid bars) or low (striped bars) in perceptual salience. From Greer, Potts, Wright, & Huston (1982).

commercials, were used as stimuli. In one study (Huston-Stein *et al.*, 1981), three cartoons were selected to represent high-action–high-violence, high-action–low-violence, and low-action–low-violence. Play behavior of pairs of children was observed before and after viewing. A control group viewed no television. The behaviors coded were aggression, imaginative play, activity level, and prosocial behavior.

The only significant treatment effect occurred for imaginative play; children who saw the two high-action programs declined in imaginative play, by comparison to the low-action viewers and a nonviewing control group. There was a tendency for high action viewers to be more aggressive than the other groups, but the difference was not significant. Again, there were no significant treatment effects on activity level or prosocial behavior.

These results suggested that high action might have some arousing effects, so a second study was designed to test arousal theory more precisely by varying environmental cues in the play situation systematically (Potts *et al.*, 1986). Programs representing all four possible combinations of high and low action with high and low violence were included. In each action–violence cell, there were two programs—one animated and one live. Pairs of preschool boys were observed in play sessions after viewing one type of television program. The environmental cues in the play setting were varied systematically. In one condition, aggression-instigating toys (such as Bobo dolls and Star Wars figures) were provided; in the other, toys designed to promote cooperation (such as a basketball set that required two players and a toy ambulance) were provided. Their behavior was coded for aggression, positive social interaction, imaginative play, total dyadic interaction, and activity level.

According to arousal theory, if high action and/or high violence produced more general arousal, then children viewing such programs should show more aggression with aggression-instigating toys *and* more prosocial behavior with the prosocial toys. Observational learning theory would also predict increased aggression with aggressive cues, at least following high-violence programs, but it would not predict increased prosocial behavior.

The results provided modest support for arousal theory, but the major contributor to arousal appeared to be violent content rather than the high-action form. Children who saw high-violence programs were more aggressive, more active, and engaged in more positive interaction than those who saw low-violence programs. Aggression was highest with aggressive toys, but positive social interaction increased regardless of toy cues. Television action level did not increase any of these behaviors, but it may have added to the effects of violent content. The highest rates of behavior occurred for the group who saw high-action–high-violence programs.

One reason for the relatively weak effects of the program viewed on behavior was the very strong effect of toy cues. The demand qualities of certain toys were sufficiently great that virtually all children manifested the same behavior, probably obliterating the variance that might have been contributed by the television viewing conditions. As mentioned earlier, the strongest effects of rapid action as a formal feature were on attention during the presentation, rather than on social play following.

C. Summary of Findings

These three studies provide some support for the hypothesis that television forms can produce arousal that in turn affects children's social interaction, but the effect appears to be fragile or to be specific to certain circumstances. It appeared most clearly when the stimuli were commercials packed with salient forms but relatively benign in content and when children were free to select from a wide range of toys. The effect was not sufficiently robust to be manifested when strong environmental cues for particular behaviors were present.

VI. CONCLUSION

We began the study of television forms and children with two sets of questions. In what ways do forms affect how actively children process the information they receive from television? What are the contributions of form to the "effects" of content?

Distinct patterns of formal features exist in different types of programs designed for children. Cartoons and commercial children's programs contain high rates of perceptually salient action, noise, and visual gimmickry. Educational programs for children use some perceptually salient techniques, but they also contain features such as moderate amounts of action, singing, and simple dialogue that promote comprehension and rehearsal of content messages. The popular stereotype of *Sesame Street* and related programs as a sensory barrage is not an accurate rendering of the forms used.

We have taken issue with those who assert that television produces passive and intellectually lazy cognitive processing by virtue of its inherent properties. We argue instead that children can process television at various levels of "activity," depending on the nature of the content and form presented *and* on their own levels of cognitive development and sophistication about the medium.

One clear indication of active processing is the extensive evidence that children attend to television selectively. They attend to material that is understandable, funny, entertaining, or otherwise interesting to them. The forms used to present material are used as cues concerning the likely interest and comprehensibility of the content. In effect, children sample the forms and contents of a program and make an implicit decision about whether it is worth continuing to attend to or not. Children monitor the auditory information from a television program when they are looking away, and they use verbal and nonverbal auditory features as cues for deciding when to look back at the set. They also respond to global formats as cues for attention. For example, a program with story continuity receives more attention than a magazine format.

This view differs dramatically from the picture sometimes drawn of the child who is passively hypnotized by the sensory and perceptual pull of the television set. Children do attend to many perceptually salient features on television, but they probably do not do so simply because of the perceptual qualities of those features. Instead, such features are part of a package of humor, simple plots, and entertaining events that appeal to them.

Children also actively process the syntactic and connotative meaning of television forms, though their understanding of some uses of form develops gradually during early and middle childhood. They use their real-world knowledge of language and event sequences to interpret television portrayals. When the uses of form are consistent with real-world information (e.g., when they mimic familiar event sequences or are congruent with culturally accepted symbols of femininity and masculinity), even young children understand them reasonably well. When features are used in media-specific ways that differ from real-world possibilities, as in an instant replay, understanding of those uses comes relatively late in childhood.

Much of children's knowledge of television form is implicit rather than explicit. They do not readily articulate the meanings of form, but they can use their knowledge to interpret a content message. As a result, formal features can enhance young children's ability to understand content messages if they are used judiciously to enhance active cognitive processing. For example, features such as sound effects can aid children in selecting central content and discriminating its messages from incidental content; visual and verbal features can be used to present an organizational structure for a story or to provide conceptual tools for understanding the content presented; visual and auditory features can elicit participation by the child in a task or game. Young children are particularly apt to benefit from these "helping" functions of television form.

The efforts to separate form from content have led to more tentative conclusions. Formal features such as animation, action, and visual and auditory special effects attract and hold children's attention independently from content. There are some clear policy implications of the finding that form often has a greater effect on attention than violent content. At the same time, there is some evidence that perceptually salient forms may induce arousal for young children, which in turn increases their likelihood of aggression and other forms of social behavior, even in the absence of violent content.

Although form and content can be separated conceptually and operationally, they must eventually be reunited. Neither exists independently of the other. In most instances, they probably form a unified whole that is more than the sum of the independent parts. Children learn the common patterns of form–content associations in television very early and use that knowledge for processing what they see and hear. If those patterns are violated, they may respond to the violation. For instance, sex-stereotyped forms in the absence of gender-typed content have little effect on play preferences.

Our focus on active processing and children's uses of television differs sharply from the effects models that predominated in studies of children and television for many years. Collins (1982) was one of the first to point out the importance of understanding the attributes of the child in determining the influences of television. Others (see, e.g., Salomon, 1979) provided insightful analyses of the formal codes of the medium. A sophisticated understanding of television effects will come only from considering both the attributes of the developing child and the particular characteristics of the medium to which that child is exposed. If the medium is not really all of the message, it is at least an important part.

ACKNOWLEDGMENTS

The work reported here has been supported by grants from the Spencer Foundation; the Graduate Research Fund, University of Kansas; the National Institute of Mental Health; and the National Institute of Child Health and Human Development. The views expressed are those of the authors and not necessarily those of the sponsoring institutions. The authors would like to thank Mabel L. Rice, who served as Senior Research Associate and valued colleague for several years. The many students and employees of CRITC who contributed to our research efforts include Jerry Bova, Marilyn Bremer, Yasmeen Butt, Sandra Calvert, Toni Campbell, Jean Siegle, Rodney Dennis, Darwin Eakins, Jacquette Elwell, Lynette Forbes, Carrie Freeseman, Douglas Greer, John Helyar, Michael Hughes, Barbara Jones, Donna Kempin, Dennis Kerkman, Alice Leary, Dafna Lemish, Valeria Lovelace, Sue Malloy, Debbie Mayberry, Lynn Mittelstadt, Jake Murphee, Marites Piñon, Robert Plehal, Richard Potts, Pouran Raeissi, David Rolandelli, Larry Rosenkoetter, Rhonda Ross, Leon Szeptycki, Kathy Tomasek, Rosemarie Truglio, Tammy Waggy, Ellen Wartella, Bruce Watkins, Lee Ann Weeks, Renate Welch, Linda Woodsmall, and Luis Zapata.

REFERENCES

Alvarez, M., Huston, A. C., Wright, J. C., & Kerkman, D. (1989). Gender differences in visual attention to television form and content. *Journal of Applied Developmental Psychology*, in press.

Alwitt, L. F., Anderson, D. R., Lorch, E. P., & Levin, S. R. (1980). Preschool children's visual attention to attributes of television. *Human Communication Research, 7*, 52–67.

Anderson, D. R., Alwitt, L. F., Lorch, E. P., & Levin, S. R. (1979). Watching children watch television. In G. A. Hale & M. Lewis (Eds.), *Attention and cognitive development*. New York: Plenum.

Anderson, D. R., & Levin, S. R. (1976). Young children's attention to "Sesame Street." *Child Development, 47*, 806–811.

Anderson, D. R., Levin, S. R., & Lorch, E. P. (1977). The effects of TV program pacing on the behavior of preschool children. *AV Communication Review, 25*, 154–166.

Anderson, D. R., & Lorch, E. P. (1983). Looking at television: Action or reaction? In J. Bryant & D. R. Anderson (Eds.), *Children's understanding of television: Research on attention and comprehension*. New York: Academic Press.

Anderson, D. R., Lorch, E. P., Field, D. E., Collins, P. A., Nathan, J. G. (1986). Television viewing at home: Age trends in visual attention and time with TV. *Child Development, 37*, 1024–1033.

Anderson, D. R., Lorch, E. P., Field, D. E., & Sanders, J. (1981). The effects of TV program comprehensibility on preschool children's visual attention to television. *Child Development, 52*, 151–157.

Anderson, D. R., & Smith, R. (1984). Young children's TV viewing: The problems with cognitive continuity. In F. J. Morrison, C. Lord, & D. F. Keating (Eds.), *Advances in applied developmental psychology* (Vol. 1). New York: Academic Press.

Bandura, A. (1977). *Social learning theory*. Englewood Cliffs, NJ: Prentice-Hall.

Bandura, A., Ross, D., & Ross, S. A. (1963). Imitation of film-mediated aggressive models. *Journal of Abnormal and Social Psychology, 66*, 3–11.

Berlyne, D. E. (1960). *Conflict, arousal, and curiosity*. New York: McGraw-Hill.

Brown, A. L., Bransford, J. D., Ferrara, R. A., & Campione, J. C. (1983). Learning, remembering, and understanding. In J. H. Flavell & E. M. Markman (Eds.), P. H. Mussen (Series Ed.), *Handbook of child psychology: Vol. 3. Cognitive development* (pp. 77–166). New York: Wiley.

Bruner, J. S., Olver, R. R., & Greenfield, P. M. (1966). *Studies in cognitive growth*. New York: Wiley.

Calvert, S. L., & Gersh, T. L. (1987). The selective use of sound effects and visual inserts for children's television story comprehension. *Journal of Applied Developmental Psychology, 8*, 363–376.

Calvert, S. L., Huston, A. C., Watkins, B. A., & Wright, J. C. (1982). The relation between selective attention to television forms and children's comprehension of content. *Child Development, 53*, 601–610.

Calvert, S. L., Huston, A. C., & Wright, J. C. (1987). Effects of visual and verbal televised preplays on children's attention and comprehension. *Journal of Applied Developmental Psychology, 8*, 329–342.

Campbell, T. A., Wright, J. C., & Huston, A. C. (1987). Form cues and content difficulty as determinants of children's cognitive processing of televised educational messages. *Journal of Experimental Child Psychology, 43*, 311–327.

Chaffee, S. H., & McLeod, J. M. (1972). Adolescent television use in the family context. In G. A. Comstock & E.A. Rubinstein (Eds.), *Television and social behavior: Vol. 3. Television and adolescent aggressiveness* (pp. 149–172). Washington, DC: U.S. Government Printing Office.

Christy, P. R., Gelfand, D. M., & Hartmann, D. P. (1971). Effects of competition-induced frustration on two classes of modeled behavior. *Developmental Psychology, 5*, 104–111.

Collins, W. A. (1982). Cognitive processing in television viewing. In D. Pearl, L. Bouthilet, & J. Lazar (Eds.), *Television and behavior: Ten years of scientific progress and implications for the eighties: Vol. 2. Technical reviews* (pp. 9–23). Washington, DC: National Institute of Mental Health.

Collins, W. A. (1983). Interpretation and inference in children's television viewing. In J. Bryant & D. R. Anderson (Eds.), *Children's understanding of television: Research on attention and comprehension*. New York: Academic Press.

Collins, W. A., Sobol, B. L., & Westby, S. (1981). Effects of adult commentary on children's comprehension and inferences about a televised aggressive portrayal. *Child Development*, 52, 158-163.

Dennis, R. W. (1981, April). *Prompting viewer interaction with televised instruction*. Paper presented at the biennial meeting of the Society for Research in Child Development, Boston.

Dorr, A. (1983). No shortcuts to judging reality. In J. Bryant & D. R. Anderson (Eds.), *Children's understanding of television: Research on attention and comprehension*. New York: Academic Press.

Dorr, A. (1985, April). *Developmental changes in reactions to television content*. Paper presented at the biennial meeting of the Society for Research in Child Development, Boston.

Edelsky, C. (1977). Acquisition of an aspect of communicative competence: Learning what it means to talk like a lady. In S. Ervin-Tripp & C. Mitchell-Kernan (Eds.), *Child discourse*. New York: Academic Press.

Faulkender, P., Wright, J. C., & Waldron, A. (1974). Generalization of habituation of concept stimuli in toddlers. *Child Development*, 45, 1002-1010.

Feshbach, S. (1972). Reality and fantasy in filmed violence. In J. P. Murray, E. A. Rubinstein, & G. A. Comstock (Eds.), *Television and social behavior: Vol. 2. Television and social learning* (pp. 318-345). Washington, DC: U.S. Government Printing Office.

Field, D. E., & Anderson, D. R. (1985). Instruction and modality effects on children's television attention and comprehension. *Journal of Educational Psychology*, 77, 91-100.

Flavell, J. H. (1985). *Cognitive development* (2nd ed.). Englewood Cliffs, NJ: Prentice-Hall.

Friedrich, L. K., & Stein, A. H. (1975). Prosocial television and young children: The effects of verbal labeling and role playing on learning and behavior. *Child Development*, 46, 27-36.

Gelman, R., & Baillargeon, R. (1983). Overview of some Piagetian concepts. In J. H. Flavell & E. M. Markman (Eds.), P. H. Mussen (Series Ed.), *Handbook of child psychology: Vol. 3. Cognitive development* (pp. 167-230). New York: Wiley.

Gibbons, J., Anderson, D. R., Smith, R., Field, D., & Fischer, C. (1986). Young children's recall and reconstruction of audio and audiovisual narratives. *Child Development*, 57, 1014-1023.

Greer, D., Potts, R., Wright, J. C., & Huston, A. C. (1982). The effects of television commercial form and placement on children's social behavior and attention. *Child Development*, 53, 611-619.

Hawkins, R., & Pingree, S. (1982). Television's influence on social reality. In D. Pearl, L. Bouthilet, & J. Lazar (Eds.), *Television and behavior: Ten years of scientific progress and implications for the eighties: Vol. 2. Technical reviews* (pp. 224-247). Washington, DC: U.S. Government Printing Office.

Hayes, D. S., & Birnbaum, D. W. (1980). Preschoolers' retention of televised events: Is a picture worth a thousand words? *Developmental Psychology*, 16, 410-416.

Hayes, D. S., Chemelski, B. E., & Birnbaum, D. W. (1981). Young children's incidental retention of televised events. *Developmental Psychology*, 17, 230-232.

Himmelweit, H. T., Oppenheim, A. N., & Vince, P. (1958). *Television and the child*. London: Oxford University Press.

Hunt, J. McV. (1961). *Intelligence and experience*. New York: Ronald.

Huston, A. C. (1983). Sex typing. In E. M. Hetherington (Ed.), P. H. Mussen (Series Ed.), *Handbook of child psychology: Vol. 4. Socialization, personality, and social behavior* (4th ed., pp. 387-468). New York: Wiley.

Huston, A. C., Greer, D., Wright, J. C., Welch, R., & Ross, R. (1984). Children's comprehension of televised formal features with masculine and feminine connotations. *Developmental Psychology*, 20, 707-716.

Huston, A. C., & Wright, J. C. (1983). Children's processing of television: The informative functions of formal features. In J. Bryant & D. R. Anderson (Eds.), *Children's understanding of TV: Research on attention and comprehension* (pp. 37-68). New York: Academic Press.

Huston, A. C., Wright, J. C., Leary, A., & Eakins, D. (1985, August). *The relations of cognitive development and viewing history to children's comprehension of television forms.* Paper presented at the annual meeting of the American Psychological Association, Los Angeles.

Huston, A. C., Wright, J. C., Wartella, E., Rice, M. L., Watkins, B. A., Campbell, T., & Potts, R. (1981). Communicating more than content: Formal features of children's television programs. *Journal of Communication, 31*(3), 32-48.

Huston-Stein, A., Fox, S., Greer, D., Watkins, B. A., & Whitaker, J. (1981). The effects of action and violence in television programs on the social behavior and imaginative play of preschool children. *Journal of Genetic Psychology, 138,* 183-191.

Jaglom, L. M., & Gardner, J. (1981). The preschool television viewer as anthropologist. In H. Kelly & H. Gardner (Eds.), *Viewing children through television.* A quarterly sourcebook in the series, *New directions in child development.* San Francisco: Jossey-Bass.

Krull, R., & Watt, J. H., Jr. (1975, May). *Television program complexity and ratings.* Paper presented at the American Association for Public Opinion Research Conference.

Krull, R., Watt, J. H., Jr., & Welty, L. W. (1977). Structure and complexity: Two measures of complexity in television programs. *Communication Research, 4,* 61-85.

Leary, A., Huston, A. C., & Wright, J. C. (1983, April). *The influence of television production features with masculine and feminine connotations on children's comprehension and play behavior.* Paper presented at the biennial meeting of the Society for Research in Child Development, Detroit.

Leary, A., Wright, J. C., & Huston, A. C. (1985, April). *Young children's judgments of the fictional/nonfictional status of television programming.* Paper presented at the biennial meeting of the Society for Research in Child Development, Toronto.

Lesser, H. (1977). *Television and the preschool child.* New York: Academic Press.

Lorch, E. P., Anderson, D. R., & Levin, S. R. (1979). The relationship of visual attention to children's comprehension of television. *Child Development, 50,* 722-727.

Mandler, J. M. (1979). Categorical and schematic organization in memory. In C. R. Puff (Ed.), *Memory organization and structure* (pp. 259-299). New York: Academic Press.

Mandler, J. M. (1983). Representation. In J. H. Flavell & E. M. Markman (Eds.) P. H. Mussen (Series Ed.), *Handbook of child psychology: Vol. 3. Cognitive development* (pp. 420-494). New York: Wiley.

Martin, C. L., & Halverson, C. F., Jr. (1981). A schematic processing model of sex typing and stereotyping in children. *Child Development, 52,* 1119-1134.

Mayberry, D., & Wright, J. C. (1981). *Children's detection of scene changes as a function of form and content cues.* Unpublished manuscript, Center for Research on the Influence of Television on Children, University of Kansas, Lawrence.

Meringoff, L. K. (1980). Influence of the medium on children's story apprehension. *Journal of Educational Psychology, 72,* 240-249.

Morison, P., Kelly, H., & Gardner, H. (1981). Reasoning about the realities on television: A developmental study. *Journal of Broadcasting, 25,* 229-242.

Palmer, E. L. (1978, June). *A pedagogical analysis of recurrent formats on Sesame Street and Electric Company.* Paper presented at the International Conference on Children's Educational Television, Amsterdam.

Palmer, E. L., & McDowell, C. N. (1979). Program/commercial separators in children's television programming. *Journal of Communication, 29,* 197-201.

Pezdek, K., & Hartman, E. F. (1983). Children's television viewing: Attention and comprehension of auditory versus visual information. *Child Development, 54,* 1015-1023.

Pezdek, K., & Stevens, E. (1984). Children's memory for auditory and visual information on television. *Developmental Psychology*, **20**, 212–218.

Postman, N. (1979). *Teaching as a conserving activity*. New York: Delacourt.

Potts, R., Huston, A. C., & Wright, J. C. (1986). The effects of television form and violent content on boys' attention and social behavior. *Journal of Experimental Child Psychology*, **41**, 1–17.

Raeissi, P., & Wright, J. C. (1983). *Training and generalization of number conservation by teachers for preschoolers*. Paper presented at the biennial meeting of the Society for Research in Child Development, Detroit.

Rice, M. L. (1983). The role of television in children's language acquisition. *Developmental Review*, **3**, 211–224.

Rice, M. L. (1984). The words of children's television. *Journal of Communication*, **28**, 445–461.

Rice, M. L., & Haight, P. L. (1986). The "motherese" of Mr. Rogers. *Journal of Child Language*, **51**, 282–287.

Rice, M. L., Huston, A. C., & Wright, J. C. (1982). The forms of television: Effects on children's attention, comprehension, and social behavior. In D. Pearl, L. Bouthilet, & J. Lazar (Eds.), *Television and behavior: Ten years of scientific inquiry and implications for the eighties: Vol. 2. Technical reviews* (pp. 24–38). Washington, DC: U.S. Government Printing Office.

Rice, M. L., Huston, A. C., & Wright, J. C. (1986). Replays as repetitions: Young children's interpretation of television forms. *Journal of Applied Developmental Psychology*, **7**, 61–76.

Rolandelli, D. R., Wright, J. C., & Huston, A. C. (1982, April). *Auditory attention to television: A new methodology*. Paper presented at the biennial meeting of the Southwestern Society for Research in Child Development, Galveston.

Rolandelli, D. R., Wright, J. C., & Huston, A. C. (1985, May). *Children's auditory and visual processing of narrated and nonnarrated television programming*. Paper presented at the annual meeting of the International Communication Association, Honolulu.

Ross, R. P., Campbell, T., Huston-Stein, A., & Wright, J. C. (1981). Nutritional misinformation of children: A developmental and experimental analysis of the effects of televised food commercials. *Journal of Applied Developmental Psychology*, **1**, 329–345.

Ross, R. P., Campbell, T., Wright, J. C., Huston, A. C., Rice, M. L., & Turk, P. (1984). When celebrities talk, children listen: An experimental analysis of children's responses to TV ads with celebrity endorsements. *Journal of Applied Developmental Psychology*, **5**, 185–202.

Ross, R. P., Wartella, E., & Lovelace, V. O. (1982, April). *A conceptual framework for describing children's television viewing patterns*. Paper presented at the biennial meeting of the Southwestern Society for Research in Human Development, Galveston, TX.

Salomon, G. (1977). Effects of encouraging Israeli mothers to co-observe "Sesame Street" with their five-year-olds. *Child Development*, **48**, 1146–1151.

Salomon, G. (1979). *Interaction of media, cognition, and learning*. San Francisco: Jossey-Bass.

Salomon, G. (1981). *Communication and education: Social and psychological interactions*. Beverly Hills, CA: Sage.

Salomon, G. (1983). Television watching and mental effort: A social psychological view. In J. Bryant & D. R. Anderson (Eds.), *Children's understanding of television: Research on attention and comprehension* (pp. 181–198). New York: Academic Press.

Schramm, W., Lyle, J., & Parker, E. B. (1961). *Television in the lives of our children*. Stanford, CA: Stanford University Press.

Singer, J. L. (1980). The power and limits of television: A cognitive–affective analysis. In P. Tannenbaum (Ed.), *The entertainment function of television*. Hillsdale, NJ: Erlbaum.

Singer, J. L., & Singer, D. L. (1983). Psychologists look at television: Cognitive, developmental, personality, and social policy implications. *American Psychologist*, **38**, 826–834.

Smith, R., Anderson, D. R., & Fischer, C. (1985). Young children's comprehension of montage. *Child Development*, **56**, 962–971.

Stein, A. H., & Friedrich, L. K. (1975). The impact of television on children and youth. In E. M. Hetherington (Ed.), *Review of child development research* (Vol. 5, pp. 183–256). Chicago: University of Chicago Press.

Watkins, B. A., Calvert, S. L., Huston-Stein, A., & Wright, J. C. (1980). Children's recall of television material: Effects of presentation mode and adult labelling. *Developmental Psychology*, **16**, 672–674.

Watkins, B. A., Huston-Stein, A., & Wright, J. C. (1981). Effects of planned television programming. In E. L. Palmer & A. Dorr (Eds.), *Children and the faces of television: Teaching, violence, selling* (pp. 49–69). New York: Academic Press.

Watt, J. H., Jr., & Krull, R. (1974). An information theory measure of television programming. *Communication Research*, **1**, 44–68.

Watt, J. H., Jr., & Krull, R. (1975, April). *Arousal model components in television programming: Form activity and violent content*. Paper presented at the annual meeting of the International Communication Association, Chicago.

Welch, R. L., Huston-Stein, A., Wright, J. C., & Plehal, R. (1979). Subtle sex-role cues in children's commercials. *Journal of Communication*, **29**, 202–209.

Winn, M. (1977). *The plug-in-drug: Television, children, and the family*. New York: Viking.

Wright, J. C., Calvert, S. L., Huston, A. C., & Watkins, B. A. (1980, May). *The effects of selective attention to television forms on children's comprehension of content*. Paper presented at the annual meeting of the International Communication Association, Acapulco, Mexico.

Wright, J. C., & Huston, A. C. (1981). The forms of television: Nature and development of television literacy in children. In H. Gardner & H. Kelly (Eds.), *Children and the worlds of television*. A quarterly sourcebook in the series, *New Directions in Child Development*. San Francisco: Jossey-Bass.

Wright, J. C., & Huston, A. C. (1983). A matter of form: Potentials of television for young viewers. *American Psychologist*, **38**, 835–843.

Wright, J. C., Huston-Stein, A. C., Potts, R., Thissen, D., Rice, M., Watkins, B. A., Calvert, S., Greer, D., & Zapata, L. (1980, March). *Formal features of children's programs as predictors of viewership by age and sex: A tale of three cities*. Paper presented at the meeting of the Southwestern Society for Research in Human Development, Lawrence, KS.

Wright, J. C., Huston, A. C., Ross, R. P., Calvert, S. L., Rolandelli, D., Weeks, L. A., Raeissi, P., & Potts, R. (1984). Pace and continuity of television programs: Effects on children's attention and comprehension. *Developmental Psychology*, **20**, 653–666.

Wright, J. C., & Vlietstra, A. G. (1975). The development of selective attention: From perceptual exploration to logical search. In H. W. Reese (Ed.), *Advances in child development and behavior* (Vol. 10, pp. 196–236). New York: Academic Press.

Wright, J. C., & Watkins, B. A. (1978, August). *Active vs. passive television viewing: A model of the development of TV information processing in children*. Paper presented at the annual meeting of the American Psychological Association, Toronto.

Zillmann, D. (1982). Television viewing and arousal. In D. Pearl, L. Bouthilet, & J. Lazar (Eds.), *Television and behavior: Ten years of scientific inquiry and implications for the eighties: Vol. 2. Technical reviews* (pp. 53–67). Washington, DC: U.S. Government Printing Office.

Sexually Violent Media, Thought Patterns, and Antisocial Behavior*

NEIL M. MALAMUTH
Communications Studies
University of California, Los Angeles
Los Angeles, California 90024

I. Introduction	160
A. The 1986 Pornography Commission	160
B. The Focus of This Chapter	161
II. Theorized Effects	163
A. An Indirect-Effects Model	163
B. Hypothesized Processes Affecting Thought Patterns	165
III. Media Characteristics and Diffusion	167
A. The Anatomy of Media Sexual Violence	167
B. Availability and Frequency of Exposure	168
IV. Sexually Violent Media and Arousal	169
A. Does Sexual Violence Stimulate Arousal in the Audience?	169
B. The Etiology of Sexual Arousal to Aggression	172
C. Does Media Exposure Change Sexual Responsiveness?	178
V. Media Exposure, Thought Patterns, and Antisocial Behavior	180
A. From Media Exposure to Thought Patterns	180
B. From Thought Patterns to Antisocial Behavior	185
VI. Other Relevant Data	194
A. Nonsexual Media Violence	194
B. The Media and Social Attitudes	195
C. Longitudinal Research in Other Areas	195

*A briefer version of this article was presented at the Surgeon General's Workshop on Pornography and Public Health, June 22-24, 1986, Washington, DC. It was entitled "Do sexually violent media indirectly contribute to antisocial behavior?" and was reprinted in M. R. Walsh (Ed.), 1987, *The psychology of women: Ongoing debates*. New Haven, CT: Yale University Press. In addition, an earlier version was presented at the International Communication Association Meetings in Montreal, Canada, May 1987, where it received a "top five" rating by the Mass Communication Division.

D. Jury Studies... 196
E. Sexual Harassment and Wife Beating..................... 196
VII. Summary and Conclusions 197
References.. 198

I. INTRODUCTION

A. The 1986 Pornography Commission

The Attorney General's Commission on Pornography (1986) generated a storm of public debate with a recently published report. This Commission's conclusions were very different from those of the earlier Commission on Obscenity and Pornography (1970). Although the 1986 Commission used various sources of information and distinguished among several categories of pornography, it appeared to rely heavily on social scientific data on sexually violent material.[1] "It is with respect to material of this variety," the Commission explained, "that the scientific findings and ultimate conclusions of the 1970 Commission are least reliable for today, precisely because material of this variety was largely absent from that Commission's inquiries" (1986, p. 324).

With regards to such material, there are three primary elements included in the overall conclusions of the 1986 Commission's Report (pp. 323-355). The first concerns the frequency of such sexually violent materials. The Commission indicates that increasingly these are the "most prevalent forms of pornography" (p. 323). On the basis of the data reviewed later in this article, this is an inappropriate conclusion because violence (or aggression), as defined by social scientists (see, e.g., Baron, 1977; Goldstein, 1986), is not frequently portrayed in sexually explicit media (see also Linz, Donnerstein, & Penrod, 1987). However, more inclusive definitions of violence (see, e.g., MacKinnon, 1987) lead to perceptions of much higher frequency in sexually explicit media.

The second element concerns the link between sexually violent media and violent behavior. The Commission concluded that "In both clinical and experimental settings, exposure to sexually violent materials has indicated an increase in the likelihood of aggression. More specifically, the research, which is described in much detail later in this Report, shows a causal relationship between exposure to material of this type and aggressive behavior towards

---

[1] The term *pornography* is used in this article to refer to sexually explicit media without any pejorative meaning intended. Also, the terms *aggression* and *violence* are used interchangeably herein, as are the terms *sexually violent media* and *violent pornography*. Although I recognize that meaningful distinctions may be made between such terms, I have not chosen to do so here.

women" (p. 324). The Commission concludes that the increase in aggressive behavior occurs not only in research settings but also includes unlawful sexually violent behavior by some subgroups of the population.

The experimental research that the Commission is referring to are studies that have shown short-term increases in laboratory aggression, following exposure to sexually violent media (see, e.g., Donnerstein & Berkowitz, 1981; Malamuth, 1978). However, this part of the 1986 Commission's report fails to include the findings of the only study examining possible long-term effects of repeated exposure to sexually violent media on laboratory aggression (Malamuth & Ceniti, 1986). That study did not find any such long-term effects. It is noteworthy that it is cited in a different section of the 1986 Commission's report—the "Social and Behavior Science Research Analysis" section (p. 985), prepared separately by a social scientist. Obviously, this information was available to the Commission. In general, the Commission's generalization from the limited data in laboratory settings to infer direct effects of sexually violent media on real-world violence is certainly questionable.

The third element of the Commission's conclusions most closely relates to the material reviewed in the present chapter. The Report concludes that the most recent evidence is "strongly supportive of significant attitudinal changes on the part of those with substantial exposure to violent pornography.... We have little trouble concluding that this attitude is both pervasive and profoundly harmful" (1986, pp. 326–327).

The new evidence on the effects of violent pornography on attitudes came primarily from research and testimony provided by my associates and I. My purpose here is to synthesize this research. However, this article is in no way intended as an endorsement of the 1986 Commission's conclusions or legal recommendations.

B. The Focus of This Chapter

The research described below analyzed media stimuli by the "messages" or meanings they convey. Meaning is, of course, a function of both the message and the receiver's interpretations of it. The message given the most attention here involved the consequences of sexual aggression. A series of experiments described here found that rape depictions that showed the victim ultimately deriving physical pleasure from her experience fostered attitudes more condoning of aggression against women. Rape depictions that portrayed the victim abhorring the experience, on the other hand, were less likely to have such effects.

According to these findings, a PG-rated film showing rape in a positive light could be more socially detrimental than an X-rated film not showing sexual violence. The degree of sexual explicitness may be less relevant than the "message" conveyed by the depiction of sexual aggression.[2]

Besides discriminating among differing "messages" in studying media stimuli, the research presented differentiates among media consumers and attempts to consider the role of other contributing factors. No influence works in a vacuum, and media influences are viewed as combining and interacting with a variety of other individual and cultural factors—sometimes counteracting them, sometimes reinforcing them, and at other times, not having much of any effect.

The current strong interest in exploring a possible relationship between pornography and crime has led to a search for direct links between exposure and deviant behavior. People have sought an immediate causal connection between media action and audience imitation. For example, a civil suit brought against NBC alleged that a rape portrayal in a television movie, *Born Innocent*, resulted in an imitation rape by some juvenile viewers (*Olivia v. NBC*, 1978). However, because of the ethical constraints against researchers' creating conditions that might increase serious aggression (e.g., exposing individuals to large doses of violent pornography and then seeing if some commit rapes), experimentation to study direct effects can only be used to a very limited extent.

Beyond the dramatic popular notion of violent pornography spurring a minority of sexual deviants and "weirdos" to criminal acts lies the far grayer, more complex, but also potentially far more pervasive area of indirect effects. The evidence in this article suggests the prospect of a wide range of media affecting the general population in a variety of different ways. In particular, it looks at how an aggregate of media sexual violence could affect a person's thought patterns (e.g., attitudes, beliefs, perceptions, schemas), which are concurrently being shaped by family, peers, other media messages, and a host of other influences. If other factors exist in the person and the environment, such thought patterns might contribute to stranger and date rape. In the absence of other factors that contribute to aggression or due to the existence of forces that inhibit (e.g., fear of punishment) or are incompatible with (e.g., empathy) violence, there is still some likelihood that these thought patterns will be expressed in other ways, such as a not-acted-upon desire to be sexually aggressive, sanctioning the sexual aggression of others, or sexist,

---

[2] Of course, sexual explicitness in and of itself should not be ignored as a conveyance of messages. Based on cultural and personal background and experience, sexual explicitness may be interpreted in many different ways, and media may convey messages about social roles and power relations even if there is no actual violence shown. For example, the uncovering of a woman's body may be perceived by some as debasing her. Similarly, the public display of sex may break taboos that could be interpreted as sanctioning other restricted behaviors (Malamuth, Feshbach, & Jaffe, 1977). However, such interpretations are not inherent to sexually explicit media, whereas a positive depiction of rape or child molestation is not equally a matter of interpretation.

discriminatory, and/or harassing behavior. Even when not translated into violent behavior, such effects have wide social implications.

II. THEORIZED EFFECTS

A. An Indirect-Effects Model

Malamuth & Briere (1986) described an indirect-effects model of hypothesized environmental influences on the development of antisocial behavior against women (see Fig. 1). To summarize this model briefly, individual conditions and the broader social climate are postulated as the originating environmental influences on the individual. The mass media are considered one of the *many* social forces that may, in interaction with a variety of other cultural and individual factors, affect the development of intermediate attributes, such as thought patterns, sexual arousal patterns, motivations, emotions, and personality characteristics. These intermediate variables, in complex interactions with each other and with situational circumstances, such as alcohol consumption or acute arousal, may precipitate behaviors ranging from passive support to actual aggression.[3] In addition to having relatively

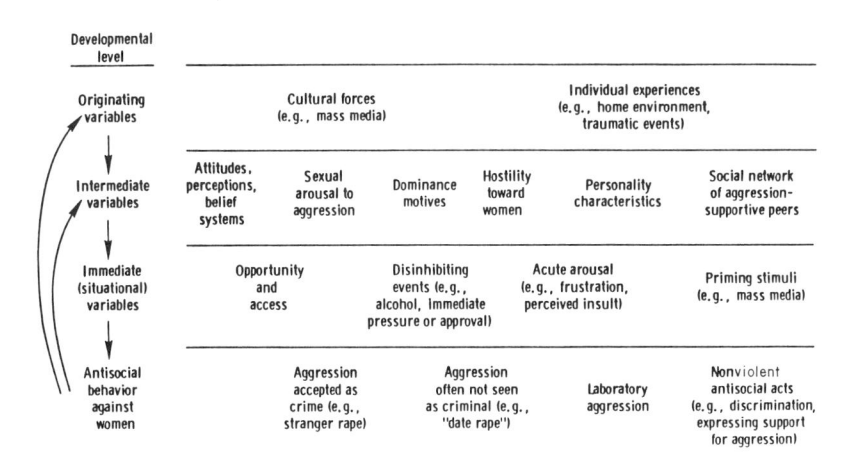

Fig. 1. Hypothesized environmental influences on antisocial behavior against women.

[3] The focus of this model is on the factors that may contribute to the development of antisocial behavior. Obviously, there may be varied factors, including some media portrayals, leading to the development of attributes stimulating prosocial behavior and reducing antisocial responses. Also, this model does not necessarily exclude other possible effects of sexually violent media, some of which may not necessarily be judged harmful by many observers.

long-term influences, the mass media may temporarily increase the recall of (or may "prime") antisocial thoughts, feelings, or behavioral urges that were previously formed (Berkowitz, 1984).

For some individuals, antisocial acts may take the form of violence that comes to the attention of the law, such as "stranger" rape or wife-battering. For others, these same underlying factors may contribute to responses that are not typically prosecuted, but instead are manifested as aggression in dating situations or in laboratory settings, a reported desire to commit acts of sexual violence, sexual harassment, discrimination against women, and/or expressed support for the sexual aggression of others. We are not lumping illegal violence together with all other antisocial behaviors, but we are suggesting, in keeping with feminists' writings (see, e.g., Russell, 1984), that all these behaviors may share some underlying causes, including media influences.

This model indicates possible avenues by which cultural forces such as the media may change a person's intermediate responses and how such changes may ultimately affect his own aggressive behavior under some circumstances. This model also suggests that changes in the thought patterns of some people may affect the aggressive behavior of others. For example, if a person becomes more tolerant of violence against women as a result of media exposure or other factors, he may change his reactions to the sexual aggression of others even if his own aggressive behavior is not altered. His reactions to others' aggression might significantly influence their actions.

This general model does not suppose a linear sequence of events, but a reciprocating system of mutually influencing factors—as indicated by the upward arrows in Fig. 1. For example, mass media portrayals of sexual violence may contribute to attitudes and perceptions, which, in combination with personality characteristics derived from aversive childhood experiences, may result in sexual aggression on a "date." This aggression, especially if unpunished, might produce a further alteration in attitudes and perceptions (including those of self), which could attract the individual to a peer network supportive of sexual aggression. These peers, themselves a product of "originating" and "intermediate" variables, might then provide greater support and approval for further sexual aggression.

I suggest two possible routes culminating in sexual aggression. First, an individual may "progress" through the stages hypothesized to produce sexual violence. Second, mass media stimuli and other cultural influences may impact on individuals not sexually violent themselves, but who nevertheless, because of their thought patterns, support and reinforce sexual violence in others. Such support may manifest itself by blaming a rape victim, supporting another man's aggression in a "locker room" conversation, or even deciding about guilt as a jury member in a rape trial. The idea of such thought patterns encouraging sexual violence is reminiscent of the "cultural climate" concept suggested by Brownmiller (1975). It argues that the media influences that increase cultural supports for sexual aggression need not produce immediate violence to have seriously harmful effects. Of course, the indirect model need not be restricted to sexual aggression but may apply to nonsexual aggression as well. For example, media depictions of violent vigilantes as heroes (e.g., the *Death Wish* series of movies) may contribute to a cultural climate condoning similar behavior in real-world settings.

The indirect effects model provides the basis for this article's twin hypotheses that may be empirically verified or falsified: (1) exposure to some sexually violent media may contribute in some individuals to the development of thought patterns that support aggression against women, and (2) such thought patterns, in combination with other influences and circumstances, may contribute to sexually violent acts in some cases and to other antisocial, but not necessarily violent, responses in others.

B. Hypothesized Processes Affecting Thought Patterns

Obviously, most viewers of media sexual violence distinguish between fantasy and reality and do not necessarily perceive the media as an absolute model for behavior. However, there is considerable research indicating that even when people recognize an event as fictional, for some it can nonetheless affect their perceptions of reality (see, e.g., Carroll, 1978). Such media influences may be more likely when the sexual violence is presented in a positive light or when the audience is sexually aroused by it.

Figure 2 summarizes several possible processes by which media sexual violence might affect thought patterns that facilitate violence against women. These have been adapted from Bandura's (1977, 1986, 1988) description of ways by which normally censured acts become more intellectually and emotionally acceptable. They include the following:

1. Labeling sexual violence more as a sexual rather than a violent act
2. Adding to perceptions that sexual aggression is normative and culturally acceptable
3. Altering perceptions of the consequences of sexual aggression—in particular, minimizing the seriousness of the consequences to the victim and reinforcing the myth that victims derive pleasure from sexual assaults
4. Changing attributions of responsibility to place more blame on the victim
5. Elevating the positive value of sexual aggression by associating it with sexual pleasure and a sense of conquest
6. Reducing negative emotional reactions to sexually aggressive acts.

MEDIA EXPOSURE: Sexual aggression depicted in a "positive" fashion and/or associated with sexual arousal

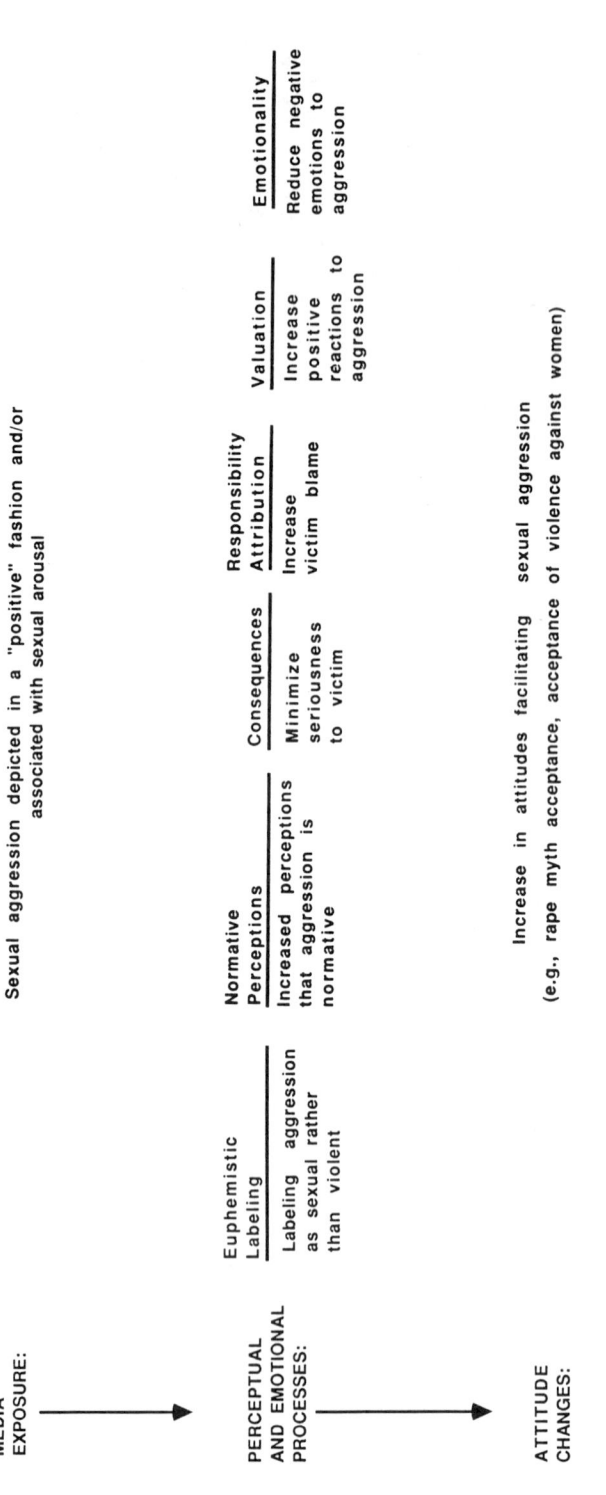

PERCEPTUAL AND EMOTIONAL PROCESSES:

Euphemistic Labeling	Normative Perceptions	Consequences	Responsibility Attribution	Valuation	Emotionality
Labeling aggression as sexual rather than violent	Increased perceptions that aggression is normative	Minimize seriousness to victim	Increase victim blame	Increase positive reactions to aggression	Reduce negative emotions to aggression

ATTITUDE CHANGES: Increase in attitudes facilitating sexual aggression (e.g., rape myth acceptance, acceptance of violence against women)

Fig. 2. Hypothesized processes mediating impact of media sexual violence on attitudes.

Some of the studies discussed later investigate these cognitive and emotional processes.

III. MEDIA CHARACTERISTICS AND DIFFUSION

A. The Anatomy of Media Sexual Violence

A comparison of sexual versus nonsexual media violence helps to isolate the characteristics of sexually violent depictions. Of course, males act against females in the vast majority of sexually aggressive depictions (see, e.g., Smith, 1976a,b; Yang, 1987), whereas the victim is usually male in nonsexual portrayals of violence (Gerbner, 1972). Two other important differences distinguish sexual and nonsexual violence. First, victims of nonsexual aggression are usually shown as outraged by their experience and intent on avoiding victimization. They, and at times the perpetrators of the aggression, suffer from the violence. However, when sexual violence is portrayed, there is frequently the suggestion that, despite initial resistance, the victim secretly desired the abusive treatment and eventually derived pleasure from it. This provides a built-in justification for aggression that would otherwise be considered unjustifiable. Sexual violence is often presented without negative consequences for either the victim or the perpetrator. For example, less than 3% of the rapists in "adult" books surveyed by Smith (1976a,b) suffered negative consequences, and their victims were seldom shown to have regrets about having been raped. Similarly, in a recent content analysis of videos, Palys (1986) found that the majority of sexual aggressors were portrayed in a positive fashion and only seldom did their violence result in negative consequences (see also Yang, 1987).

The second distinction between sexual and nonsexual violence involves the element of sexual arousal. Such arousal in response to sexually violent depictions might result in subliminal conditioning and cognitive changes in the consumer by associating physical pleasure with violence. Therefore, even sexual aggression depicted negatively may have harmful effects because of the sexual arousal induced by the explicitness of the depiction. For example, a person who views a sexually violent scene might feel that the violence is immoral but may nonetheless be sexually aroused by it. Such arousal might motivate him to rationalize the aggression or to minimize its seriousness or its consequences.

Given these issues, particular concern about sexual aggression in the media is not only based on the frequency of sexual as compared to nonsexual violent portrayals. Instead, the positive manner in which sexual violence is portrayed and its potential to positively link or reinforce sex and violence justifies special concern. Nevertheless, it is important to consider the frequency of sexually violent media and the level of exposure to such images.

B. Availability and Frequency of Exposure

1. Availability in Media

Most of the research pertaining to the availability issue has been conducted with media stimuli that are sexually explicit, although there has also been some research on the frequency of sexually aggressive portrayals in the non-sexually explicit media. Content analyses indicate considerable variability of sexual aggression in differing types of sexually explicit media, with "adult" books having about 30% (Smith, 1976a,b), "adult" movies about 10-15% (Palys, 1986; Slade, 1984; Yang, 1987), and "soft core" magazines about 5% (Malamuth & Spinner, 1980; Winick, 1985). In contrast, the levels of sexual aggression have been found to be very high in detective magazines (Dietz & Evans, 1982), but these are typically not sexually explicit (e.g., featuring nudity) portrayals.

Content analyses of daytime "soap operas" have yielded quite different patterns. On the one hand, Lowry, Love, and Kirby (1981) reported that sexual aggression was the second most frequent type of sexual activity, although it was typically implied rather than actually portrayed. On the other hand, Greenberg and D'Alessio (1985) reported that the results of a content analysis of soap operas found that references to rape were not common, occurring about once in every 11 hours of broadcasting. In contrast, the sexual activity most frequently referred to—verbal mention of intercourse—occurred 1.5 times in an hour of soap opera broadcasting. There are many differences between these studies in the time periods, shows analyzed, and the sampling and analysis techniques that could account for the differing conclusions.

Baxter, De Riemer, Landini, Leslie, and Singletary (1985) conducted a content analysis of a random sample of music videos aired on MTV during a week in 1984. They found that the separate portrayals of either violence or depiction of sexual feelings or impulses were very frequent. However, the actual fusion of sex and violence was relatively rare. For example, sadomasochism occurred in 5% of the videos and sexual bondage in 2%.

2. Frequency of Exposure

Demare, Briere, and Lips (1988) surveyed 222 Canadian undergraduate males regarding their exposure to various types of sexually explicit media. Thirty-six percent reported that within the past year they were exposed at least once to sexually violent pornography (which consisted of materials showing a man forcing a woman to perform a sexual act against her will or a rape of a woman). Thirteen percent reported having viewed such materials more than twice within the past year. These data suggest that exposure to some sexually aggressive images is not limited to a very small segment of the population.

Another important question concerns the age of exposure to such materials. Although there is little research specifically on sexually violent media, potentially relevant research suggests that exposure probably occurs quite early. Research focusing on exposure to sexually explicit media per se found that about 20% of males had their first exposure by age 12 (Abelson, Cohen, Heaton, & Suder, 1970). More recently, on the basis of a small national probability sample of Canadians, Check (1985) reported that more than a third of youths between the ages of 12 and 17 years reported viewing sexually explicit films at least once a month. There is no reason to assume that these youths are not exposed to the violent portions contained within the sexually explicit media, as well as within nonexplicit media.

A recent survey of Great Britain assessed, in a representative sample of children and adolescents, the frequency of exposure to video films that are legally classified as obscene in that country (many of these would not receive such a classification in the United States). Because these films are banned in Great Britain, they were not viewed in theaters but in private homes by the use of videos. The investigators report that

> It is a matter of grave concern that in the formative years, 45% of children... have seen one or more video films which would legally be classified as obscene in this country on account of the morbid, sadistic and repugnant nature of the violence they portray. The first knowledge of sexual life acquired by these children may come from viewing films in which sexual conduct is inextricably entwined with violence, hatred, coercion and the humiliation of women in particular. (Roth, 1985, p. 3)

It is important to consider both the actual media frequency of sexually violent materials and their availability to the public, including children. Although there may or may not have been very large increases in the frequency of such media stimuli over the past three decades, new media technologies, such as cable or video recorders, may have led to much wider dissemination in recent years. Unfortunately, there are not any scientific studies (that I am aware of) that examine this possibility.

IV. SEXUALLY VIOLENT MEDIA AND AROUSAL

A. Does Sexual Violence Stimulate Arousal in the Audience?

An issue with important implications for the attraction to and effects of sexually violent media concerns whether such stimuli are likely to be sexually arousing to the consumer. If such materials are particularly arousing sexually to substantial segments of the population, there may be an economic incentive for their continued production. However, if these materials are sexually arousing to only a small fringe element of society, then such an incentive is far less likely. The research described in this section is relevant to this arousal issue, beginning with work that seemed to show that only a small segment of men are aroused by sexual violence.

1. Rape Index

Abel and associates (Abel, Barlow, Blanchard, & Guild, 1977; Abel, Blanchard, & Becker, 1976, 1978; Abel, Blanchard, Becker, & Djenderedjian, 1978) reported that rapists showed relatively high and about equal levels of penile tumescence to audiotapes portraying rape and consenting sexual acts. Although there was some indication that the more violent rapists were more aroused sexually by rape than by consenting scenes (Abel et al., 1977), the conclusion about rapists in general was that they were equally as aroused by rape as by mutually consenting depictions. In contrast to rapists, these studies found that nonrapists showed relatively little sexual arousal to rape depictions.

On the basis of their data, Abel and colleagues (1977) developed the rape index, which is a ratio of sexual arousal to rape portrayals compared with arousal to consenting sex portrayals. With this index, a man whose sexual arousal toward rape is similar to or greater than his arousal to consenting depictions would be considered to have an inclination toward rape. Various investigators have used this measure in the diagnosis and treatment of rapists and have recently extended it to child molesters by contrasting sexual arousal to depictions of child molestation with arousal to consenting-adult depictions (see, e.g., Abel, Becker, Murphy, & Flanagan, 1981; Avery-Clark & Laws, 1984; Quinsey, Chaplin, & Carrigan, 1980). Quinsey and colleagues (1980) provided some support for the predictive validity of this assessment technique by showing that it successfully predicted recidivism of child molesters following discharge from a psychiatric institution.

2. Mass Media and Sexual Violence

As was noted, the development of the rape index was based on findings that nonrapists showed relatively little sexual arousal to rape depictions. However, the information presented earlier in this chapter indicates that some sexually explicit mass media have incorporated, to a certain degree, rape portrayals and other sexually violent images. This suggests that such themes may be sexually arousing to some media consumers, many of whom are not likely to be actual rapists. There would therefore appear to be a conflict between the impressions created by studies of media content versus research using the rape index regarding whether nonrapists are sexually aroused by rape portrayals.

In explanation of these differing impressions, Malamuth and colleagues suggested that the type of sexual violence found in the mass media may differ in content from that used in the research with rapists and that only certain types of rape depictions may be highly arousing to some nonrapists (Malamuth, Heim, & Feshbach, 1980). To assess this possibility empirically, we systematically manipulated the content of rape and consenting depictions presented to college students. These findings and those of subsequent experiments (see, e.g., Malamuth & Check, 1980, 1983) implicated the victim's reactions within rape scenes to be of critical importance: Rape depictions were found to stimulate relatively little sexual arousal when the victim was portrayed as continuously abhorring the assault; when the victim was perceived as becoming involuntarily aroused sexually, on the other hand, sexual arousal to rape was as high, and even tended to be nonsignificantly higher than arousal to consenting depictions (Malamuth & Check, 1983). These data appear to help reconcile the aforementioned conflicting conclusions because both content analytical studies (see, e.g., Smith, 1976b) and somewhat less systematic observations (see, e.g., Brownmiller, 1975) have noted that sexually violent pornography portrayals frequently depict the victim as becoming aroused sexually when assaulted. Of course, the victim's reactions would not be the only content dimension likely to affect the degree of sexual arousal elicited. An example of another dimension likely to have a significant impact is the degree to which extreme, vicious violence (with descriptions of "blood and gore") is included in the content (see also Quinsey & Chaplin, 1984; Quinsey, Chaplin, & Upfold, 1984).

3. Individual Differences

Although manipulations in the content of stimuli yielded information about the type of rape depictions that inhibit the sexual arousal of nonrapists, it is also important to consider the potential mediating role of individual differences among subjects. The classification of subjects into either a rapist or nonrapist grouping may obscure important information. Consideration of individual differences among the nonrapist group seems particularly necessary (although similar analyses examining individual differences among rapists also are needed) in light of the theorizing (see, e.g., Clark & Lewis, 1977; Russell, 1975, 1984) and research (see, e.g., Malamuth, 1981) that suggest that within the unincarcerated male population, there are men with varying degrees of inclinations to aggress against women.

Findings in this area are well illustrated by the data of Malamuth and Check (1983). In a preliminary session, males were administered questionnaires concerning their sexual attitudes and behaviors. One item inquired about the likelihood that the subject himself would rape if he could be assured of not being caught and punished (i.e., the likelihood of raping or LR item). On the basis of this item, 62 subjects were classified as low LR (a rating of 1 = "not at all likely" on the 5-point scale). Forty-two subjects were classified as high LR (a rating of 2 or higher). This distribution is similar to that of earlier studies (Malamuth, 1981; Malamuth, Haber, & Feshbach, 1980; Malamuth & Check, 1980; Tieger, 1981).

Several days later, these subjects listened to one of eight audiotapes of an interaction involving sexual intercourse between a man and a woman. The content of these depictions was systematically manipulated along the dimensions of consent (woman's consent vs nonconsent), pain (woman's pain vs no pain), and outcome (woman's arousal vs disgust).

As is indicated in Fig. 3, the data highlighted the importance of the interaction between individual differences among subjects and variations in the depiction content. The pattern of the data on both self-report and tumescence measures indicated that when the woman was portrayed as experiencing disgust, both low and high LR subjects were less aroused sexually by the nonconsenting as compared with consenting depictions. However, when the woman was perceived as becoming aroused sexually, a very different pattern emerged: Low LR subjects were equally aroused to the consenting and the nonconsenting depictions, whereas high LR subjects showed *greater* arousal to the nonconsenting scenes.

These data suggest that the presence of sexual violence within the mass media may indeed reflect interest among some segments of consumers (see Murphy, Coleman, & Haynes, 1986, for a replication of some of these data with a nonstudent community sample). The findings show that a sizable minority of the population (e.g., high LR subjects) are more aroused by a certain type of rape depiction (i.e., that portraying victim arousal) than by consenting portrayals. It is important to examine the cultural and individual reasons why some men are highly aroused sexually to certain types of rape depictions.

B. The Etiology of Sexual Arousal to Aggression

The etiology of such arousal to aggression might be understood within the framework of theoretical approaches to the causes of rape. There are two general types of theories relevant to this issue. The first emphasizes cultural attitudes, roles, and beliefs that justify sexual coercion (see, e.g., Brownmiller, 1975; Burt, 1978, 1980; Clark & Lewis, 1977; Russell, 1975, 1984). According to this view, our culture's socialization often defined some degree of coercive sexuality as the normal standard, reflecting a "macho" dominant role for men and a submissive role for women. Rape is therefore seen as an extreme point of a continuum of forced sexuality rather than a discrete, deviant act committed by only a few mentally ill men. Sexual arousal in response to aggression, therefore, might be similarly seen as falling along a continuum whereby nonrapists evidence differing levels of similarity to rapists.

WOMAN'S AROUSAL

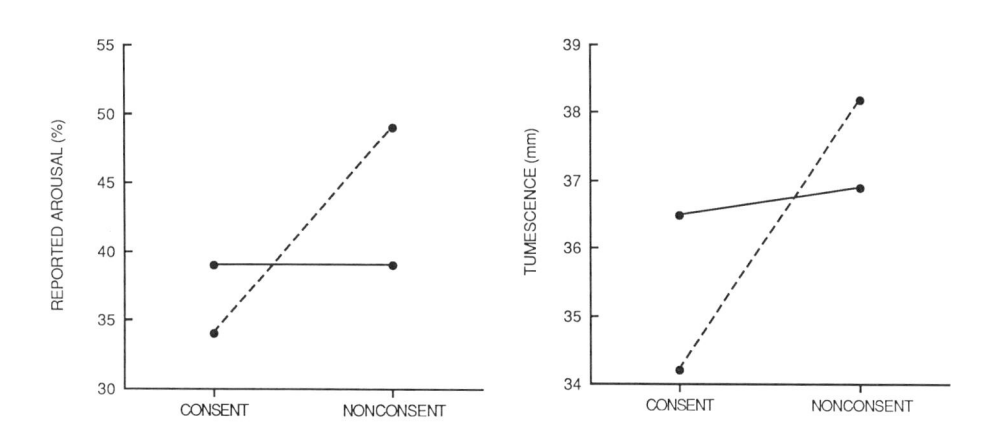

WOMAN'S DISGUST

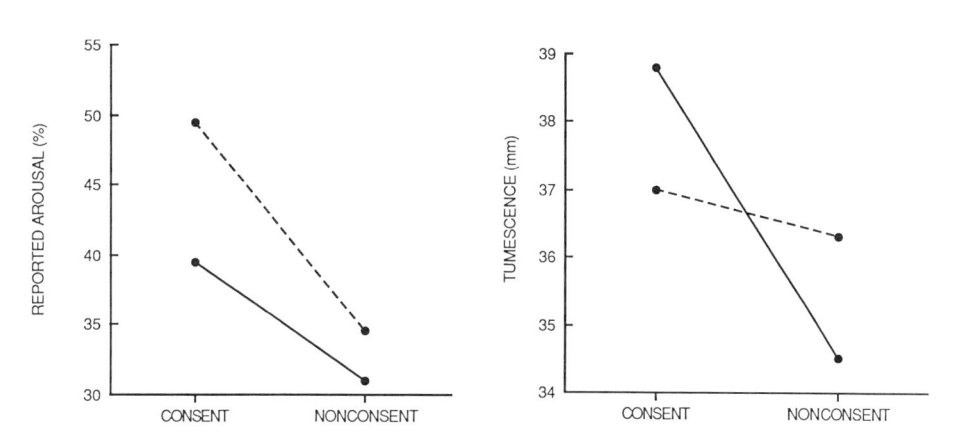

Fig. 3. Penile tumescence and self-reported sexual arousal as a function of depiction of content and subjects' likelihood of raping (LR) classification. Broken line, high LR; solid line, low LR. From Malamuth & Check (1983). Reprinted by permission.

On the basis of such cultural theories, sexual arousal from aggression would be expected to be associated with a general set of beliefs or ideology in which male dominance and female submissiveness are perceived as natural and justified, which adheres to a perception of male–female relationships as fundamentally adversarial and includes attitudes described as "rape supportive" (Burt, 1980). Furthermore, according to this approach, to the extent that arousal from aggression reflects a "macho" orientation, it would be associated with a general acceptance of aggression in nonsexual situations (see, e.g., Sanday, 1981). Lastly, on the basis of the cultural approach, one would expect that sexual arousal from aggression is not an isolated response but is related to other measures of inclinations toward violence against women.

According to the second approach, in contrast, rape is viewed primarily as being sexually motivated. There are several variants to such an approach. According to one, rape is a form of sexual pathology, as presented in some psychoanalytic analyses (see, e.g., Hammer, 1957). Another variant is the contention that rape is motivated by overwhelming sexual impulses (Cohen, Garofalo, Boucher, & Seghorn, 1971). Sociobiological approaches (Shields & Shields, 1983; Thornhill & Thornhill, 1983; Thornhill, Thornhill, & Dizinno, 1986) suggest an additional variant theorizing that men who are unsuccessful in obtaining sexual access to women by other strategies are more likely to use force. What these variants have in common is the prediction that differences in men's inclinations to rape, such as those that may be reflected in sexual arousal from aggression, would be related to differences in sexual factors, such as sexual deprivation, sexual inhibitions, and so on.

In an analysis of a representative sample of tribal societies, Sanday (1981) found evidence consistent with a cultural approach to the etiology of rape. In cultures with higher rates of rape, there was greater acceptance of a social ideology of male dominance over women and of intergroup and interpersonal aggression. In contrast to the predictions of a sexual approach, however, she did not find a relation between indices of sexual repression and cross-cultural differences in rape rates. In our research, similar predictor variables were used within the same culture.

To identify individual differences, Malamuth and colleagues asked subjects to indicate how sexually aroused they thought they would be by forcing a woman to do something against her will (Malamuth, Check, & Briere, 1986). We used the phrase *force* rather than terms such as *violence* or *aggression* because these might provide information only about the more extreme end of the continuum predicted by cultural theories of rape. We later examined whether reported arousal from force was indeed predictive of sexual arousal from rape and from nonsexual aggression. In addition, we analyzed whether differences in sexual arousal to force were associated with four general areas: (1) *ideological attitudes* concerning areas such as adversarial male–female relations, rape, and male dominance; (2) *aggressive attitudes* about interpersonal and international aggression; (3) *sexual responses* such as attitudes, inhibitions, experiences, and knowledge; and (4) *self-ratings* regarding whether the subject himself might engage in sexually aggressive acts, and how attractive he found such acts, as well as his reactions to mutually consenting intercourse.

The results extended the earlier findings showing that aggression may be a sexual stimulant for some individuals from the general population. The data confirmed that men's reported sexual arousal from forcing a woman (assessed in a preliminary session) is predictive of their actual sexual arousal that was assessed in a later session by both self-reports and penile tumescence. More specifically, three subgroups were identified (see Fig. 4): For those who reported no arousal or moderate arousal from force (approximately 70% of the male subjects), the presence of aggression inhibited sexual arousal. In contrast, for those who reported a relatively high level of arousal from force (about 30% of the subjects), aggression was indeed found to enhance sexual arousal, particularly when assessed via penile tumescence.

In examining the correlates of sexual arousal from force, we found that those indicating higher levels of such arousal were more accepting of an ideology that justifies male aggression against and dominance over women, assessed on a variety of scales (see Table I). As further indicated in this table, arousal from force was also found to be associated with greater acceptance of aggression in nonsexual situations. In addition, we found that arousal from

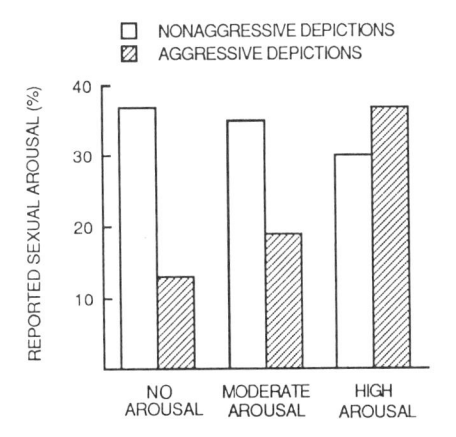

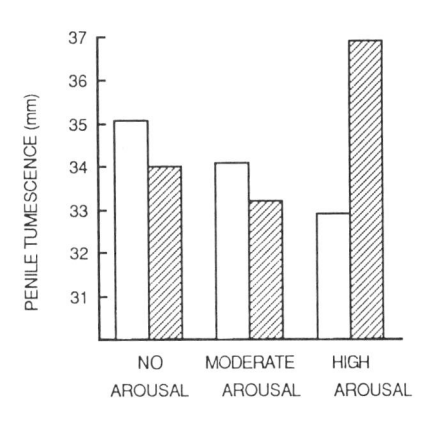

Fig. 4. Reported sexual arousal and penile tumescence as a function of relative arousal from force grouping (no, moderate, and high) and the depictions' aggressiveness (aggressive vs nonaggressive). From Malamuth, Check, & Briere (1986). Reprinted by permission.

TABLE I

Means and Statistical Significance of Ideological, Aggressive, and Sexual Scales and Self-Ratings for Three Levels of Reported Arousal from Force[a]

Scale	Arousal from force (means)			F[b]	p	DFA[c]	Trend[d]
	No	Moderate	High				
Ideological attitudes							
Disbelief of rape claims	12.91ₐ	14.15ₐ	14.10ₐ	3.41	.05	**.37**	linear
Victim responsible for rape	24.15ₐ	25.58ₐ	29.37_b	8.65	.0002	**.64**	linear
Rape reports as manipulation	4.32ₐ	5.08_b	5.26_b	5.84	.003	**.54**	linear
Rape only happens to certain women	2.22	2.46	2.19	1.00	ns	−.01	—
Male dominance is justified	12.75ₐ	14.53_b	15.55_b	9.62	.0001	**.72**	linear
Adversarial sexual beliefs	8.84ₐ	9.55_{a,b}	10.28_b	3.74	.03	**.49**	linear
Women enjoy sexual violence	8.01ₐ	9.16_b	10.58_c	12.58	.0001	**.82**	linear
Acceptance of domestic violence	6.18ₐ	7.00_b	7.20_b	3.45	.03	**.42**	linear
Acceptance of vengeance	2.89	3.20	2.97	1.07	ns	.06	—
Sex for procreation	9.21	8.46	9.00	1.33	**ns**	−.08	—
Sexual conservatism for women	14.65	14.64	15.91	2.49	—	.28	—
Stronger male sex drives	6.29	6.22	6.61	0.78	—	.14	—
Sex and menstruation	4.68	4.46	4.59	0.55	ns	.07	—
Stereotyped roles for women in relationships	15.97ₐ	16.68ₐ	19.13_b	7.34	.001	**.57**	linear
Rules regarding traditional male and female behavior	11.73ₐ	12.86ₐ	13.27ₐ	3.05	.05	**.40**	linear

Aggressive attitudes						
Support for personal and institutional aggression	23.04 ₐ	24.55 ᵦ	26.22 ᵦ	9.02	.0002	**.83** linear
Opposition to hunting and use of guns by public	11.13	10.20	10.17	1.74	ns	.34 —
Physical punishment for children	3.71	4.03	3.91	1.19	ns	.22 —
Support for use of nuclear weapons	1.79 ₐ	2.27 ₐ,ᵦ	2.62 ᵦ	5.72	.004	**.66** linear
Sexual responses						
Sexual permissiveness	0.00	−0.47	0.40	0.56	ns	—
Acceptance of masturbation	0.11	0.02	−0.01	0.05	ns	—
Sex inhibited by contraception problems	−0.34	0.10	0.30	2.54	.08	—
Acceptance of explicit sexual materials	−0.04	−0.32	0.47	1.42	ns	—
Sexual experience and knowledge	−0.14	0.08	0.13	0.33	ns	—
Importance of sex	−0.04	−0.22	0.11	1.01	ns	—
Sex inhibited by disapproval	−0.16	0.03	0.12	0.48	ns	—
Sex inhibited by fear	−0.14	−0.01	0.19	1.49	ns	—
Adequacy of sexual knowledge	0.08	0.01	−0.12	0.86	ns	—
Self-ratings						
Idea of rape is attractive	1.05 ₐ	1.36 ᵦ,꜀	1.52 ꜀	12.72	.0001	.28 linear
Idea of forcing a woman is attractive	1.08 ₐ	1.67 ᵦ	2.24 ꜀	75.55	.0001	**.71** linear
Likelihood of raping	1.06 ₐ	1.51 ᵦ	2.07 ꜀	30.58	.0001	**.45** linear
Likelihood of forcing	1.14 ₐ	2.13 ᵦ	3.19 ꜀	115.14	.0001	**.87** linear
Idea of intercourse is attractive	3.29	3.14	3.00	1.41	ns	−.10 —
Own arousal to sexual intercourse	75.25	77.17	72.68	0.043	ns	−.03 —

[a] Means not sharing a common subscript are different at $p < .05$ by Scheffé test. From Malamuth, Check, & Briere (1986).
[b] Degrees of freedom for the F tests ranged from 2300 to 2356. Differences were due to some subjects' not answering individual questions.
[c] Discriminant function analysis structure coefficients, considered meaningful (italicized) at $|c| \geq .35$.
[d] Trends significant at $p < .05$.

force related to attraction to sexually coercive acts and the belief that subjects themselves might actually engage in such acts in the future. In contrast, arousal from force did not relate to noncoercive sexual responses, including attitudes, inhibitions, or sexual experience and knowledge; it was also not related to subjects' self-ratings regarding attractions, intentions, and reactions to mutually consenting intercourse. However, it should be noted that the assessment of sexual responses was based on subjects' self-perceptions that may not adequately enable assessing variables such as unconscious sexual conflicts. [The reader is referred to Malamuth *et al.* (1986) for a more detailed description of the instruments and procedures used.]

These data are consistent with those of Briere and Malamuth (1983), who found that self-reported likelihood of sexual aggression was related to rape-supportive attitudes but not to variables reflecting sexual drive or sexual inhibitions. The findings are also consistent with Sanday's (1981) analysis of tribal societies in implicating ideological and aggressive variables but not sexual variables as linked to aggression against women (although she examined rape rates, whereas we focused on sexual arousal in response to coercion).

On the whole, the data are supportive of theoretical approaches, such as a feminist one (see, e.g., Brownmiller, 1975), that implicate cultural attitudes and roles as causes of aggression against women, but they are not supportive of theoretical approaches that implicate sexual causes. On the basis of the correlation between ideological beliefs and sexual arousal from force, we may speculate about one possible etiology of such arousal. In adolescence, when many youth experience their first sexual fantasies and activities, individuals who are more accepting of an adversarial ideology, especially in male–female relationships, may be more likely to experience sexual arousal in the context of aggressive and adversarial relations. For example, a man who believes that women must be coerced into sexual acts and/or who perceives social relations generally as adversarial, may experience sexual arousal and pleasure while engaging in an act of real or imagined aggression or dominance. Through the frequent pairing of sexual arousal with aggressive acts and feelings, the person may experience conditioning of arousal in response to sexual aggression and, by extension, to aggressive behavior.

C. Does Media Exposure Change Sexual Responsiveness?

Is there actual empirical evidence that exposure to the fusion of sexual and aggressive images in media materials produce conditioning of sexual arousal? I am not aware of any scientific evidence showing that exposure to violent pornography or similar materials produces sustained changes in people's sexual responsiveness to such stimuli. Only one study I know of directly addressed whether repeated exposure to sexually violent media changes people's arousal by such stimuli (Ceniti & Malamuth, 1984). Because of ethical barriers against exposing minors to pornography, the research was conducted solely with adults even though they are probably not the optimal subjects. Because first experiences with pornography usually take place in adolescence (see earlier discussion), and because sexual arousal patterns are probably established prior to adulthood, media exposures that may have profound effects in childhood may not have comparable effects during adulthood.

Ceniti and Malamuth (1984) classified 69 adult males into force-oriented, non-force-oriented, and unclassifiable categories, based on their penile tumescence when presented with portrayals of rape and consensual sex during a preexposure session. Those classified as force oriented had shown relatively high levels of sexual arousal to rape depictions. Those classified as non-force-oriented had shown relatively little arousal to rape depictions, but they had become aroused to consensual sex portrayals. Subjects labeled as unclassifiable had shown little arousal to either type of depiction. Following this classification, subjects were randomly assigned to one of three exposure groups: sexually violent, sexually nonviolent, or control. Those assigned to the sexually violent condition were exposed to 10 sexually violent stimuli (including feature-length films, and written and pictorial depictions) over a period of 4 weeks. Subjects in the sexually nonviolent condition were exposed to 10 presentations of sexually nonviolent activities only. Subjects in the control condition were not exposed to any stimuli. Soon after their exposure, subjects returned to the laboratory and were presented with depictions similar in theme to the preexposure session. Penile tumescence and self-reported sexual arousal were measured again.

Force-oriented subjects, whether exposed to sexually violent or nonviolent media, became *less* aroused to the rape depictions in the postexposure session than those in the control condition. They also tended to be less aroused by the postexposure nonviolent depictions, although this effect was considerably less pronounced. Both non-force-oriented and unclassifiable subjects, however, showed no significant effects of exposure. The reduced arousal of force-oriented subjects appears similar to the temporary habituation effects frequently found in studies using nonviolent sexual material (see, e.g., Mann, Berkowitz, Sidman, Starr, & West, 1974; Zillmann & Bryant, 1984).

Although the research data have not shown evidence of increased sexual arousal to aggression as a result of repeated exposure to sexually aggressive media depictions, the research described in the next section provides some support for the indirect-effects model's two interrelated hypotheses that exposure to media depictions can help form thought patterns supportive of real-life sexual aggression, and that such patterns may in turn contribute to actual antisocial behavior, including aggression against women.

V. MEDIA EXPOSURE, THOUGHT PATTERNS, AND ANTISOCIAL BEHAVIOR

A. From Media Exposure to Thought Patterns

1. Survey Data

Several studies assessed the correlation between degree of men's exposure to sexually explicit media and their reactions to violence against women. Such correlational studies can only reveal associations between the amount of media people reported consuming and their cognitions. They cannot indicate whether these media were responsible for their thoughts. Unfortunately, these studies did not distinguish between sexually violent and sexually nonviolent media. Had they focused specifically on sexually violent media rather than sexually explicit media in general, it is likely that the links to thought patterns condoning aggression would have emerged as strongly, if not more strongly.

In most studies, higher levels of reported exposure to sexually explicit media correlated with reactions more supportive of violence against women. For example, in a sample of college men, Malamuth and Check (1985a) found that higher readership of sexually explicit magazines was correlated with more beliefs that women enjoyed forced sex. Similar associations were found by Koss and Dinero (1988) with a national sample of university students. Further, among a diverse sample of Canadian men, Check (1984) found that more exposure to sexually explicit media was correlated with higher acceptance of rape myths, of violence against women, and of general sexual callousness. Briere, Corne, Runtz, and Malamuth (1984) reported similar correlations in a sample of college males. However, Demare *et al.* (1988) did not find significant associations between attitudes supporting violence against women and amount of exposure either to nonviolent or to violent sexually explicit media. These investigators did find that the latter, but not the former, was significantly associated with men's reports that there was a likelihood they would commit sexual aggression if they could be assured that they would not be punished for such acts (for a description of this measure, see Malamuth, 1981, 1984).

On the other hand, Malamuth (1988c) did not find a statistically significant correlation between levels of exposure to sexually explicit media and attitudes concerning violence against women. However, additional analyses yielded interesting findings. That study asked subjects to indicate how much information about sexuality they obtained in their childhood from various sources, such as peers, parents, church, educational media, educational courses, sexually explicit media, and doctors. Sexually explicit media emerged as the second most important source of information, second only to peers. Subjects who reported obtaining more information from explicit media also held attitudes more supportive of violence against women. Such a correlation was not found with the other sources of information about sexuality. Information from some, such as educational courses, actually correlated with lower levels of attitudes supportive of violence against women. In fact, sexually explicit media's link to antisocial attitudes tended to be stronger when compared to other sources of sexual information than when measured alone; in other words, such media's "predictive" power was unaffected or actually increased when other variables were controlled for.

Focusing only on quantity of exposure, therefore, may be an oversimplified approach. Sexually explicit media's degree of influence on a person may largely depend on how that exposure interacts with other influences. People raised with little education about sexuality, or in families where sex was treated as "taboo," may be more susceptible to the influences of explicit media than those reared with considerable education about sex (Malamuth, 1978; Malamuth & Billings, 1985). It makes sense that those with other sources of sex information can more accurately assess the myths about women and sexuality portrayed in some pornography. However, those without much sex education might be more apt to use explicit media as a primary source of information.

2. *Experimental Research*

A growing body of experimental research complements the survey data. The following studies have shown connections between sexually violent media and thought patterns supportive of sexual aggression, but they have not revealed similar relations with equally explicit, nonviolent stimuli that portrayed both sexes in equal power roles. Here, it is possible to consider a causal link because other factors have been controlled. Still, caution must be exercised in generalizing findings from controlled situations to naturally occurring settings.

Research has examined the impact of positive versus negative rape portrayals in two ways. One series of studies assessed how either victim arousal or abhorrence at the end of a rape depiction changed the way in which the assault was perceived when the rape itself remained identical in the two versions. When the rape victim became aroused, male subjects labeled the assault more as a sexual act. They also perceived greater justification for it, reported a greater likelihood that they and other men would commit such an act, and saw the victim as more responsible for what had occurred (Donnerstein, 1984; Rapaport, 1984). These effects have been particularly pronounced for more sexually aggressive men.

These experiments show that changing the outcome of a rape affects the way it is perceived. They do not show that these perceptions carry over to perceptions of rape in general. In another series of studies, the carryover effects of perceptions of and attitudes toward rape were directly examined. These studies assessed whether rapes depicting victim arousal changed subjects' perceptions of other rapes, altered their beliefs about women's reactions to sexual assaults, and increased their acceptance of violence against women.

In two experiments, male subjects were either exposed to depictions of mutually consenting sex, rape in which the female victim eventually became aroused, or rape abhorred by the victim. Afterward, the subjects were shown a rape depiction and asked about their perceptions of the act and the victim. In one of these studies, those subjects exposed to the "positive" rape portrayal perceived the second rape as less negative than those first exposed to the other depiction (Malamuth & Check, 1980). It also found some indication that exposure to rape depicting victim arousal may have led men to perceive rape as a more normative act (Malamuth & Check, 1980). Subjects in the second experiment were asked how women in general would react to being victimized by sexual violence (Malamuth & Check, 1985a). Those exposed to a positive rape portrayal believed that a higher percentage of women would derive pleasure from being sexually assaulted. This effect of the portrayal was particularly apparent in men with higher inclinations to aggress against women.

A third experiment conducted outside the laboratory yielded similar results (Malamuth & Check, 1981). Male and female undergraduates were randomly assigned to one of two exposure conditions. Participants in the experimental condition were given free tickets to view feature-length films on two different evenings that included portrayals of women as victims of aggression in sexual and nonsexual scenes. These films suggested that the aggression was justified and/or had positive consequences. On the same evenings, subjects in the control condition were given tickets to other films that did not contain any sexual violence. The movies shown in both exposure conditions have been aired with some editing on national television. Subjects viewed these films with moviegoers who purchased tickets and were not part of the research. Classmates of the recruited subjects who did not see the films were also studied as an "untreated" control group. Several days after the films were viewed, a "Sexual Attitude Survey" was administered to the entire class. (Subjects were not aware of the relationship between this survey—purportedly administered by a polling agency—and the earlier movies some students had seen as part of an ostensibly unrelated study.)

Subject responses were assessed by scales developed by Burt (1980). They included Acceptance of Interpersonal Violence (AIV) against women (e.g., acceptance of sexual aggression and wife battering), Rape Myth Acceptance (RMA) (e.g., the belief that women secretly desire to be raped), and Adversarial Sexual Beliefs (ASB) (e.g., the notion that women are sly and manipulating when out to attract a man). These measures were embedded within many irrelevant items intended to disguise the purpose of the survey.

As is shown in Fig. 5, exposure to the films portraying positive effects significantly increased the scores of male but not female subjects on the AIV scale.[4] A similar pattern was observed on the RMA scale, although the effect only approached acceptable levels of statistical significance. The ASB scores were not at all affected. Taken together, the data demonstrated effects of sexually violent movies on men's acceptance of violence against women that were sustained for at least a few days. Moreover, the results were obtained in a nonlaboratory setting seemingly devoid of "demand characteristics" (i.e., researchers' subtly conveying their hypotheses to subjects). Demare (1985) replicated these results using very similar procedures. Unfortunately, however, there are no longitudinal data available that might enable the study of potential effects of sexually violent media on attitudes over relatively long periods of time.

An earlier experiment by Malamuth, Reisen, and Spinner (1979) found no changes in thought patterns following exposure to media sexual violence that did not depict victim arousal. In the experiments showing significant media effects, the stimuli were specifically selected because they clearly depicted violence against women as having positive consequences. These findings suggest that certain antisocial effects may be limited to media stimuli depicting positive consequences of sexual aggression.

Still, sexually violent films that do not portray positive consequences may nonetheless affect consumers in undesirable ways. For example, Linz (1985) studied the effects of repeated exposure to X- and R-rated feature-length films

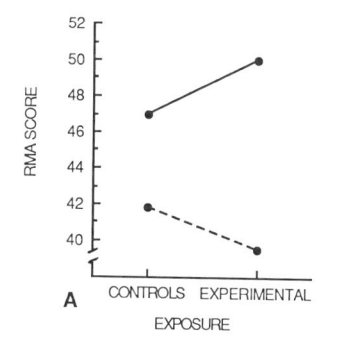

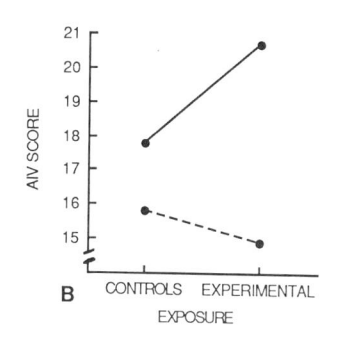

Fig. 5. Rape Myth Acceptance scores (A) and Acceptance of Interpersonal Violence scores (B) as a function of exposure and gender. Solid line, males; broken line, females. From Malamuth & Check (1981). Reprinted by permission.

---

[4]Some might argue that the use of college students in these and similar studies limits the ability to generalize from the findings. That implies that college students are more susceptible to media influences than noncollege students or younger people. In fact, less educated and younger groups might be more susceptible to such influences.

portraying sexual violence with primarily negative consequences to victims. He found that these movies had desensitizing effects on viewers. In one experiment, male college students who viewed five such movies had fewer negative emotional reactions to such films. There was even a tendency for the subjects' "desensitization" to carry over to their judgments of a rape victim in a simulated trial presented following their exposure to the films. In a second experiment, Linz again found that males exposed to several R-rated, sexually violent films became less sympathetic to a rape victim in a simulated trial and were less able to empathize with rape victims in general.

It is important to keep in perspective the nature of the effects that have been found for sexually violent media. These effects have not been the wide, sweeping changes that some seem to assume. It would be unparalleled in media research if they were. Given the type and duration of exposures involved and the fact that subjects are adults with relatively established thought patterns, the most that can be expected (if effects exist) is that they would be detected only with very careful and precise assessment that is specifically geared to the manipulations used. The effects found following brief laboratory exposure (Malamuth & Check, 1985a) were based on the concept of temporarily priming (Wyer & Srull, 1981) previously formed cognitions and attitudes.

The study that has shown changes that persisted over a period of days (Malamuth & Check, 1981) used two unedited feature-length films that suggested that violence against women was justified or led to positive consequences. As noted, significant effects were found on one of three scales and a marginal effect was found on another scale. Also, a relatively large sample was used (over 50 subjects in each condition), creating considerable power to detect any effects.

The foregoing is particularly relevant to a recent study ostensibly attempting to replicate the effects reported here. Fisher and Grenier (1987; reported in Fisher & Barack, 1988) edited 5 minutes of videotapes to create four types: neutral, erotic nonviolent, a rape in which the victim seemed to enjoy her plight, and a rape abhorrence condition. Male subjects were exposed to one of these versions. Then the subjects were given several multidimensional scales, including the Attitudes Toward Women Scale (ATWS; Spence & Helmreich, 1972), the Acceptance of Women as Managers Scale (AWMS; Peters, Terborg, & Taynor, 1974), and the AIV and RMA scales (Burt, 1980). The authors report that no significant effects were found as a function of the exposure manipulation.

In my opinion, this research hardly constitutes an "attempted replication."

Let us imagine that an effect had been found as a result of this brief exposure, as measured by the multidimensional ATWS or AWMS. How credible would it be that a 5-minute exposure (with the manipulation in the rape victim's reactions probably lasting less than a minute) produced fundamental changes in the way men view women or their beliefs about the role of women as business managers? It is difficult to conceive of any brief exposure that would have such effects. The only scale (as distinguished from key individual items) that has been found significantly to show effects in our previous research is the brief AIV scale (Malamuth & Check, 1981) that measures relatively few dimensions (Briere, Malamuth, & Check, 1985). This scale's content is closely linked to the content of the two feature-length films used by Malamuth and Check (1981). Although Fisher and Grenier (1988) also used the AIV scale, it appears to have been presented after the other two lengthy multidimensional scales inquiring about women's roles. Even if their brief exposure might have had some effect on the AIV scale, it is difficult to know what impact there may have been due to presenting it following the other scales.

There is no question that it is essential for other investigators to attempt to replicate the types of effects reported here. It is necessary, however, that they create comparable conditions that maximize the opportunity of detecting any effects that might exist. The research of Fisher and Grenier (1988) has, quite to the contrary, created a set of conditions that made it extremely unlikely that any significant effects would be found.

B. From Thought Patterns to Antisocial Behavior

1. *Hypothesized Connections*

Although psychologists have demonstrated that there is seldom a strong, direct link between thought patterns, such as attitudes, and behavior (Ajzen & Fishbein, 1977), several researchers have contended that beliefs and attitudes accepting or justifying sexual aggression are an important cause of aggression against women (see, e.g., Brownmiller, 1975; Russell, 1984). Burt has presented the most influential theoretical perspective in this area (1978, 1980, 1983). She contends that a cultural matrix that encourages rigid sex roles and supports male dominance over females generates attitudes supportive of rape. These attitudes act as "psychological releasers or neutralizers, allowing potential rapists to turn off social prohibitions against injuring or using others" (1978, p. 282). To assess such attitudes and beliefs, Burt (1980) developed the scales used in the experiments described earlier, including the AIV, RMA, and ASB.

It is ethically impossible to test in a completely satisfactory way the proposition that certain thought patterns contribute causally to the occurrence of rape and other forms of serious sexual aggression. To do so would require some experimental manipulation that would intentionally increase such thought patterns, particularly in those most likely to commit sexual aggression.

By observing whether those exposed to such a manipulation were more sexually aggressive than a comparable control group, the researcher would be able to establish with confidence whether a cause and effect relationship existed. Particularly useful for the focus of the present article would be a manipulation whereby exposure to sexually violent media was used to determine whether it resulted in changed thought patterns, and then to observe whether these led to aggression. It would be unconscionable to conduct such research if the experimenter believed that there was a reasonable likelihood that the manipulation might increase aggression outside the laboratory. In fact, the studies described earlier, which examined the effects of exposure to sexually aggressive media on thought patterns, employed countereducation debriefings soon after exposure. Typically, such debriefings are now required by ethics committees that grant permission to conduct this type of research. In some research, there was also exclusion of a substantial percentage of subjects judged most likely to be adversely affected by the exposure (see, e.g., Linz, 1985). Assessments of the effectiveness of these debriefings in reducing acceptance of violence against women and similar thought patterns has been indicated in several studies (Check & Malamuth, 1984; Donnerstein & Berkowitz, 1981; Linz, 1985; Malamuth & Check, 1984).

Because it is neither feasible nor conscionable to conduct the ideal design, research relevant to the connection between thought patterns and sexual aggression can only provide suggestive data. Before turning to such research, it is instructive to consider the conclusions of a wide range of studies in other areas that have examined the connection between thought patterns, such as attitudes, and behavior. In reviewing this general area, Zanna and Fazio (1982) characterized the historical development of research on attitudes and behavior as consisting of three generations of research. In the first, researchers were concerned with demonstrating whether attitudes affected behavior. Zanna and Fazio feel that this question has been settled and that research has moved to the second and third generations by asking "when" and "how" do such effects take place. Another investigator (Ajzen, 1982) has pointed out that research that failed to show connections between attitudes and behavior typically studied global rather than specific attitudes. "Global attitudes toward an object . . . are of little value if we are interested in predicting a particular action with respect to the object. To predict a single behavior we have to assess the person's attitude toward the behavior in question" (Ajzen, 1982, p. 13).

Although the general literature on the relationship between attitudes and behavior strongly implicates a causal connection, it is obviously important to qualify that by the nature of the behavior in question. Behavior that is condemned in the culture is probably less likely to be strongly connected with thought patterns than a behavior that is supported by the culture. This is because the expression of antisocial behavior is likely to be inhibited by potential social sanctions. As Hearold (1986) suggests, this may partly explain the findings of her meta-analysis on the effects of television on social behavior, in which she found significant effects on both antisocial and prosocial behaviors, but with the latter averaging about twice as high as the former.

In connection with this distinction, I would like to stress an aspect of the model described earlier. Although it may indeed be the case that the expression of serious aggressive behavior will be inhibited in most individuals with thought patterns that facilitate such behavior, some other less socially prohibited behaviors may nonetheless be affected. I disagree, therefore, with the statements by reviewers such as Sears, Freedman, and Peplau (1985), who appear to accept the validity of the findings that thought patterns are affected, but who write that "The key, though, is whether or not violent pornography increases behavioral aggression" (p. 294). Although the possibility that in some individuals aggressive behavior may be affected by changed thought patterns is indeed an important aspect of the issue, it is not the "key." After examining research relevant to the aggressive behavior question, I discuss more fully the potential for effects on nonviolent behaviors.

Studies by my colleagues and I provide some support for the perspective that thought patterns relate to inclinations to aggress against women. They show a significant relationship between Burt's rape-condoning attitude and belief scales and men's self-reported likelihood of engaging in a wide range of violence against women as long as the men suffered no negative consequences (see, e.g., Briere & Malamuth, 1983; Malamuth, 1981, 1984). However, some commentators have contended that the linkage between thought patterns and actual aggressive behavior is assumed too facilely in such studies (see, e.g., Vance, 1985).[5] Fortunately, several studies have recently examined this connection and have found consistently that the attitude and belief scales can predict actual aggressive behavior. This, of course, does not mean that everyone with attitudes condoning aggression will act on them, nor do these studies establish a causal connection.

2. Laboratory Aggression

Malamuth (1983) tested whether men's thought patterns could predict their aggressive behavior in a laboratory setting. He also examined whether men's arousal to rape depictions, as compared to their arousal to consensual sex depictions, predicted laboratory aggression.

About a week after both thought patterns (on the AIV and RMA scales) and sexual arousal to rape were measured, subjects participated in what they

[5] It has been recently demonstrated that using information from both men's reported likelihood of forcing sex (if they could avoid negative consequences) and their actual sexually aggressive behavior is a more comprehensive approach than using either dimension alone (Malamuth, 1988a).

believed was a totally unrelated "extrasensory perception" experiment. In that session, they were angered by a female aide of the experimenter, who pretended to be another subject. Later in the session, subjects could vent their aggression against her by administering unpleasant noise as punishment for her incorrect responses. They were told that punishment was thought to impede rather than aid extrasensory transmission, but they were given the option of trying it out. Subjects were also asked how much they wanted to hurt their cosubject with the noise. Men with beliefs and attitudes more supportive of aggression and with higher levels of sexual arousal to rape were more aggressive against the woman and wanted to hurt her to a greater extent.

Malamuth and Check (1982) successfully replicated these results in a similar experiment that did not consider the subjects' arousal to rape but did assess thought patterns. Later, Malamuth (1988b) examined the extent to which several measures related to real-world violence against women (including thought patterns) predicted laboratory aggression against both female and male targets. As expected, significant relationships were found for female targets only. Taken together, these three experiments consistently showed that thought patterns supportive of aggression against women related to objectively observable behavior—laboratory aggression against women.

Although such laboratory assessments of aggression have the advantage of being an objective measurement not relying on subjects' self-reports, they have the disadvantage of using a setting that some researchers argue is artificial and lacking in ecological validity (see, e.g., Kaplan, 1983). The case for linking thought patterns with actual aggressive behavior is strengthened by studies that have measured naturally occurring behavior.

3. Aggression in Naturalistic Settings

These studies have used samples of men from the general population as well as convicted rapists. The importance of thought patterns such as attitudes toward violence is confirmed by the data showing that men's aggressiveness against women is linked with their own attitudes as well as those of their peers.

Ageton (1983) gauged the extent to which a variety of measures predicted levels of sexual aggression. Subjects, 11–17 years old, drawn from a representative national sample, were interviewed in several consecutive years in the late 1970s. The sexual aggression focus was added to a study primarily designed to focus on other issues (see, e.g., Elliott, Huizinga, & Ageton, 1985), creating some limitations in the extent to which longitudinal predictions concerning sexual aggression could be properly assessed. However, the study's design allowed the predictor measures (e.g., attitudes, involvement with peers, etc.) to be obtained before the occurrence of sexual aggression, which was assessed by self-reports.

Analyses were conducted by identifying "offenders" and comparing them to a matched control group on a variety of measures. The results showed that a variety of variables discriminated between the two groups, but in a discriminant analysis (conducted in a manner similar to stepwise regression), it was found that involvement with delinquent peers at a young age was the best single predictor of sexual aggression later in life. Personal attitudes toward sexual assault was another of the factors found to differentiate significantly between those who became sexually aggressive and those who did not. However, the contribution of the attitude factor was small after the role of involvement with delinquent peers was considered. These data were interpreted by Ageton to show that the same factors predicting general delinquency (i.e., peer influences) also predict sexual aggression.

Although Ageton's research has made an important contribution by virtue of being the first (and to date the only) longitudinal study of sexual aggression, at least a couple of limitations should be noted. First, Ageton did not specifically assess acceptance of sexual aggression or attitudes regarding violence against women. According to our research and that of others (Demare *et al.*, 1988), these attitudes are most likely to be associated with sexually aggressive behavior rather than the type of attitudes assigned by Ageton (i.e., sex-role stereotyping, beliefs in rape myths, and attitudes about aggression in general).

Second, the definition of sexual aggression used by Ageton to classify offenders versus nonoffenders was very encompassing. It included "all forced sexual behavior involving contact with the sexual parts of the body" including rape, incest, sodomy, forced fondling, and attempted sexual coercion where the force component was as mild as verbal pressure or as severe as a physical beating or injury from a weapon. Although we believe that it was appropriate to consider the range of behaviors Ageton studied within the general rubric of sexual aggression, it seems inappropriate to group together such diverse acts. Considerable research has indicated some important distinctions between differing gradations of sexual aggression (see, e.g., Koss, Leonard, Beezley, & Oros, 1985; Malamuth, 1988a). Indeed, the majority of the offenders in Ageton's sample indicated that the highest level of sexual aggression in which they had engaged consisted of pressuring someone to do more sexually than they wanted to do. The author refers to this as "date rape," a term that she uses to include behaviors that are clearly not legally defined as rape (because there may not have been any sexual intercourse and because in a high proportion of the cases, the pressure did not have the intended results).

Ageton's findings regarding the role of peers are certainly consistent with other research indicating that there are some general factors that affect a variety of antisocial behaviors. However, it would seem inappropriate to conclude on the basis of that research that peer influences are the only important factors here. It may have been particularly difficult in that study to disentangle highly interrelated factors. For example, one's attitudes are likely to form part of a constellation of factors, including a person's choice of friends. Research by Hepburn (1977) suggests that having attitudes supportive of delinquent acts may contribute to the selection of delinquent associates, although a bidirectional process is obviously likely.

In a cross-sectional study, Alder (1985) used a subsample from a larger representative sample of men from a particular county in Oregon to assess variables potentially predictive of sexual aggression. These included family background, social class, educational attainment, war experience, peer behavior, and personal attitudes toward sexual aggression. The findings suggested that the most important factor relating to sexual aggression was having sexually aggressive friends. The other two factors found likely to contribute to sexual aggression were attitudes legitimizing such aggression and military service in the Vietnam war.

Several studies using samples of college men also reported significant links between attitudes and actual sexual aggressiveness (Briere *et al.*, 1984; Koss *et al.*, 1985; Mosher & Anderson, 1986; Rapaport & Burkhart, 1984). These studies measured self-reported sexual aggression on a continuum of behaviors ranging from psychological pressure on women to rape. Similar results were reported by Kanin (1985), who compared the attitudes of 71 university students who admitted committing rape with a control group of nonaggressive college males. He found that a much higher percentage of rapists justified rape in general than did control subjects. Moreover, he found that rapists were far more likely to believe their reputations would be enhanced among their peers by sexually aggressive behavior toward women, particularly those perceived as "pick-ups," "loose," "teasers," or "economic exploiters."

Using a sample of 155 men, Malamuth (1986) divided the variables that might contribute to sexual aggression into three classes: (1) Motivation for sexual aggression included sexual arousal to aggression (measured by penile tumescence), hostility toward women, and dominance as a motive for sex; (2) disinhibition to commit sexual aggression included attitudes supporting aggression and antisocial personality characteristics, measured by Eysenck's psychoticism scale; and (3) opportunity to aggress sexually was assessed by sexual experience. These predictors were then correlated with self-reports of sexual aggression. Data were available for 95 subjects on all of the six predictors, and for 155 on all of the measures except penile tumescence (60 subjects did not wish to participate in that type of assessment).

Three interrelated questions were addressed by Malamuth:

1. Would the predictor factors relate significantly to reported sexual aggression?

All the predictors except psychoticism were significantly related to naturalistic aggression, with psychoticism showing a marginally significant relationship.

2. Would the factors provide "redundant prediction" or would a combination of factors predict better than each alone?

The predictors did not, on the whole, provide "redundant information," in that a combination of them was superior to any individual ones for predicting levels of sexual aggressiveness. With all of the six predictors "force" entered into the equation, four made significant unique contributions (tumescence rape index, HTW, AIV, and sexual experience).

3. If a combination of factors were superior, would an additive or an interactive combination yield the best prediction?

Regression equations containing interactive effects accounted for a significantly greater percentage of the variance (45% of all 155 subjects and 75% for the 95 subjects) than equations containing additive effects only (30% and 45%, respectively) (see Table II).

To illustrate and further examine the data, the following analysis was performed: For each predictor, a relatively high score was defined as above the median of its distribution. Subjects were then divided according to the number of predictors for which they scored either *high* or *low*. This approach is analogous to classifying a characteristic as present or not by defining presence as a relatively high score. A person scoring above the median on all the variables would be considered as possessing all the characteristics. In keeping with the regression results, for the 155 subjects, the dominance, HTW, AIV, psychoticism, and the sexual experience predictors were used for this classification, whereas for the 95 subjects, these variables, as well as the tumescence rape index, were used.

Figure 6 shows the average level of sexual aggression according to this classification scheme, with the top graph showing the results for the entire sample of 155 subjects and the bottom graph for the 95 participants for whom data were also available on penile tumescence. In both instances, analyses of variance on these data yielded highly significant effects ($p < .0001$).

The data pattern appeared to show a synergistic process whereby the combined action of several variables yielded considerably higher levels of sexual aggression than would be expected by the additive combination of them.

Malamuth and Check (1985b) attempted a partial replication of these findings. They administered to 297 males the same measures used by Malamuth

TABLE II

Multiple Regression Analyses on Sexual Aggression with Tumescence Index ($n = 95$)[a]

Predictor	Data from analysis accounting for additive combinations of factors only Beta[b]	sr[2c]	Data from analysis including factor interactions Beta[b]	sr[2c]
TUMRAPE	.329	.100***	.206	.026**
DOM	.085	.006	.170	.017*
HTW	.209	.032*	.037	.001
AIV	.207	.035*	.168	.022*
PSYCH	.027	.001	.016	.000
SEXEXP	.026	.066**	.111	.010
AIV × SEXEXP	—	—	.166	.025**
TUMRAPE × DOM × AIV × PSYCH	—	—	.200	.029
TUMRAPE × DOM × HTW × AIV	—	—	.493	.151****
TUMRAPE × DOM × HTW × AIV × SEXEXP	—	—	.445	.158****
Multiple R	.619****		.865****	
R^2	.383		.748	

[a] TUMRAPE = Tumescence Arousal to Rape Index; DOM = dominance motive; HTW = Hostility Toward Women scale; AIV = Acceptance of Interpersonal Violence (against women) scale; PSYCH = psychoticism scale; SEXEXP = sexual experience measure. From Malamuth (1986).
[b] Standardized regression coefficient.
[c] Squared semipartial correlation coefficient indicating unique contribution of variable.
*$p < .05$. **$p < .005$. ***$p < .001$. ****$p < .0001$.

(1986), except for the sexual arousal indices and for psychoticism. The results replicated successfully Malamuth's (1986) conclusions: The predictors related significantly to sexual aggression, a combination of predictors was superior to individual ones, and an equation including interactions was preferable to an additive one only. Taken together, the findings of these two studies suggest that a person's thought patterns supporting violence against women may be one of several important contributors to sexually aggressive acts, but that each contributor alone is unlikely to produce serious sexual aggression.

The data on unincarcerated subjects point clearly to a relationship between sexual aggression and thought patterns supportive of violence against women, although they also highlight the importance of other contributing factors. One of these other factors, peer support, might also be influenced by the impact of media exposure on the audience's attitudes. The findings on unincarcerated men are reinforced by research on incarcerated rapists.

Using DOM, HTW, AIV, PSYCH, SEXEXP
(n = 155)

Using TUMRAPE, DOM, HTW, AIV, PSYCH, SEXEXP
(n = 95)

SEXUAL AGGRESSION

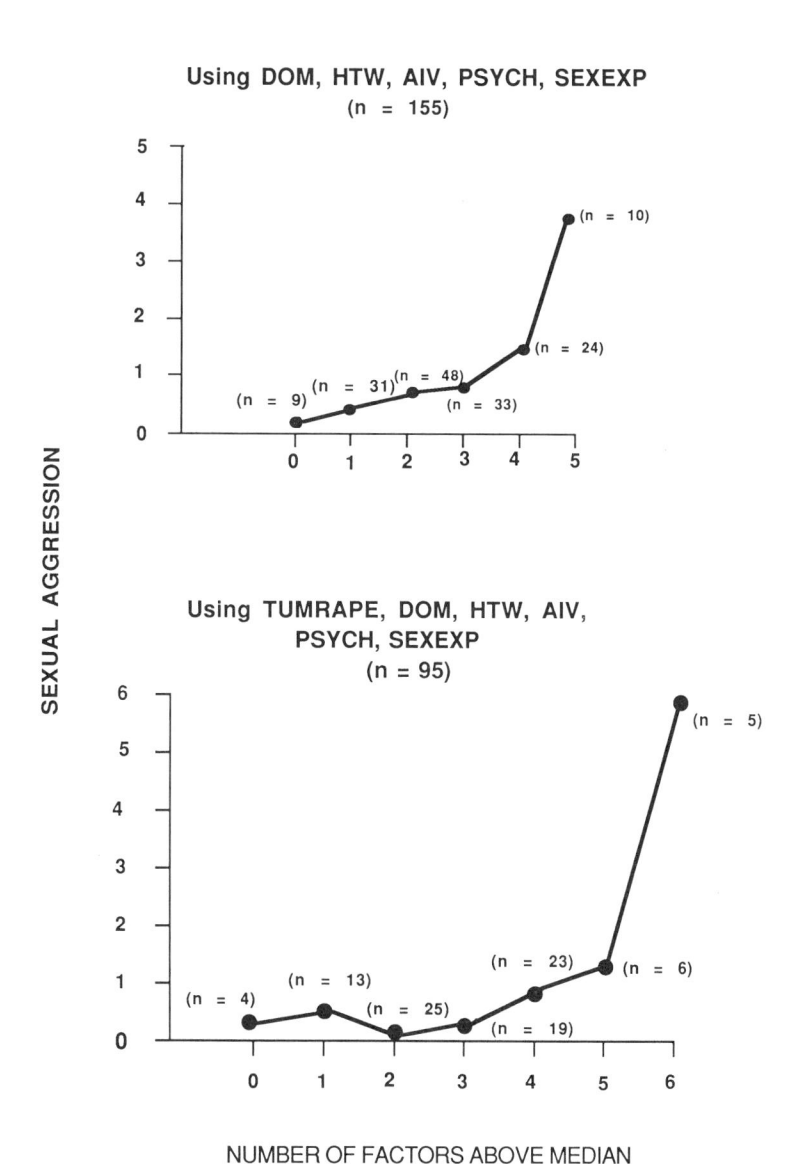

NUMBER OF FACTORS ABOVE MEDIAN

Fig. 6. Mean levels of sexual aggression as a function of factors on which subjects scored above median. *Note:* TUMRAPE = Tumescence Arousal to Rape Index; DOM = dominance motive; HTW = Hostility toward Women scale; AIV = Acceptance of Interpersonal Violence (against women) scale; PSYCH = psychoticism scale; SEXEXP = sexual experience measure. From Malamuth (1986). Reprinted by permission.

4. Convicted Rapists

Many clinical studies report that convicted rapists frequently hold callous attitudes about rape and believe in rape myths to a relatively high degree (see, e.g., Gager & Schurr, 1976). Data from more systematic studies of rapists' thought patterns tend to collaborate the clinical reports. For example, Wolfe and Baker (1980) studied the beliefs and attitudes of 86 convicted rapists and reported that virtually all believed that their actions did not constitute rape or were justified by the circumstances. Unfortunately, these investigators did not distinguish between general endorsement of rape myths and rationalizations of the rapists' personal crimes. Burt (1983) found that although rapists perceived the same degree of violence as the general public in vignettes describing aggression against women, they were less likely to perceive the violence as "bad" and more likely to justify it. Scully and Marolla (1984, 1985) found that rapists tended to believe in rape myths, particularly those justifying violence against women, more than control groups composed of other felons. Finally, Hall, Howard, and Boezio (1986) compared the rape attitudes of three groups: rapists, men convicted of other violent crimes, and a control group from the general population. Although the rapists' scores on degree of tolerance of rape appeared on the average to be the highest of the three groups, statistical analyses revealed that the two offender groups did not significantly differ from each other, but both were more tolerant than the general population group.

VI. OTHER RELEVANT DATA

A. Nonsexual Media Violence

Although research on nonsexual media violence has not devoted much attention to the formation and importance of thought patterns (Rule & Ferguson, 1986), some relevant findings exist. The research of Huesmann, Eron, Klein, Brice, and Fischer (1983) attempts the most direct assessment of cause and effect relations in this area. After involving elementary schoolchildren in a program designed to change their attitudes about television violence, the researchers studied whether changed attitudes translated into less aggressive behavior. The students were randomly divided into experimental and control groups. Over a 2-year span, the experimental group was educated about harmful aspects of television violence, while the control group received neutral treatments. Although the frequency of the children's free-time viewing of violence did not change, their attitudes about the violence did. In addition, their peers reported reduced aggression in the experimental group but no change in the behavior of the control group. These data suggest that changed attitudes about TV violence led to a reduction in personal aggression by children, as reported by their peers.

Another relevant study published by Van der Voort (1986) assessed whether individual differences in children's perceptual, emotional, and attitudinal reactions to TV violence predicted peer-reported aggression. Significant relationships were found between the predictors (measured 1 year earlier) and actual aggression. The more children approved of the violence of "good guys" on TV, the higher their aggression, even after factors such as socioeconomic levels and school achievement were controlled. Van der Voort also found that parents who were less concerned that their children viewed violence had more aggressive children. Although these findings suggest a relationship between attitudes and behavior, they do not justify cause-and-effect conclusions. In addition, it should be noted that some studies have not found significant effects of viewing television violence on attitudes (see, e.g., Belson, 1978), although reviews of the literature in this area have concluded that, on the whole, research on media violence generally indicates significant relationships (see, e.g., Rule & Ferguson, 1986).

B. The Media and Social Attitudes

Christenson and Roberts (1983) reviewed the research focusing on the impact of television on the formation of children's social attitudes in areas other than violence, including political, gender-role, and racial attitudes. They concluded that overall, impressive effects have been clearly demonstrated. On the other hand, McGuire's (1986) review of media effects generally concludes that there are few, if any, areas where consistent media effects have been empirically demonstrated.

C. Longitudinal Research in Other Areas

A major shortcoming of the current literature on the relationship between thought patterns and antisocial behavior against women is the absence, with the single exception noted earlier (Ageton, 1983), of longitudinal research.[6] Fortunately, longitudinal studies in other areas provide data about the role of thought patterns that seem relevant to the present focus. For example, Jessor and Jessor (1977) conducted a large-scale longitudinal project in which several hundred high school and college youths, both males and females, were followed for 4 consecutive years. They assessed the role of various factors in affecting problem behaviors, including excessive use of alcohol, drug use,

---

[6] As discussed earlier, this is also a shortcoming of the research regarding the relation between sexually violent media and the formation of thought patterns.

and general deviance (e.g., aggression, stealing, and lying).[7] Among the predictor variables studied were general attitudes toward deviance, as well as the extent to which positive attitudes toward particular behaviors prevail over negative attitudes toward them. The findings were strongly suggestive of a causal effect of both types of attitudes, in interaction with other factors, on the timing of initial onset and on the actual occurrence of problem behavior. This study provides a model for research on sexual aggression that might be ethically acceptable and yet may yield considerable information regarding causal influences.

In another longitudinal study, Newcomb and Bentler (1988) assessed the relative importance of three types of factors—family context, emotional distress, and socially deviant attitudes—on adolescent drug use. They concluded that socially deviant attitudes were the most powerful influence on teenage substance use. Although the other two types of variables also exerted some influences, these were largely mediated by socially deviant attitudes.

D. Jury Studies

One aspect of the model presented in Fig. 1 is the idea that changes in thought patterns may be important even if these do not increase the likelihood that the person himself will commit aggressive acts. Jury decisions, for example, involve reactions to aggression and not aggressive behavior.

Feild and Bienen (1980) examined the impact of personal juror characteristics on reactions to a simulated rape case. The "jurors" in the simulated trials were groups of citizens, police officers, rape counselors, and rapists. Jurors' attitudes and beliefs about rape were found to be highly predictive of their decisions in the rape trial. For example, people who believed that rape victims often precipitate rape were more lenient toward the rapist. If such beliefs result in milder punishment of rapists, the deterrence against rape may be reduced by social attitudes.

E. Sexual Harassment and Wife Beating

Attitudes and beliefs about rape have also been shown to relate to other forms of inclinations to engage in antisocial behavior against women. For example, Pryor (1986) extended Malamuth's earlier work on men's self-

---

[7] Some of the acts included by Jessor and Jessor (1977) in the general heading of "problem behaviors" might be labeled very differently by other observers, particularly by today's standards. For example, included in this category were protest behaviors or activism, as well as premarital sexual intercourse. Fortunately, the investigators presented separate analyses on the various categories of "problem behaviors," enabling specific focus on those for which more consensus might be reached regarding the appropriate labeling. The conclusions discussed here apply to behaviors such as aggression when assessed separately.

reported likelihood of raping (Malamuth, 1981, 1984) to studying the likelihood of sexually harassing. He developed 10 hypothetical scenarios portraying a male who could sexually exploit a woman by virtue of his social role (e.g., professor–student, executive–secretary). Male undergraduates were asked to imagine themselves in each of these roles and to consider what they would do if they could avoid any negative consequences to themselves from sexually harassing the woman. Respondents indicated the likelihood that they would choose such behavior on a scale ranging from 1 (not at all likely) to 5 (very likely). Pryor found that men's reported likelihood of exploitative behavior was similar in the 10 situations, enabling the computation of an overall likelihood of sexual harassment (LSH) score for each subject.

Pryor obtained data supporting the validity of the LSH reports in an ostensibly unrelated laboratory task where subjects were asked to teach a woman how to putt in a golf game. It was found that those with higher LSH scores more frequently used the golf task to sexually touch the woman.

Of particular relevance to the present chapter were Pryor's findings that men's LSH ratings correlated strongly with their reported likelihood of raping as well as with measures of their beliefs and attitudes regarding violence against women (e.g., the AIV and RMA scales). These data are consistent with the view that diverse violence and nonviolent antisocial acts against women (e.g., rape and sexual harassment) relate to, and are possibly caused by, similar factors (see Fig. 1).

Briere (1987) also extended the self-reported likelihood approach to the area of wife battering. He found that a large percentage of a sample of university males indicated at least some likelihood of hitting a hypothetical wife in one or more of five situations. He also found that scales labeled Attitudes Toward Wife Abuse, Attitudes Toward Women, and Acceptance of Interpersonal Violence Against Women were correlated with self-reported likelihood of wife battering.

Importantly, there are also supportive data in research assessing actual behavior rather than reported likelihood. Kantor and Straus (1987) used interview data from a national representative sample of 5159 families to examine the relationship between three factors and the occurrence of wife abuse. The three factors were alcohol drinking, socioeconomic status, and attitudes approving of wife abuse. They found that the attitude factor had the strongest association with the occurrence of wife abuse, although all three factors had some association. Moreover, they found that a combination of the three factors (i.e., interaction effects) enabled the best "prediction" of wife abuse.

VII. SUMMARY AND CONCLUSIONS

The research presented has provided some support for the model hypothesizing indirect causal influences of media sexual violence on antisocial behavior against women. Data were described that indicate (1) linkages between exposure to media portrayals of sexual violence and resultant changes in thought patterns supportive of sexual aggression, and (2) a relationship between such thought patterns and a variety of antisocial behaviors against women. The data suggest that such thought patterns may contribute to high levels of sexual aggression if combined with other factors such as peer support for aggression, sexual arousal to aggression, antisocial personality characteristics, and hostility toward women. Clearly, much additional research is needed to further develop and test this model.[8]

As with many behaviors, it is apparent that antisocial behavior against women is a function of many interacting causal factors. It is very difficult to gauge the relative influence, if any, of media exposure alone. However, by itself, it is likely to exert only a small influence, if any. But, this may be true, to some degree, for all potentially contributing causes. Only in interaction with other factors might they have substantial influences. Research concerned with the reduction of antisocial behavior against women, therefore, requires attention to all potentially contributing factors, including the mass media.

ACKNOWLEDGMENTS

I thank Albert Bandura, Timna Horowitz, and Susan Holley for valuable comments on earlier drafts of this article and Rebecca Lipa and Nancy Rhan for excellent typing.

REFERENCES

Abel, G. G., Barlow, D. J., Blanchard, E., & Guild, D. (1977). The components of rapists' sexual arousal. *Archives of General Psychiatry*, 34, 895-903.

Abel, G. G., Becker, J., Murphy, W., & Flanagan, B. (1981). Identifying dangerous child molesters. In R. B. Stuart (Ed.), *Violent behavior: Social learning approaches to prediction, management and treatment* (pp. 116-137). New York: Brunner-Mazel.

Abel, G. G., Blanchard, E. B., & Becker, J. V. (1976). Psychological treatment of rapists. In M. Walker & S. Brodsky (Eds.), *Sexual assault: The victim and the rapist* (pp. 99-115). Lexington, MA: Lexington Books.

Abel, G. G., Blanchard, E. B., & Becker, J. V. (1978). An integrated treatment program for rapists. In R. Rada (Ed.), *Clinical aspects of the rapist* (pp. 161-214). New York: Grune & Stratton.

Abel, G. G., Blanchard, E. B., Becker, J. V., & Djenderedjian, A. (1978). Differentiating sexual aggressiveness with penile measures. *Criminal Justice and Behavior*, 5, 315-332.

Abelson, H., Cohen, R., Heaton, E., & Suder, C. (1970). National survey of public attitudes toward and experience with erotic materials. In *Technical report of the Commission on Obscenity and Pornography* (Vol. 6, pp. 1-25). Washington, DC: U.S. Government Printing Office.

Ageton, S. S. (1983). On behaving in accordance with one's attitudes. In M. Zanna, E. T. Higgins, & C. P. Herman (Eds.), *Consistency in social behavior: The Ontario Symposium* (Vol. 2, pp. 3-16). Hillsdale, NJ: Erlbaum.

---

[8]Some suggestions for future research are made by Malamuth and Briere (1986).

Ajzen, I. (1982). On behaving in accordance with one's attitudes. In M. P. Zanna, E. T. Higgins, & C. P. Herman (Eds.), *Consistency in social behavior: The Ontario symposium* (Vol. 2, pp. 3-16). Hillside, NJ: Erlbaum.

Ajzen, I., & Fishbein, M. (1977). Attitude–behavior relations: A theoretical analysis and review of empirical research. *Psychological Bulletin*, **84**, 888-819.

Alder, C. (1985). An exploration of self-reported sexually aggressive behavior. *Crime and Delinquency*, **31**, 306-331.

Attorney General's Commission on Pornography. (1986). *Report of the Attorney General's Commission on Pornography: Final report*. Washington, DC: U.S. Government Printing Office.

Avery-Clark, C. A., & Laws, D. R. (1984). Differential erection response patterns of sexual child abusers to stimuli describing activities with children. *Behavior Therapy*, **15**, 71-83.

Bandura, A. (1977). *Social learning theory*. Englewood Cliffs, NJ: Prentice-Hall.

Bandura, A. (1986). *Social foundations of thought and action: A social cognitive theory*. Englewood Cliffs, NJ: Prentice-Hall.

Bandura, A. (1988). Social cognitive theory of moral thought and action. In W. M. Kurtines & J. L. Gewirtz (Eds.), *Moral behavior and development: Advances in theory, research and applications* (Vol. 1). Hillsdale, NJ: Erlbaum, in press.

Baron, R. A. (1977). *Human aggression*. New York: Plenum Press.

Baxter, R. L., De Riemer, C. D., Landini, A., Leslie, L., & Singletary, M. W. (1985). A content analysis of music videos. *Journal of Broadcasting and Electronic Media*, **29**, 333-340.

Belson, W. A. (1978). *Television violence and the adolescent boy*. London: Saxon House, Teakfield Ltd.

Berkowitz, L. (1984). Some effects of thoughts on anti- and prosocial influence of media events: A cognitive neoassociation approach. *Psychological Bulletin*, **95**, 410-427.

Briere, J. (1987). Predicting self-reported likelihood of battering: Attitudes and childhood experiences. *Journal of Research in Personality*, **21**, 61-69.

Briere, J., Corne, S., Runtz, M., & Malamuth, N. M. (1984, August). *The Rape Arousal Inventory: Predicting actual and potential sexual aggression in a university population*. Paper presented at the annual meeting of the American Psychological Association, Toronto.

Briere, J., & Malamuth, N. M. (1983). Self-reported likelihood of sexually aggressive behavior: Attitudinal versus sexual explanations. *Journal of Research in Personality*, **17**, 315-323.

Briere, J., Malamuth, N. M., & Check, J. V. P. (1985). Sexuality and rape—supportive beliefs. *International Journal of Women's Studies*, **8**, 414-423.

Brownmiller, S. (1975). *Against our will: Men, women and rape*. New York: Simon & Schuster.

Burt, M. R. (1978). Attitudes supportive of rape in American culture. *House Committee on Science and Technology, Subcommittee on Domestic and International Scientific Planning, Analysis and Cooperation, Research into violent behavior: Sexual assaults* (Hearing, 95th Congress, 2nd session, January 10-12, 1978) (pp. 277-322). Washington, DC: U.S. Government Printing Office.

Burt, M. R. (1980). Cultural myths and support for rape. *Journal of Personality and Social Psychology*, **38**, 217-230.

Burt, M. R. (1983). Justifying personal violence: A comparison of rapists and the general public. *Victimology: An International Journal*, **8**, 131-150.

Carroll, J. D. (1978). The effect of imagining an event on expectations for the event: An interpretation in terms of the availability heuristic. *Journal of Experimental Social Psychology*, **14**, 88-96.

Ceniti, J., & Malamuth, N. M. (1984). Effects of repeated exposure to sexually violent or nonviolent stimuli on sexual arousal to rape and nonrape depictions. *Behaviour Research and Therapy*, **22**, 535-548.

Check, J. V. P. (1984). *The effects of violent and nonviolent pornography* (Contract No. 95SV 19200-3-0899). Ottawa, Ontario: Canadian Department of Justice.

Check, J. V. P. (1985). *A survey of Canadians' attitudes regarding sexual content in media*. Report to the Lamarsh Research Programme on Violence and Conflict Resolution and the Canadian Broadcasting Corporation, Toronto.

Check, J. V. P., & Malamuth, N. M. (1984). Can participation in pornography experiments have positive effects? *Journal of Sex Research*, 20, 14-31.

Christenson, P. G., & Roberts, D. F. (1983). The role of television in the formation of children's social attitudes. In M. J. Howe (Ed.), *Learning from television: Psychological and educational research* (pp. 79-99). New York: Academic Press.

Clark, L., & Lewis, D. (1977). *Rape: The price of coercive sexuality*. Toronto: The Women's Press.

Cohen, M. L., Garofalo, R., Boucher, R. B., & Seghorn, T. (1971). The psychology of rapists. *Seminars in Psychiatry*, 3, 307-327.

Commission on Obscenity and Pornography. (1970). *Report of the Commission on Obscenity and Pornography*. New York: Random House.

Demare, D. (1985). *The effects of erotic and sexually violent mass media on attitudes toward women and rape*. Unpublished manuscript. University of Winnipeg, Winnipeg, Manitoba.

Demare, D., Briere, J., & Lips, H. (1988). Violent pornography and self-reported likelihood of sexual aggression. *Journal of Research in Personality*, 22, 140-153.

Dietz, P. E., & Evans, B. (1982). Pornographic imagery and prevalence of paraphilia. *American Journal of Psychiatry*, 139, 1493-1495.

Donnerstein, E. (1984). Pornography: Its effects on violence against women. In N. M. Malamuth & E. Donnerstein (Eds.), *Pornography and sexual aggression* (pp. 53-81). New York: Academic Press.

Donnerstein, E., & Berkowitz, L. (1981). Victim reactions in aggressive-erotic films as a factor in violence against women. *Journal of Personality and Social Psychology*, 41, 710-724.

Elliott, D. S., Huizinga, D., & Ageton, S. (1985). *Explaining delinquency and drug use*. Newbury Park, CA: Sage.

Feild, H., & Bienen, L. (1980). *Jurors and rape: A study in psychology and the law*. Lexington, MA: D. C. Heath.

Fisher, W. A., & Barak, A. (1988). Sex education as a corrective: Immunizing against possible effects of pornography. In D. Zillmann & J. Bryant (Eds.), *Pornography: Recent research, interpretations, and policy considerations*. Hillsdale, NJ: Erlbaum.

Fisher, W. A., & Grenier, G. (1988). *Failures to replicate effects of pornography on attitudes and behavior: The emperor has no clothes*. Manuscript in preparation, University of Western Ontario, London, Ontario.

Gager, N., & Schurr, C. (1976). *Sexual assault: Confronting rape in America*. New York: Grosset & Dunlap.

Gerbner, G. (1972). Violence in television drama: Trends and symbolic functions. In G. Comstock & E. A. Rubinstein (Eds.), *Television and social behavior: Vol. 1. Media content and control* (pp. 28-187). Washington, DC: U.S. Government Printing Office.

Goldstein, J. H. (1986). *Aggression and crimes of violence*. Oxford: Oxford University Press.

Greenberg, B. S., & D'Alessio, D. (1985). Quantity and quality of sex in the soaps. *Journal of Broadcasting and Electronic Media*, 29, 309-321.

Hall, E. R., Howard, J. A., & Boezio, S. L. (1986). Tolerance of rape: A sexist or antisocial attitude? *Psychology of Women Quarterly*, 10, 101-118.

Hammer, E. F. (1957). A psychoanalytic hypothesis concerning sex offenders. *Journal of Clinical and Experimental Psychology*, 18, 177-184.

Hearold, S. (1986). A synthesis of 1043 effects of television on social behavior. In G. Comstock (Ed.), *Public communication and behavior* (Vol. 1, pp. 65-133). New York: Academic Press.

Hepburn, J. B. (1977). Testing alternative models of delinquency causation. *Journal of Criminal Law and Criminology*, 67, 450-460.

Huesmann, L. R., Eron, L. D., Klein, R., Brice, P., & Fischer, P. (1983). Mitigating the imitation of aggressive behaviors by changing children's attitudes about media violence. *Journal of Personality and Social Psychology*, **44**, 899-910.

Jessor, R., & Jessor, S. L. (1977). *Problem behavior and psychosocial development: A longitudinal study of youth.* New York: Academic Press.

Kanin, E. J. (1985). Date rapists: Differential sexual socialization and relative deprivation. *Archives of Sexual Behavior*, **14**, 219-231.

Kantor, G. K., & Straus, M. A. (1987). The "drunken bum" theory of wife beating. *Social Problems*, **34**, 213-231.

Kaplan, R. (1983). The measurement of human aggression. In R. Kaplan, V. Koencni, & R. Novaco (Eds.), *Aggression in children and youth.* Rijn, Netherlands: Sijthoff & Noordhoff.

Koss, M. P., & Dinero, T. E. (1988). Predictors of sexual aggression among a national sample of male college students. In R. A. Pentky & V. L. Quinsey (Eds.), *Sexual aggression: Current perspectives. Annals of the New York Academy of Sciences* (pp. 133-147). New York: New York Academy of Sciences, in press.

Koss, M. P., Leonard, K. E., Beezley, D. A., & Oros, C. J. (1985). Nonstranger sexual aggression: A discriminant analysis of psychological characteristics of nondetected offenders. *Sex Roles*, **12**, 981-992.

Linz, D. (1985). *Sexual violence in the media: Effects on male viewers and implications for society.* Unpublished doctoral dissertation, University of Wisconsin, Madison.

Linz, D., Donnerstein, E., & Penrod, S. (1987). The findings and recommendations of the Attorney General's Commission on Pornography: Do the psychological "facts" fit the political fury? *American Psychologist*, **10**, 946-953.

Lowry, D. T., Love, G., & Kirby, M. (1981). Sex on the soap operas: Patterns of intimacy. *Journal of Communication*, **31**, 90-96.

MacKinnon, C. A. (1987). *Feminism unmodified: Discourses on life and law.* Cambridge, MA: Harvard University Press.

Malamuth, N. M. (1978, September). *Erotica, aggression and perceived appropriateness.* Paper presented at the 86th annual convention of the American Psychological Association, Toronto.

Malamuth, N. M. (1981). Rape proclivity among males. *Journal of Social Issues*, **37**, 138-157.

Malamuth, N. M. (1983). Factors associated with rape as predictors of laboratory aggression against women. *Journal of Personality and Social Psychology*, **45**, 432-442.

Malamuth, N. M. (1984). Aggression against women: Cultural and individual causes. In N. M. Malamuth & E. Donnerstein (Eds.), *Pornography and sexual aggression* (pp. 19-52). New York: Academic Press.

Malamuth, N. M. (1986). Predictors of naturalistic sexual aggression. *Journal of Personality and Social Psychology*, **50**, 953-962.

Malamuth, N. M. (1988a). A multidimensional approach to sexual aggression: Combining measures of past behavior and present likelihood. In R. A. Prentky & V. L. Quinsey (Eds.), *Sexual aggression: Current perspectives. Annals of the New York Academy of Sciences* (pp. 123-132). New York: New York Academy of Sciences.

Malamuth, N. M. (1988b). Predicting laboratory aggression against female vs. male targets: Implications for research on sexual aggression. *Journal of Research in Personality*, **22**, 474-495.

Malamuth, N. M. (1988c). *Sources of information about sexuality and their correlates: With particular focus on pornography.* Unpublished manuscript, University of California, Los Angeles.

Malamuth, N. M., & Billings, V. (1985). The functions and effects of pornography: Sexual communication versus the feminist models in light of research findings. In J. Bryant & D. Zillmann (Eds.), *Perspectives on media effects.* Hillsdale, NJ: Erlbaum.

Malamuth, N. M., & Briere, J. (1986). Sexual violence in the media: Indirect effects on aggression against women. *Journal of Social Issues*, **42**, 75-92.

Malamuth, N. M., & Ceniti, J. (1986). Repeated exposure to violent and nonviolent pornography: Likelihood of raping ratings and laboratory aggression against women. *Aggressive Behavior*, **12**, 129-137.

Malamuth, N. M., & Check, J. V. P. (1980). Penile tumescence and perceptual responses to rape as a function of victim's perceived reactions. *Journal of Applied Social Psychology*, **10**, 528-547.

Malamuth, N. M., & Check, J. V. P. (1981). The effects of mass media exposure on acceptance of violence against women: A field experiment. *Journal of Research in Personality*, **15**, 436-446.

Malamuth, N. M., & Check, J. V. P. (1982, June). *Factors related to aggression against women*. Paper presented at the annual meeting of the Canadian Psychological Association, Toronto.

Malamuth, N. M., & Check, J. V. P. (1983). Sexual arousal to rape depictions: Individual differences. *Journal of Abnormal Psychology*, **92**, 35-67.

Malamuth, N. M., & Check, J. V. P. (1984). Debriefing effectiveness following rape depictions. *Journal of Sex Research*, **20**, 1-13.

Malamuth, N. M., & Check, J. V. P. (1985a). The effects of aggressive pornography on beliefs in rape myths: Individual differences. *Journal of Research in Personality*, **19**, 299-320.

Malamuth, N. M., & Check, J. V. P. (1985b). *Predicting naturalistic sexual aggression: A replication*. Unpublished manuscript, University of California, Los Angeles.

Malamuth, N. M., Check, J. V. P., & Briere, J. (1986). Sexual arousal in response to aggression: Ideological, aggressive, and sexual correlates. *Journal of Personality and Social Psychology*, **50**, 330-340.

Malamuth, N. M., Feshbach, S., & Jaffe, Y. (1977). Sexual arousal and aggression: Recent experiments and theoretical issues. *Journal of Social Issues*, **33**, 110-133.

Malamuth, N. M., Haber, S., & Feshbach, S. (1980). Testing hypotheses regarding rape: Exposure to sexual violence, sex differences, and the "normality" of rapists. *Journal of Research in Personality*, **14**, 121-137.

Malamuth, N. M., Heim, M., & Feshbach, S. (1980). Sexual responsiveness of college students to rape depictions: Inhibitory and disinhibitory effects. *Journal of Personality and Social Psychology*, **38**, 399-408.

Malamuth, N. M., Reisin, E., & Spinner, B. (1979, August). *Exposure to pornography and reactions to rape*. Paper presented at the 86th annual convention of the American Psychological Association, New York.

Malamuth, N. M., & Spinner, B. (1980). A longitudinal content analysis of sexual violence in the best-selling erotic magazines. *Journal of Sex Research*, **16**(3), 226-237.

Mann, J., Berkowitz, L., Sidman, J., Starr, S., & West, S. (1974). Satiation of the transient stimulating effect of erotic films. *Journal of Personality and Social Psychology*, **30**, 729-735.

McGuire, W. J. (1986). The myth of massive media impact: Savagings and salvagings. In G. Comstock (Ed.), *Public communication and behavior* (Vol. 1, pp. 173-257). New York: Academic Press.

Mosher, D. L., & Anderson, R. D. (1986). Macho personality, sexual aggression, and reactions to guided imagery of realistic rape. *Journal of Research in Personality*, **20**, 77-94.

Murphy, W. D., Coleman, E. M., & Haynes, M. R. (1986). Factors related to coercive sexual behavior in a nonclinical sample of males. *Violence and Victims*, **4**, 255-278.

Newcomb, M. D., & Bentler, P. M. (1988). The impact of family context, deviant attitudes, and emotional distress on adolescent drug use: Longitudinal latent-variable analyses of mothers and their children. *Journal of Research in Personality*, **22**, 154-176.

Olivia, N. v. National Broadcasting Co., Inc. (1978). *California Reporter*, **141**, 511-515.

Palys, P. S. (1986). Testing the common wisdom: The social content of video pornography. *Canadian Psychology*, **27**, 22-35.

Peters, L. H., Terborg, J. R., & Taynor, J. (1974). Women As Managers Scale (WAMS): A measure of attitudes toward women in management positions. *JSAS Catalogue of Selected Documents in Psychology*, **4**, 27.

Pryor, J. B. (1986). Sexual harassment proclivities in men. *Sex Roles*, **17**, 269-289.

Quinsey, V. L., & Chaplin, T. C. (1984). Stimulus control of rapists' and non-sex offenders' sexual arousal. *Behavioral Assessment*, **6**, 169-176.

Quinsey, V. L., Chaplin, T. C., & Carrigan, W. F. (1980). Biofeedback and signaled punishment in the modification of inappropriate sexual age preferences. *Behavioral Therapy*, **11**, 567-576.

Quinsey, V. L., Chaplin, T. C., & Upfold, D. (1984). Sexual arousal to nonsexual violence and sadomasochistic themes among rapists and non-sex offenders. *Journal of Consulting and Clinical Psychology*, **52**, 651-657.

Rapaport, K. (1984). *Sexually aggressive males: Characterological features and sexual responsiveness to rape depictions*. Unpublished doctoral dissertation, Auburn University, Auburn, AL.

Rapaport, K., & Burkhart, B. R. (1984). Personality and attitudinal characteristics of sexually coercive college males. *Journal of Abnormal Psychology*, **93**, 216-221.

Roth, M. (1985). Introduction: The social-psychological phenomenon of violence. In G. Barlow & A. Hill (Eds.), *Video violence and children*. London: Hodder & Stoughton.

Rule, B., & Ferguson, T. (1986). The effects of media violence on attitudes, emotions and cognitions. *Journal of Social Issues*, **42**, 29-50.

Russell, D. E. H. (1975). *The politics of rape*. New York: Stein & Day.

Russell, D. E. H. (1984). *Sexual exploitation: Rape, child abuse and workplace harassment*. Newbury Park, CA: Sage.

Sanday, P. R. (1981). The socio-cultural context of rape. *Journal of Social Issues*, **37**, 1-27.

Scully, D., & Marolla, J. (1984). Convicted rapists' vocabulary of motive: Excuses and justifications. *Social Problems*, **31**, 530-544.

Scully, D., & Marolla, J. (1985). Riding the bull at Gilley's: Convicted rapists describe the rewards of rape. *Social Problems*, **32**, 251-263.

Sears, D. O., Freedman, J. L., & Peplau, L. A. (1985). *Social psychology* (5th ed.). Englewood Cliffs, NJ: Prentice-Hall.

Shields, W. M., & Shields, L. M. (1983). Forcible rape: An evolutionary perspective. *Ethnology and Sociobiology*, **4**, 115-136.

Slade, J. W. (1984). Violence in the hard-core pornographic film: A historical survey. *Journal of Communication*, **34**, 148-163.

Smith, D. G. (1976a, August). *Sexual aggression in American pornography: The stereotype of rape*. Paper presented at the annual meeting of the American Sociological Association, New York.

Smith, D. G. (1976b). The social content of pornography. *Journal of Communication*, **26**, 16-33.

Spence, J. F., & Helmreich, R. (1972). The Attitudes Toward Women scale: An objective instrument to measure attitudes toward the rights and roles of women in contemporary society. *JSAS Catalog of Selected Documents in Psychology*, **2**, 66.

Thornhill, R., & Thornhill, N. W. (1983). Human rape: An evolutionary analysis. *Ethology and Sociobiology*, **4**, 137-173.

Thornhill, R., Thornhill, N. W., & Dizinno, G. (1986). The biology of rape. In S. Tomaselli & R. Porter (Eds.), *Rape* (pp. 102-121). New York: Basil Blackwell.

Tieger, T. (1981). Self-rated likelihood of raping and the social perception of rape. *Journal of Research in Personality*, **15**, 147-158.

Vance, C. S. (1985, April). What does the research prove? *Ms. Magazine*, **XIII**(10), 40.

Van der Voort, T. H. A. (1986). *Television violence: A child's-eye view*. Amsterdam: Elsevier.

Winick, C. (1985). A content analysis of sexually explicit magazines sold in adult bookstores. *Journal of Sex Research*, **21**, 206-210.

Wolfe, J., & Baker, V. (1980). Characteristics of imprisoned rapists and circumstances of the rape. In C. G. Warner (Ed.), *Rape and sexual assault*. Germantown, MD: Aspen Systems.

Wyer, R. S., & Srull, T. K. (1981). Category accessibility: Some theoretical and empirical issues concerning the processing of social stimulus information. In E. T. Higgens, C. P. Herman, & M. P. Zanna (Eds.), *Social cognition: The Ontario Symposium* (Vol. 1, pp. 161-197). Hillsdale, NJ: Erlbaum.

Yang, N. (1987). *Sexual, violent, sexually violent, and prosocial behaviors in R-, X-, and XXX-rated films and videos*. Unpublished doctoral dissertation, S. I. Newhouse School of Public Communications, Syracuse University, Syracuse, NY.

Zanna, M. P., & Fazio, R. H. (1982). The attitude-behavior relation: Moving toward a third generation of research. In M. P. Zanna, E. T. Higgins, & C. P. Herman (Eds.), *Consistency in social behavior* (pp. 283-302). Hillsdale, NJ: Erlbaum.

Zillmann, D., & Bryant, J. (1984). Effects of massive exposure to pornography. In N. M. Malamuth & E. Donnerstein (Eds.), *Pornography and sexual aggression* (pp. 115-138). New York: Academic Press.

Parallel Content Analysis: Old Paradigms and New Proposals

W. RUSSELL NEUMAN
Massachusetts Institute of Technology
Cambridge, Massachusetts 02139

I. Introduction: Weber, Lasswell, Lazarsfeld, and Hovland	205
II. The Strategy of Parallel Content Analysis	209
III. Rethinking the Communications Effects Paradigm	213
A. The Limits of Experimental Research	214
B. The Limits of Survey Research	217
C. The Limits of Content Analysis	220
D. The Limits of Field Research	226
E. The Nature of Communications Effects	231
IV. Emerging Models for Communications Research	235
A. Beyond Attitudes	236
B. Beyond Direct Effects	241
C. Toward Time-Series Analysis	249
V. Parallel Content Analysis	253
A. Common Elements in the New Research Perspectives	253
B. Parallel Content Analysis as a Strategy for Research	257
C. Some Exemplary Studies	264
D. Conclusion	277
References	280

I. INTRODUCTION: WEBER, LASSWELL, LAZARSFELD, AND HOVLAND

At the peak of his powers in 1910, Max Weber addressed the first congress of the German Society of Sociology in Frankfurt. Weber, like many of the other seminal scholars in the emerging disciplines of sociology and political science, was centrally concerned with the evolution of social and cultural institutions. He had published studies of the interaction of religious culture and social institutions and the evolution of bureaucratic authority, which became models of how such research ought to be conducted for generations of social scientists to come.

As he stood before the first organized gathering of this young field, he proposed a bold new cooperative research effort. This would be a critically important enterprise to draw together scholarship in the field and to demonstrate its relevance for current social and political issues. What did Weber propose? He called for a systematic study of the press and public opinion:

> Gentlemen, the first subject deemed suitable by the Society for a purely scientific treatment is a sociology of the press.... A committee will be formed which soon will try to gain the cooperation of press experts, numerous theoreticians of the press—as you know, we have already some brilliant theoretical publications in this field...and the practitioners of the press...
>
> We must examine the press first to this end: What does it contribute to the making of modern man? And second: how are the objective, supra-individual cultural values influenced, what shifts occur, what is destroyed and what is newly created of the beliefs and hopes of the masses?
>
> You will ask now: Where is the material to begin such studies? Material consists of the newspapers themselves, and we will now, to be specific, start with scissors and compasses to measure the quantitative changes of newspaper content of the last generation.... From these quantitative analyses we will proceed to qualitative ones. We will have to pursue the kind of stylistic approach to the newspaper, the way in which the same problems are discussed in newspapers and outside of them. (Weber, cited in H. Hardt, pp. 174, 181-182 in *Social Theories of the Press*. Copyright © 1979. Reprinted by permission of Sage Publications, Inc.)

Weber's speech was based on a research proposal,[1] *Preliminary Report of a Suggested Survey of the Sociology of Newspapers*, which outlined a co-ordinated parallel content analysis of press coverage of political issues over time and the content of the public response, mixing quantitative and qualitative research approaches. Neither content analysis nor survey research had been developed as formal methodologies by 1910, and it is interesting to speculate on how the emergence of those methodologies might have been influenced by the research Weber proposed.

But the project was never to be completed. Weber had won some cooperation from the German Press Association and had worked diligently on the project for a year and a half, but he ultimately abandoned it. Hanno Hardt (1979), who has studied the emergence of German social science during this period, concludes that it was not a loss of interest but an unfortunate coincidence of outside circumstances that forced Weber to abandon his original plans. The circumstances included a bitter battle between Weber and a colleague at his university, and a libel suit involving Weber's wife, Marianne.

---

[1] The proposal is summarized in Hardt (1979) on pages 171-173.

Marianne later described her husband's efforts to persuade his colleagues to cooperate with him. A few small-scale studies were conducted on the Prussian press and the evolution of the feature story format. Another study focused on the role of classified advertising. The largest study involved a quantitative content analysis of 10 newspapers of various types over the course of a year. But Weber's colleagues were preoccupied with other matters, and shortly, the outbreak of the First World War overtook his efforts to stimulate and coordinate research (Marianne Weber, 1926).

There was another strikingly similar effort by an influential social scientist to stimulate a coordinated research effort along these lines. The scholar in this case was Harold Lasswell. The intriguing history of Lasswell's efforts is traced in Morris Janowitz's essay, "Content Analysis and Study of the 'Symbolic Environment' " (1969). Janowitz described Lasswell's (1935) book, *World Politics and Personal Insecurity*, as a groundbreaking study that proposed a continuing "world attention survey," a cooperative program of content analysis of the world's press and world public opinion.

For two decades, Lasswell published studies supporting this approach and directed a number of colleagues in the War Time Communications Project sponsored by the Library of Congress during the 1940s. Through this period, his colleagues included Gabriel Almond, Nathan Leites, Ithiel de Sola Pool, Daniel Lerner, and Alexander George. Lasswell's efforts were considerably more successful than Weber's. In this case, the intervening world war became a stimulus rather than an impediment to research. Lasswell managed to engage some exceptionally bright and active young scholars, who joined in the publication of *The Language of Politics* in 1949 and continued similar work as they scattered to universities around the country in the 1950s. But the critical threshold of scholarly attention was not reached, and the work became narrowly associated with the notion of wartime propaganda. Further efforts at institutionalized data collection failed, and Lasswell himself ultimately abandoned the effort. Janowitz (1969) concluded simply that "Content analysis. . . failed to emerge as a device for describing the essence of mass communications on a long-term trend and social change basis" (p. 156). Janowitz was struck by the irony that in Lasswell's later effort, *The Future of Political Science* (1963), which outlined his views on the future goals and promising methodologies of political science, he made not a single reference to content analysis.

There were two other coordinated efforts to study communications and propaganda effects of a somewhat different character, which were marked by considerably greater success. The first was coordinated by Carl Hovland, an experimental psychologist at Yale. His work also emerged out of concern with World War II propaganda, but, in this case, it spawned a burgeoning literature on attitude change. Among the classic studies were *Experiments on*

Mass Communication by Hovland, Lumsdaine, and Sheffield (1949), and *Communication and Persuasion* by Hovland, Janis, and Kelley (1953). Hovland and colleagues focused their attention on experimentally manipulated change of opinion derived primarily in laboratory studies with soldiers and students, and he and his graduate students were prolific and tremendously influential. [McGuire's (1968, 1986) literature reviews, for example, cite literally thousands of studies closely following in this research tradition.]

Another mentor and model in the study of communications research effects was the sociologist Paul Lazarsfeld. The founder of the Bureau of Applied Social Research at Columbia University, pioneer in survey research and voting studies, and collaborator with Frank Stanton, Robert Merton, Bernard Berelson, Elihu Katz and many others, he set forth a model heavily emphasizing survey research for assessing the impact of advertising and political campaigns. The key studies include Lazarsfeld, Berelson, and Gaudet (1948), *The People's Choice: How the Voter Makes Up His Mind in a Presidential Campaign*; Berelson, Lazarsfeld, and McPhee (1954), *Voting: A Study of Opinion Formation in a Presidential Campaign*, and Katz and Lazarsfeld (1964), *Personal Influence: The Part Played by People in the Flow of Communications*. Lazarsfeld's work and his use of survey methodology were also tremendously influential, setting forth a model for two generations of researchers in communications, political science, and sociology (Glock, 1967).

This portrait of the origins of communications research is drawn with a particular point in mind. Four distinguished scholars set forth models for communications effects research in the first half of the twentieth century. Weber and Lasswell failed to win acceptance for their research paradigms and ultimately abandoned their efforts. Hovland and Lazarsfeld, however, succeeded in generating paradigms for experimental and survey research studies of communications effects that were to dominate scholarship for four decades. For abundant evidence of this pattern in the communications field, one might examine the literature reviews compiled by Klapper (1960); Weiss (1968); McGuire (1968); Kraus and Davis (1976); Comstock, Chaffee, Katzman, McCombs, and Roberts (1978); or G. E. Lang and Lang (1981). The underlying reasons for these relative successes and failures present an interesting challenge for intellectual historians. Most active scholars in the field, however, take the success of Hovland's and Lazarsfeld's paradigms as self-evidently appropriate for understanding the social phenomenon at hand. Most are only vaguely aware of Weber's and Lasswell's efforts.

Hardt (1979) and Janowitz (1969), who carefully examined Weber's and Lasswell's failures, argue convergently that miscellaneous historical and personal factors intervened. Had historical circumstances and personal energies been only slightly altered, Weber and Lasswell might well have succeeded in capturing the imagination of their colleagues and initiating a new self-sustaining research tradition. The character of modern communications research could have been dominated by the study of long-term social and political trends—a rigorous, institutionalized scientific effort in monitoring the content of the ongoing media flow with parallel efforts to monitor the public's response.

This chapter has a single thesis that draws explicitly on this historical prologue. Growing frustration with the limits of orthodox experimental and survey methods in the study of short-term communications effects may yet lead to the reemergence of the Weber–Lasswell paradigm. Using Klapper's (1960) characterization of minimal communications effects as the central symbol of the old orthodoxy, a new generation of communications researchers in the 1960s, 1970s, and 1980s has grown increasingly uncomfortable with the dominant paradigm and has been pushing and poking around with new methods and theories in an attempt to revitalize and reformulate the practice of research.

Thomas Kuhn's historical work (1962) has produced a seductively simple and attractive model of how scientific paradigms evolve. It evokes a wonderful imagery of a "palace revolution" as a new generation of scholars discovers a new set of variables and appropriate new methodologies and dramatically ousts their orthodox elders to rewrite the textbooks. Perhaps it works that way sometimes in the physical sciences. The recent history of communications research, however, suggests that we are witnessing a much more complicated process, involving multiple false starts, profound confusion, a great deal of sympathy and encouragement from elder scholars, and an old paradigm that dies very hard. As it is said, we live in interesting times.

The following pages attempt to characterize and formalize some elements of the evolving paradigm of communications research. There is increasing agreement that more of what Weber and Lasswell had originally proposed ought to be explored. The "new paradigm," of course, will not replace but rather complement existing models of appropriate research design. In fact, a key development is a self-consciously multimethod model of research.

II. THE STRATEGY OF PARALLEL CONTENT ANALYSIS

In 1977, Steven Chaffee wrote a memo to the Social Science Research Council's Committee on Television and Social Behavior. The committee had been struggling with the narrowly defined model of communications effects, especially the increasingly routine research concerning the effects of violent programming on children. Chaffee's memo attempted to explain why communications research had gotten into a rut. His basic argument was that communications researchers could be divided into two groups, the media-centric and the effects-centric researchers.

Media-centric research is conducted by those who are primarily interested in the structure of the communications industries and media content. Media-centric research examines the traditional structures and the complex patterns of media content in rich detail, but it also tends to take the issue of effects as a given. A small sampling of recent books and this tradition might include Curran, Gurevitch, and Woollacott (1977), *Mass Communication and Society*; Adams and Schreibman (1978), *Television Network News*; Gans (1979), *Deciding What's News*; Newcomb (1979), *TV: The Most Popular Art*; Gitlin (1980), *The Whole World is Watching*; Greenberg (1980), *Life on Television*; Cantor (1980), *Prime-Time Television*; Paletz and Entman (1981), *Media Power Politics*; Bagdikian (1981), *The Media Monopoly*; M. Robinson and Sheehan (1983), *Over the Wire and on TV*; and Lichter, Rothman, and Lichter (1986), *The Media Elite*. This group includes both humanists and social scientists who conduct literary or quantitative content analyses of the media (such as Newcomb, Greenberg, Gans, Cantor, Robinson and Sheehan, and Adams and Schreibman). The other prominent cluster includes sociologists and radical critics of the organizational structure of American mass media, and especially the news media (notably, Curran, Gurevitch, Woollacott, Bagdikian, Gans, Paletz and Entman, and Gitlin).

Effects-centric researchers, however, focus on audience effects and take the complexity of media content and structural organization as a given. Recent research in this tradition includes Comstock *et al.* (1978), *Television and Human Behavior*; Kraus and Davis (1976), *The Effects of Mass Communication on Political Behavior*; Adler *et al.* (1980), *The Effects of Television Advertising on Children*; Bishop, Meadow, and Jackson-Beeck (1978), *The Presidential Debates*; Patterson (1980), *The Mass Media Election*; Himmelweit, Humphreys, Jaegers, and Katz (1981), *How Voters Decide*; MacKuen and Coombs (1981), *More Than News*; Rice and Paisley (1981), *Public Communication Campaigns*; Weaver, Graber, McCombs, and Eyal (1981), *Media Agenda-Setting in a Presidential Election: Issues, Images, and Interest*; Milavsky, Kessler, Stipp, and Rubens (1982), *Television and Aggression: Results of a Panel Study*; Ball-Rokeach, Rokeach, and Grube (1984), *The Great American Values Test*; and Bryant and Zillmann (1986), *Perspectives on Media Effects*. Here, experimental and survey research methodologies dominate; the rigor of scientific design keeps the attention of researchers on other matters, and as a result, most researchers treat the issue of complex media messages as an inconvenience. Researchers are likely to make use of whatever media content is handy or to design artificial, simplistic persuasive messages.

This gap between media-centric and effects-centric research has been noted by a number of reviewers in the field (Comstock, 1980; Katz, 1980; McLeod & Reeves, 1980). McLeod and Reeves, in particular, develop the argument further and suggest that what is missing is an "isomorphism" between the measurement of content and the measurement of effects. Although they do not develop one, they suggest that a new theoretical perspective and corresponding new measurement model ought to be devised to bridge the gap. It is precisely that gap that the strategy of Parallel Content Analysis attempts to address.

The accumulated reviews of the field of mass communication research reveal a number of consistent themes about the status of the field, what is known, and why research designs need to be improved (see, Becker, McCombs, & McLeod, 1975; Chaffee, 1977; Clarke & Kline, 1974; Comstock *et al.*, 1978; Davison & Yu, 1974; De Fleur & Ball-Rokeach, 1982; Katz, 1977, 1980; Kraus & Davis, 1976; G. E. Lang & Lang, 1981; Lemert, 1981; Lowery & De Fleur, 1983; McLeod & Reeves, 1980; McQuail, 1977, 1983; Pearl, Bouthilet, & Lazar, 1982; Pietila, 1977; Reeves & Wartella, 1982; Roberts & Bachen, 1981; Zukin, 1981). These essays have titles such as "On the Nature of Mass Media Effects," "Media Effects Reconsidered: Some New Strategies for Communications Research," "On Conceptualizing Media Effects," "Does Mass Communications Change Public Opinion After All?" Each essay reviews the prominent research studies numbering in the hundreds—sometimes in the thousands—and on the basis of its assessment of weaknesses and strengths, each puts forward recommendations for future work. Almost unanimously, these reviews call for more natural settings of measurement, longer-term measurement, a better appreciation of the complexity of the "message-as-stimulus," and a better appreciation of the salience and meaning of particular messages for different audience members.

Some of these new directions of research have emerged already as schools of research complete with a unique vocabulary, several widely cited seminal studies, and articulate defenders of the new faith. A list of emergent schools of communications effects research might include uses and gratifications, agenda setting, information diffusion, and cultivation analysis.

The term *Parallel Content Analysis* is used here to identify an evolving paradigm for research. It is perhaps an awkward choice of labels for several reasons, one of which is that content analysis occupies a rather modest position in the pantheon of social science methodologies. The term *content analysis* has an unfortunate association with atheoretical "number-crunching" research. It conjures up imagery of counting for counting's sake—perhaps typified by the awkwardly written and unenthusiastic master's thesis that is more scholarly in appearance than in substance. In other words, its bad reputation is too often soundly justified. The term is used, however, because although content analytic research has tended to be atheoretical, it need not be. Indeed, the research design outlined in the following pages attempts explicitly to link content analytic data through causal analysis to other measures of social behavior.

Parallel content analysis is defined as the systematic and simultaneous measurement of media content and audience response. Media content and audience response are monitored and recorded as fully as possible and archived for later parallel content analysis by communities of interested researchers. The character of parallel content analysis lends itself to large-scale, cooperative data collection and data analysis. The first part, archiving media content, is easy. In fact, many of the broadcast and print media have been carefully maintaining archives of their own work, as have independent organizations such as the Vanderbilt Television News Archives and the Museum of Broadcasting. The more difficult task is trying to derive a systematic sample of the mix of print and broadcast news and entertainment content representative of what an average American might have seen in a given year.

Audience response is assessed using a mixture of closed- and open-ended survey interviews, depth interviews, and perhaps focus-group techniques to generate a parallel archive of natural language responses of a representative sample of the citizenry. This is the unique, but also frustratingly difficult, aspect of the proposed research strategy. There would seem to be an almost limitless variety of current events, values, and beliefs that individuals could talk about. Most communications effects research, of course, focuses very narrowly on a specific content stimulus and a corresponding before-after attitude measure. But the pioneering depth interview work by Lane (1962) and more recent work by Graber (1984) and Gamson (1988) does demonstrate the viability of amassing and systematically analyzing hours of depth interview transcripts.

What follows will draw attention to a number of taken-for-granted methodological traditions and illustrate how the choice of methodology influences the development of theory. It is a traditional review of research, but it is self-consciously selective in reviewing and exaggerating the shortcomings of previous research in order to make a point. Parallel content analysis is not a new method. It is a systematic extension and integration of existing methods along the lines proposed by George Comstock at the conclusion of the massive review he and his colleagues completed on television effects (Comstock *et al.*, 1978). Though methodology is emphasized, it is hoped that this is not done in such a way as to neglect the underlying theoretical concerns that motivate concern with these methods in the first place. Theory and method interact. The search for an abstract and freestanding "theory of human communications" is unlikely to be a promising strategy. The process of mass communications, for example, is an element in the maintenance of modern industrial democracies, in the economic development of the Third World, and in the transmission of values and beliefs across generations. It is inappropriately seen as an independent and unique field of social scientific scholarship. Such a position resonates with the early writings of Weber and

Lasswell—mass communications in modern times is an integral part of social, cultural, and political change.

III. RETHINKING THE COMMUNICATIONS EFFECTS PARADIGM

Experimental research, survey research, content analysis, and field research each have their widely celebrated shortcomings. It is not that the data produced by each method is without value, but rather that each is, in itself, incomplete. The experimental tradition, for example, is helpful in understanding certain types of communications effects. Take as an illustration an individual who has been puzzling for several days over what gift to buy for a close friend's birthday. A television ad provides information on an ideally appropriate gift. The "persuasive" information provided in the advertisement fits neatly with the expectations and needs of the individual. It represents a short-term process that is subject to meaningful manipulation through experimental designs. But such methods are less appropriate to the study of persuasive political communications in a national election. The accumulation of bits of political information from months of half-attentive monitoring of the news media, the evaluation of several years of an incumbent's performance, the interpretation of complex political symbolism linked to party identifications passed on from parents and grandparents, for example, does not lend itself to realistic laboratory simulation.

Because most researchers are trained in only one methodological tradition, they tend to apply it to each substantive issue they confront. The advantages and disadvantages of a given method are well known and acknowledged by its practitioners, but they tend, over time, to develop a taken-for-granted quality. As a result, it may be appropriate to give special emphasis to the complementary nature of the different approaches.

Figure 1 uses the traditional notions of internal and external validity as organizing concepts to illustrate the complementary character of four dominant methodological traditions (Babbie, 1986; Ball-Rokeach, Grube, & Rokeach, 1984; Wimmer & Dominick, 1983).

Experimental research, by limiting the variation to manipulated variables, is in a position to conclude that any differential effects are the unambiguous result of the manipulated variables. Thus, the inference of effect is high on internal validity. But such manipulations are obtrusive and artificial, least like social phenomena in natural settings, and thus low on external validity. In contrast, content analysis unobtrusively monitors social phenomena as they take place (higher external validity) but is much less able to infer causal structure (internal validity). Survey and field research fall somewhere in between.

```
        Experimental      Survey         Field         Content
          Designs        Research       Studies        Analysis


                    Increasing   Internal   Validity
         ◄─────────────────────────────────────────────────


                    Increasing   External   Validity
         ─────────────────────────────────────────────────►
```

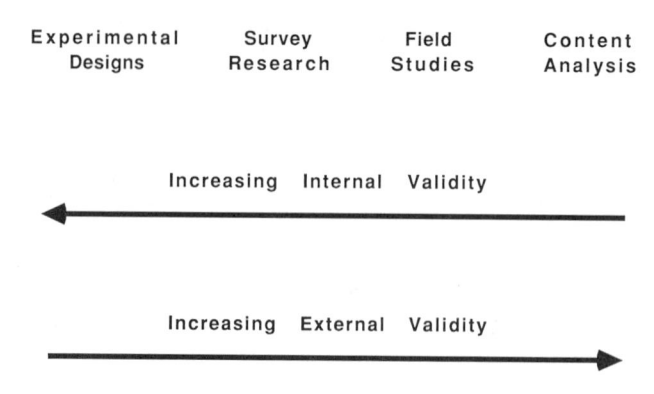

Fig. 1. Research methods in communications effects research.

Most reviews of methodology and of accumulated research studies conclude, appropriately, that scientific consensus emerges out of convergent findings across methodological designs. This is explicitly incorporated in Campbell and Fiske's (1959) widely cited notion of convergent validity. Parallel content analysis attempts to draw on these complementarities by combining elements of survey research, field research, and content analysis. Experimental research is not included and, as a result, there are potential problems of causal inference and internal validity. Time-series measurement is emphasized in an effort to compensate for that weakness.

A. The Limits of Experimental Research

Picture, if you will, a platoon of soldiers in garrison during World War II rising as usual before dawn. The noncommissioned officers direct the platoon to a classroom. The soldiers are given what looks like an examination asking about their personal opinions on military strategy. The soldiers are shown a film entitled "The Battle of the Britain" and are asked to fill out a follow-up questionnaire while sergeants stand with crossed arms at the rear of the room.

Was the film persuasive? Did it change opinions? Perhaps. Unfortunately, the psychological dynamics of the experimental situation are close to those of routine military training films and examinations, a familiar script by which soldiers as students try to figure out the right answers as they complete the questionnaire. We may be able to learn something about the highly structured and institutionalized communications processes from such research but relatively little about the long-term accumulation of information and the process of social attitude change among citizens.

Another classic experiment in this field is the Bobo doll study (Bandura, Ross, & Ross, 1963). Children were randomly assigned to groups, one of which observed aggressive behavior performed by a live actor, and another of which saw films of aggressive behavior sometimes involving actors dressed up as cartoon characters. A control group saw neither. The children were put in a room that contained toys and a three-foot, inflated Bobo doll, the type designed to be punched and bounce back to an upright position because of the weighted base of the doll. Observers coded children's behavior and found that the aggressive acts performed by the live and filmed actors resulted in increased levels of aggressive play, including sitting on the Bobo doll's head and hitting it with a mallet.

The experiment has the advantage of relying on observed behavior rather than attitudes. But Bobo dolls are designed to be hit. Rather than "learned behavior," the children might in part have been stimulated to higher levels of activity and energy which, in the absence of Bobo dolls, might not have been defined as aggressive behavior. Further, it is not clear that aggressive play with toys translates to aggressive or antisocial behavior with real people such as hitting a playmate over the head with a mallet. To build on these examples and extend the argument, we will identify nine components to the problem of external validity in experimental design.

1. *The Complexity of the Stimulus*

A half-hour film on military strategy or even a short skit illustrating aggressive behavior represents an extremely complex social stimulus. Different aspects of the stimulus might be recalled or interpreted in very different ways by different audience members. Such experimental stimuli are designed to make a particular point, but they inevitably communicate other subtle and unintended messages as well. Traditionally, in experimental design, researchers treat the character of the stimulus as a given and treat the varying interpretation and misinterpretation of the stimulus as measurement noise.

Some experiments have addressed the complexity of the stimulus and in doing so dramatically illustrate its importance. Cooper and Jahoda (1947), for example, studied the reactions of individuals to cartoons designed to poke fun at bigotry. An intent was to use gentle humor to demonstrate to individuals the error of their prejudiced ways. But the researchers found that the creative ability of prejudiced subjects to restructure and reinterpret these cartoons in light of their own beliefs far exceeded the intended persuasive effects.

2. *Artificiality of the Stimulus*

A related problem drawing from the effects-centric orientation of the experimental approach is a casual approach to selecting experimental stimuli. The accumulated "persuasive messages" on which the corpus of attitude change theory is built is a somewhat bizarre mix of stimuli including comic book preferences (Kelman, 1953), attitudes toward toothaches (Hovland *et al.*, 1953), and attitudes toward eating fried grasshoppers (Zimbardo, Weisenberg, Firestone, & Levy, 1965). Subject matter is selected most often as a matter of convenience. The impact of the character of the subject matter on the success of the persuasive messages is simply not defined as problematic (Hovland, 1959). This reinforces the next point.

3. *Attitude Creation versus Attitude Change*

Experimental researchers in search of attitude change tend to select topics in which firm attitudes and beliefs have not already been established. Thus, important beliefs about religion, politics, race relations, patriotism, or perhaps gender-role stereotypes are typically avoided. But such are topics on which true attitude change over time would be most relevant, both theoretically and politically. The early work by the Hovland team, for example, explored attitude change on steel industry industrial policy, the selling of antihistamines by pharmacists without a doctor's prescription, the future of atomic-powered submarines, and the effect of the growth of television on the number of movie theaters in the year 1955 (Hovland *et al.*, 1953). Such matters were of marginal concern to the typical subject, and, as a result, the phenomenon at hand might be more accurately characterized as attitude creation rather than attitude change (McGuire, 1968).

4. *The Artificiality of the Context*

Perhaps the most widely acknowledged problem of experimental research is the artificiality of the laboratory context. The Hawthorne Effect, experiment effect, or "demand characteristics" of the experiment may significantly distort the conclusions. In the classic examples, of course, respondents falsely exhibit what they perceive as expected behavior in an attempt to please the observing researchers (Rosenthal, 1966).

5. *Artificially High Levels of Attentiveness*

The attentiveness of students, soldiers, and experimental subjects generally tends to be at an unrealistically high level, compared with patterns of exposure to communicated messages in the real world. Typically, there is no competition for the experimental subject's attention by either distracting or competing messages. As a result, experimentally induced attitude change may be exaggerated (Hovland, 1959).

6. *Short Time Frames*

In the foregoing example of the television viewer pondering a gift selection, a behavioral effect follows closely upon exposure to a brief message. But such phenomena represent a relatively rare breed of communications effects. To fully understand advertising effects, for example, one needs to trace the long-term accumulation of impressions and purchase behaviors associated with competing brands (Comstock *et al.*, 1978).

7. Limited Samples

Because the experimental perspective growing from the tradition of psychological research attempts to characterize human behavior in general, students and soldiers are simply seen as representative of the human species. But, to the extent that such demographic variables as age and educational level intervene, as they often do with regard to social and political attitudes, one hesitates to generalize from a subject universe of college sophomores (McGuire, 1968).

8. Attitudes versus Beliefs and Behavior

Although some experiments have attempted to assess knowledge and behavior, the great bulk of studies in this tradition focus on opinion and opinion change as measured by questionnaires. This is traditional but not inherent in experimental design. The repeated call (in many of the recent reviews of the communication effects literature) for a much broader definition of dependent variables, including beliefs, knowledge, more broadly defined cultural norms, and behavior, reflects a growing and appropriate concern (Fishbein, 1965; Schuman & Johnson, 1976).

9. Individual-Level Analysis

The experimental paradigm by its nature focuses on individual differences and psychological processes. The study of organizational and group processes, as well as broader cultural and historical phenomena, is generally not amenable to experimental analysis (Comstock *et al.*, 1978; Durkheim, 1964; Katz, 1977).

10. Summary

The failure of experimental research lies not with the methodology itself but with the failure of experimental researchers to move their theory-building beyond the bounds of the experimental paradigm, to address and integrate data collected by other methods, and to examine communications processes other than those amenable to laboratory research.

B. The Limits of Survey Research

The quintessential example of the survey research tradition would probably be an election study such as Berelson and associates' *Voting* (1954). The strengths and weaknesses of the survey are quite similar to those of the experiment. In fact, most experimental work in communications uses a survey-style questionnaire for before-and-after attitude measures. In the survey tradition, however, the interviewing takes place in the home and attempts to assess the accumulated impact of real-world communications. Berelson and his colleagues interviewed 1029 residents in Elmira, New York over the summer of 1948 and traced changes in knowledge about and attitudes toward the candidates and issues of the presidential election of that year. They concluded that the media coverage of the presidential campaign seemed to have surprisingly little impact on voters' knowledge of underlying political issues or on voters' evaluation of the candidates. Berelson and his colleagues reported on what was to become in subsequent election studies a familiar pattern of low levels of political interest, limited familiarity with the issue positions of the candidates, and a general reliance on inherited party identification in voting decisions. In a concluding chapter, Berelson suggested that perhaps the limited political involvement of the mass citizenry may prove to be a long-term benefit of systemic political stability.

Are such conclusions and speculations about the process of American political communications truly justified by data of this sort? Perhaps not. Berelson and his associates conducted their first interviews in June of the election year and found opinions of the candidates to be quite stable through the summer to the election in November. They concluded that the media had not swayed many voters. What they did not study was the process by which those impressions of candidates Dewey and Truman had evolved through longer-term exposure to media coverage. Dewey, who had been governor of New York and had run a fairly close race against Roosevelt in 1944, was a well-known national political figure, and especially well known to the sample from Elmira, New York. Truman, of course, had been Vice President under Roosevelt and President since Roosevelt's death in 1945. Furthermore, the researchers selected a half dozen political issues from international relations to economic policy they thought might prove to be important in voting decisions. But evidence that these preselected issues were not critical in the voters' calculus does not mean that no issues were. For the most part in survey research, respondents can only agree or disagree with a predetermined and preformulated list of issues. There is scant opportunity for interviewees to reformulate an issue, to explain whether an issue is perceived as relevant, or to raise a new issue.

The authors of *Voting* were careful and clearly competent researchers. The larger sample size and real-world environments of their data collection represent clear-cut advantages over experimental designs. But, in turn, they have a constrained ability to make unambiguous inferences about underlying causal structures. The data from any single-method design must be put in perspective.

1. Attitude Measurement

The problem is again one of artificiality. In this case, it is the artificiality of the "attitude" as measured by surveys in contrast to attitudes and beliefs as they are manifested in day-to-day behavior. As with experimental design, many survey studies may mistake the phenomenon of attitude creation for that of attitude change. When an earnest young interviewer drives all the way out to one's house to ask one's opinion on some issue of economic policy or foreign affairs, most respondents try to oblige. If they have not given the matter much thought, they will look for a cue in the interviewer's behavior or a clue in the question wording that might enable them to express an opinion. Technical studies of survey responses reveal that slight changes in question wording or in the order questions are asked can significantly alter the distribution of responses (Berelson, 1966; Bogart, 1972; Payne, 1951; Schuman & Presser, 1981). When the same questions are asked of the same respondents in later interviews, significant proportions give the opposite response or opt for a no-opinion response. In one famous study, Philip Converse (1970) demonstrated that only one fifth of the respondents in a national study had stable opinions over time on a basic issue of political policy despite the fact that over two thirds would offer an opinion each time they were asked. George Bishop, Oldendick, Tuchfarber, and Bennett (1980) found that a almost a third of their respondents expressed opinions on a nonexistent Public Affairs Act of 1975 (Incidentally, they were evenly split in favoring and opposing the act.).

2. Measurement Error

As a result of these problems of getting respondents to admit they do not have a meaningful attitude on some issues, survey data is plagued with considerable measurement noise—a mixture of true attitudes, quasi attitudes, and artificially invented pseudo-opinions. Despite the fact that in aggregate, an apparently consistent 60% of the population support a particular issue in repeated polls, a closer analysis reveals that it is not the same 60% each time the question is asked. There is a consistent churn of opinion at the individual level. Thus, when survey researchers report the results to a decimal point or two, they convey a misleading and false sense of rigor and precision.

Because the actual effect of a single exposure to a message in the mass media may only involve a small percentage of the audience (Naples, 1979), the assessment of such effects through survey research is likely to become completely overwhelmed by measurement noise. These problems are compounded by a general confusion among many casual users of survey research between traditional statistical sampling error, which is typically in the range of ±3% and the more subtle and more fundamental forms of attitude measurement error in the range of 20–30% (Schuman & Presser, 1981; Selvin, 1968). An interesting debate in the field continues over whether this substantial measurement error is primarily the fault of ambiguous question wording or the ambiguous thinking of the typical respondent (Achen, 1975; Popkin, Gorman, Phillips, & Smith, 1976).

3. The Power of Prophecy

As with biblical quotations, most full-scale surveys will provide at least some support for almost any hypothesis one might care to test. The problem here is the ratio between reported findings and collected data.

The typical survey will include between 100 and 200 items. The typical research article based on survey data will report results on fewer than a dozen items. In selecting items, combining them into scales, and labeling indexes, there is considerable room for art amidst the science. This is distinctly different from experimental research in which the experimental design predetermines and limits the number of variables and the form of statistical analysis.

Selvin (1968), in his discussion of data-dredging in survey research, raised an important further question about the ultimate effect of selecting items from lists of available items on the interpretation of traditional sampling statistics. This problem compounds the measurement noise issue and may lead to a consistent pattern of *Type II statistical error*—that is, false positive conclusions.

There is another element to the power of prophecy in survey research. It is a corollary of always finding at least some evidence to support one's hypothesis. It might be described as the pattern of only finding what one is looking for. In survey research (as with experimental research) all of the variables of analysis are predetermined when the questionnaire is designed, so the analyst is unable to assess the effects of any unanticipated variables. The classic example here might be the extensive literature on television's possible effects on children's antisocial behavior. Over two decades, researchers concerned about the possible effects of violence in broadcasting looked for evidence that children's behavior might be affected, and indeed, from experimental and survey studies, found such evidence (Comstock *et al.*, 1978; Pearl *et al.*, 1982). But in the midst of the process, a new group of researchers raised a new question. Perhaps television has prosocial effects, teaching appropriate social behavior, cooperative behavior, and the like. When research was designed to assess prosocial effects, such effects were also found (Comstock *et al.*, 1978).

Survey data, like experimental data, will continue to be an important element in the scientific assessment of communications processes. The thrust of the argument here is simply that to rely exclusively on either, as have the great majority of communications effects studies in the literature, is ill advised.

C. The Limits of Content Analysis

Content analysis is a generic label for scientific attempts to assess the symbolic environment. P. J. Stone, Dunphy, Smith, and Oglivie (1966, p. 6) define content analysis as "any research technique for making inferences by systematically and objectively identifying specified characteristics within text." The classic study of the content analysis tradition would have to be an analysis of propaganda. One might take, for example, "May Day Slogans in Soviet Russia" (Yakobson & Lasswell, 1949), which attempted to trace shifting political strategies of the Soviet elite through the 1930s. Throughout this period, the Soviet Communist Party published a list of political slogans as part of the annual May Day celebrations. These slogans were authoritative and rich in political symbolism. American analysts intrigued by shifting Soviet political strategies decided to quantify and analyze trends in types of slogans propagated each year. Yakobson and Lasswell uncovered a clear trend away from calls for world revolution toward a more parochial concern with domestic policy and development of the Soviet economy (see Fig. 2).

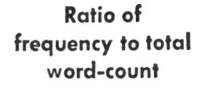

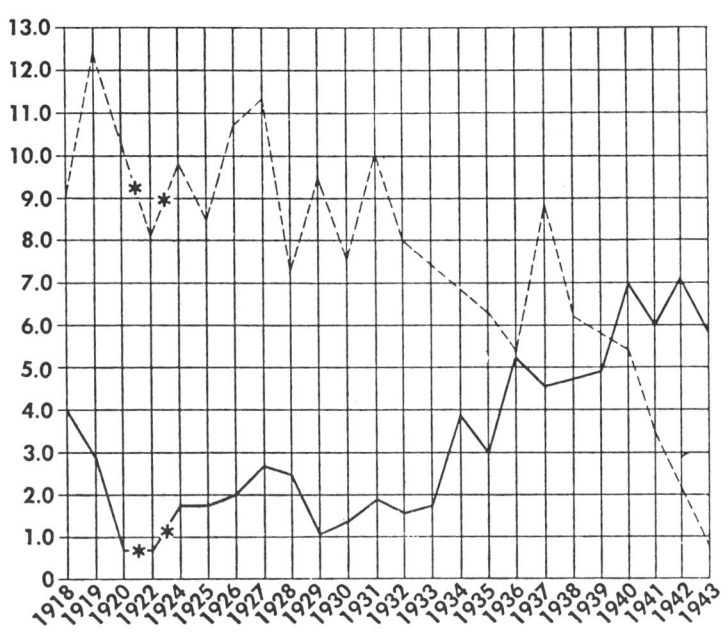

Fig. 2. Analysis of trends in the occurrence of national (solid line) and universal-revolutionary (broken line) symbols in May Day slogans of the Communist Party (USSR). Asterisks indicate that no slogans were issued in 1921 and 1923. Reprinted with permission from Yakobson & Lasswell (1949). In H. D. Lasswell, N. Leites, and associates (Eds.), *The language of politics* (p. 243). Cambridge, MA: MIT Press.

It is an exemplary study in several respects. First of all, by carefully coding and quantifying the political slogans, the content analysis clarifies a pattern that might not have been evident to an observer simply reviewing the texts. Second, by tracking content over an extended period of time, a trend not necessarily evident comparing any 2 successive years is evident.

The study of propaganda per se has receded from the forefront of social science. The tradition of content analysis proceeds, however, focusing on such matters as bias in news coverage and racial and gender stereotypes in entertainment content. One characteristic example of the new type of work would be the CASTLE study (children and social television learning) conducted at Michigan State University and sponsored by the United States Office of Child Development and the Department of Health, Education, and Welfare. Bradley Greenberg (1980) and associates analyzed the portrayal of antisocial and prosocial behaviors, black Americans, the American family, and traditional gender roles in prime-time entertainment television series in the mid-1970s. Greenberg reports on 13 studies resulting from the research. They found, for example, that blacks were represented on entertainment television programs in rough proportion to their presence in the population as a whole, but they were generally younger than whites, very unlikely to be portrayed as professionals, and very seldom cast in the role of villain. Hispanic Americans were found to be represented on television in proportions much lower than their presence in the population as a whole. And there were very few television roles for older Americans—less than 3% of characters were in the 65-and-over category.

M. Robinson and Sheehan's (1983) *Over the Wire and On TV* analyzed television and wire service coverage of the 1980 election campaign and typifies modern political content analysis. Their staff of coders measured the fairness, seriousness, comprehensiveness, and balance of coverage for different candidates, with special attention to the differences between television and print journalism. They found that on the whole the news media were objective and fair, but the broadcast media dealt more with candidate personalities and devoted more time to interpreting than describing political events.

1. The Failure to Stimulate Scholarly Interest

Content analysis is surprisingly little known and little used. To the extent that it does have a reputation, it is not a terribly good one. So, while it may seem unfair to blame those intrepid scholars who continue to work in these fields for a failure to have attracted much general scholarly attention, the method seems to have fallen even further short of its promise than experimental and survey research. Such a conclusion may sound a little strange because in the overviews of the field (Berelson, 1952; Gerbner, Holsti, Krippendorff, Paisley, & Stone, 1969; Holsti, 1968; Pool, 1959; Rosengren, 1981), one finds a generally cheery enthusiasm about progress in the field. But the more candid analyses of Janowitz (1969) and Markoff, Shapiro, and Weitman (1974) tell a truer story.

Janowitz, as noted previously, focused on Lasswell's ill-fated proposal for a world attention survey, based on an ongoing content analysis of the world's press, concluding that content analysis has failed to emerge as a common research tool. Markoff, Shapiro and Weitman describe content analysis as a methodological ghetto, isolated from developments in the philosophy of social science and social science methodology.

Only a few scattered courses devote primary attention to the methodology of content analysis despite dramatic growth in the academic field of communications research. *The General Inquirer*, a general use content analysis program, is in use in only a few research universities around the country despite the fact that it has been available for 20 years. Social science methodology textbooks, if they mention content analysis at all, dismiss the topic in a few pages, usually as an illustration of unobtrusive measurement. Content analysis, it appears, simply remains outside the mainstream of social science.

2. *The Central Problem of Inference*

Holsti's (1968) review of the field and Krippendorff's (1980) book make the same argument. Content analytic data, they assert, has to be used in conjunction with other types of data. If the issue is communications effects, data on the context of communications and changing attitudes, knowledge, or behavior must be collected. Content analysis data by itself can only be descriptive.

Such principles are clear and well-articulated but all too frequently lost in practice. Take, for example, Greenberg's (1980) *Life on Television*. The study was designed to measure not only content but also to involve field surveys of young people and their mothers and the relationship between viewing and behavior in different family contexts. The book, however, reports only on the content analysis and leaves the difficult matter of television effects and causal inference to a later, unspecified report.

George Gerbner and his colleagues have attempted to move beyond content analysis and have integrated several existing surveys with content analytic data. The effort is well motivated, but the disjuncture between the content analytic data and the available survey data has proven to be extremely problematic and fraught with technical difficulties. Much of the argument Gerbner and his colleagues make is that those who report watching a great deal of television have distinct social attitudes and beliefs. But the causal effect might work in the opposite direction—that is, people with certain distinctive world views might tend to watch a great deal of television. It is also quite possible that the relationship is spurious (i.e., other variables such as education explain heavy viewing and particular attitudes). A number of contradictory findings have also emerged recently. And the lack of coordinated measurement and the lack of time series measures have proven to be persisting problems (Gerbner, Gross, Morgan, & Signorielli, 1980, 1981a,b; Hirsch, 1980, 1981a,b; Hughes, 1980; McDonald, 1983).

3. *The Lack of Convergent Findings*

Unlike the collegial traditions of experimental and survey research, content analysis tends to be conducted by individual scholars working independently. There is little sense of a community of scholars or a scholarly organization that might be called upon to refine measurement and theory cooperatively. Each analyst tends to start anew, developing a unique coding scheme and a new sample of communications content. The conclusions are restricted to the particular content at hand, and the scientific tradition of replication is almost nonexistent in this field.

4. *The Distraction of Adversarial Content Analysis*

One of the reasons the content analytic tradition has not settled on some standardized codes to measure fundamental political, social, and cultural variables is that for those who are trying to make an adversarial point, it is more convenient to shape the coding process to dramatize the findings one seeks to uncover.

One well-known example of adversarial content analysis is Edith Efron's (1971) *The News Twisters*. Ms. Efron is a free-lance journalist, and was a frequent contributor to *TV Guide* while writing the book. She monitored the 1968 presidential campaign and recorded her impressions of when reporters were particularly snide or critical in their coverage of Nixon and Humphrey. She was convinced that the networks were biased and that they had favored Humphrey over Nixon. When she translated her impressions into quantitative form, the results struck her as damning empirical evidence, but her measures were never clearly defined and the whole process only vaguely approximated a systematic content analysis.

More recently, unions have asked members to watch TV and record evidence of antiunion content in the mass media and publish the results in their union publications. Also, business-sponsored, private research groups such as the Media Institute, "a tax-exempt research organization supported by a wide range of foundations, corporations, associations, and individuals (with the) objective of improving the level and quality of media coverage of business and economic affairs" have sought and found evidence through content analysis that businessmen are not treated as positively as they might be in the media (see, e.g., Theberge, 1981). As long as adversarial content analysis remains strong, its existence weakens the prospect that rigorous, systematic, and scientific content analysis will be taken seriously.

5. Lack of a Central Archive

Expanding on the point made previously about the failure of convergence, Janowitz (1969) argues that small-scale content analyses conducted by individual scholars tend to focus only on short-term trends over a few months or a few years. He argues that important social, economic, and cultural phenomena involve more gradual change that requires the analysis of data over years or decades. Such analyses require the coordinated efforts of numerous scholars and the existence of central archives. The Vanderbilt Television News Archives represents one positive development in this direction, but other efforts of longer-term measurement, such as the work of Naisbitt cited in Janowitz (1976) and the work of Gerbner and colleagues at the University of Pennsylvania (Gerbner, 1969, 1973; Gerbner & Gross, 1976; Gerbner *et al.*, 1980), have not been made generally available for analysis by other scholars.

6. The Unfulfilled Promise of Computerized Content Analysis

In 1966, Philip Stone and his associates published *The General Inquirer*, which described a new approach—computerized content analysis. Sponsored by the National Science Foundation and working with an enthusiastic young crew of sociologists, psychologists, and linguists at Harvard, Stone developed a general-use computerized system for content analysis of text. Their book included a provocatively diverse collection of studies, but the computer program had significant limitations, was difficult to use, and ultimately, was used only infrequently outside of the original circle of Harvard researchers.

Markoff and colleagues (1974) use rather strong language to argue that its disuse is as it should be. They describe computerized content analysis as "waiting for Golum." They argue that the complexities of language and meaning analysis require human coders in the content analysis process. Until linguistic and semantic theory and artificial intelligence advance computerized analysis significantly, they assert, rigorous content analysis using human judgment will continue to offer more promise.

7. Simplistic Coding Schemes

Markoff *et al.* (1974) make a more general point:

> It is apparent to us that content-analytic methodology today more often impoverishes documentary work than it enriches it. Social scientists who come upon an interesting collection of documents which they would like to analyze discover that the procedures most often and most forcefully recommended by specialists enable them to translate the contents of their text only in such ways as to yield results uninteresting at best and absurd at worst. (p. 2)

They point out that this is not an inherent part of content analysis but an artifact of simplistic and atheoretical attempts to quantify text for analysis.

It is a bit of a Catch-22. Theories about long-term social, political, and cultural trends are widely acknowledged as central to social scientific research. Over the years, small-scale content analyses addressing limited issues in limited contexts over short time periods have resulted in a small and undistinguished literature. Content analysis is relevant to the study of broader social trends, but because the connection between the two has not been well articulated, progress on both sides has been slow. Content analysis, unlike survey research and experimental work, lends itself to the quick and dirty. It is too easy to do a bad content analysis. The promise of content analysis as a central social science methodology has been stillborn. As Berelson (1952) puts it:

> Content analysis, as a method, has no magical qualities—you really get out of it no more than you put in, and sometimes you get less. In the last analysis, there is no substitute for a good idea. (p. 518)

D. The Limits of Field Research

The goal of field research in communications is to accumulate reliable and generalizable data on communications processes and effects in real-world settings. This often involves the use of such techniques as participant observation, field observation, or case studies (Babbie, 1986). Given the central problems of artificiality of setting and biases in research intervention in experimental and survey studies, systematic field data collection offers an important corrective.

One classic example of field research in communications is Star and Hughes (1950). They attempted to assess the effects of a public information campaign intended to educate the public in Cincinnati, Ohio on the purposes and goals of the newly founded United Nations. With the cooperation of the advertising community, the newspapers, and radio stations, a series of public service announcements and ads repeated the central themes of the campaign for several months. The research team carefully surveyed opinion and knowledge before, during, and after the campaign. They concluded that the campaign had little effect. Roughly one third of the population had a clear idea of the origins and purposes of the United Nations before the campaign, and the number was substantially the same at its conclusion. Those who were most familiar with the specific content of the public service announcements were those who already knew about the United Nations, and those uninterested in and uninformed about such matters appeared to be completely unaffected by the campaign.

Although there were literally hundreds of print and broadcast messages communicated, the researchers concluded that these messages represented only a small fraction of the flow of information to the citizenry of Cincinnati. It was an important and frequently cited lesson. Outside the laboratory, there is little motivation for audience members to pay attention to information, the relevance of which has not already been made clear. Thus, although the researchers used a survey technique in data collection, the public service campaign was a naturally occurring event characteristic of the field research tradition.

A more recent and much more elaborate communications campaign on health information provides another exemplary field study. It was conducted by a team of researchers from the Institute for Communications Research at Stanford and funded by the National Heart, Lung and Blood Institute. The researchers selected three matched communities in Northern California and developed an intense multimedia information campaign concerning the relationship of smoking and other health-related habits to heart disease. Group activities were also initiated to provide interpersonal reinforcement for the information in one community. The media campaign without group activities took place in the second community. The third community served as a control group. The health-related attitudes and behavior of residents were tracked at all three sites. The results revealed that the campaign was dramatically successful in influencing both behavior and attitudes when reinforced by interpersonal and group activities, and these effects persisted beyond the end of the campaign. In the community where the media campaign did not include interpersonal reinforcement, small positive changes in attitudes and behavior turned out not to be statistically or substantively significant (Comstock, 1983; Farquhar *et al.*, 1977; Maccoby & Farquhar, 1975; Maccoby, Farquhar, Wood, & Alexander, 1977; Maccoby & Solomon, 1981).

Although field research provides an important complement to data and hypotheses generated by other methods, its own limitations are significant.

1. *The Constraints of Convenience*

Perhaps the central problem of field research is that of external validity: the difficulty of inferring from one or two field sites to a meaningful universe of social settings. One hesitates, for example, to overgeneralize from the Cincinnati study (Star & Hughes, 1950). The quality and character of the public service announcements and the nature of the issue selected limit generalization. The conservative and perhaps partly isolationist Cold War mood following World War II may have meant that the United Nations campaign was ill timed, leading to unduly restrained conclusions about communication effects. In turn, the growth of health consciousness in California in the late 1970s may have resulted in misleadingly strong results in the Stanford study because, in a very unique way, the message put forward by these researchers about social behavior and health turned out to be the right message at the right time.

Indeed, much of what we know about the successful information campaigns is a result of the existence of interested sponsors willing to both conduct the research and make it available to the broader scientific community. The recent volume published by Sage on public communication campaigns (Rice & Paisley, 1981), for example, resulted from a conference sponsored by the National Wildlife Coordinating Group of the U.S. Department of Agriculture, Department of the Interior, the U.S. Fish and Wildlife Service, and the National Association of State Foresters (among others). Not surprisingly, the two most frequently cited entries in the index are Everett Rogers and Smokey the Bear. Behavioral generalizations would benefit from a more systematic and theoretically grounded sampling of field research sites rather than an aggregation of available studies. We know something about seat belt campaigns and the attempts to market soy ice cream because the results have been published. However, few proprietary advertising or political advertising research reports generally ever work their way into the compendium of accumulated scientific findings.

2. *Problematic Causal Inference from Field Studies*

This is, of course, the classic complaint of the experimentalist who looks with concern, and frequently, some befuddlement at the attempt to figure out what is related to what from field data. Among the classic examples frequently used to engage the curiosity of communications students is the problem of whether an observed correlation between exposure to violent television and aggressive behavior among children is the result of the propensity of aggressive children to watch action-oriented television programming or whether the causal direction might run the other way (Chaffee, 1972). The ecological fallacy of causal inference from aggregated data is widely recognized (W. S. Robinson, 1950).

Even time-series data from field settings require great care in causal inference. The classic example of words of warning along these lines was put forth by statisticians Yule and Kendall (1950). They became intrigued by the apparent evidence that the growth of radio caused increased mental deficiency. (The historical data are illustrated in Fig. 3.) They concluded, of course, that those were simply coincidental trends. Other scholars, however, have noted that the growth of television parallels a distinct decline in the strength of the political party system and an equally dramatic decline in the average Scholastic Aptitude Test (SAT) scores of the high school population in the United States. Such relationships are plausible and generate an appropriate call for research, but such evidence is far from unassailable.

3. *Small Effects Lost in Measurement Noise*

McLeod and Reeves (1980) comment on a generic problem of nonexperimental designs—they depend on "natural variation":

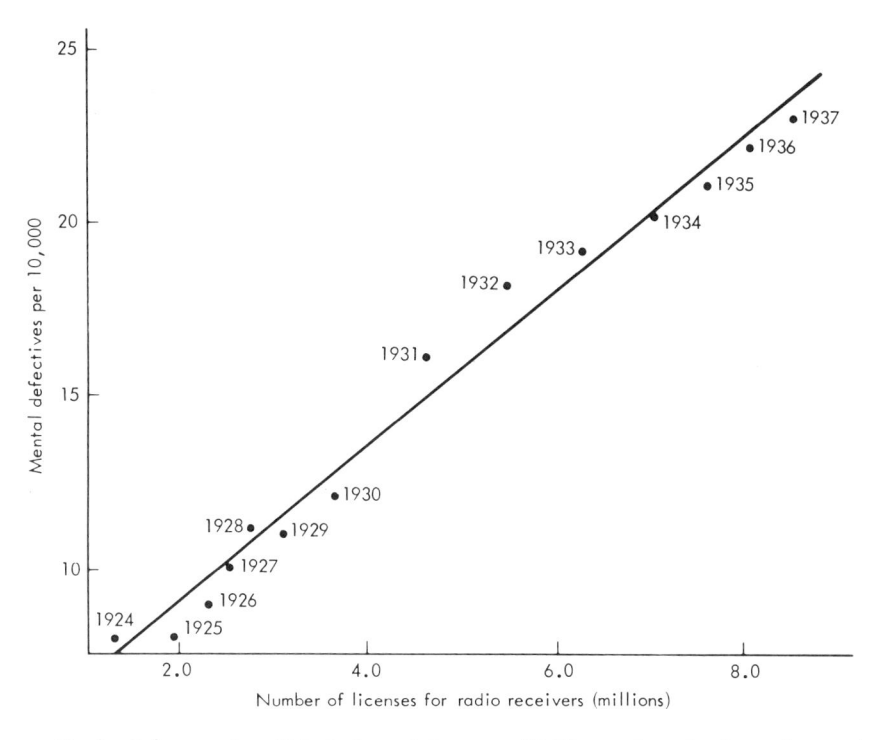

Fig. 3. Inferences from historical correlation, $r = .99$. The number of radio receivers and number of mental defectives in Great Britain, 1924-1937. From Tufte (1974). Reprinted with permission.

> There is an old dictum in experimental research that urges the researcher to "start strong" in manipulating the differences between conditions. The nonexperimental counterpart of this dictum is to find sufficient variance in natural conditions of the stimulus such that the significant relationships of the effects might be obtained. This is a potential problem for mass media research where the level of exposure is being measured...this would markedly lower the likelihood of finding any strong association with the effect variables. (p. 31)

McLeod and Reeves are not alone in making such assertions. Such arguments are frequently found in reviews of the literature. But it is a troubling bit of advice, in that it seems to blame the methodology for the existence of small effects and to call for a systematic emphasis on atypical field settings. If, in the majority of real-world circumstances, there are only small differences in stimulus level, one might well expect communications effects to be relatively small, and that is generally going to be true for any single message or short-term information campaign. The purpose of well-designed research is not to demonstrate that effects are larger than they really are.

230   W. Russell Neuman

The true problem is that single-exposure communications effects tend to be so small that they are difficult to separate from measurement noise. The appropriate response is to try to improve the precision of measurement and study effects over longer periods of time where they might accumulate to sufficient size.

In one of the few cases where large-scale field research on advertising effects using precise measures of consumer behavior has been made public, we find that, indeed, effects tend to be quite small (Naples, 1979). Figure 4 shows that among those who have regularly used a household product, the likelihood of purchase over a 4-week period moves up gradually 2 percentage points after

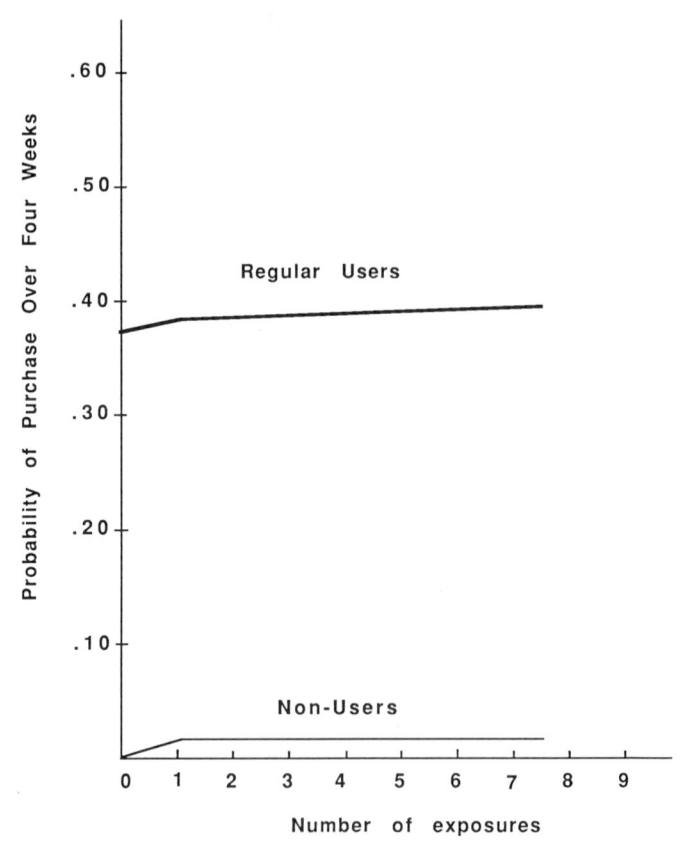

Fig. 4. The size of communications effects: increase in probability of purchasing a household product as a result of multiple commercial exposures. From Naples (1979). Reprinted with permission.

seven exposures to the ad campaign, and among those who do not regularly use the product, probability of purchase increases 2 percentage points after one exposure and not at all thereafter. With random measurement error in the range of ±3% and systematic measurement several times that in most field studies, it is no wonder that the demonstration of single-exposure, short-term effects is fraught with frustration.

4. Narrowly Defined Dependent Variables

Most field research, especially when it is sponsored by agencies such as the Forestry Service or the Transportation Department, has a clear-cut interest in explicitly intended, narrowly defined effects of information campaigns. Thus, we have some data on how Smokey the Bear and his colleagues have influenced public knowledge and perception of forest fire dangers, but it is not known whether any of the dramatic public service announcements may have unintentionally inspired a few cases of pyromania or generated an increased fear of camping in national parks among other viewers.

The strong tradition in this research paradigm is to document the presence or absence of intended effects. Perhaps, in time, designs will be modified to explore a fuller mix of intended or unintended results of persuasive campaigns. Phillips (1986), for example, has made creative and productive use of what he calls the "found experiment," focusing thus far on the impact of widely publicized suicides, accidents, and executions on rates of violent behavior. Hopefully, his work will stimulate a broader array of field research.

E. The Nature of Communications Effects

In the late 1950s, Wilbur Schramm started to use the phrase "the bullet theory" to characterize simple-minded, stimulus–response notions of communications effects. Since then, no review of the field has been complete without a ritualized acknowledgment of how simplistic the early bullet theories were in thinking about communications effects and how much more sophisticated we have become since then.

1. The Bullet Theory

In De Fleur and Ball-Rokeach's *Theories of Mass Communication* (1982), for example, bullet theory is explained as follows:

> *Media Messages as Magic Bullets.* In the aftermath of the war, there emerged a quite general belief in the great power of mass communication. The media were thought to be able to shape public opinion and to sway the masses toward almost any point of view desired by the communicator.... But in retrospect it has come to be called the "magic bullet theory." In more contemporary times it has also been called by other colorful names, such as the "hypodermic needle theory" and the "transmission belt theory." The basic idea behind

these names is that media messages are received in a uniform way by every member of the audience and that immediate and direct responses are triggered by such stimuli. (pp. 160-161)

It is a rich metaphor.[2] Bullets are nasty, fast-moving, unavoidable, life-threatening little things. The metaphor draws on the mythology of war-time propaganda, the parallel notions of wars of bullets and wars of words. For propaganda to affect audience members, it need only hit them. There is no room for the individual to interpret or ignore the message. This perspective also resonates with the social problem orientation of students of mass communications—the general concern that the mass media "cause" juvenile delinquency, passivity, lower grades, antisocial behavior, sexual promiscuity, and so forth.

Despite the numerous pronouncements about how far communications research has come, the bullet theory continues to dominate the communications effects paradigm. Researchers continue to study the effects of individual messages on audience members. We have come to understand that individuals may interpret or ignore a message, but for the most part, theories have advanced only to allow different types of audience members to be differentially affected once they are "hit." Theorizing about advertising effects continues to count how many "bullets" it takes (as measured in exposures or gross ratings points) to increase brand share. Researchers rely as heavily as ever on before-and-after attitude change measures.

2. The Notion of Communications Flow

There is, however, an alternative metaphor—one based on the notion of communications flow.[3] It conjures up the notion of a steady stream of information, ideas, and images that, over a long period of time, influence public thinking as the flow of a river etches clearly discernable patterns in the rock of the river bed.

Rather than focus on an individual message or a series of messages, researchers might analyze the shifting character of flows of information and ideas. Some types of people and institutions—like some types of soil and rock—may be more influenced by the complex chemistry of water. But to conduct experiments by watching droplets of water bounce off rocks in laboratory has limited value.

---

[2] G. E. Lang and Lang (1981) have argued that bullet theory never really existed as such. They may well be correct, but it is such a powerful metaphor and convenient way of characterizing the process in communications theory that the Langs are unlikely to succeed in changing the way the field characterizes itself.

[3] The term is drawn from the recent work of Ithiel de Sola Pool (Pool, Inose, Takasaki, & Hurwitz, 1984).

3. Five Principles

There are five principles concerning the complex accumulative character of communications effects that might inform measurement and theory building:

a. The Complexity of Communications Content. Understanding the effect of bullets is like eighteenth-century physics. The question is how much damage is caused by a given amount of mass accelerated by a given amount of kinetic energy. The understanding of communications processes might more fruitfully be based on twentieth-century analytic chemistry. Each message, even when taken singly, represents a complex compound with dominant elements and traces of other chemicals structured in complex ways. The job of the analytic chemist is to try to analyze the compound by watching the way it interacts with a series of other chemicals. The key, of course, is to discover a *pattern* of interaction effects. Too often in communications research, conclusions are drawn from a single interaction.

Furthermore, following the notion of communications flow, one wants to look beyond the effects of a single message to the effect of a large accumulated series of messages. An experimentalist is likely to be puzzled by such a suggestion. Could researchers possibly assess the effect of a whole library of messages rather than a single message? Only a tiny fraction of the library's content is actually read by any one individual. But it is true, nonetheless, that by content analyzing a sample of books from a typical library in the United States and one in the Soviet Union or the Third World, one would uncover profound differences in the character of the ideas emphasized and how they are structured. Further, one could take two identical libraries in different communities and find that what the public chose to read in each revealed consistent and meaningful patterns of public interest. From such a perspective, one moves away from individual attitude change toward a broader definition of accumulated effects.

b. The Complexity of the Interpretation of Communication. In the early 1950s, when Talcott Parsons and his colleagues at Harvard attempted to formalize a model of human behavior, the "theory of action," they gave a great deal of thought to how the modeling of social behavior differed from the modeling of physical phenomena (Parsons & Shils, 1951). One of the ideas they emphasized was that individuals do not simply respond to the pressures in their social environment; they interpret those pressures. The importance of human interaction in communications was widely incorporated into social science theory, including the notions of cognitive dissonance (Festinger, 1957), prejudice and racism (Adorno, Frankel-Brunswik, Levinson, & Sanford, 1950), political ideology (Lane, 1962), and symbolic communications (Goffman, 1974), to name a few.

But in communications effects modeling, the dominant formulation focuses on the notion of media uses and gratifications. This formulation draws attention to individual motivations in media exposure broadly defined, such as selecting television viewing over book reading. It is clearly a step in the right direction but moves research, so far at least, only a few steps toward understanding the critical importance of the interpretation of communications. We need to move further toward understanding the uses, gratifications, and interpretations of specific messages.

c. The Complexity of the Behavioral Response. The more recent reviews of the communications effects literature have begun to assert that researchers have begun not only to move beyond the bullet theory, but also to rely less often on attitudes as the dependent variable. Communications researchers, it is asserted, are looking now to more broadly defined "cognitive effects." Again, it is clearly a step in the right direction, but attitudes as measured by traditional questionnaires are still so much more convenient to assess than complex patterns of cognitive structure or behavior that they continue to dominate research reports in the literature.

d. The Complexity of the Communications Environment. A number of thoughtful observers have commented on the importance of understanding not only the communications process but also the environment in which it takes place (Freidson, 1953; Riley & Riley, 1959). They have pointed out, for example, that the classic Lasswell model of "who says what to whom with what effect" omits the element "in what environment." A given message is likely to have a differential impact if it is placed in an entertainment as opposed to a news program. It is likely to have a differential impact if it is said either by a teacher in a classroom or by a close friend. It is likely to have a different impact in the context of different national political systems. This is all painfully obvious and frequently acknowledged, but in the accumulation of scientific evidence on communications effects, the communications environment remains a source of concern but not an analytic variable. Laboratory and field experiments are designed to be exemplary and typical. It is not supposed to make any difference if you replicate the experiment in a different laboratory. It is prohibitively expensive to attempt to sample multiple field settings and systematically compare results across them. But if researchers are to take the widely recognized importance of the communications environment seriously, this problem must eventually move from the status of exogenous annoyance to analytic variable.

e. The Time Frame of Effects. Again, as noted in the notion of communications flow, the nature of communications effects is likely to be slow and cumulative over long periods of time. Bullets move quickly. Ideas and information do not. The dominant methodologies of communications research allow researchers to assess effects over a few hours or perhaps a few weeks or months. The curious result is that 90% of methodological effort in this field is focused on 10% of the communications process.

4. The Social Problems Orientation of Communications Research

There are several historical treatments of how the history of communications research is tied to the history of emerging social problems (Lowery & De Fleur, 1983; Neuman, 1981; Reeves & Wartella, 1982).

It makes sense. Why would the government or foundations pay for studies of successful and routine communications processes? As a result, we find abundant research on how movies cause juvenile delinquency, propaganda distorts citizen judgment, advertising hypnotizes consumers, comic books seduce the innocent, radio programs cause panics, and television stunts the intellectual growth of our children.

Perhaps it would be naive for researchers to refuse funding from agencies and citizens concerned about a particular social problem, but, in turn, researchers should try to avoid the crisis mentality of hurriedly conducted, short-term research and attempt to address longer-term social, cultural, and political trends.

An artifact of the social problem orientation is a special concern with children as an audience. This emerges from the traditional collective responsibility for the education of children and the need to pass on one's cultural heritage and social traditions. Also, children are seen as especially helpless in protecting themselves from the onslaught of persuasive messages. As a result, about half of the research in the field of communications focuses on children (Comstock & Lindsey, 1975)—a group that, in effect, represents a relatively small fraction of the audience.

The ebb and flow of communications research will continue to follow immediate social concerns. For a while, in the early 1980s, it looked as though we were about to witness a shift from the effects of television to the effects of videogames on children, but the videogame fad proved to be short lived and the effects of personal computers emerged as a hot topic (Greenfield, 1984). It is hoped that some of these energies can be harnessed to address the underlying questions of communications flows through evolving communications technologies.

IV. EMERGING MODELS FOR COMMUNICATIONS RESEARCH

Each "school" of communications research fits within the general communications effects paradigm but emphasizes a subset of variables and methods. There are variations, but the emergence of a new school usually follows a pattern. A seminal study incorporating a new catchphrase such as "agenda setting" or "uses and gratifications" and a new twist in research design is published. The original scholars, their students, and a few others generate a follow-on literature expanding and refining the original themes and measurement techniques. Within 4 or 5 years, the school becomes recognized and labeled in reviews of research and in textbooks as a new research perspective. The distinctive character of these research schools is that they respond explicitly to a perceived weakness in the existing research paradigm and draw attention to new variables and new methods. If the school is successful in promulgating its basic idea and methods, it begins to lose its distinctiveness and the urgency of its original mission. Thus, after time, the boundaries blur, and the research school is integrated into the general paradigm of communications effects research.

As the notion of research "schools" implies, each perspective has its devoted converts and equally devoted critics, both of whom emphasize the perspective's distinctive rather than common features with respect to the underlying paradigm of research. Thus, what is less often addressed is how the schools relate to one another and how the insights of each might eventually converge back into a central paradigm of communications research.

A. Beyond Attitudes

1. *Cognition and Learning*

One of the most frequently and approvingly noted observations about the development of communications research during the late 1970s and 1980s is the growing emphasis on the cognitive, learning, and knowledge effects of the media. This "cognitive" perspective emerged from America's heartland in the mid-1970s, emphasized by a number of scholars, including Peter Clarke and Jerry Kline (1974) at the University of Michigan, Steven Chaffee (1975) and Jack McLeod at the University of Wisconsin, and Lee Becker and Maxwell McCombs at Syracuse (Becker *et al.*, 1975). The cognitive perspective deviated from the typical school of research because there was no single seminal empirical study. In this case, the seminal work was a review of research published by Clarke and Kline (1974) in the second edition of a new journal entitled *Communication Research*. They were straightforward in announcing their intentions:

> Our purpose has been to stimulate imagination about mass communication and effects variables that can help disclose ways that media contribute to learning.... Arguments are presented for looking at cognitive outcomes as dependent variables in communications research rather than placing emphasis only on affective realms. (p. 238)

These arguments were expanded in Becker and associates' (1975) "The Development of Political Cognitions." Becker and his associates felt that it was ironic that the literature of political communications had focused so heavily on attitude change and the persuasive function of the media while ignoring the transmission of information through the news media. They concluded that the emphasis on persuasive effects was an outgrowth of historical concern with propaganda during the wars and a special concern of political scientists and political sociologists with political campaigns. They reviewed the existing corpus of research and drew attention to an intriguing pattern in the findings. Because of the widely acknowledged phenomena of selectivity and cognitive dissonance, audiences were not exhibiting massive attitude-change effects. This had led to the celebrated minimal effects hypothesis (Klapper, 1960). But, they observe, throughout the literature, there is abundant evidence of learning effects.

Clarke and Kline (1974) reinforce this argument, drawing on Patterson and McClure's study of the 1972 election (Patterson & McClure, 1976), which revealed that although political attitudes typically shifted only 1 or 2 percentage points, there were more dramatic increases in the range of 10–20% in voter knowledge about candidate positions over the course of the campaign, and that, importantly, increased media exposure was clearly linked to these knowledge increases.

Becker *et al.* (1975) cited emerging work on information gaps, political knowledge, and agenda setting, and concluded that by 1975:

> These recent studies dealing with media effects on information holding, together with the increasing body of research on agenda setting, manifest a major shift in the field away from studies of attitude effects. (p. 57)

This view was also emphasized by Roberts and Bachen's (1981) review of the literature and extended to the field of television and social behavior in the 1982 report published by the National Institute of Mental Health (NIMH) (Pearl *et al.*, 1982). In the NIMH report, Yale psychologist Jerome Singer (1982) characterized this as part of a major paradigm shift in psychology toward a broader-gauged cognitive orientation. By 1984, Chaffee concluded,

> I wouldn't be surprised to see it [the attitude change research tradition] die out completely once those researchers reared on Hovland and oblivious to the many theoretical innovations since have retired from the research scene. (S. H. Chaffee, personal communication, 1984)

On the one hand, one is hard-pressed to disagree with the notion that it is appropriate to examine cognitive–knowledge-dependent variables as well as attitude–persuasion variables. On the other hand, the celebration of a paradigm shift as indicated by Singer and Chaffee may be a bit premature. But researchers have not yet come very far in refining appropriate methods and theories for understanding cognitive and learning effects. The term "cognitive effects" has become increasingly popular, but the research designs and theories are still very dependent on the old persuasion, attitude-change model.

Take, for example, *The Presidential Debates*, edited by Bishop, Meadow, and Jackson-Beeck (1978), which presented studies of the 1976 Ford–Carter debates. The introduction of the book emphasizes new theoretical and empirical questions that evolved since the original studies of the Kennedy–Nixon debates (see, e.g., Ellsworth, 1965; Kraus, 1962; Middleton, 1962); these new questions emphasize voters' need for information about candidates' issue positions rather than a journalistic concern with attitude change and the perception of winners and losers. The central section of the book is entitled "Cognitive and Behavioral Consequences of the Debates." Yet, the studies reported in the book rely heavily on traditional before-and-after attitude change measures (Becker, Sobowale, Cobbey, & Eyal, 1978; Bishop, Oldendick, & Tuchfarber, 1978; Hagner & Rieselbach, 1978; G. E. Lang & Lang, 1978; Nimmo, Mansfield, & Curry, 1978; Steeper, 1978).

Two fundamental difficulties continue to plague this well-motivated and entirely appropriate impulse to refine the research paradigm. The first is a continuing reluctance of survey researchers to measure knowledge. The survey research tradition has continued to emphasize a need to maintain rapport with respondents and to maximize the expression of opinions by assuring respondents that there are no right or wrong answers and that each person's opinion is as important as the next person's. Accordingly, when it comes time to ask veridical questions of political knowledge, respondents are reluctant to have their ignorance clearly demonstrated, and interviewers are hesitant.

The second problem is that the information effects in question are, in a sense, tautological, and theoretically less interesting. If a television documentary or a newspaper news article straightforwardly presents 10 matters of fact that are correctly perceived by only 50% of the audience, what is one to make of such a finding? Either the journalists are incompetent in clearly presenting the information or large segments of the audience are inattentive or cognitively deficient. The conclusion that journalists should write more clearly or that citizens should be more attentive are less than satisfying.

The way in which the cognitive perspective will be most influential is in broadening the definition of the dependent variable in communications effects research to move beyond textbookish facts to deeper issues of political knowledge and sophistication and to the cognitive organization of beliefs (Neuman, 1986). Accordingly, research methods will have to move away from the educational model of teaching and testing toward a more open-ended approach, to understand how audiences come to interpret, understand, and organize information.

2. Cultivation Analysis

The most prominent model here is the cultivation analysis approach promulgated by George Gerbner and his associates at the Annenberg School of Communication at the University of Pennsylvania. The basic rationale for this approach was developed in papers by Gerbner in 1969 and 1973 and the reports of the Violence Profile, a content analysis of entertainment television (Gerbner & Gross, 1976). Generally, this perspective sets itself apart from the experimental model and proposes to examine the long-term linkages between media content and the audience response rather than a narrowly focused, short-term, cause-and-effect process. Five distinctive aspects of this approach to communications effects research can be identified.

a. A Broader Definition of the Dependent Variable. Gerbner and his colleagues defined the audience member's world view as the dependent variable. They seek to understand the

> Cultivation of issues, conceptions, and perspectives that gives meaning to all ideas and actions.... The "effects" of communications are not primarily what they make us "do" but what they contribute to the meaning of all that is done—a more fundamental and ultimately more decisive process.... All animals "behave" but only humans act in a symbolic context. (Gerbner, 1973, p. 568)

This has been characterized by McQuail (1977), drawing on Lippmann (1922), as the "definition of social reality." As Lippmann might characterize it, it is studying how media represent a conduit between the complex world outside and the (corresponding) pictures in our heads.

b. Emphasis on Symbolic Communications. Gerbner and his associates, whose work focuses primarily on television, argue that it is as important to study entertainment as it is to study informational media content. They note that the television world of situation comedies and cops and robbers creates a synthetic world of human behavior that cannot help but influence the viewing audience. Gerbner refers to them as standardized images or cultural stereotypes. The process of transmission and adoption of these organizing stereotypes is labeled a "cultivation" process in order to distinguish it from persuasion-type processes.

c. The Notion of a Symbolic System. Cultivation analysis emphasizes the coherent structuring of images into a symbolic system. In a vein similar to the agenda-setting notion, Gerbner (1973) argues that by emphasizing and ignoring certain elements of the real world consistently in media portrayals, the media come to communicate not only what is, but also what is important.

d. The Accumulation of Effects over Time. The cultivation school explicitly distinguishes itself from short-term experimental research by emphasizing longer-term, cumulative effects of media content. It is argued that an important effect of media patterns is reinforcement of existing beliefs and that evidence of effects need not require evidence of attitude change.

e. Unintentional Communications. This perspective emphasizes that numerous effects may involve phenomena neither intended by the communicator nor directly perceived by the receiver. The established institutions of mass communications are organized to maximize audience size and advertising revenue. Although such structural incentives may reinforce political and cultural orthodoxies, it is not necessarily self-consciously intended. In turn, the average audience member is seen as turning to the media for entertainment and information rather than out of a motivation to have cultural norms reinforced.

The perspective of the cultivation school resonates with the leftist critics of capitalist media, the so-called "critical school," which includes the work of Marcuse (1964), Mattelart (1980), Schiller (1973), Miliband (1969), and Curran *et al.* (1977), among others. Katz (1980) described this as the study of ideological effects of the media and traces the roots of this research to Horkheimer and Adorno (1944/1973) and the early speculations of Paul Lazarsfeld and Robert Merton (1948).

As with the general emphasis on cognitive effects, most observers applaud the incorporation of cultural effects into the communications research paradigm, and especially an explicit-linkage, general-exposure hypothesis and research oriented around exposure to specific messages.

The central problem for this school of research arises from numerous shortcomings of its initial empirical outings. Gerbner and his colleagues have chosen to keep the data within the University of Pennsylvania's walls and have developed a somewhat stylized approach to data analysis that, as one might have predicted, has led to a small storm of criticism (Doob & McDonald, 1979; Gerbner *et al.*, 1980, 1981a,b; Hirsch, 1980, 1981a,b; Hughes, 1980).[4] It is hoped that these methodological problems and distracting debates will not exhaust the researchers but will energize new efforts to broaden and strengthen measurements of these important and long-term social phenomena.

---

[4] The bottom line of these methodological dialogues seems to be that Gerbner's conclusions that television reinforces fears about crime and social-role stereotypes are not supported by other work. Because there are a number of other social and demographic correlates of heavy television viewing, it is very difficult to demonstrate that television's "view of reality" has cultivated a distinctive world view among heavy television viewers or whether it is caused by the other social factors. It turns out, according to Hirsch, that similar world views are also held by people who watch extremely little television, which suggests that it may be the other factors. Hirsch also criticizes the concepts of mainstreaming and resonance developed recently by Gerbner and his colleagues as contradicting the original thrust of the research perspective.

B. Beyond Direct Effects

1. Uses and Gratifications

The most prominent school of research based on the premise that communications effects depend on audience attitudes and expectations is referred to as the "uses and gratifications approach." It is a somewhat awkward label, but it seems to have stuck. Katz, Blumler, and Gurevitch (1974) characterize this perspective as follows:

> Compared with the classical effects studies, the uses and gratifications approach takes the media consumer rather than the media message as its starting point, and explores his communications behavior in terms of his direct experience with the media. It views members of the audience as actively utilizing media contents, rather than being passively acted upon by the media. Thus, it does not assume a direct relationship between messages and effects, but postulates instead that members of the audience put messages to use, and that such usages act as intervening variables in the process of effect. (p. 12)

The two principal premises, then, are (1) the active audience—active participants in the communications process, selectively exposing themselves to the communications flow, filtering and interpreting the messages in accordance with their own needs and interests, and (2) differential effects—the impact of a flow of communications or of a particular message will not necessarily be uniform across the entire audience.

The origins of this school draw on functional theory in sociological analysis, particularly as developed by Paul Lazarsfeld, Robert Merton, and Elihu Katz at Columbia University in the 1940s and 1950s (Wright, 1975). There are a number of classic studies from the early years of communications research that are still frequently cited to clarify the relationship between the uses and gratifications perspective and the more linear, stimulus–response effects model from which it emerged. Herzog (1944), for example, studied the audiences for daytime radio soap operas. She combined in-depth interviews and survey research techniques to explore the interests and motivations of housewives in the Midwest. In addition to the expected patterns of escape, emotional release, and entertainment, Herzog discovered that many listeners felt that they extracted a lot of practical advice from these programs. Listeners noted a great variety of helpful information, including hints on raising children, strategies for avoiding divorce, manners, fashion, and as one put it, "how to win friends and influence people" (p. 51). Similar results have been demonstrated more recently for television soap operas (Katzman, 1972). However, Herzog's pioneering work is still cited as an example of the importance of taking the view of the audience member in understanding the complexities of communications processes, the mixture of intended and unintended consequences of communications, and the blurring of the boundaries between informational and entertainment content.

In another classic study conducted by Berelson (1949), a newspaper strike in New York City provided a natural field experiment to explore what "missing the newspaper" means. Like Herzog, Berelson found that the habit of newspaper reading exists in a complex social milieu that involves a great deal more than simply keeping informed about public affairs. Berelson noted that newspapers in many ways function as an informational tool for daily living. Such routine information as radio schedules, financial information, and even advertising content were perceived as important elements in people's daily lives. The psychological importance of feeling informed and the relevance of public affairs information for maintaining social prestige became evident in Berelson's open-ended interviewing.

In a more recent study in this tradition, Katz, Gurevitch, and Haas (1973) conducted an elaborate survey of motivations for media use on an Israeli sample and developed a model of characteristic uses of the major mass media, including television, radio, newspapers, books, and motion pictures. Through factor analysis and the use of individual-level data to characterize the central media institutions, Katz and his colleagues developed a heuristic map of similarities of use across the media (see Fig. 5). The map represents, in two-dimensional space, the correlations for eight uses for each of five media (the closer two points are, the higher the correlation). In turn, the diagram creates a circle of the five media, with each being perceived as most like its adjacent neighbors. The dashed lines in Fig. 5 separate the political and personal needs satisfied by each medium.

One of the most impressive results of the empirical literature is the consistency with which the same four central motivations for media exposure turn up again and again in different settings. Although the terminologies and definitions vary, these represent the core concepts: (1) *diversion*—emotional release and escape from burdens and problems; (2) *surveillance of the environment*—the need to feel and to be informed about current events, social trends, so forth; (3) *personal identity*—the reinforcement of personal values, putting one's life in perspective; and (4) *personal relationships*—media as substitutes for personal companionship.

Most of the research thus far has focused on understanding the relationship of these fundamental motives to use of a particular medium and such unexciting findings as the observation that newspapers are heavily used for surveillance. Little is known about whether motivations are consistent for individuals or vary with moods and circumstances or how motivations

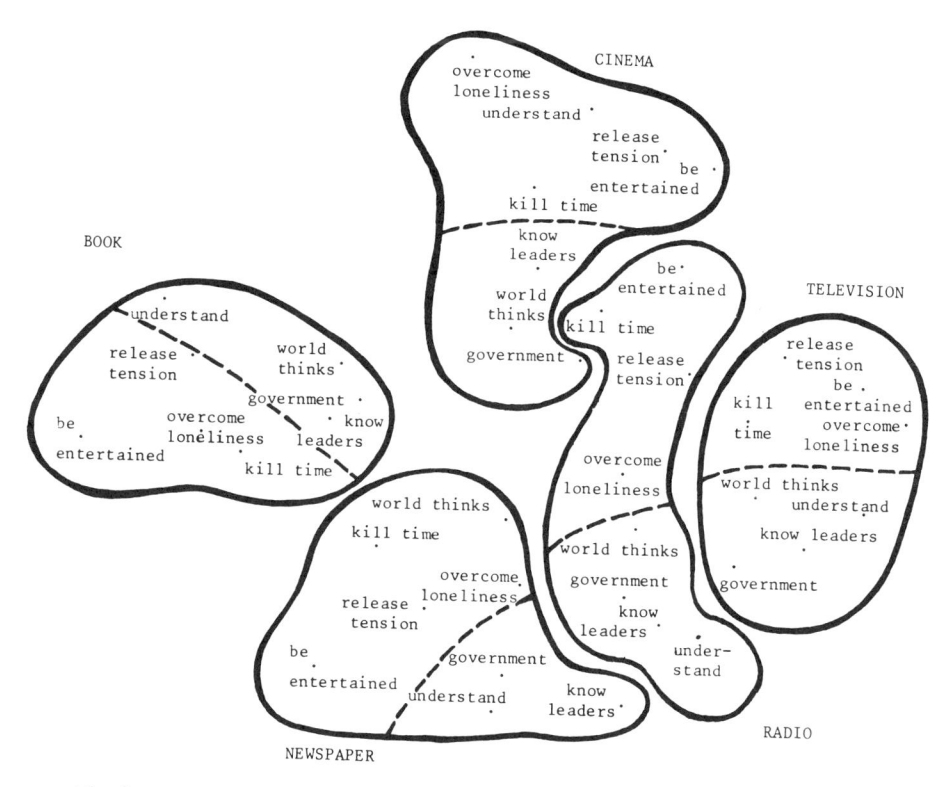

Fig. 5. A map of media uses and gratifications. From Katz, Gurevitch, & Haas (1973). Reprinted with permission.

influence patterns of exposure to types of content within a medium. More importantly, little is known about whether a different motivational set influences the perception and retention of content (Becker, 1979; Elliott, 1974; Swanson, 1979; Weiss, 1976).

A specialized methodological problem associated with this research is the difficulty of respondents to introspectively assess why they do what they do. Bem (1970), for example, warns that the imputation of personal motives involves a complex "psychologic" that may generate misleading results, frequently tainted by the individual's perception of what is socially desirable. As McQuail, Blumler, and Brown (1972) note,

> The relationship between content categories and audience needs is far less tidy and more complex than most commentators have appreciated.... One man's source of escape from

> the real world is a point of anchorage for another man's place in it. There is neither a one-to-one correspondence between communications content and audience motivation nor any such correspondence between the place on a presumed scale of cultural worth to which a program of material may be assigned...and the depth of meanings that may be drawn from them by many of their most keen attenders. (pp. 162-163)

But it should be noted that even among the critics of the uses and gratifications tradition, there is a consistent strain of sympathy for the approach. Critics support the attempt to study communications as a conditional, interactive process and criticize particular studies for not being methodologically rigorous or theoretically complete enough. The premise of uses and gratifications resonates strongly within the research community. As a result, it appears again and again under a number of rubrics as a central theme in the literature.

Clarke and Kline's (1974) notion of message discrimination represents an interesting example. They propose abandoning measures of media use, such as inventories of time spent with various media, and substituting a new measure they label "media discrimination." The new measure is based on what symbols and information respondents can recall seeing or reading about in the media. Clarke and Kline propose an open-ended interview technique by which individuals nominate important problems and describe what of relevance to those problems they may have learned from the media, the nature of their interest, and motives for paying attention. Such an approach, of course, emphasizes the audience's initiative and selective recall and interpretation. Given the current levels of media exposure and the size of the daily flow of information through the media, their proposal to start first with what audience members can interpret as salient would seem to be a promising strategy. Other similar efforts to derive new terminologies and approaches to measurement from the uses and gratifications notion have emerged recently.[5]

2. *Contingent Effects*

Another terminology, more general than uses and gratifications, has come into use recently. The term is "contingent effects." It simply draws attention to the fact that other variables intervene in the communications-effects process. One class of variables is, of course, the uses and gratifications orientation of the audience member. Other classes of variables include the context of communication, the reactions of other audience members, the age or

[5] In what appear to be independent efforts to introduce a new concept of communications effect, for example, both Kraus and Davis (1976) and McCombs (1981a) selected the term "transactional" to characterize the two-way nature of communications flow and audience interpretation. In another case, Windahl (1981) introduced the term "conseffects" as a combination of consequences and effects to emphasize the interactive process of media content and audience use.

educational level of the audience member, and so forth. Comstock *et al.* (1978) and McLeod and Reeves (1980) developed general models and a series of examples to demonstrate the potential importance of contingent conditions in communications effects.

3. Agenda Setting

When Maxwell McCombs and Donald Shaw, two young journalism professors at the University of North Carolina, Chapel Hill, set out to conduct a small study of local voters in 1968, they may have felt that they were onto some interesting new ideas, but they did not know that they were about to found a new research perspective. They drew on a phrase from an earlier study of the press and foreign policy (Cohen, 1963), which posited that, "the press may not be successful much of the time in telling people what to think, but it is stunningly successful in telling its readers what to think *about* [emphasis in original]." (p. 13)

This new perspective offered an attractive alternative to the model of persuasive attitude change. McCombs and D. L. Shaw (1972) content analyzed the local and national media coverage of the 1968 political election, quantifying the relative attention to such issues as public welfare, civil rights, fiscal policy, foreign policy, and the war in Vietnam. They also measured the relative attention given to these issues in aggregate from a small sample of Chapel Hill voters. (The central findings are displayed in Table I.) They concluded that these correlations represented reasonably strong evidence of an agenda-setting effect. They noted appropriately that because of the limits of the data, no causal relationship could yet be established, but it seemed to be enough evidence to sustain further inquiry. And further inquiry there was, involving several hundred papers and books, including D. L. Shaw and McCombs (1977), *The Emergence of American Political Issues*; Weaver *et al.* (1981), *Media Agenda-Setting in a Presidential Election*; and McCombs (1981a,b), "The Agenda-Setting Approach" and "Setting the Agenda for Agenda-Setting Research."

One of the most prominent elements of this research tradition is its emphasis on the cognitive processes associated with media effects. The approach is characterized by Weaver *et al.* (1981):

> Agenda-setting involves a learning process. People familiarize themselves with mass media images of the political world and learn through a variety of cues how important particular stories are deemed by the media. Learning story content and internalizing salience appear to be neither automatic nor uniform for different people or different subject matter or in different contexts. To fully understand agenda-setting, we need to know the scope of these variations. We also should know whether agenda-learning involves considerable thought and evaluation, or whether it is a comparatively mindless form of rote learning whereby people memorize media priorities and emphases without absorbing any of the information on which those priorities are based. (p. 20)

TABLE I

The Seminal Agenda-Setting Findings: Rank Order Correlations between Media Coverage and Voters' Ordering of Issue Salience[a,b]

	Correlation value	
	Major items	Minor items
Raleigh Times	.80	.73
Raleigh News & Observer	.91	.93
Durham Sun	.82	.96
Durham Morning Herald	.94	.93
New York Times	.96	.97
NBC news	.89	.91
CBS news	.63	.81
Newsweek	.30	.53
Time	.30	.78

[a] Modified from McCombs & D. L. Shaw (1972). *Public Opinion Quarterly*, **36** (2), 176–178. University of Chicago Press.

[b] 1968 presidential campaign, 100 respondents from Chapel Hill, North Carolina.

Like a number of the other emerging perspectives, agenda setting has its critics. Also, as with the other perspectives, the critics tend to support the basic impulse of the research and emphasize the need for more consistent and rigorous measurement and more clearly drawn lines between the findings and the underlying theoretical concerns.

Perhaps the most troubling difficulty is the problem of what Miller, Goldenberg, and Erbring (1979) call "real world cues." Some issues like high interest rates, inflation, gasoline shortages, and other phenomena have the character of impinging upon the daily life of citizens and being interpreted as serious national problems whether or not the media confirm such a perception with large-scale coverage. Although other events (such as the war in Vietnam), may not impinge directly on the daily lives of many citizens, they are of clear national importance and are still likely to be perceived as significant national issues by the citizenry, even during a lull of battlefield news or hiatus in antiwar controversy. Thus, the real test of media agenda setting requires attention to specialized issues, the significance of which are relatively unclear and the existence of which are unaccessible except for the media. Accordingly, more recent research has addressed the interaction over time of media coverage, public attention, and independently derived "real world measures" to sort out causes and effects (Erbring, Goldenberg, & Miller, 1980; MacKuen, 1981; Miller *et al.*, 1979; Neuman & Fryling, 1985).

There is an interesting tension in the agenda-setting approach between the individual and the aggregate level of analysis. At its root, the perception of cues about the political salience of issues is a psychological, individual-level process. The research methods of the original McCombs and D. L. Shaw (1972) study and the great majority of those following it, however, have relied on aggregated survey interview data. Only Doris Graber's most recent book (1984), *Processing the News: How People Tame the Information Tide*, relies heavily on depth interviews and a disaggregated approach to cognitive processes. But, this tension between the individual and the aggregate level yet may prove to be a productive one (Neuman & Fryling, 1985). Increasingly, the field is incorporating the ideas of Noelle-Neumann's (1984) spiral-of-silence notion, which emphasizes that each individual's opinions on public issues are perceived by individuals as either being consonant with or at some distance from the central tendencies of public opinion in general. Furthermore, McCombs himself in a recent article (1981b) has made the case that no single methodology is exclusively appropriate for agenda-setting research, but that a mixture of individual and aggregated approaches ought to be pursued.

Although there is considerable interest in the underlying metaphor of agenda setting and the associated research methods, the accumulated empirical findings thus far have been ambiguous and conflicting. Even within the two major book-length studies—D. L. Shaw and McCombs (1977) and Weaver *et al.* (1981)—there remain unresolved conflicts and contradictions in the data including those that bear directly on the agenda-setting hypothesis itself. In the Weaver *et al.* study, for example, parallel surveys were conducted in Lebanon, New Hampshire; Indianapolis, Indiana; and Evanston, Illinois. There was such a complicated pattern of confirmation and disconfirmation of the agenda-setting hypothesis, using identical methodologies at the different sites, at different time periods in the campaign, and with various dependent variables, that the authors had to compile charts to report the complex pattern of positive and negative results. Reviewing the full corpus of research studies reveals further conflicting findings, but in this case, the problem is further complicated by the diversity of methodological approaches. As Winter (1981) puts it: "The drive for total innovation has overwhelmed the scientific prerequisite of at least partial replication" (p. 240).

The general response of researchers in the field has been to try to sort out in which media, about which types of issues, and for which types of individuals the agenda-setting phenomenon is most clearly in evidence. It is not clear whether television or newspapers have stronger agenda-setting effects

(McCombs & D. L. Shaw, 1972, vs. D. L. Shaw & McCombs, 1977; see also Weaver *et al.*, 1981). There are conflicting findings on whether high-interest voters are more susceptible to agenda-setting effects or not. Mullins (1973) finds no difference; E. F. Shaw (1974) finds a positive relationship between interest level and agenda-setting effects; and McLeod, Becker, and Byrnes (1974) find a negative relationship. It is unclear whether intervening, interpersonal discussion lessens the agenda-setting effect of the media. McCombs and D. L. Shaw (1972) conclude that it does. Mullins (1973) concludes that it does not. Even McCombs's graduate students working together at Syracuse were unable to converge on an optimal time frame and time lag to demonstrate agenda-setting effects (G. Stone, 1975 versus Winter, 1979).

With the publication of several overview assessments of the literature in 1981, including those by Weaver *et al.* and McCombs (1981a,b), there was a clear-cut call for coordinated collegial efforts to develop a consistent approach to measurement. There is strong agreement that rather than attempting to infer effects from single-time surveys, every effort should be made to collect continuous time series data. And finally, the field must address the question of overall issue agendas, as well as the unique patterns in the rise and fall of issues over time. As McCombs (1981a) puts it, the agenda-setting metaphor is a powerful one, but we are early yet in the process of moving metaphor to theory.

4. *The Spiral of Silence*

Elisabeth Noelle-Neumann (1977, 1984) has been developing just such a theory for research on the dynamics of agenda setting. She uses the notion of a spiral of silence as her key concept. Her emphasis is on understanding public opinion as a public phenomenon, rather than a simple summary of private opinions. Most individuals, she argues, are inclined to weigh their own opinion against their perception of the climate of opinion before expressing their views publicly. If individuals believe they are in a small minority on a particular issue, they are less likely to express their view, or they will at least weaken their stand somewhat so as not to appear isolated or out of touch. Thus, emphasizing the negative side of such a dynamic, she notes that there may be a spiraling effect toward an increasingly isolated minority opinion resulting ultimately in public silence on an issue. Noelle-Neumann draws on the classic work of psychologists Solomon Asch (1952) and Stanley Milgram (1961) to illustrate the potential importance of perceived group pressures toward conformity in the evolution of public opinion. It could also work in the opposite direction, of course, as people realize over time that others share their views, and what was once an unacceptable or extreme position gains legitimacy over time. In either case, it raises an important element in the measurement of public opinion over time—changes in perception of the overall climate of opinion.

A key element in the process is, of course, media coverage of public issues and public reporting of opinion poll results. Individuals have impressionistic notions of the climate of opinion from talking to neighbors and friends, but on such matters as national elections and fundamental political issues, they must rely on the media and polling results for a sense of who is most likely to win and whether the public as a whole is increasingly concerned about a particular issue. Noelle-Neumann notes that perceptions of the climate of opinion can diverge sharply from the reality (as measured by polling data over time). In one case, she demonstrated that public perception of who would win the Bundestag elections of 1965 shifted dramatically in favor of the Christian Democrats despite polls that revealed a continuing tight race between the Christian Democrats and the Social Christian Democrats. It is not clear what caused this bandwagon effect (the Christian Democrats did end up winning the most votes) (Noelle-Neumann, 1977). But, in any case, such phenomena clearly merit closer scrutiny. Such an enterprise is custom-designed for parallel content analysis.

C. Toward Time-Series Analysis

1. Information Diffusion

A somewhat older and larger research tradition spanning several disciplines focuses on the diffusion of information and innovation over time. The field has its roots in rural sociology and the study of agricultural innovation. The seminal study is generally credited to Ryan and Gross (1943), who tracked the patterns and the adoption of a new high-yield hybrid corn seed developed at Iowa State University by farmers in the area. Between 1928 and 1941, they plotted the cumulative curve of adoption over time and found evidence of an S-shaped curve. Adoption, after a slow start, shot up 40% between 1933 and 1936 and then leveled off, approaching full penetration asymptotically. Ryan and Gross found that early adopters had higher incomes, had larger farms, and were more cosmopolitan, as measured by the number of trips they had taken to Des Moines. They found that the role of communications channels shifted over time, with early adopters receiving most of their information from salespersons and later adopters learning about hybrid corn from neighbors. Rogers (1983), who has participated in and monitored this field, described their study as establishing the research paradigm and putting an indelible stamp on the studies to follow.

A particularly interesting element of this research tradition is its emphasis on the failure, as well as the success, of innovation and communication campaigns. Rogers (1983), for example, traced the failure of an intensive 2-year campaign by public health workers in the remote Peruvian village of Los Molinos to promote the boiling of drinking water because of the impure water system. After 2 years, only 5% of the families of Los Molinos adopted the regular practice of drinking only boiled water in response to the health workers' efforts. Research revealed that the boiling of water had strong symbolic meaning in local custom for reasons not at all related to sanitation. The villagers believe that only the sickly should drink boiled water and that it was unthinkable that a person not yet sick would do such a thing. The villagers, Rogers reports, were resistant to attempts to explain the existence of germs in the water. They insisted that if the germs were so small, how could they possibly harm humans.

The role of the mass media in the diffusion process is perhaps best characterized by the classic study conducted by Neurath (1960). He studied the patterns of agricultural innovation in India. In this study, villagers listened to an agricultural radio forum describing basic and innovative farming techniques appropriate to their area. In one village, farmers simply listened to broadcasts. In another, they listened and discussed the relevance of the broadcasts among themselves. In a third control village, neither the radio programs nor the discussions were available. Neurath found that only with the reinforcement of local discussion were there significant innovation effects.

The underlying model of communications effects in the information diffusion perspective can be straightforwardly summarized: "Diffusion is the process by which an innovation is communicated through certain channels over time among the members of a social system" (Rogers, 1983, p. 5). The emphasis is on the flow of new information or innovation and its accumulative effect over time. Figure 6 illustrates the now-classic S-shaped diffusion curve and the traditional typology of early and late adopters. There is an intriguing pro-innovation orientation of this research, which labels those who adopt late as "laggards". Rogers explains that this research tradition results primarily from sponsored research of change agents and such an orientation is a natural outgrowth of that history. More recent research has attempted to take a more balanced view of the positive and negative impacts of various innovations (Rogers, 1983, pp. 92–103).

2. *The Two-Step Flow Theory*

This research tradition is, in effect, a subset of the information-diffusion school. It reflects another characteristic of new work on communications effects, in that it pays close attention to the social characteristics of those who are most receptive to new information rather than treating the audience as an undifferentiated mass. The two-step flow model emerged out of the Columbia voting studies of the 1940s and 1950s and focused on the flow of information from the media through opinion leaders to the mass audience. Despite extensive coverage in the mass media, voters appeared to be relatively uninformed about the issue positions of the candidates. The Columbia researchers emphasized the reassuring findings that better educated citizens

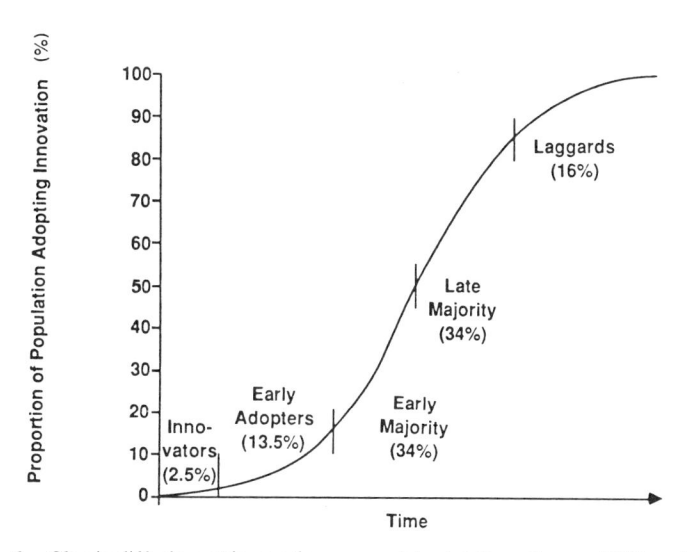

Fig. 6. Classic diffusion-of-innovation curve. Adapted from Rogers (1983, p. 247).

spent significantly more time attending to the media, were better informed about issues, and played the role of opinion leader in interpreting, explaining, and passing on information from the media to friends, colleagues, and family members. More recent studies have expanded the original two-step formulation to a multistep flow and a more complex process, with different types of people playing leadership roles in different issue areas (Katz & Lazarsfeld, 1955; Rogers, 1973; Troldahl & Van Dam, 1965).

Figure 7 summarizes the convergent findings of research in this field. As one might expect, education, social participation, media exposure, and other similar variables associated with social status are positively correlated with receptivity to innovation and new information. Early innovators, however, although demographically upscale, tend to be a self-reliant and independent lot, and accordingly are somewhat less likely to socialize and play the role of opinion leaders.

The more recent studies that reformulate one-way, two-step flow to a multistep, interactive process of discussion and interpretation among interested citizens converge with other emerging research models and blur the distinctive character of the original two-step model.

3. *The Information Gap Theory*

Another related model, which has emerged from the work of Tichenor and colleagues (Tichenor, Donohue, & Olien, 1970, 1980; Ettema & Kline, 1977), combines the idea of information diffusion and an educationally differentiated audience:

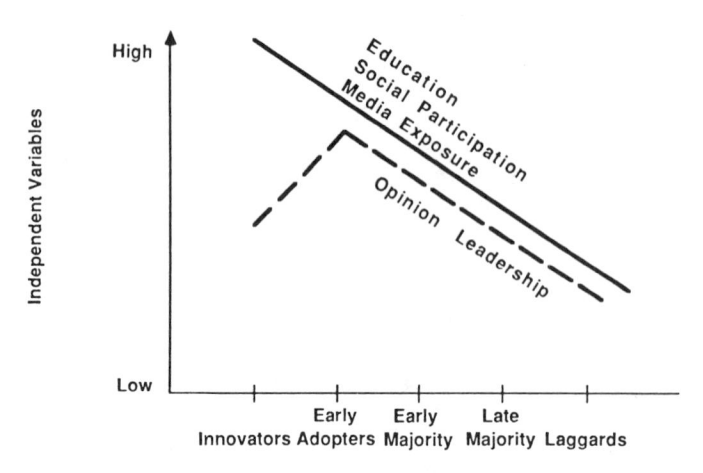

Fig. 7. Demographic correlates of innovation. Adapted from Rogers (1983, p. 262).

> As the infusion of mass media information into the social system increases, segments of the population with higher socio-economic status tend to acquire this information at a faster rate than lower status segments, so that the gap in knowledge between these segments tends to increase. (From Tichenor et al., 1970. *Public Opinion Quarterly*, **34**, p. 159. Reprinted by permission of University of Chicago Press.)

In their original study, they demonstrated that after several years of heavy media attention to space rocketry and satellites, the gap in knowledge about the space program across educational strata increased. Similar widening knowledge gaps were found for new information on the relationship between smoking and cancer. It is an important extension of the basic information diffusion model because of its emphasis on the possibility that widening gaps in political perceptions among different class strata could lead to increasingly polarized political confrontations.

In a thoughtful review of the information-gap model in 1977, Ettema and Kline expanded the research paradigm to include the corresponding and opposite *ceiling-effect phenomenon*—the prospect that over time, as a result of repeated coverage of an issue, the information is fully penetrated in the upper social strata and the lower social strata may, in effect, catch up. Ettema and Kline report a number of conflicting findings in their review of the relevant studies, and they appropriately turn their attention to the conditions and types of issues for which knowledge gaps or ceiling effects in the diffusion of information over time are likely to be in evidence.

Tichenor and colleagues (1970) had assumed that the knowledge gap would be primarily a result of less-developed cognitive skills and lower levels of media exposure among lower status groups. Ettema and Kline offer an intriguing alternative explanation, focusing on the motivations of different social groups to attend to such issues. They suggest that lower class individuals might well conclude that certain kinds of economic information is simply not relevant to them because they are effectively excluded from employment in certain realms. They suggest that the motivation–relevance variable as perceived by the different social strata be added into the theoretical model.

Rogers' (1983) overview notes that the information diffusion field has grown dramatically in the years following the seminal studies of agricultural innovation and now includes over 3000 studies across a range of social science disciplines. Three fundamental tenets of the research approach persist (1) a clear reliance on the element of time in communications; (2) an explicit recognition that communications take place in a social environment, with close attention to the structural characteristics and cultural values of that environment; and (3) a recognition that communications take place against a pattern of resistance. Perhaps one of the reasons that the interest in information diffusion is so strong is that innovation attempts so frequently fail.

V. PARALLEL CONTENT ANALYSIS

A. Common Elements in the New Research Perspectives

The inherent limitations of the experimental, survey, content analysis, and field research traditions have been outlined here. Communications scholars are, for the most part, well aware of these limitations. They criticize them in the work of others and attempt to overcome them in refining their own research designs. A number of new schools of research have also been reviewed. In each case, the evolving methodologies of the research schools self-consciously and explicitly attempt to overcome methodological limitations of previous work. The common elements of these evolving research perspectives provide a basis for a convergent approach.

1. A Broader Definition of Communications Effects

There has been a steady pattern of movement away from the narrowly circumscribed attitude-change paradigm as characterized in the work of Carl Hovland and his associates. The new work moves toward an exploration of the effects of communication on cognitive structures, political and cultural assumptions, knowledge, images, stereotypes, political agendas and ideologies. For the most part, these new research approaches are intended to supplement rather than replace the original attitude change model. The impact of mass-communicated messages on attitude change remains a matter of considerable concern. But increasingly, researchers are attempting to explore the interaction of attitudes with cognitive styles, perceptual schemata, and cultural premises.

Researchers are moving beyond a narrow focus on the intended effects of persuasive and advertising messages to explore a variety of unintended effects. Perhaps an appropriate example here would be the study of advertising effects. Initial work, naturally enough, focused on the ability of advertisements to increase product sales. Increasingly, however, scholars have become concerned with cumulative effects, especially the commercialization of American culture (Schudson, 1984).

The cultivation model notes that television producers structure their programs to develop a narrative denouement, and, of course, to maximize commercial popularity. They and their sponsors may be a bit curious about the long-term, accumulative, cultural effects of situation comedies and action-adventure shows, but such matters lie outside of their day-to-day concerns and outside of the purview of the research the industry sponsors. Such effects are subtle and difficult to measure.

The agenda-setting model notes that the process of gathering, editing, and presenting the daily news involves a complex interaction of professional journalistic norms and commercial considerations. Journalists do not gather at editorial meetings with the conspiratorial intent to set anybody's political agenda. They see themselves as reporting the day's news, not filtering, structuring, and interpreting complex and ambiguous events. But, over time, the effect of professional norms about what is and is not newsworthy may well come to structure political debate and public opinion.

There is also a clear shift from a linear, one-directional notion of communications effects toward an interactional model. A notion of an active audience, of uses and gratifications, of the interpretation of communicated messages, and of patterns of selective recall all draw attention to the interactional nature of the communications process.

2. Multimethod Models

In tandem with a growing belief that it is necessary to define communications effects more broadly, there is increasing recognition that any single approach is by itself incomplete. The fable of the blind men and the elephant comes to mind. For a while, experimentalists and survey researchers, each relying on their own data, debated the true character of the communications process. It may be that the eyesight of no single researcher has improved a great deal over the past 20 years, but there is at least an increased recognition that a consensual assessment, including the participation of each method, is needed. The concluding note of Comstock *et al.*'s (1978) massive assessment of the field focuses on this issue:

> In a single laboratory-type experiment, the role of statistical tests is to insure that a particular finding is highly unlikely to be the result of sampling anomalies. That role cannot be filled by replication in order to make inferences about events outside study. Replication

does increase confidence that within the limits of the method the finding is real, and it can expand the categories of persons for which a finding can be said to hold; but it does not ensure generalizability to real life events.

The unhappy fact is that no single method can provide unambiguous evidence of a real-life causal relationship. There is typically a trade off between lack of ambiguity for causal inference and the certainty of real-life applicability. There is also typically a tradeoff between flexibility, in terms of ability to study an issue and the diversity of issues that can be studied, and the certainty of real-life applicability. The laboratory-type experiment is strong for causal inference and in flexibility, but direct extrapolation to real life events is hazardous. The difficulty is that a finding may always in some way be attributable to the artificiality of the circumstances, so that what is "real" within an experiment may not be real in terms of actual events. [Reprinted from pages 491 and 492 of *Television and Human Behavior* by the RAND Corporation (New York: Columbia University Press, 1978). Copyright 1978 by the RAND Corporation. Used by permission.]

In resonance with that point of view, the agenda-setting model calls for a comparative analysis of media content data and survey data on public agendas. The work in the field has recently been expanded to include depth-interview methods (Graber, 1984; Weaver *et al.*, 1981) and field data on so-called "real world cues" (Ebring *et al.*, 1980; Zucker, 1978). The cultivation-analysis model integrates the use of content analysis, survey research, and, in some cases, field data. Other work on the structural characteristics of mass media institutions, such as that of Gans (1979), combines participant observation in the field with content analysis. All in all, these efforts appear to be a widely accepted and strongly encouraged development.

3. Research in Natural Environments

Another way of characterizing this trend is the movement from the laboratory to the field. It is not an abandonment of the laboratory but rather a growing recognition that laboratory data should be validated against field results. In addition to the growth of multimethod research designs, there is increasing use of field experiments. Ball-Rokeach, Grube, and Rokeach (1984), for example, have recently reviewed the increasing attention to naturalistic settings for media-effects research. This is also reflected in the agenda-setting tradition. The work by Iyengar and Kinder (1987) provides another important example.

4. Renewed Attention to Communications Content

This, too, grows out of the broader definition of communications effects and concerns about natural environments. In the experimental tradition, researchers commonly refer to communications content as the "stimulus." Such a terminology is revealing. It emphasizes the generic qualities of the message being studied. The message/stimulus is seen as a sample message taken to be reasonably representative of a general class of messages. Thus, any convenient persuasive message or segment of violent television content might well make a suitable stimulus for research in much the same way that college sophomores make suitable and convenient representatives of the human species. This reflected the long-standing effects-centric orientation of communications research. But researchers increasingly came to see the subtleties of meaning within the communications stimulus as worthy of closer attention. Comstock *et al.* (1978), for example, trace how research on children and television first used rather informal and approximate measures of overall television exposure and attempted to correlate them with behavior patterns. Increasingly, designs became more sophisticated, and measurement focused on the character of the television programming viewed rather than simple aggregated viewing time. These differences in measurement, they argue, lead to significant differences in the kind of conclusions reached.

5. *The Importance of Time-Series Measurement*

Katz's (1980) overview of the field gets right to the point:

> Discovery of the link between the mass media and interpersonal networks [the research on two-step flows] revealed that the process of change cannot be represented as a straight line between a persuasive media message and individual action. Just as the media do not act directly on decisions they do not act immediately. Influence takes time. Introduction of the notion of time into the conceptualization of the media effects reoriented empirical research from media campaigns to the diffusion of innovation, i.e., the study of acceptance *over time* [emphasis in original] of some new idea or new thing as it makes its way through a social structure via media and interpersonal networks. (p. 122)

James Coleman (1964, 1981) has been trying to convince his colleagues in the social sciences to include time explicitly in their models and theorizing. Kline (1977), MacKuen (1981), and Fan (1985) have more recently developed this argument with particular attention to communications processes. It is not that the research community is unpersuaded. The relative sparsity of time-series measurement is primarily a function of administrative difficulty and expense. Measurement over time measurement is integral to the models of agenda setting, information diffusion, information gap, and two-step flow. Time is also an explicit element in cultivation theory and, as Roberts and Bachen (1981, p. 328) point out, it is ironic that so much of the cultivation research conducted by the Annenberg group has relied on inference from cross-sectional analyses.

6. *A Flexible Approach to Units of Analysis*

The classic studies relied on either experimental or survey designs. In each case, the measurement was of individual attitudes or behavior. The individual-level data was aggregated and analyzed statistically to make inferences about the propensities of human behavior. Such aggregation averages out potentially differential interpretation of media content by different individuals or different types of individuals. Multimethod approaches, however, by their nature, are more flexible and allow the analyst to move back and forth between individual- and aggregate-level data. McLeod and Reeves (1980) deal with this issue at some length. They characterize communications research as more like political science than psychology, in that it must deal with both institutions and behavior rather than with just behavior. They suggest that as a result, the development of theory in communications research comes more slowly and in smaller "islands" than the grand theories of such single-level fields as psychology or organizational behavior (pp. 38–40).

7. The Blurring of Boundaries

As a result of the common elements in these new research perspectives, each is becoming somewhat less distinct, perhaps even moving toward integration. Agenda-setting studies, for example, increasingly emphasize the analysis of time-series data in a manner quite akin to the diffusion tradition. Furthermore, the agenda-setting work has incorporated contingent variables such as the need orientation of audience members, expressly linked to the uses and gratifications tradition (McCombs, 1981a,b). Cultivation analysis has also developed a uses and gratifications component, the notion of resonance—"the amplification of issues particularly salient to certain groups of viewers" (Gerbner *et al.*, 1980)—and having collected time-series data, they will no doubt move in that direction as well. Ultimately, each perspective may increasingly cite the other literatures.

B. Parallel Content Analysis as a Strategy for Research

The idea of parallel content analysis is not new but rather represents a convergence of research ideas and a reformulation of the new communications-effect paradigm in progress. Table II presents a list of eight proposals for new paradigms in communications research. Each of them involves elements of parallel content analysis. The first two are those by Weber and Lasswell, reviewed at the beginning of this chapter.

The third proposal was put forward by Morris Janowitz. In his 1969 essay, Janowitz reviewed Lasswell's proposal for quantitative research on political values in the world's major mass media and the circumstantial, administrative, and substantive reasons why Lasswell's call to arms failed to inspire a significant following. In that article, Janowitz simply observed the failure with disappointment and left it at that.

In 1976, however, Janowitz was moved to present a proposal of his own. He published an article in the *Journal of Communication* entitled "Content Analysis and the Study of Socio-Political Change." He had become intrigued

TABLE II

A 70-Year Tradition of Calls for Programmatic Research

Proponent	Key terminology	Central theoretical concerns	Proposed methodology
Max Weber (1910)	Sociology of the press	Press economics and public opinion, cross-national comparisons	Content analysis of press, institutional analyses
Harold Lasswell (1935); Lasswell, Leites, & associates (1949);	Quantitative semantics, world attention survey	Propaganda, political ideology, political symbolism	Comparative and time-series content analysis
Morris Janowitz (1969, 1976)	Content analysis of sociopolitical change	Social, political, cultural change	Time-series media content analysis
Philip Stone (1972)	Social indicators based on communications content	Social indicators, value change	Time-series content analysis
George Gerbner (1973)	Cultural indicators	Political and social symbolism, media effects	Time-series media content analysis, depth interviews, surveys
Steven Chaffee (1975)	Diffusion of political information	Public opinion, information diffusion, political socialization, media effects	Programmatic time-series media content analysis and coordinated field research
James Beniger (1978)	Greenfield index	Agenda-setting, public opinion, media effects	Time-series analysis of extent social trend and extant media index data
Karl Erik Rosengren (1980)	Cultural indicators	Long-term cultural trends, interaction of culture and social structure	Time-series analysis of social trend data and media content analysis

by a relatively obscure commercial service called "The Trend Report," generated by the Center for Policy Process. The Center had accumulated trend content analysis data over the preceding 5 years from a weighted representative sample of 200 American newspapers. The director of the center, John Naisbitt, later became quite well known with the publication of *Megatrends* (1982), a mass-audience book that drew on trend data. In his proposal, Janowitz called for a revitalization of time-series content analysis and coordinated efforts to utilize systematically coded media data in the study of long-range political, social and cultural trends. Janowitz, however, has not been active in this area, and Naisbitt's status as a best-selling author has kept him busy with public speaking engagements.

Shortly after Janowitz published his initial essay, Philip Stone published a paper that expanded on his own pioneering work on *The General Inquirer* (P. J. Stone, 1972) and that proposed an ongoing computerized content analysis of both media content and a sampling of significant social documents. Stone's proposal was based on the idea of extending the notion of social indicators (Bauer, 1966). Stone observed,

> Most social indicator discussions focus on statistics similar to economic indicators. A classic case is Durkheim's study of the analysis of suicide rates. Another kind of social indicator, which we will consider in this paper, is based on changes in the content of the mass media and other public distributions of information such as speeches, sermons, pamphlets, and textbooks. (p. 211)

He pointed out the potential relevance of such data to Karl Mannheim's (1936) work on cultural heterogeneity, Deutsch's (1963) work on political feedback patterns, and Johnson, Sears, and McConahay's (1971) study of "black invisibility" in media coverage and changing racial attitudes. He pointed out that automated optical text readers and growing computerized text processing by the media themselves increase the ease and lower the costs of computerized monitoring. His proposal has been expanded and developed by De Weese (1976), Firestone (1972), and R. P. Weber (1984) and has stimulated considerable interest in Europe (Melischek, Rosengren, & Stappers, 1984; Mochmann, 1980).

George Gerbner's 1973 paper on cultural indicators, published in the proceedings of an international conference on the future of content analysis, is one of the grandest and most expansive of this series of proposals. He also began by drawing on the social-indicators tradition in noting that private and governmental commissions since the 1930s had called for systematic efforts at monitoring the media and media effects. Gerbner argues that few policy matters as significant as communications policy are determined with so little reliable systematic cumulative information about actual trends:

> We know very little about trends in the composition and structure of the mass-produced systems of messages that define life in urbanized societies. We know no more about the

institutional processes that compose and structure those systems. Most of our research on how people respond and behave in specific situations lacks insight into the dynamics of the common control context in which and to which they respond...

How is this massive flow managed? How does it fit into or alter the existing cultural context? What perspectives on life and the world does it express and cultivate? How does it vary across time, societies and cultures? Finally, how does the cultivation of collective assumptions relate to the conduct of public affairs, and vice versa? [From Gerbner (1973). In G. Gerbner, L. Gross, & W. Melody (Eds.), *Communications Technology and Social Policy: Understanding the New "Cultural" Revolution* (pp. 555, 558). Copyright © 1973. Reprinted by permission of John Wiley & Sons, Inc.]

Also in this essay, Gerbner developed the concept of cultivation analysis, which became integrated into his studies of television violence. Gerbner's strategy apparently was to follow up on the call for ongoing monitoring of television violence made in the 1972 Surgeon General's report on television and children (Surgeon General's Scientific Advisory Committee on Television and Social Behavior, 1972) and develop a seed project for a broader inquiry into cultural trends and media effects. Three setbacks hindered this strategy. First, the funding available for monitoring television violence turned out to be very limited. Second, the research effort, as it turned out, became an exclusive enterprise of Gerbner and his colleagues at the University of Pennsylvania and did not develop into a cooperative effort of scholars in the field. Third, because of these first two constraints, the theoretical and methodological scope of the research as originally proposed was never fully executed.

Steven Chaffee, responsible for the next in this series of proposals, published a keystone theoretical chapter entitled "The Diffusion of Political Information" in his book, *Political Communication* (1975). Drawing on David Easton's general model for a political system (1953, 1965a,b), Chaffee assembled an inspiring agenda for research focusing on political communication. Like Gerbner's proposal, his proposal outlined a broad front of coordinated research and data collection over time. Chaffee particularly emphasized the relevance of the information-diffusion model for the maintenance of authority and support in political systems. He noted the importance of appropriate time-series data for refining current theories of political socialization and political mobilization. In the conclusion, he noted sagely,

The preceding discussion of methodological ideals and pragmatic realities makes it clear that the kind of research outlined in this paper is not going to be conceptualized, proposed, funded, and executed at one fell swoop.... Some priorities need to be set so that incremental approaches can be made toward realization of a program that will eventually, in retrospect, be seen as aiming toward development and testing of a comprehensive and empirical theory of the diffusion of political information. (pp. 123–124)

Chaffee's incremental strategy and his attempt to bridge the gap between diffusion of information and communications effects research, however, did not stimulate much of a reaction in the literature.

James Beniger's (1978) paper, "Media Content as Social Indicators," is the first in these series of calls for research to explicitly take its predecessors into account. Beniger cites Lasswell, Janowitz, and Stone and draws on both the traditions of social indicators and agenda setting to propose the use of existing periodical indexes as a cost-efficient technique for monitoring media trends:

> The idea that measures of mass media content might complement survey research in monitoring survey research is as old as public opinion polling itself.... The limited success of past attempts to monitor social change using media content on a large scale, continuing basis would seem to be due to the prohibitive cost of the data collection efforts, rather than any shortcoming of the underlying idea. A better strategy might be to develop and test media indicators on a more modest scale. (pp. 450-451)

He proposed the general term "Greenfield Index," after journalist Meg Greenfield who first used it in the early 1960s to trace the trends in media attention to religious institutions and moral conditions. Beniger noted approvingly that Greenfield did not naively equate media attention with cultural trends or public opinion but, as a practicing journalist, was very much aware of the fads and fashions of journalistic coverage. Beniger's extension of Greenfield's technique was to compare the time-series media index data with national statistics and public opinion data.

The most recent proposal in this tradition was advanced by Karl Erik Rosengren, who heads up a Swedish research team studying cultural trends and agenda setting in post-World War II Sweden. Rosengren (1980) reestablished the roots of this research in the German tradition of sociology of knowledge, drawing on questions raised by Marx, Weber, and Mannheim: "Perhaps the first thing to question about media as agents of social change or the status quo is a special case of the old question of the relationship between culture and social structure" (p. 169).

Rosengren's model of the interrelationships between social structure and culture ties several strands of the European philosophical tradition to recent empirical work on social and cultural indicators. The final report of the Swedish cultural indicators research program is not yet published, but some of the scattered research reports published thus far will no doubt whet the appetite of the research community (see Rosengren, 1981).

One might note, in the progression of proposals summarized in Table II, from Weber in 1910 to Rosengren in 1980, that up until the last two, each of the others emphasized itself as the beginning of a new tradition rather than the most recent manifestation of an ongoing movement in social science. Some of these scholars emphasized the analysis of media trends as an indicator of social trends, whereas others seemed to be more interested in the media as a causal agent in the agenda-setting sense. Some emphasized broad cultural norms, whereas others centered on the rise and fall of more narrowly defined political issues. Some emphasized methodological precision and rigorous modeling, whereas others emphasized a less formal and more open-ended approach. But, there are also strong common themes to each of these proposals. They all emphasized the empirical measurement of trends in media content over time and the systematic comparison of those trends to other forms of behavioral or public opinion data. Each shared a central theoretical concern with the role of the media in social and political change.

The present case for parallel content analysis draws on and extends this tradition of proposals in calling for a programmatic research effort on long-term trends in mass communication and public opinion. The term parallel content analysis emphasizes the need for flexible but isomorphic measures of trends in media and other indicators of public and political life. Elsewhere, it has been referred to as the "Input–Output Model" (Neuman, 1982) or simply as "agenda-setting" (Neuman, 1979).

A consistent and perhaps ultimately debilitating shortcoming of the content analysis tradition is its ad hoc character. A basic principle of the accumulation of scientific knowledge is the comparability of studies. Both the experimental and the survey research traditions have developed a reasonable tradition of accumulated findings and ultimately, on some issues, scientific consensus through the use of systematically comparable methods. Given that each new attempt at content analysis started with a unique content sample and almost always a unique coding scheme, an accumulation of convergent findings has been all but impossible. The two key requirements for content analysis to take its place among the other research traditions are (1) a programmatic effort of the research community to develop a general-use representative sampling of media content, and (2) the development of some standardized codes for central theoretical constructs.

Clearly, no sampling of media content or coding scheme, regardless of how expansive or flexible it might be, could be appropriate for all research issues. But a programmatic effort to establish a single archived set of raw content data and at least a standard set of common codes against which individual scholars could compare their findings and to which they could contribute, would be essential. It would take time, no doubt, for a reasonably refined set of codes for measuring social and cultural and political change to emerge, but a special advantage of archived content data is that newly refined codes could always be applied to archived raw data.

The six principles put forward in this call for research are as follows:

1. A programmatic effort for coordinated, archived data collection
2. A general-use representative sample of mass media content
3. A corresponding general-purpose audience sample of loosely structured depth interviews and standard survey items

4. The coordinated collection of extant data on aggregate social behavior from a variety of institutional sources (real-world data)
5. The development of a battery of standardized content codes that can be applied to both the media and the public interview samples
6. Continuous data collection over an extended period of time.

The primary mass media would be defined as television, radio, motion pictures, newspapers, magazines, and books. A procedure would be designed to generate a sample of available content in each of these media, weighted by audience exposure, so that the content collected represented what American citizens are most likely to read and see. The raw materials would be permanently archived on audio- and videotape and microfilm, and the audio component of the broadcast and motion picture sample would be transcribed. The sampling interval would be monthly. Standardized codes would include broadly defined values, the depiction of violence, the ratio of information to entertainment, the proportion of foreign versus domestic news, the treatment of specific issues and events, and so on. As the theoretical relevance of new values or issues became clear later on, analysts could return to the earlier data and add new time series to the accumulated data base.

Public opinion would be tracked by a parallel system of open-ended monthly depth interviews with a representative sample of perhaps 200 individuals in a rolling panel design (whereby a subset are reinterviewed at regular intervals and others are freshly integrated into the sample). The interview would last one hour or a bit longer and would involve a series of general probes, including current concerns facing the individuals and their families and the nation as a whole, what the individual had seen or read about in the media lately, and other probes about their perception of their social and political environment, as well as standardized indicators of trust in government, evaluation of the economy, evaluation of the president's handling of his or her job, and other such indicators that have proven valuable in polling research. The use of open-ended techniques leads to a smaller proportion of the population commenting on any given issue. In a 1-hour interview, even with appropriate probing, any number of prominent and important issues may not come up. Such an approach is, in that sense, inefficient, compared with standard closed-ended survey items. But given such trade-offs, interviewing techniques can be designed to include both formats, starting with very broad undirected probes, leading to a list of standard probes, and then ending with closed-ended survey questions.

The kinds of theoretical concerns potentially addressed by a data resource of this type would include the rise and fall of political issues from public attention; changing political institutions such as political parties, unions, and other voluntary organizations; political mobilization; the role of the media in following, reinforcing, or initiating changing values and beliefs; strategies of citizens for processing large amounts of complex information about public affairs; and so forth.

Perhaps the best argument for the promise of this approach is noting the achievements of individual attempts along these lines thus far.

C. Some Exemplary Studies

Despite their diversity, each of the following studies involves a significant subset of the six principles of parallel content analysis noted above. In an effort to overlay some structure on an unruly literature, the studies are organized along the seven research-tradition headings in Table III. The first four, taken together, represent the basic model of parallel content analysis. The fifth, refraction analysis, reflects the non-time-series approach, and the sixth and seventh represent examples of additional studies that apply these principles in a more narrowly focused theoretical domain.

1. *Cultural Indicators*

The emphasis here is on broadly defined, long-term cultural trends. Increasing or decreasing emphases on particular values or symbols over periods from several decades to several centuries long are contrasted with aggregate data on changing social behavior. Practitioners here trace their roots to Sorokin's class work on cultural dynamics (1937–1941) and George Gerbner's more recent theoretical work (1969, 1973). A symposium on cultural indicators was held in Vienna, Austria, in the winter of 1982, under the auspices of the Australian Academy of Sciences, and it resulted in *Cultural Indicators* (Melischek *et al.,* 1984). Plans are currently being discussed for another international symposium.

If there is a classic and seminal study, perhaps it is the analysis of popular magazine biographies conducted by Leo Lowenthal (1944) and reprinted in his more recent book, *Literature, Popular Culture, and Society* (1961). Lowenthal noted that biographies had become increasingly prevalent in popular magazines in the first half of the twentieth century. He found that the classic American symbolism of the Horatio Alger myth was indeed heavily emphasized and that a systematic content analysis of these biographies over time might reveal some intriguing cultural trends. Indeed they did. Lowenthal found a correspondence between the economic transition from the early smokestack, production-oriented stage to the mass-consumption stage that followed in midcentury and the trends in magazine heroes (see Fig. 8).

The early biographies included those of J. P. Morgan, railroad president; James J. Hill, pioneer in aviation and the inventor of the torpedo; and James C. Davis, the director general of the U.S. railroad administration. These biographies had such headings as "Unknown Captains of Industry" and "Wall Street Men." From a representative sketch of Theodore Roosevelt, Lowenthal quotes,

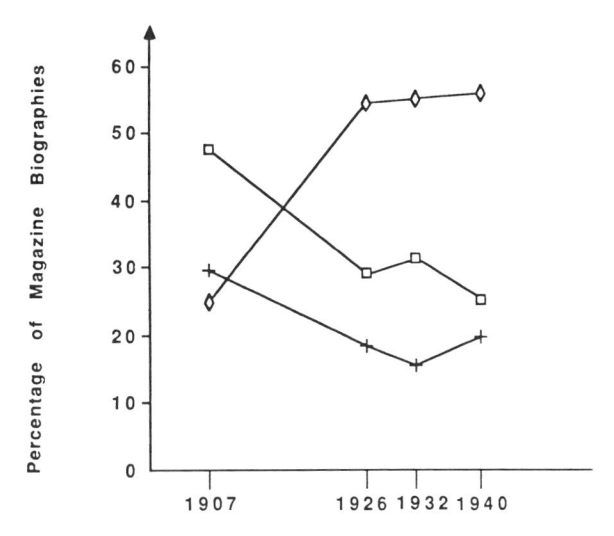

Fig. 8. Lowenthal's data on shift from idols of production to idols of consumption. □, Political life; +, business and professional; ◊, entertainment. From Lowenthal (1944).

> It is possible for a young man to go as a laborer into the steel business and before he has reached his mature prime become, through his own industry and talent, the president of a vast steel association.... (Lowenthal, 1961, p. 113)

But, the emerging pattern of later biographies looks much more like the personality journalism of today and includes,

> ...movie stars, sports heroes, newspaper men and radio commentators, a pair of munitions traders, a quack doctor, a horse race gambler, a woman sailor, the owner of an island resort, and the retired rector of a swanky society prep school. (Lowenthal, 1961, p. 115)

These are, as Lowenthal puts it, the heroes of the society of leisure.

Lowenthal did not develop an explicit comparison to aggregate economic data, although such data existed, but his pioneering work set a model of the promise of time-series analysis to connect media content to shifting cultural and economic values of significance.

An example of a more recent study in this tradition could be drawn from Rosengren's Cultural Indicators of the Swedish Symbol System Project. This particular study was conducted by Eva Block (1984), head of the research office at the Swedish Archive for Sound and Pictures in Stockholm. Block's analysis tracks the emphasis in newspaper editorials over this period and reveals a distinct trend in the emphasis of equality over freedom and in the emphasis on the environment (see Fig. 9). Block hypothesized that the growing concern with the environment might result in a loss of emphasis on economic growth, but the data revealed that the emphasis on economic growth was relatively

TABLE III
Models of Parallel Content Analysis

Research tradition	Exemplary studies	Theoretical focus	Principal methodology	Limitations	Principal contribution
Cultural trends	Hart (1933); Lowenthal (1944); Rosengren (1981); Melischek, Rosengren, & Stappers (1984)	Long-term cultural change, value trends, values of production vs. consumption, science vs. religion, women in labor force, freedom & equality, capitalism & liberalism, international relations	Time-series content analyses of periodicals, newspapers, public speeches, books, advertisements, editorials	Work tends to be descriptive, neglects systematic measurement of variables outside of cultural-media sphere	Draws attention to long-term trends, broadly defined values
Time-series agenda setting	Funkhouser (1973b); Beniger (1978); Neuman (1979); Erbring, Goldenberg, & Miller (1980); Smith (1980); MacKuen (1981); Neuman & Fryling (1985)	Media effects, interplay between real-world cues, media issue coverage, & public opinion: Vietnam, race relations, drugs, pollution, inflation, unemployment	Time-series content analyses of news media, coupled with time-series opinion poll data & national economic, crime statistics, etc.	Short time periods, media sampling problems, very incomplete public opinion & national statistics, problems of noncomparable data sets	Promising practical model for parallel content analyses, moves beyond description, data allow for some causal analyses & sophisticated time-series techniques
Political cognition	Gans (1979); Neuman (1981); Graber (1984); Gamson & Modigliani (1989); Gamson (1988)	Political cognition, ideology, information processing, schemata, political values, news institutions	Depth interviews with mass sample loosely coupled with content analyses of news media	Not time series, nonparallel content analyses of media & public responses	Moves away from closed-ended survey questions of public response toward depth-interview response

Communication flow	Neuman (1982); Pool (1983); Pool, Inose, Takasaki, & Hurwitz (1984); Neuman & Pool (1986)	Aggregate flow of information through mass media, media use behavior, information overload, media technology, economics & policy	Secondary analyses of extant time-series data on media use, coupled with analyses of quantity (but not content) of information in various media	Dependent on industry data, which is incomplete & frequently not comparable across media; does not deal with media content or public response	Emphasizes long-term trends, aggregate patterns; lays groundwork for large-scale content analysis
Refraction analysis	K. Lang & Lang (1953); Breed (1955); Gerbner (1973); Neuman (1976, 1982)	Media effects, especially bias; filtering; interpreting real-world events; cultivation; gatekeeper effects	Methods vary, comparing observation of real event with media coverage, or different stages of media coverage or media coverage & audience recall	Nonparallel analyses of reality & media, or media & audience response	Complements time-series analyses through in-depth, snapshot study of successive stages of filtering & interpreting from source to audience
Short-term media effects	Bollen & Phillips (1981, 1982); Phillips (1983)	Media effects, behavioral modeling, media & aggressive behavior	Time-series comparison of media content & short-term increases in national statistics on suicide and homicide rates	Difficulties of causal inference, limited available data on appropriate dependent variables, limited to short-term effects	Alternative to laboratory-based studies of media & aggressive behavior, pioneering efforts at using extant aggregate statistics
Presidential popularity	P. F. Stone & Brody (1970); Brody & Page (1975); Haight & Brody (1977)	Media effects, presidential political strategies, political support & ability to govern	Time-series content analyses of balance between positive & negative news coverage & poll data on presidential job performance	Limited time frames & relatively narrow theoretical focus	Sophisticated modeling, causal analysis

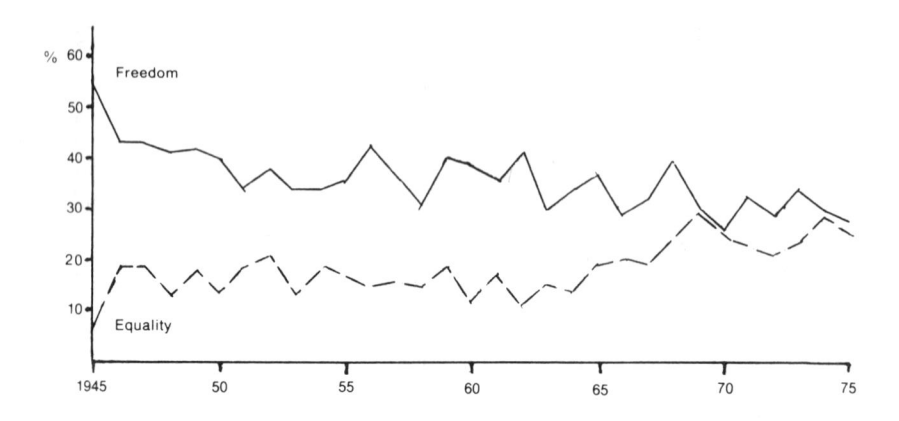

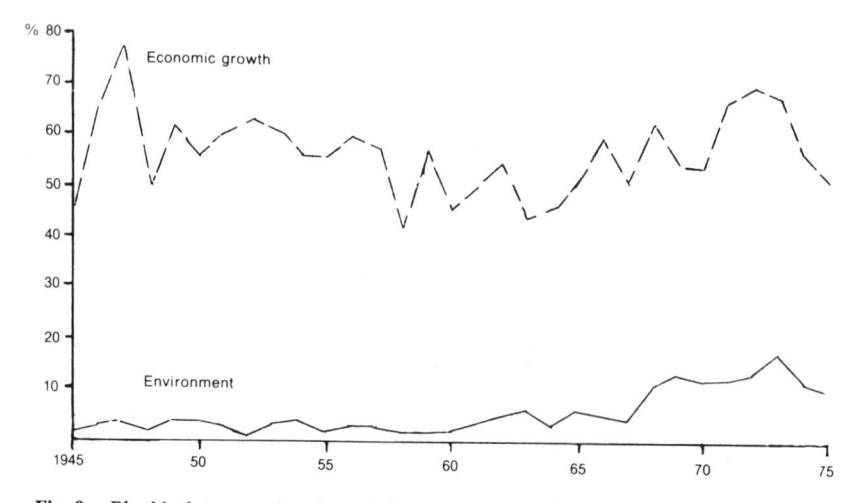

Fig. 9. Block's data on cultural trends in Sweden: political values in newspaper editorials. Ordinate, percentage of newspaper editorials; abscissa, year. From Block (1984).

constant in Sweden throughout this period. Block compared these findings with economic trends and Swedish voting patterns.

Robert Weber's (1981) study of cycles of political symbolism from 1795 to 1972 is particularly interesting and complements this research tradition. He uncovered a 52-year cycle of changing thematic emphases, which appears to be correlated with the Kondratieff economic cycle (Kondratieff, 1935). He analyzed the British speeches from the throne delivered at the opening of each British parliamentary session, corresponding to the American State of the Union address, and discovered a recurring cycle back and forth between progressive and conservative ideologies and also between cosmopolitan and parochial emphasis on national policy. Weber explicitly ties these patterns and political symbolism to business cycles as follows:

> During each depression, there is debate within society on alternative courses of action. The Parochial theme represents this discussion. First, the realization occurs that the present situation differs from normal business cycles and thus requires strong action. Second, some action is chosen. Third, the decision must be justified. The justification is couched in terms of the greatest good for the greatest number of people, even if some classes benefit more than others. As the economy begins to expand, a part of the additional profits and wealth is redistributed to workers. Some social ills are ameliorated. This occurs in such a way that inequities in the distribution of power and wealth are not seriously jeopardized. These actions are discussed in the Progressive theme.
>
> Following two decades of increasing output and real but limited gains for workers, the Cosmopolitan phase represents increased attention to the relations between the political center and periphery. This is a period of increasing concern with foreign affairs. There are calls for greater political and economic activity in the international arena partly justified by the promise of additional benefits to workers and capitalists alike. However, as new contradictions build and profits decline, a conservative theme encompasses a discussion of the restoration of profits and capital accumulation. (p. 1142)

Weber goes on to describe how further economic pressures lead to a return to parochial themes. He finds strikingly similar patterns in an analysis of American political speeches over the same period and ties these political cycles and economic correlates to Wallerstein's "world system" concept of the increasing interconnection of the world's nation states. Kondratieff's model has been challenged, and Weber's intriguing interpretation may too be subject to fundamental criticism. Nonetheless, such attempts as his and Block's to address long-term trends in fundamental values of equity and economic structure within societies offer an important link between the field of communications research and the fields of history, political economy, and comparative politics.

The weakness of this research tradition is its descriptive emphasis. With the exception of Weber's work and a few other studies, most analysts are content to systematically document long-term cultural trends and relate them in a loose and informal way to historical and economic phenomena. There is, however, wide recognition in the research literature (including Rosengren, 1981, and Melischek *et al.*, 1984) that systematic measurement of other domains of social behavior must be integrated with the cultural trend data if the field is ever to really blossom as an area of scientific inquiry.

2. *Time-Series Agenda-Setting Research*

Time-series agenda-setting research represents a natural evolution from the original single-time correlational measurement methodology developed by McCombs and D. L. Shaw (1972). McCombs and his colleagues at Syracuse were acutely aware of the importance of the time element in the agenda-setting process and address the issue in a number of studies, most of which are reviewed and summarized in Eyal, Winter, and De George (1981).

The first time-series agenda-setting study, however, was conducted by another scholar working independently in California. Raymond Funkhouser published two articles in 1973, reviewing trends in the media coverage of political issues in the 1960s. His *Journalism Quarterly* article (1973a) is particularly interesting because he explicitly contrasts trends in media coverage with "real-world" statistics collected by federal agencies. He found a surprising independence between patterns of growth and decline in media coverage and the federal statistics covering such issues as Vietnam, crime, and racial unrest. Funkhouser reviewed a series of explanations for these disjunctures, emphasizing the regularized and structured demand for news by the commercial news media, in contrast to the random patterns of real-world events.

Zucker (1978), like Funkhouser, found a complex pattern of correlation and independence between media coverage and public opinion, and he developed a theory of variable news media influence based on the obtrusiveness of issues—that is, whether individuals have means other than the media to monitor these issues. Such matters as inflation and gas shortages would represent examples of obtrusive issues. Zucker also developed a theory of issue duration, positing that media influence would be strongest at the early stages of public attention to new issues.

Michael MacKuen's (1981) study is also convergent. MacKuen started from a simple time-series correlation model and extended it with appropriate mathematical adjustments to account for the inertial character of news coverage, which significantly improved the level of correlation between public concern and media coverage. But MacKuen's findings strongly support the other recent studies in this tradition in demonstrating that the media–public-opinion linkage is much more subtle and complex than originally posited by the agenda-setting model:

> We move away from a sense that much of the public's attentions derive passively from the weight of contemporary news coverage and adopt the notion that citizens evaluate political events and respond to them selectively and differentially. That is not to say that

the press plays no role at all. . . . However, the evidence clearly suggests that the bulk of the symbolic impact [of the media] may more properly be attributed to the *character* [emphasis in original] of events and their portrayal, particularly the continuity-breaking ones, and not to the simple *amount* [emphasis in original] of news coverage allocated to the problems. [From MacKuen, p. 122 in M. B. MacKuen & S. L. Coombs (Eds.), *More Than News: Media Power in Public Affairs*. Copyright © 1981. Reprinted by permission of Sage Publications, Inc.]

Similar work has also been conducted by Beniger (1978), Erbring *et al.* (1980), Neuman (1979), Neuman and Fryling (1985); and Smith (1980). A significant shortcoming of the time-series agenda-setting research thus far has been its reliance on available data, and especially archived Gallup data on the public perception of the most important problems facing the country.

3. *Political Cognition*

Political cognition represents a third research tradition that contributes to the concept of parallel content analysis. This literature is quite different from the first two. Cultural trends and time-series agenda-setting both emphasize aggregate long-term trends and a quantitative methodology. Work on political cognition, in contrast, tends to focus on small-scale, detailed content analysis or depth interviews. Gans's (1979) content analysis of thematic political values in American news media illustrates this approach. He found a number of persistent symbolic themes, including altruistic democracy, responsible capitalism, small-town pastoralism, and individualism. He also found a strong and persistent journalistic aversion to political extremes, which he labeled "moderatism." Gans did not couple this analysis with a depth-interview study of audience responses, although he had conducted such work in other studies (Gans, 1962, 1968, 1974), but he focused on the structural constraints of modern American news organizations and emphasized persisting themes rather than recent trends.

William Gamson's ongoing work, although it does not involve a time-series design, perhaps comes closest to parallel content analysis (Gamson, 1988, Gamson & Modigliani, 1989). He and his associates thus far have focused their attention on four issues: affirmative action, troubled industry, nuclear power, and the Arab–Israeli conflict. They use a multiperson depth-interview procedure, called "peer group conversations," in which small groups respond to and discuss political cartoons and news stories. The discussions are recorded, transcribed, and content analyzed. Central to Gamson's work is a model of political schemata—cognitive structures that shape the processing, interpretation, and recall of political events and issues (Neisser, 1976; Abelson, 1981). He contrasts his approach with the agenda-setting model as follows:

> In our model, it is not simply information that is tuned in, but packages that interpret information. People construct and modify their understanding in an environment that is

constantly offering them potential schemata, suggesting how an issue is to be understood and what should be done about it. One might better say that we adopt a schema rather than construct it, fleshing it out as we use it over time.

If this model is accurate, it gives the media an important and subtle role in shaping our thinking about public events. If a metaphor seems dramatic and compelling, one might adopt it without recognizing the taken-for-granted assumptions it contains. One cannot quarrel with unrecognized assumptions. The core of a package can be boot-legged into one's schema without the kind of awareness that allows for critical examination. (Gamson, 1988)

Such a perspective offers a fresh look at the issue of attitude change and the acquisition of political knowledge.

Doris Graber's *Processing the News* (1984) uses similar methods to develop models of citizens' strategies for, as she puts it, "taming the information tide." She conducted her study on 21 residents of Evanston, Illinois, organized into groups with varying levels of political interest and varying levels of media exposure. She developed a detailed model of the role of political schemata, with special attention to the relatively low level of political information exhibited by most citizens.

This line of research has been limited by short time frames of analysis, relatively small samples, and a loose fit between content analysis and depth-interview methodologies, but its potential contribution to parallel content analysis should be clear.

4. *Communications Flow*

As a result of some pioneering work by Ithiel de Sola Pool at the Massachusetts Institute of Technology and some of his colleagues at Tokyo University, another quite different approach has been put forward. The seminal publication was an article by Pool published in *Science* in 1983 and a booklength study by Pool and his associates, published by the University of Tokyo Press and North Holland Press in 1984 (Pool, Inose, Takasaki, & Hurwitz, 1984). Reviewing the importance of economic and industrial indicators, Pool argued that to understand the interaction of social communications and media technology, efforts should be undertaken to track the aggregate flow of information over time. Pool noted that the proportion of the work force working in the information sector has been rising from about 5% in 1870 to about 33% in 1915 to about 50% of all employees today.

Pool and his colleagues compiled statistics from a variety of industry and government sources and found that the flow of communications was increasing at a rate of twice that of a gross domestic product in constant dollars, but that the per capita consumption of words was not growing at an equivalent rate, generating an increasing gap between the flow of mass media information and the amount of media consumed. One of his most intriguing findings was the discovery of a law-like correlation between price of communications and communications flow, as illustrated in Fig. 10. At the upper left of the figure are the mass media producing between 10^9 and 10^{14} words per year in the United States, at cost of a fraction of 1 cent per 1000 words. In the lower right-hand corner are the point-to-point media, with prices in the range of 10 cents to 100 dollars per 1000 words, and, accordingly, much smaller levels of use.

The other conclusion clearly evident in this trend data from 1960 to 1980 is the decreasing price and increasing quantity of communications. Print media such as newspapers, magazines, mail, and books have changed relatively little in price and quantity, while facsimile, data communications, and cable television have moved several orders of magnitude in decreased price and increased quantity. In other related papers, the attempt was made to address the issue of communications overload and to extend the model with content analysis to track the growth and decline of broad categories of information rather than a simple aggregate level of words flowing through the media system (Neuman, 1982; Neuman & Pool, 1986).

5. Refraction Analysis

Refraction analysis is a term developed by G. E. Lang and Lang (1981). There has been surprisingly little empirical work along these lines, especially

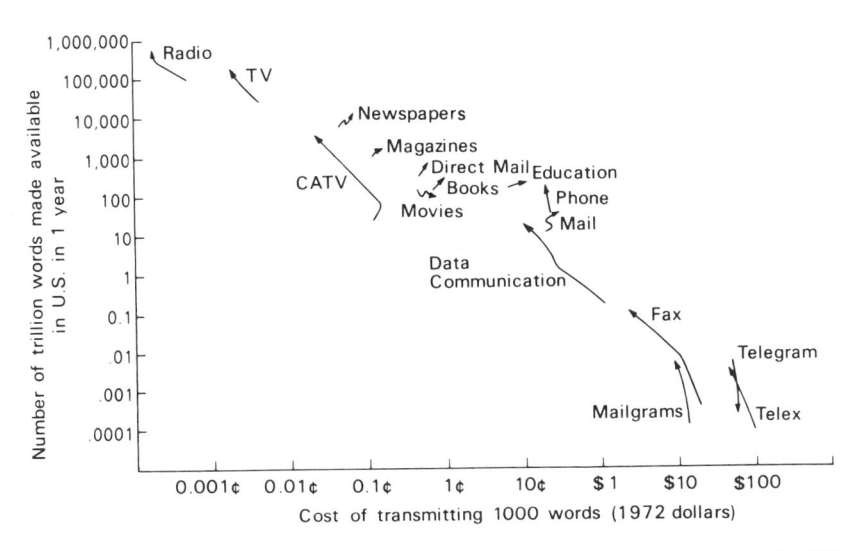

Fig. 10. Pool's data on trends in media use and media costs in the United States, 1960–1980. From Pool, Inose, Takasaki, & Hurwitz (1984).

considering the strong theoretical concerns with bias, filtering, and gatekeeping by the media. Refraction analysis refers to the systematic comparison of real-world events with their coverage and characterization to the mass media. We are adopting the term *refraction analysis* here to identify non-time-series parallel content analysis.

The classic study here might well be the Langs' analysis of the MacArthur Day parade, published in 1953. Thirty-one participant observers were recruited to observe General MacArthur's triumphant airport arrival, motorcade, and parade in Chicago in April, 1951. The Langs compared the accumulated field notes with the television coverage of the event. They discovered that television coverage systematically distorted and exaggerated the character of the event. The coverage emphasized the enthusiasm and the size of the crowd and, through interviews and carefully selected camera angles, dramatized the ceremonial aspects of the General's visit. Given the straightforward research design of systematically comparing participant observation with media coverage, it is surprising that few scholars have followed in the Langs' footsteps.

Another approach to refraction analysis is exemplified by Breed's study (1955), in which he systematically analyzed the decision-making process of editors as they function as information gatekeepers, deciding to print some stories from the wire services and ignore others. Breed analyzed the patterns of selection and had the editors return to each of the rejected, as well as accepted, stories to explain their editorial reasoning.

Perhaps the most widely noted research tradition that falls under the refraction rubric is the work by George Gerbner and colleagues on cultivation analysis. The comparison of the demographics of television characters with the American population is important and provocative. The strongly critical judgment of the management and structure of American television that is associated with this research, however, may prove to be ill advised. The emphasis in television on certain character types may be primarily a result of the exigencies of drama and comedy rather than a reflection of systematic racial, gender-based, or age bias. One wonders, for example, whether the demography of Elizabethan England closely paralleled the casts of Shakespeare's plays, and if not, whether the bard's work would deserve equivalent criticism. The close linkage of the analysis of communications flow to media reform at this early stage of research may actually inhibit both enterprises.

Other studies have content analyzed television news and entertainment programming and have conducted depth interviews with viewers following broadcasts to systematically compare what elements of the programming were most easily recalled and how they were interpreted. Neuman (1976) revealed that although recall rates of network television news are rather low (reaching levels of 50% of the stories broadcast only after considerable prompting and cues of story "headlines"), the rate of recall is quite similar for different educational groups. Recall of types of stories varies. As one might expect, human interest stories and visually explicit stories about unusual weather phenomena such as hurricanes are most easily remembered, whereas abstract discussions of the economy, ecology, or political commentaries are recalled at a lower rate.

Table IV reviews these stories and reports the proportions of stories presented compared to storied recalled. The content categorization is crude, and the viewer response is measured only in terms of recall, but the basic model of parallel data collection is demonstrated.

There seems to be a greater variation in responses to entertainment television. Table V reports the responses of viewers interviewed by telephone after watching 1 of 30 programs selected to be representative of the commercial and public television schedules (Neuman, 1982; Neuman & Keegan, 1980). Rather than measure simple recall of entertainment programs, the methodology in this case asked respondents what thoughts came to mind and made a distinction between analytic responses (responses regarding the program itself, focusing on plot, character development in the script, etc.) and interpretive responses (responses that related the content of the program to other ideas or events in the viewer's life).

Table V reports the relative rates of analytic and interpretive responses (indexed at 100, the overall average level of response for the 30 programs sampled) for different program types. Given that 30 programs represent only a tiny fraction of the full flow of broadcast content, one hesitates to draw

TABLE IV

Short-Term Recall of Television News Stories[a]

Story content	Recall rate (%)	Percentage of stories actually presented	Percentage of stories actually recalled
Weather	63.7	3.2	4.0
Human interest	58.7	5.9	6.6
U.S. politics	53.9	11.1	11.5
Race relations	53.0	2.6	2.6
Foreign affairs	53.0	25.5	26.0
Vietnam	52.3	26.8	26.8
Economy	50.5	15.0	14.7
Ecology	45.2	6.5	5.7
Commentaries	34.1	2.6	1.8

[a]Source: Neuman (1976).

TABLE V

Short-Term Response to Entertainment Television[a]

Television type	Analytic response	Interpretive response
Commercial television		
Situation comedies	106	86
Action–adventure	103	83
Drama	139	140
Public affairs	108	143
Public television		
Drama	101	25
Public affairs	43	124

[a]Source: Neuman & Keegan (1980).

firm conclusions about these program types. Nevertheless, the results demonstrate an intriguing pattern across program types. As one might expect, commercial situation comedies and action–adventure programs generate an average or below-average level of response, but the rare commercial dramatic and public affairs programs do as well or better at stimulating the thinking of the audience, as do their public broadcasting counterparts. Such results are fragmentary and reflect the early stages of the development of research methodology in this field. Gerbner has thus far come closest to developing systematic samples in analytic categories that would lend themselves to programmatic efforts at refraction analysis.

6. Short-Term Media Effects

This is the sixth cluster of research. David Phillips is a prominent practitioner of research in this area. The approach calls for an examination of extant data for evidence of short-term effects of prominent news events. Bollen and Phillips (1981, 1982) studied rates of imitative suicide in response to prominent television news stories, and Phillips (1983) found evidence that nationally televised heavyweight championship prize fights trigger a brief but sharp increase in homicides in the United States. This work in natural settings offers an intriguing alternative to the tradition of laboratory research on television and aggressive behavior, but the limitations of extant data and the analysis of only short-term effects is constraining (Phillips, 1986).

7. Presidential Popularity

Presidential popularity represents a final cluster of research. Richard Brody and colleagues at Stanford (Brody & Page, 1975; Haight & Brody, 1977; P. F. Stone & Brody, 1970) have studied patterns of media coverage of

American presidents and the interaction of that coverage with presidential popularity, as measured by opinion polls. They have studied both the amount of coverage and the relative balance of positive and negative statements about presidential performance. Brody and Page (1975), for example, analyzed the trends of popularity of the Johnson and Nixon administrations and found evidence of a great deal of inertia in public evaluations of presidents. They developed a news discrepancy theory of opinion change, which draws attention to disjunctures between developing news and the level of past evaluations. Haight and Brody (1977) demonstrated an interaction between the public response to presidential behavior, in this case in the Nixon administration, and the timing of presidential press conferences to try to shore up lagging support.

The work on presidential popularity represents a small subset of issues, but further demonstrates the potential of parallel content analysis.

D. Conclusion

The definition of a "communications effect" must be understood as a central problem in the field. Communications effects have taken on a quality of taken-for-granted self-evidence.

1. A Definition of Communications Effects

The communications research community has been rather cavalier about the definition of what is or is not a communications effect. Like the judiciary trying to struggle with a precise definition of pornography, researchers seem to take the position that they cannot define it in the abstract, but they know it when they see it. Whatever the viability of such definitions of pornography in legal circles, such a premise has clearly been detrimental to systematic communications research. Some researchers find that data on behavior induced from exposure to a stimulus in a laboratory is meaningful and generalizable evidence of communications effects. Other researchers find that differential media exposure of social groups exhibiting different patterns of behavior provides reliable evidence of effects. Other researchers consider the coincidence of certain values and ideas in the media and in the beliefs of the mass population to be further evidence of effects.

But consider the proposition that communications effects are a special case of the general social phenomena of power and influence effects. A number of distinguished scholars in the social sciences have wrestled mightily with the problem of the definition and systematic measurement of such phenomena. This tradition of research was developed by Max Weber (1925/1968) and includes Carl Friedrich (1937), Bertrand Russell (1938), Harold Lasswell and Abraham Kaplan (1950), Robert Dahl (1963), and William Gamson (1968). The central questions are the following: How can you tell if an attempt to influence an individual's behavior has been successful? What would the subject of the influence have attempted to have done otherwise? It is inherently difficult to tell. When professional lobbyists return to their sponsoring organizations and argue, whatever the outcome, that it would have been much worse had they not participated in the influence process, who could prove them wrong?

Experimental data, because of the control group, does speak to the issue of what targets of influence would otherwise have done, but it is not necessarily generalizable to real-world settings. The other forms of data, although from real-world settings, are plagued by the difficulty of causal inference.

Parallel content analysis attempts to respond to these problems. It involves time-series analysis. It suggests that the best way to sort out *what* is causing *what* is to study natural variations over long periods of time, with an eye to when changing patterns of behavior either precede or follow changing communications flow and when behaviors remain unchanged. Therein lies the naturalistic answer to the question of what audiences would have done otherwise. It also allows for the possibility that small but consistent effects over time will rise to levels reliably measured by our crude instruments.

2. *The Communications Effects Pendulum*

Many scholars, in reviewing the communications field, have noted a cycle of emphasis moving back and forth between minimal and maximal communications effects (McQuail, 1977; Katz, 1977, 1980; Pietila, 1977; Comstock *et al.,* 1978; McLeod & Reeves, 1980; Gerbner, 1983). Briefly, the early research dominated by the bullet theory posited strong communications effects, followed by skepticism and qualifications (as summarized in Klapper's work, 1960), and followed, in turn, by a strong and energetic movement back toward the conclusion of significant effects. One is tempted to conclude that the culture of such pendulum swings represents an unproductive environment for addressing fundamental scientific questions. But, then again, if one appreciates that the energy of the debate might be fruitfully harnessed to motivate serious, systematic research, perhaps it is a blessing in disguise. One strategy is to use the polarized debate over minimal versus significant effects as a means to an end. It becomes a symbol and a heuristic device for engaging the curiosity of students and laypersons who might be puzzled by the need to conduct systematic research on what common sense reveals to be obviously true.

3. *The Social-Problems Orientation of Communications Research*

A very similar phenomenon in the history of communications research is its association with particular social problems. As noted, the advent of comic books and motion pictures was associated with juvenile delinquency, and the emergence of television drew forth strong voices of concern over its potential antisocial and anti-intellectual influences on an easily influenced youthful audience. Again, one is tempted to distance oneself from the types of short-term, narrowly focused, and adversarial research that such social-problem concerns seem to generate. But perhaps the appropriate response of the research community might be to take this national concern and attempt to translate it into a sustained research effort on long-term communications effects.

Henry Aaron's study, *Politics and the Professors* (1978), although it does not deal with communications issue per se, offers an interesting perspective on the interaction of politically salient social problems and the social science research community. Aaron studied the Great Society programs of the early 1960s, the social science research on which they were based, and the further research that they spawned. Reviewing this process from the perspective of the following decade, Aaron's conclusions are somewhat pessimistic. The time scale necessary to conduct research, the identification of key variables, and the definitions of effects in social sciences stand at some distance from the immediate and unqualified conclusions Washington policy makers would prefer.

Indeed, it is widely recognized that the input of social science to policy making represents a frustratingly loose linkage, but communications researchers need not throw up their hands in despair. Perhaps the research community could be strategically prepared when government authorities, foundations, and concerned citizens next crystallize their attention on a particular social problem related to communications effects. True, previous attempts to translate immediate policy concerns into programmatic long-term social science research have failed—one thinks first of the social indicators movement (Aborn, 1984; Social Science Research Council, 1983)—but perhaps the communications field will prove more amenable to programmatic time-series research.

4. *Measuring the Success or Failure of Communications Research*

How can we tell if we are making progress? At several points in this review, it has been argued that the sense of progress—for example, the movement away from the simplistic bullet theory—has been illusory. The accumulation of additional incomplete, noncomparable, and conflicting findings is a weak form of progress. One is drawn to the hopeful promise of new coordinated efforts, new forms of data collection, and the evolution of a new paradigm of communications effects.

When Max Weber addressed his fellow social scientists in 1910, he put forward a rather grand plan for the coordinated measurement of media content and public response. He indicated that he had been in contact with the German Press Association and was confident that the data could be made available. Different members of the audience would suggest different approaches to analysis. Would the social science community be able to sustain a cooperative and coordinated effort at data collection and analysis? Weber concluded presciently, "You can see immediately, honored members of the audience, the road to the answers to such questions is extremely long."

REFERENCES

Aaron, H. J. (1978). *Politics and the professors*. Washington, DC: Brookings Institution.
Abelson, R. P. (1981). The psychological status of the script concept. *American Psychologist*, **36**, 715-729.
Aborn, M. (1984, September). The short and happy life of social indicators at the National Science Foundation. *Items* (Social Science Research Council).
Achen, C. (1975). Mass political attitudes and the survey response. *American Political Science Review*, **69**, 1218-1231.
Adams, W., & Schreibman, F. (Eds.). (1978). *Television network news*. Washington, DC: George Washington University Press.
Adler, R., Lesser, G. S., Meringoff, L. K., Robertson, T. S., Rossiter, J. R., & Wood, S. (1980). *The effects of television advertising on children*. Lexington, MA: Lexington Books.
Adorno, T. W., Frankel-Brunswik, E., Levinson, D. J., & Sanford, R. N. (1950). *The authoritarian personality*. New York: Harper & Row.
Asch, S. E. (1952). Group forces in the modification and distortion of judgments. In *Social psychology* (pp. 450-473). Englewood Cliffs, NJ: Prentice-Hall.
Babbie, E. (1986). *The practice of social research* (4th ed). Belmont, CA: Wadsworth.
Bagdikian, B. (1981). *The media monopoly*. Boston: Beacon Press.
Ball-Rokeach, S. J., Grube, J. W., & Rokeach, M. (1984). *A method for assessing media effects on self-selected audiences in natural settings*. Paper presented at the American Sociological Association conference, San Antonio, TX.
Ball-Rokeach, S. J., Rokeach, M., & Grube, J. W. (1984). *The great American values test*. New York: Free Press.
Bandura, A., Ross, D., & Ross, S. A. (1963). Imitation of film-mediated aggressive models. *Journal of Abnormal and Social Psychology*, **66**, 3-11.
Bauer, R. A. (Ed.). (1966). *Social indicators*. Cambridge, MA: MIT Press.
Becker, L. B. (1979). Measurement of gratifications. *Communications Research*, **6**, 54-73.
Becker, L. B., McCombs, M. E., & McLeod, J. M. (1975). The development of political cognitions. In S. H. Chaffee (Ed.), *Political communication* (pp. 21-64). Newbury Park, CA: Sage.
Becker, L. B., Sobowale, I. A., Cobbey, R. E., & Eyal, C. H. (1978). Debate's effects on voters' understanding of candidates and issues. In G. F. Bishop, R. G. Meadow, & M. Jackson-Beeck (Eds.), *The presidential debates: Media, electoral, and policy perspectives* (pp. 126-139). New York: Praeger.
Bem, D. J. (1970). *Beliefs, attitudes, and human affairs*. Belmont, CA: Wadsworth.
Beniger, J. R. (1978). Media content as social indicators. *Communication Research*, **5**(4), 437-453.
Berelson, B. (1949). What "missing the newspaper" means. In P. Lazarsfeld & F. Stanton (Eds.), *Communication Research, 1948-49*. New York: Harper & Row.
Berelson, B. (1952). *Content analysis in communications research*. New York: Free Press.
Berelson, B. (1966). Content analysis in communications research. In B. Berelson & M. Janowitz (Eds.), *Reader in public opinion and communication* (pp. 260-266). New York: Free Press.

Berelson, B., Lazarsfeld, P., & McPhee, W. (1954). *Voting: A study of opinion formation in a presidential campaign.* Chicago: University of Chicago Press.

Bishop, G. F., Meadow, R. G., & Jackson-Beeck, M. (Eds.). (1978). *The presidential debates: Media, electoral, and policy perspectives.* New York: Praeger.

Bishop, G. F., Oldendick, R. W., & Tuchfarber, A. J. (1978). The presidential debates as a device for increasing the "rationality" of electoral behavior. In G. F. Bishop, R. G. Meadow, & M. Jackson-Beeck (Eds.), *The presidential debates: Media, electoral, and policy perspectives* (pp. 179-196). New York: Praeger.

Bishop, G. F., Oldendick, R. W., Tuchfarber, A. J., & Bennett, S. (1980). Pseudo-opinion on public affairs. *Public Opinion Quarterly,* **44,** 198-209.

Block, E. (1984). Freedom, equality, et cetera. In G. Melischek, K. E. Rosengren, & J. Stappers (Eds.), *Cultural indicators* (pp. 159-176). Vienna: Verlag Der Osterreichischen Akademie Der Wissenschaften.

Bogart, L. (1972). *Silent politics.* New York: Wiley.

Bollen, K. A., & Phillips, D. P. (1981). Suicidal motor vehicle fatalities in Detroit: A replication. *American Journal of Sociology,* **87,** 404-412.

Bollen, K. A., & Phillips, D. P. (1982). Imitative suicides: A national study of the effects of television news stories. *American Sociological Review,* **47,** 802-809.

Breed, W. (1955). Social control in the newsroom. *Social Forces,* **33,** 326-335.

Brody, R. A., & Page, B. I. (1975). The impact of events on presidential popularity. In A. B. Wildavsky (Ed.), *Perspectives on the presidency* (pp. 136-148). Boston: Little, Brown.

Bryant, J., & Zillmann, D. (Eds.). (1986). *Perspectives on media effects.* Hillsdale, NJ: Erlbaum.

Campbell, D. T., & Fiske, D. W. (1959). Convergent and discriminant validation by the multitrait/multi-method matrix. *Psychological Bulletin,* **56,** 81-105.

Cantor, M. G. (1980). *Prime-time television.* Newbury Park, CA: Sage.

Chaffee, S. H. (1972). Television and adolescent aggressiveness. In G. A. Comstock & E. A. Rubinstein (Eds.), *Television and social behavior: Vol. 3. Television and adolescent aggressiveness* (pp. 1-34). Washington, DC: U.S. Government Printing Office.

Chaffee, S. H. (1975). The diffusion of political information. In S. H. Chaffee (Ed.), *Political communication* (pp. 85-128). Newbury Park, CA: Sage.

Chaffee, S. H. (1977). Mass media effects. In D. Lerner & L. Nelson (Eds.), *Communication research* (pp. 210-241). Honolulu: University of Hawaii Press.

Clarke, P., & Kline, F. G. (1974). Media effects reconsidered. *Communication Research,* 1(2), 224-240.

Cohen, B. (1963). *The press and foreign policy.* Princeton, NJ: Princeton University Press.

Coleman, J. S. (1964). *Introduction to mathematical sociology.* New York: Free Press.

Coleman, J. S. (1981). *Longitudinal data analysis.* New York: Basic Books.

Comstock, G. (1980). *Television in America.* Newbury Park, CA: Sage.

Comstock, G. (1983). The mass media and social change. In E. Seidman (Ed.), *Handbook of social interaction* (pp. 268-288). Newbury Park, CA: Sage.

Comstock, G., Chaffee, S., Katzman, N., McCombs, M., & Roberts, D. (1978). *Television and human behavior.* New York: Columbia University Press.

Comstock, G., & Lindsey, G. (1975). *Television and human behavior: The research horizon, future and present.* Santa Monica, CA: Rand Corporation, R-1748-CF.

Converse, P. (1970). Attitudes and non-attitudes. In E. Tufte (Ed.), *The quantitative analysis of social problems* (pp. 168-189). Reading, MA: Addison-Wesley.

Cooper, E., & Jahoda, M. (1947). The evasion of propaganda. *Journal of Psychology,* **23,** 15-25.

Curran, J., Gurevitch, M., & Woollacott, J. (Eds.). (1977). *Mass communication and society.* Newbury Park, CA: Sage.

Dahl, R. A. (1963). *Modern political thought.* Englewood Cliffs, NJ: Prentice-Hall.

Davison, W. P., & Yu, F. T. C. (Eds). (1974). *Mass communication research*. New York: Praeger.
De Fleur, M. L., & Ball-Rokeach, S. (1982). *Theories of mass communication* (4th ed.). New York: Longman.
Deutsch, K. W. (1963). *The nerves of government*. New York: Free Press.
De Weese, L. C., III. (1976). Computer content analysis of printed media. *Public Opinion Quarterly*, 40(1), 92-100.
Doob, A., & MacDonald, G. E. (1979). Television viewing and fear of victimization. *Journal of Personality and Social Psychology*, 37(2), 170-179.
Durkheim, E. (1964). *The rules of sociological method*. New York: Free Press.
Easton, D. (1953). *The political system*. New York: Knopf.
Easton, D. (1965a). *A framework for political analysis*. Englewood Cliffs, NJ: Prentice-Hall.
Easton, D. (1965b). *A systems analysis of political life*. New York: Wiley.
Efron, E. (1971). *The news twisters*. New York: Nash.
Elliott, P. (1974). Uses and gratifications research. In J. G. Blumler & E. Katz (Eds.), *The uses of mass communication* (pp. 249-268). Newbury Park, CA: Sage.
Ellsworth, J. W. (1965). Rationality and campaigning: A content analysis of the 1960 presidential campaign debates. *Western Political Quarterly*, 18, 794-802.
Erbring, L., Goldenberg, E. N., & Miller, A. H. (1980). Front page news and real-world cues. *American Journal of Political Science*, 24(1), 16-49.
Ettema, J. S., & Kline, F. G. (1977). Deficits, differences, and ceilings. *Communication Research*, 4(2), 179-202.
Eyal, C. H., Winter, J. P., & De George, W. F. (1981). The concept of time frame in agenda-setting. In G. C. Wilhoit & H. de Bock (Eds.), *Mass communication review yearbook* (Vol. 2; pp. 212-218). Newbury Park, CA: Sage.
Fan, D. P. (1985). Ideodynamics: The kinetics of the evolution of ideas. *Journal of Mathematical Sociology*, 11, 1-24.
Farquhar, J. W., Maccoby, N., Wood, P. D., Alexander, J. K., Breitrose, H., Brown, B. W., Jr., Haskell, W. L., McAlister, A. L., Meyer, A. J., Nash, J. D., & Stern, M. P. (1977). Community education for cardiovascular health. *Lancet*, i, 1192-1195.
Festinger, L. (1957). *A theory of cognitive dissonance*. Evanston, IL: Row Peterson.
Firestone, J. M. (1972). The development of social indicators from content analysis. *Policy Sciences*, 3, 249-283.
Fishbein, M. (1965). A consideration of beliefs, attitudes, and their relationships. In I. D. Steiner & M. Fishbein (Eds.), *Current studies in social psychology* (pp. 107-120). New York: Holt.
Freidson, E. (1953). The relation of the social situation of contact to the media in mass communication. *Public Opinion Quarterly*, 17, 230-238.
Friedrich, C. J. (1937). *Constitutional government and politics*. New York: Harper & Row.
Funkhouser, G. R. (1973a). Trends in media coverage of the issues of the '60s. *Journalism Quarterly*, 50(3), 533-538.
Funkhouser, G. R. (1973b). The issues of the sixties. *Public Opinion Quarterly*, 37(1), 62-75.
Gamson, W. A. (1968). *Power and discontent*. Homewood, IL: Dorsey Press.
Gamson, W. A. (1984, Fall). A constructionist approach to mass media and public opinion. *Symbolic Interaction*.
Gamson, W. A., & Modigliani, A. (1986, July). Media discourse and public opinion on nuclear power: A constructionist approach. *American Journal of Sociology*.
Gans, H. J. (1962). *The urban villagers*. New York: Free Press.
Gans, H. J. (1968). *The uses of television and their educational implications*. New York: Center for Urban Education.
Gans, H. J. (1974). *Popular culture and high culture*. New York: Basic Books.

Gans, H. J. (1979). *Deciding what's news.* New York: Pantheon.
Gerbner, G. (1969). Toward "cultural indicators": The analysis of mass mediated public message systems. In G. Gerbner, O. R. Holsti, K. Krippendorff, W. J. Paisley, & P. J. Stone (Eds.), *The analysis of communications content.* New York: Wiley.
Gerbner, G. (1973). Cultural indicators. In G. Gerbner, L. Gross, & W. Melody (Eds.), *Communications technology and social policy* (pp. 555-573). New York: Wiley.
Gerbner, G. (1983). The importance of being critical—In one's own fashion. *Journal of Communication,* 33(3), 355-362.
Gerbner, G., & Gross, L. (1976). The scary world of TV's heavy viewer. *Psychology Today,* 9, 41-45.
Gerbner, G., Gross, L., Morgan, M., & Signorielli, N. (1980). The "mainstreaming" of America. *Journal of Communication,* 30(3), 10-29.
Gerbner, G., Gross, L., Morgan, M., & Signorielli, N. (1981a). A curious journey into the scary world of Paul Hirsch. *Communication Research,* 8(1), 39-72.
Gerbner, G., Gross, L., Morgan, M., & Signorielli, N. (1981b). Final reply to Hirsch. *Communication Research,* 8(1), 259-280.
Gerbner, G., Holsti, O. R., Krippendorff, K., Paisley, W. J., & Stone, P. J. (1969). *The analysis of communications content.* New York: Wiley.
Gitlin, T. (1980). *The whole world is watching.* Berkeley: University of California Press.
Glock, C. Y. (1967). *Survey research in the social sciences.* New York: Russell Sage Foundation.
Goffman, E. (1974). *Frame analysis.* New York: Harper & Row.
Graber, D. (1984). *Processing the news: How people tame the information tide.* New York: Longman.
Greenberg, B. S. (1980). *Life on television: Content analyses of U.S. TV drama.* Norwood, NJ: Ablex.
Greenfield, P. M. (1984). *Mind and media: The effects of television, video games, and computers.* Cambridge, MA: Harvard University Press.
Hagner, P. R., & Rieselbach, L. N. (1978). The impact of the 1976 presidential debates: Conversion or reinforcement? In G. F. Bishop, R. G. Meadow, & M. Jackson-Beeck (Eds.), *The presidential debates: Media, electoral, and policy perspectives* (pp. 157-178). New York: Praeger.
Haight, T., & Brody, R. (1977). The mass media and presidential politics. *Communication Research,* 4, 14-60.
Hardt, H. (1979). *Social theories of the press.* Newbury Park, CA: Sage.
Hart, H. (1933). Changing social attitudes and interests. *Recent Social Trends,* 342-382.
Herzog, H. (1944). What do we really know about daytime serial listeners? In P. F. Lazarsfeld & F. N. Stanton (Eds.), *Radio research, 1942-1943* (pp. 3-33). New York: Duell, Sloan & Pearce.
Himmelweit, H. T., Humphreys, P., Jaegers, M., & Katz, M. (1981). *How voters decide.* New York: Academic Press.
Hirsch, P. (1980). The "scary world" of the nonviewer and other anomalies. *Communication Research,* 7(4), 403-456.
Hirsch, P. (1981a). On not learning from one's own mistakes. *Communication Research,* 8(1), 3-37.
Hirsch, P. (1981b). Distinguishing good speculation from bad theory. *Communication Research,* 8(1), 73-95.
Holsti, O. R. (1968). Content analysis. In G. Lindzey & E. Aronson (Eds.), *The handbook of social psychology* (2nd ed., pp. 596-692). Reading, MA: Addison-Wesley.
Horkheimer, M., & Adorno, T. (1944). The cultural industry: Enlightenment as mass deception. Reprinted in *The dialectics of enlightenment* (1973). London: Allen Lane.
Hovland, C. I. (1959). Reconciling conflicting results derived from experimental and survey studies of attitude change. *American Psychologist,* 14, 8-17.
Hovland, C. I., Janis, I., & Kelley, H. H. (1953). *Communication and persuasion.* New Haven, CT: Yale University Press.
Hovland, C. I., Lumsdaine, A. A., & Sheffield, F. D. (1949). *Experiments in mass communication.* Princeton, NJ: Princeton University Press.

Hughes, M. (1980). The fruits of cultivation analysis. *Public Opinion Quarterly*, **44**(3), 287-302.
Iyengar, S., & Kinder, D. (1987). *News that matters: Television and American opinion*. Chicago: University of Chicago Press.
Janowitz, M. (1969). Content analysis and the study of the "symbolic environment." In A. A. Rogow (Ed.), *Politics, personality, and social science in the twentieth century* (pp. 155-170). Chicago: University of Chicago Press.
Janowitz, M. (1976). Content analysis and the study of sociopolitical change. *Journal of Communication*, **26**(4), 10-21.
Johnson, P., Sears, D. O., & McConahay, J. B. (1971). Black invisibility, the press, and the Los Angeles riot. *American Journal of Sociology*, **76**, 698-721.
Katz, E. (1977). *Social research on broadcasting*. London: British Broadcasting Corporation.
Katz, E. (1980). On conceptualizing media effects. In T. McCormack (Ed.), *Studies in communications* (Vol. 1, pp. 119-141). Greenwich, CT: JAI Press.
Katz, E., Blumler, J. G., & Gurevitch, M. (1974). Utilization of mass communication by the individual. In J. G. Blumler & E. Katz (Eds.), *The uses of mass communications: Current perspectives on gratifications research*. Newbury Park, CA: Sage.
Katz, E., Gurevitch, M., & Haas, H. (1973). On the use of the mass media for important things. *American Sociological Review*, **38**(2), 164-181.
Katz, E., & Lazarsfeld, P. (1955). *Personal influence*. New York: Free Press.
Katzman, N. (1972). Television soap operas. *Public Opinion Quarterly*, **36**(2), 200-212.
Kelman, H. C. (1953). Attitude change as a function of response restriction. *Human Relations*, **6**, 185-214.
Klapper, J. T. (1960). *The effects of mass communication*. New York: Free Press.
Kline, F. G. (1977). Time in communication research. In P. M. Hirsch, P. V. Miller, & F. G. Kline (Eds.), *Strategies for communication research* (pp. 187-204). Newbury Park, CA: Sage.
Kondratieff, N. D. (1935). The long waves in economic life. *Review of Economic Statistics*, **17**, 105-115.
Kraus, S. (Ed.). (1962). *The great debates*. Bloomington: Indiana University Press.
Kraus, S., & Davis, D. (1976). *The effects of mass communication on political behavior*. University Park: Pennsylvania State University Press.
Krippendorff, K. (1980). *Content analysis*. Newbury Park, CA: Sage.
Kuhn, T. (1962). *The structure of scientific revolutions*. Chicago: University of Chicago Press.
Lane, R. E. (1962). *Political ideology*. New York: Free Press.
Lang, G. E., & Lang, K. (1978). The formation of public opinion: Direct and mediated effects of the first debate. In G. F. Bishop, R. G. Meadow, & M. Jackson-Beeck (Eds.), *The presidential debates: Media, electoral, and policy perspectives* (pp. 61-80). New York: Praeger.
Lang, G. E., & Lang, K. (1981). Mass communication and public opinion. In M. Rosenberg & R. H. Turner (Eds.), *Social psychology* (pp. 653-682). New York: Basic Books.
Lang, K., & Lang, G. E. (1953). The unique perspective of television and its effect. *American Sociological Review*, **18**, 3-12.
Lasswell, H. D. (1935). *World politics and personal insecurity*. New York: Free Press.
Lasswell, H. D. (1963). *The future of political science*. New York: Atherton Press.
Lasswell, H. D., & Kaplan, A. (1950). *Power and society*. New Haven, CT: Yale University Press.
Lasswell, H. D., Leites, N., & associates. (1949). *The language of politics*. Cambridge, MA: MIT Press.
Lazarsfeld, P. F., Berelson, B., & Gaudet, H. (1948). *The people's choice: How the voter makes up his mind in a presidential campaign*. New York: Columbia University Press.
Lazarsfeld, P. F., & Merton, R. K. (1948). Mass communication, popular taste, and organized social action. In L. Brynson (Ed.), *The communication of ideas* (pp. 95-118). New York: Harper.

Lemert, J. B. (1981). *Does mass communication change public opinion after all?* Chicago: Nelson-Hall.
Lichter, S. R., Rothman, S., & Lichter, L. S. (1986). *The media elite.* Bethesda, MD: Adler & Adler.
Lippmann, W. (1922). *Public opinion.* New York: Free Press.
Lowenthal, L. (1944). Biographies in popular magazines. In P. F. Lazarsfeld & F. N. Stanton (Eds.), *Radio research 1942-1943* (pp. 507-548). New York: Duell, Sloan & Pearce.
Lowenthal, L. (1961). *Literature, popular culture, and society.* Palo Alto, CA: Pacific Books.
Lowery, S., & De Fleur, M. L. (1983). *Milestones in mass communication.* New York: Longman.
Maccoby, N., & Farquhar, J. W. (1975). Communication for health. *Journal of Communication,* **25**(3), 114-126.
Maccoby, N., & Solomon, D. S. (1981). Heart disease prevention: Community studies. In R. E. Rice & W. J. Paisley (Eds.), *Public communication campaigns* (pp. 105-125). Newbury Park, CA: Sage.
MacKuen, M. B. (1981). Social communication and the mass policy agenda. In M. B. MacKuen & S. L. Coombs (Eds.), *More than news: Media power in public affairs* (pp. 19-144). Newbury Park, CA: Sage.
MacKuen, M. B., & Coombs, S. L. (Eds.) (1981). *More than news: Media power in public affairs.* Newbury Park, CA: Sage.
Mannheim, K. (1936). *Ideology and utopia.* New York: Harcourt Brace.
Marcuse, H. (1964). *One-dimensional man.* Boston: Beacon Press.
Markoff, J., Shapiro, G., & Weitman, S. R. (1974). Toward the integration of content analysis and general methodology. In D. Heise (Ed.), *Sociological methodology, 1975* (pp. 1-58). San Francisco: Jossey-Bass.
Mattelart, A. (1980). *Mass media, ideologies, and the revolutionary movement.* Sussex, England: Harvester Press.
McCombs, M. E. (1981a). The agenda-setting approach. In D. D. Nimmo & K. R. Sanders (Eds.), *Handbook of political communication* (pp. 121-140). Newbury Park, CA: Sage.
McCombs, M. E. (1981b). Setting the agenda for agenda-setting research: An assessment of the priority ideas and problems. In G. C. Wilhoit & H. de Bock (Eds.), *Mass communication review yearbook* (Vol. 2, pp. 209-211). Newbury Park, CA: Sage.
McCombs, M. E., & Shaw, D. L. (1972). The agenda-setting function of mass media. *Public Opinion Quarterly,* **36**(2), 176-187.
McDonald, D. G. (1983). Investigating assumptions of media dependency research. *Communication Research,* **10**(4), 509-528.
McGuire, W. J. (1968). The nature of attitudes and attitude change. In G. Lindzey & E. Aronson (Eds.), *The handbook of social psychology* (2nd ed., pp. 136-314). Reading, MA: Addison-Wesley.
McGuire, W. J. (1986). The myth of massive media impact: Savagings and salvagings. In G. Comstock (Ed.), *Public communication and behavior* (Vol. 1, pp. 173-258). New York: Academic Press.
McLeod, J., Becker, L., & Byrnes, J. E. (1974). Another look at the agenda-setting function of the press. *Communication Research,* **2**, 131-166.
McLeod, J. M., & Reeves, B. (1980). On the nature of mass media effects. In S. B. Withey & R. P. Abeles (Eds.), *Television and social behavior* (pp. 17-54). Hillsdale, NJ: Erlbaum.
McQuail, D. (1977). The influence and effects of mass media. In J. Curran, M. Gurevitch, & J. Woollacott (Eds.), *Mass communication and society* (pp. 70-94). Newbury Park, CA: Sage.
McQuail, D. (1983). *Mass communication theory.* Newbury Park, CA: Sage.
McQuail, D., Blumler, J. G., & Brown, J. R. (1972). The television audience. In D. McQuail (Ed.), *Sociology of mass communications* (pp. 135-165). Baltimore, MD: Penguin Books.

Melischek, G., Rosengren, K. E., & Stappers, J. (Eds.). (1984). *Cultural indicators*. Vienna: Austrian Academy of Sciences.

Middleton, R. (1962). National TV debates and presidential voting decisions. *Public Opinion Quarterly*, 26, 426-428.

Milavsky, J. R., Kessler, R. C., Stipp, H. H., & Rubens, W. S. (1982). *Television and aggression: Results of a panel study*. New York: Academic Press.

Milgram, S. (1961). Nationality and conformity. *Scientific American*, 205, 45-51.

Miliband, R. (1969). *The state in capitalist society*. London: Weidenfeld & Nicolson.

Miller, A. H., Goldenberg, E. N., & Erbring, L. (1979). Type-set politics. *American Political Science Review*, 73(1), 67-84.

Mochmann, E. (1980). *Computerstrategien fur die kommunikationsanalyse*. Frankfurt: Campus Verlag.

Mullins, L. E. (1973). *Agenda-setting on campus: The mass media and learning of issue importance in the '72 election*. Paper presented to the Association for Education in Journalism, Fort Collins, CO.

Naisbitt, J. (1982). *Megatrends*. New York: Warner Books.

Naples, M. J. (1979). *Effective frequency*. New York: Association of National Advertisers.

Neisser, U. (1976). *Cognition and reality*. San Francisco: Freeman.

Neuman, W. R. (1976). Patterns of recall among television news viewers. *Public Opinion Quarterly*, 40, 115-123.

Neuman, W. R. (1979). *The impact of the mass media on the changing American voter*. Paper presented at the annual meeting of the American Sociological Association, Boston.

Neuman, W. R. (1981). The ebb and flow of social research on television. In W. R. Neuman (Ed.), *The social impact of television* (pp. 5-23). New York: Aspen Institute.

Neuman, W. R. (1982). Television and American culture. *Public Opinion Quarterly*, 46, 471-487.

Neuman, W. R. (1986). *The paradox of mass politics*. Cambridge, MA: Harvard University Press.

Neuman, W. R., & Fryling, A. C. (1985). Patterns of political cognition. In S. Kraus & R. Perloff (Eds.), *Mass media and political thought* (pp. 223-240). Newbury Park, CA: Sage.

Neuman, W. R., & Keegan, C. (1980). *The evaluation protocol*. Paper presented at the annual meeting of the American Association for Public Opinion Research, Cincinnati, OH.

Neuman, W. R., & Pool, I. d. S. (1986). The flow of information into the home. In S. Ball-Rokeach & M. G. Cantor (Eds.), *Media, audience and social structure*. Newbury Park, CA: Sage.

Neurath, P. M. (1960). *Radio forums in India*. Delhi: Government of India Press.

Newcomb, H. (1979). *TV: The most popular art*. Garden City, NY: Doubleday.

Nimmo, D., Mansfield, M., & Curry, J. (1978). Persistence and change in candidate images. In G. F. Bishop, R. G. Meadow, & M. Jackson-Beeck (Eds.), *The presidential debates: Media, electoral, and policy perspectives* (pp. 140-156). New York: Praeger.

Noelle-Neumann, E. (1977). Turbulence in the climate of opinion: Methodological applications of the spiral of silence theory. *Public Opinion Quarterly*, 41, 143-158.

Noelle-Neumann, E. (1984). *The spiral of science: Public opinion—Our social skin*. Chicago: University of Chicago Press.

Paletz, D. L., & Entman, R. M. (1981). *Media power politics*. New York: Free Press.

Parsons, T., & Shils, E. A. (Eds.). (1951). *Toward a general theory of action*. New York: Harper & Row.

Patterson, T. (1980). *The mass media election*. New York: Praeger.

Patterson, T., & McClure, R. D. (1976). *The unseeing eye: The myth of television power in national politics*. New York: Putnam.

Payne, S. L. (1951). *The art of asking questions*. Princeton, NJ: Princeton University Press.

Pearl, D., Bouthilet, L., & Lazar, J. (Eds.). (1982). *Television and behavior: Ten years of scientific inquiry and implications for the eighties: Vol. 2. Technical reviews*. Washington, DC: U.S. Government Printing Office.

Phillips, D. P. (1983). The impact of mass media violence on U.S. homicides. *American Sociological Review*, **48**(4), 560–568.

Phillips, D. P. (1986). The found experiment: A new technique for assessing the impact of mass media violence on real-world aggressive behavior. In G. Comstock (Ed.), *Public communication and behavior* (Vol. 1, pp. 259–307). New York: Academic Press.

Pietila, V. (1977). On the effects of mass media. In M. Berg and associates (Eds.), *Current theories in Scandinavian mass communication research* (pp. 117–146). Grenaa, Denmark: GMT.

Pool, I. d. S. (1959). *Trends in content analysis today*. Urbana: University of Illinois Press.

Pool, I. d. S. (1983). Tracking the flow of information. *Science*, **221**(4611), 609–613.

Pool, I. d. S., Inose, H., Takasaki, N., & Hurwitz, R. (1984). *Communications flows*. Tokyo: University of Tokyo Press.

Popkin, S., Gorman, J. W., Phillips, G., & Smith, J. A. (1976). Comment: What have you done for me lately? *American Political Science Review*, **70**, 779–805.

Reeves, B., & Wartella, E. (1982). *For some children under some conditions: A history of research on children and media*. Paper presented at the annual meeting of the International Communications Association, Boston.

Rice, R. E., & Paisley, W. J. (Eds.). (1981). *Public communication campaigns*. Newbury Park, CA: Sage.

Riley, M. W., & Riley, J. W. (1959). Mass communication and the social system. In R. K. Merton, L. Broom, & L. S. Cottrell, Jr. (Eds.), *Sociology today* (pp. 537–578). New York: Basic Books.

Roberts, D. F., & Bachen, C. M. (1981). Mass communication effects. *Annual Review of Psychology*, **32**, 307–356.

Robinson, M., & Sheehan, M. A. (1983). *Over the wire and on TV*. New York: Russell Sage Foundation.

Robinson, W. S. (1950). Ecological correlations and the behavior of individuals. *American Sociological Review*, **15**, 351–357.

Rogers, E. M. (1973). Mass media and interpersonal communication. In I. d. S. Pool & W. Schramm (Eds.), *Handbook of communication* (pp. 290–310). Chicago: Rand McNally.

Rogers, E. M. (1983). *Diffusion of innovations* (3rd ed.). New York: Free Press.

Rosengren, K. E. (1980). Mass media and social change: Some current approaches. In G. C. Wilhoit & H. de Bock (Eds.), *Mass communication review yearbook* (Vol. 1, pp. 168–180). Newbury Park, CA: Sage.

Rosengren, K. E. (Ed.). (1981). *Advances in content analysis*. Newbury Park, CA: Sage.

Rosenthal, R. (1966). *Experimenter effects in behavioral research*. New York: Appleton-Century-Crofts.

Russell, B. (1938). *Power*. New York: Norton.

Ryan, B., & Gross, N. C. (1943). The diffusion of hybrid seed corn in two Iowa communities. *Rural Sociology*, **8**, 15–24.

Schiller, H. I. (1973). *The mind managers*. Boston: Beacon Press.

Schudson, M. (1984). *Advertising: The uneasy persuasion*. New York: Basic Books.

Schuman, H., & Johnson, M. P. (1976). Attitudes and behavior. *Annual Review of Sociology*, **2**, 161–207.

Schuman, H., & Presser, S. (1981). *Questions and answers in attitude surveys*. New York: Academic Press.

Selvin, H. (1968). Survey research. In D. Sills (Ed.), *International encyclopedia of the social sciences*. New York: Macmillan.

Shaw, D. L., & McCombs, M. E. (1977). *The emergence of American political issues*. St. Paul, MN: West.

Shaw, E. F. (1974). *Some interpersonal dimensions of the media's agenda-setting function*. Paper presented at the Conference on the Agenda-Setting Function of the Press, Syracuse University, Syracuse, NY.

Singer, J. L. (1982). Introductory comments. In D. Pearl, L. Bouthilet, & J. Lazar (Eds.), *Television and behavior: Ten years of scientific inquiry and implications for the eighties: Vol. 2. Technical reviews* (pp. 2-8). Washington, DC: U.S. Government Printing Office.

Smith, T. W. (1980). America's most important problem—A trend analysis. *Public Opinion Quarterly*, 44(2), 164-180.

Social Science Research Council. (1983). The council's program in social indicators. *Items*.

Sorokin, P. A. (1937-1941). *Social and cultural dynamics, 1-4*. London: Allen & Unwin.

Star, S. A., & Hughes, H. M. (1950). Report on an educational campaign. *American Journal of Sociology*, 55, 389-400.

Steeper, F. T. (1978). Public response to Gerald Ford's statements on Eastern Europe in the second debate. In G. F. Bishop, R. G. Meadow, & M. Jackson-Beeck (Eds.), *The presidential debates: Media, electoral, and policy perspectives* (pp. 81-101). New York: Praeger.

Stone, G. (1975). *Cumulative effects of the media*. Paper presented at the Conference on the Agenda-Setting Function of the Press, Syracuse University, Syracuse, NY.

Stone, P. J. (1972). Social indicators based on communication content. *Proceedings of the Fall Joint Computer Conference*.

Stone, P. J., & Brody, R. A. (1970). Modeling opinion responsiveness to daily news: The public and Lyndon Johnson, 1965-1968. *Social Science Indicators*, 9, 95-122.

Stone, P. J., Dunphy, D. C., Smith, M. S., & Oglivie, D. M. (1966). *The general inquirer*. Cambridge, MA: MIT Press.

Surgeon General's Social Scientific Advisory Committee on Television and Social Behavior. (1972). *Television and growing up: The impact of televised violence*. Report to the Surgeon General, United States Public Health Service. Washington, DC: U.S. Government Printing Office.

Swanson, D. L. (1979). The continuing evolution of the uses and gratifications model: A critique. *Communication Research*, 6, 3-7.

Theberge, L. J. (1981). *Crooks, con men and clowns*. Washington, DC: Media Institute.

Tichenor, P. J., Donohue, G. A., & Olien, C. A. (1970). Mass media flow and differential growth in knowledge. *Public Opinion Quarterly*, 34, 159-170.

Tichenor, P. J., Donohue, G. A., & Olien, C. A. (1980). *Community conflict and the press*. Newbury Park, CA: Sage.

Troldahl, V. C., & Van Dam, R. (1965). Face to face communication about major topics in the news. *Public Opinion Quarterly*, 29(4), 626-634.

Tufte, E. R. (1974). *Data analysis for politics and policy*. Englewood Cliffs, NJ: Prentice-Hall.

Weaver, D. L., Graber, D. A., McCombs, M. E., & Eyal, C. H. (1981). *Media agenda-setting in a presidential election: Issues, images, and interest*. New York: Praeger.

Weber, Marianne. (1926). *Max Weber, Ein Lebensbild*. Tubingen: Mohr.

Weber, Max. (1910). Towards a sociology of the press. Reprinted in *Journal of Communication*, 1976, 26(3), 96-101.

Weber, Max. (1925). *Economy and society*. Berkeley: University of California Press. (Reprinted, 1968)

Weber, R. P. (1981). Society and economy in the Western world system. *Social Forces*, 59(4), 1130-1148.

Weber, R. P. (1984). Content analytic indicators. In G. Melischek, K. E. Rosengren, & J. Stappers (Eds.), *Cultural indicators* (pp. 301-313). Vienna: Austrian Academy of Sciences.

Weiss, W. (1968). Effects of mass media of communication. In G. Lindzey & E. Aronson (Eds.), *Handbook of social psychology* (2nd ed., Vol. 5, pp. 77-195). Reading, MA: Addison-Wesley.

Weiss, W. (1976). Review of *The uses of mass communications*. *Public Opinion Quarterly*, 40, 132-133.

Windahl, S. (1981). Uses and gratifications at the crossroads. In G. C. Wilhoit & H. de Bock (Eds.), *Mass communication review yearbook* (Vol. 2, pp. 174-185). Newbury Park, CA: Sage.

Winter, J. P. (1979). *An agenda-setting time frame for the civil rights issue, 1954-1976*. Unpublished manuscript, S. I. Newhouse School of Public Communications, Syracuse University, Syracuse, NY.

Winter, J. P. (1981). Contingent conditions in the agenda-setting process. In G. C. Wilhoit & H. de Bock (Eds.), *Mass communication review yearbook* (Vol. 2, pp. 235-244). Newbury Park, CA: Sage.

Wright, C. R. (1975). *Mass communication* (2nd ed.). New York: Random House.

Yakobson, S., & Lasswell, H. D. (1949). May Day slogans in Soviet Russia, 1918-1943. In H. D. Lasswell, N. Leites, & associates (Eds.), *The language of politics* (pp. 233-297). Cambridge, MA: MIT Press.

Yule, G. U., & Kendall, M. G. (1950). *An introduction to the theory of statistics* (14th ed.). London: Charles Griffin.

Zimbardo, P. G., Weisenberg, M., Firestone, I., & Levy, B. (1965). Communication effectiveness in producing public conformity and private attitude change. *Journal of Personality*, 33, 233-255.

Zucker, H. G. (1978). The variable nature of news media influence. In B. D. Ruben (Ed.), *Communication yearbook II* (pp. 225-240). New Brunswick, NJ: Transaction Books.

Zukin, C. (1981). Mass communication and public opinion. In D. D. Nimmo & K. R. Sanders (Eds.), *Handbook of political communication* (pp. 359-390). Newbury Park, CA: Sage.

Nuclear War on Television: The Impact of The Day After

STUART OSKAMP

Faculty in Psychology
Claremont Graduate School
Claremont, California 91711

I. Introduction	292
A. The Making of *The Day After*	293
B. Media Predictions	294
C. Conditions of Broadcasting *The Day After*	295
D. Media Verdicts	296
II. The Variety of Research Studies	297
A. Sources of Research Findings	297
B. Quantitative Analysis	298
C. Considerations in Analyzing Research Reports	298
III. The Early Instant-Analysis Reports	301
A. Topics	301
B. Evaluations of *The Day After*	304
C. Nuclear Beliefs and Attitudes	305
D. Attitudes toward Reagan	306
E. Public Opinion Changes following *The Day After*	306
IV. The More Comprehensive Studies	307
Study Characteristics	308
V. Findings of the Comprehensive Studies	309
A. Viewer Characteristics	322
B. Reactions to *The Day After*	323
C. Effects of *The Day After* on Information Learned	325
D. Effects on Attitudes and Beliefs	325
E. Differential Effects of *The Day After*, the *Viewpoint* Panel Discussion, and Other Communications	334
F. Persistence of Attitude and Belief Changes	336
G. Postmovie Differences between Viewers and Nonviewers	338
H. Demographic Comparisons	340
I. Additional Substantive Issues	341
J. Research Artifacts	342

VI. Discussion 343
   A. Summary of Findings 343
   B. Limitations and Implications of the Research Reports 345
   C. Conclusion: A Media Event 347
References.. 348

I. INTRODUCTION

The 1983 television movie about the aftermath of nuclear war, *The Day After*, was a unique and unprecedented media event. Its estimated audience of 100 million viewers watching in 46% of America's television households was the 12th largest U.S. television audience of all time and the 2nd largest for a film on television ("Fallout From," 1983; Kaatz, 1984). *The Day After* received mass public attention because it addressed a controversial and emotional topic that had formerly been taboo on network television. As a result, it generated intense political controversy between antinuclear activists and proarmaments advocates. The program also aroused widespread fears about its possible damaging effects on children and on impressionable adult viewers ("Nightmare," 1983).

For more than 1 month before *The Day After's* nationwide showing on November 20, 1983, preview articles and commentaries in news magazines and papers all over the country made its broadcast a national news event. As one typical example, a nationwide cover story trumpeted that "[The program] will reach out and detonate a thermonuclear apocalypse in our communal psyche.... The very idea of what television can do may never be the same" ("TV's Nuclear," 1983, p. 66). A survey study by a leading advertising agency concluded,

> In the history of television, no single program ever created so much controversy for such an amount of time by so many people at so many levels of society as *The Day After*. By the time it was actually aired, many people felt they had already lived through it. (J. Walter Thompson, 1983, p. 6)

Just like journalists and politicians, psychologists and other social scientists were also fascinated by *The Day After's* potential for influencing public opinion and national affairs, and they turned out in force to study it scientifically. In addition to the program's importance, it was relatively convenient to conduct research on it. National publicity and the more than 500,000 printed *Viewer's Guides* widely distributed more than one month in advance of the broadcast offered to researchers the unprecedented, perhaps never-to-be-repeated opportunity to do pretest–posttest studies of a nuclear catastrophe!

This chapter discusses the research findings concerning the public impact of this unique media event; hence, the 30 papers summarized here arguably represent the single greatest accumulation of research reports on a single media event, with the exception of the many studies of the "great debates" between U.S. presidential candidates (Katz & Feldman, 1962; Sears & Chaffee, 1979; Sigelman & Sigelman, 1984).

A. The Making of *The Day After*

The film's directors, producers, and sponsoring network undoubtedly had many motives in presenting it to the public. There were obvious commercial and financial motives in their massively publicizing the movie and broadcasting it during the "sweeps" period when the obtained Nielsen ratings of audience size determine the following season's advertising rates. However, the network president declared that "commercial success has never been ABC's prime consideration with the project" (Attanasio, 1983, p. 13). Indeed, the network lost money on the film's initial showing because many advertisers were reluctant to have their products associated with a nuclear disaster. Consequently, commercials were sold at a bargain rate, yielding only $2.3 million of the film's $7 million cost, with the remainder to be recouped from reruns, theater and foreign showings, and cable television sales (Kaatz, 1984).

Beyond the commercial motives, the producers' key aim was to provide a public service by showing "ordinary Americans what their lives would be like after a nuclear war" (Farber, 1983, p. H1). They spelled out their long-range hope for the program in "grave white letters" at its end ("Nightmare," 1983, p. 84): "It is hoped that the images of this film will inspire the nations of this earth, their people and leaders, to find the means to avert the fateful day." Pursuing this goal, the producers risked breaking two long-standing guidelines for entertainment television: "Never leave viewers politically aroused or emotionally distressed" ("TV's Nuclear," 1983, p. 70).

ABC made strenuous attempts to mute the film's political implications so that it would be seen as informative rather than propagandistic and so that the network could not be accused of political partisanship. The producer emphasized that the film concentrated on the effects of nuclear war and carefully avoided dealing with its causes or with ways of preventing it (Meyer, 1983). To accomplish this, it was purposefully unclear about how the nuclear conflict began and which side started it. The precipitating events were deliberately mentioned only in ambiguous snatches of news bulletins and conversation that were presented as background to the everyday activities of the characters' lives.

ABC also attempted to reduce the emotionally disturbing aspects of the film somewhat while remaining faithful to scientific knowledge about nuclear effects. Though some victims were shown being vaporized, the network limited the number of deaths shown by decreeing that seven inanimate objects would have to be destroyed for every three human deaths portrayed ("TV's Nuclear," 1983). Though hospital scenes showed many injured, views of open wounds and sounds of cries and screams were minimized. Though suffering, sores, and hair loss were shown, the vomiting and diarrhea that accompany radiation sickness were not (Schofield & Pavelchak, 1985). The extent of gory scenes and physical violence depicted was probably less than in most films of violence, crime, or war. In a subsequent nationwide poll of viewers, 80% said that the effects of a nuclear war would be worse than those portrayed in the film (Sussman, 1983). In fact, ABC acknowledged its sanitization of the nuclear aftermath by broadcasting a printed message at the end of the film, which said that its scenario was "in all likelihood less severe than what would actually occur" (W. C. Adams *et al.*, 1984, p. 18).

B. Media Predictions

Despite attempts by the producers to render the film nonpolitical and reduce its emotionally disturbing aspects, it became the subject of intense public controversy. Most commentators who previewed the film found it impressively dramatic and expected it to have a striking public impact. Representative quotations declared:

> No one will be able to forget it.... As has rarely happened in television history, a work of fiction has achieved the urgency and magnitude of live coverage of a national crisis. (Shales, 1983, p. C1)

> People turn where they stand into living X rays just before they disintegrate entirely. Fire storms swallow up towns. The images of destruction, mild for a theatrical movie and practically gentle by a factual measure, are still striking.... They pack force. ("Nightmare," 1983, p. 86)

> What the film did was to make our abstract knowledge of nuclear devastation concrete: personal, individual, and therefore terrible. It made us aware of reality. (Lewis, 1983, p. 19)

Organizations on both ends of the political spectrum geared up either to promote the film or to fight it. The director of the Campaign Against Nuclear War predicted a boost for the nuclear-freeze movement, calling the film "a $7 million advertising job for our issue" (quoted in W. C. Adams *et al.*, 1984). The antinuclear group Ground Zero distributed 300,000 viewer's guides in over 500 cities. Several antinuclear groups combined to sponsor the Day Before Project, which organized more than 500 community meetings in which 25,000 participants discussed their nuclear concerns and their reactions to the film (Schofield & Pavelchak, 1985). Viewing parties were held in churches, schools and colleges, and community centers all over the nation. A piggyback publicity campaign sponsored television commercials stressing the nuclear danger and giving a toll-free number that viewers could call to obtain more information and action suggestions; by the end of the week, about 50,000 people had called the number ("Fallout From," 1983).

At the other extreme, conservative groups also saw the film's impact as potentially explosive and attacked it strenuously. Phyllis Schlafley and leaders of Young Americans for Freedom labeled it as blatant propaganda. Henry Kissinger called it simple-minded and complained, "Are we supposed to make policy by scaring ourselves to death?" ("Fallout From," 1983). The leader of the Moral Majority, Jerry Fallwell, considered the film a challenge to the Reagan administration's defense policies and condemned it as "a threat to our national security." His organization wrote to many clergymen urging them to preach sermons against the film. The Moral Majority also threatened to start a boycott against companies that advertised on the program and actually wrote to over 100 major advertisers warning them not to buy commercial time during the movie (Mermigas, 1983). White House spokesmen admitted their concern over the effects of the film. Some advisers suggested that President Reagan should go on television to counter the film, and Secretary of State Shultz eventually made a solo appearance on the discussion show that followed the film, in which he stressed how actively the administration was working for nuclear arms control ("Fallout From," 1983).

Another general expectation of commentators was that the film would be emotionally devastating to many viewers, and particularly to children. The American Academy of Child Psychiatry and the American Academy of Pediatrics recommended that no one should watch the film alone because they might be overwhelmed by reactions of despair, fear, or anxiety, and most of the widely distributed *Viewer's Guides* emphasized this warning (Malcolm, 1983). Educators for Social Responsibility urged that children under 12 not be allowed to watch the film, and they sponsored several thousand advance showings of a brief version of the film to help teachers and parents understand and handle children's nuclear fears (Schofield & Pavelchak, 1985). Both ABC and groups of parents and psychologists initiated studies of children's reactions to the film and publicized recommendations designed to avoid any distress reactions (Lometti & Feig, 1984; Singer, 1984). In addition, crisis centers put on extra staff members for the night of the broadcast, and in many cities, special hot lines were set up to handle calls from traumatized viewers. However, as it turned out, there were very few such calls, and the film produced far less emotional disturbance than had been predicted, perhaps partly because of all the preparatory work that had been done to forestall such reactions (W. C. Adams *et al.*, 1984; Lometti & Feig, 1984; "Fallout From," 1983).

C. Conditions of Broadcasting *The Day After*

The Day After was shown all across America on Sunday evening, November 20, 1983; it was the first time that this controversial topic had been handled in network television entertainment. The film lasted 2 hours and 15 minutes, including commercials, but the commercials were bunched in several groups during the first hour (before the rockets were fired and the bombs exploded on Kansas City) and at the very end of the program. A 1-hour-and-15-minute *Viewpoint* program immediately followed. It was broadcast without commercial interruption and featured a panel discussion about the film and about nuclear war issues, moderated by ABC news anchorman Ted Koppel. Of the 100 million who viewed *The Day After*, about three quarters remained tuned in for the first portion of the *Viewpoint* program, and about half saw most or all of it (Kaatz, 1984).

In contrast with the film itself, the *Viewpoint* program focused largely on how nuclear war could be prevented, though it also included reactions to the film and new information about the aftermath of nuclear war. The first speaker was Secretary of State George Shultz, who appeared alone to present the administration's view on how the government was working to avoid nuclear war. The participants in the panel discussion that followed were former U.S. cabinet officers Henry Kissinger, John Schlesinger, Robert McNamara, and Lieutenant General Brent Scowcroft, authors William Buckley and Elie Wiesel, and astronomer Carl Sagan. Sagan discussed the then-brand-new scientific findings about the "nuclear winter" that would follow a major nuclear exchange (Turco, Toon, Ackerman, Pollack, & Sagan, 1983). Wiesel, who has written about the Nazi Holocaust, emphasized the overriding importance of avoiding nuclear genocide by eliminating nuclear weapons. McNamara also spoke in favor of a nuclear freeze and a phased reduction in nuclear arms. The other four panelists all gave general support to the administration's reliance on nuclear deterrence and opposition to a nuclear freeze, thus probably blunting the antinuclear movement's hopes that the program would reap a dividend of nuclear freeze advocates.

D. Media Verdicts

After the intense buildup of media publicity and commercial hype, some commentators felt the film itself was anticlimactic and disappointing. A typical judgment was that

> With all the hoopla, the film was anti-climactic, even naive. Those under 25 seemed more affected than their elders.... The national anxiety attack predicted beforehand by freeze advocates never came to pass. ("Fallout From," 1983)

Polls of high school and college students elicited comments such as, "The movie was underplayed. Not enough gruesome effects. Too many people still alive after the bombs" (Schofield & Pavelchak, 1985), and "There weren't a lot of people with their faces melting away" ("Fallout From," 1983). Headlines read: "*Day After* Reaction Minimal," "Movie Changed Few Opinions," and "*Day After* Didn't Hurt Reagan" (Schofield & Pavelchak,

1985). These seemed to be the most frequently voiced reactions, though other headlines emphasized "TV Atom War Spurs Vast Discussion" (McFadden, 1983) or "An Audience of 100 Million" ("Audience of," 1983). The White House was reported to be vastly relieved that the film had not converted viewers to antinuclear positions.

Many of the headlines about minimal effects were based on several instant-analysis polls whose findings were reported a day or 2 after the film's screening. Though these polls generally did find some changes in people's opinions, the conclusion typically publicized was " 'Day After' Impact Slight, Poll Finds" (Knap, 1983).[1]

II. THE VARIETY OF RESEARCH STUDIES

A. Sources of Research Findings

At the time of the initial writing of this chapter, none of the detailed original research reports on *The Day After* had been published, though a few were in press and some brief articles of general commentary had been published (see, e.g., Comstock, 1984; Kaatz, 1984; Lometti & Feig, 1984). Consequently, I have relied almost entirely on unpublished preprints solicited from their authors. I learned of these papers through informal channels, by following up every lead of which I became aware, for a formal search of the usual abstracting services would have been fruitless.

One open symposium that I chaired at the 1984 American Psychological Association annual meeting collected together 10 of the papers; 5 others were presented in other sessions at the same convention. Other papers were given at meetings of the American Association for Public Opinion Research, the International Communications Association, and the Midwest Political Science Association. All of these reports were solicited, and all but a few of them, which were not sent, are summarized in this chapter. Similarly, copies of all original research reports that were mentioned in the popular media accounts of *The Day After*'s impact were requested. In addition, the major national commercial polls and academic survey organizations (Gallup, Harris, National

---

[1] Some of the factors that led the popular media to conclude that *The Day After* had little impact have been discussed by Schofield and Pavelchak (1985). They emphasize unrealistic public expectations encouraged by advance publicity, the similarity of the script to standard "disaster movies," and the film's lack of clear behavioral directions on what viewers could do to help prevent nuclear war. For each of these factors, they present social psychological research evidence as to why it would be likely to diminish changes in public opinion and behavior stemming from the film. They also mention another factor leading to the "no impact" conclusion—a factor which is discussed at length in this chapter—namely, the early polls' focus on aspects of attitudes which were unlikely to be changed by the film.

Opinion Research Center, and the Survey Research Center at the University of Michigan) were contacted, but it appears that no studies of *The Day After* were done by them. A few foreign studies conducted in England and Australia are also included in this review.

B. Quantitative Analysis

Ideally, it would have been desirable to conduct a metanalysis of the research on *The Day After*, as advocated by Glass, McGaw, and Smith (1981) or Cooper (1984). However, the data available in these as-yet-unpublished reports were insufficient to allow a meaningful metanalysis to be conducted. The total number of studies is relatively small for a metanalysis, and because different studies investigated quite different dependent variables, the number of studies on any given type of variable was further reduced. Moreover, a few studies did not report statistical tests, and many studies reported mean scores without standard deviations, or significance intervals without means, but they did not present the more precise statistical data such as standard deviations, ts or Fs, and degrees of freedom, which are needed for metanalysis. In the cases in which enough information was available, the stated significance intervals and sample sizes have been used to make a conservative estimate of t values and then of effect sizes for dependent variables that were significant, using estimation formulas presented by Cooper (1984, pp. 99–100). In such studies, the range of effect sizes for significant variables is shown in Tables I and III later in this chapter.

C. Considerations in Analyzing Research Reports

1. A Package of Stimuli

No one knew beforehand what topics the discussion in the *Viewpoint* program would cover, and very few researchers were able to see *The Day After* before its national screening in order to gain detailed knowledge of its contents. Thus, researchers were not able to tailor their questions to the exact contents of the programs. Indeed, most did not know about the showing of the *Viewpoint* program far enough in advance to ask about it separately from the film. Consequently, in all but a very few research reports, the two programs must be considered as a package, with their effects inextricably interwoven.

A further part of the media "package" for many research studies was the preprogram publicity and controversy. The nationwide media coverage of the film and the nuclear issues it raised began as much as a month beforehand ("Nightmare," 1983), and they became especially intense during the week prior to the broadcast, in news magazine cover stories and newspaper articles (see, e.g., "Nuclear," 1983; "Hard Look," 1983). Thus, it is highly likely that many Americans displayed anticipatory attitude change in the week or so before the program (Cialdini & Petty, 1981). According to past research findings, the effect of this would be to polarize them further toward their current position if they were highly emotionally involved in the issue (Jerry Fallwell's reaction would be one example), or to moderate their attitude in the direction of the expected message if they were not highly involved in the issue. The latter effect would be expected to be typical of most Americans if they heard discussion about the program beforehand.

2. Timing

As a result of the likelihood of anticipatory attitude change, the timing of the research pretests becomes a crucial consideration in analyzing findings. The few studies with pretests several weeks or more before the program (see, e.g., Mayton, 1984; Sussman, 1983) probably captured most of the anticipatory attitude change effects, combined with the specific effects of the two programs themselves; but of course, they may also have reflected the results of other world events, such as changing tensions in the Middle East. Studies with pretests about a week beforehand probably caught some of the anticipatory change, combined with the specific program effects; whereas the few studies with pretests only hours before the program probably missed the anticipatory changes altogether (see, e.g., W. C. Adams *et al.*, 1984).

Timing of the posttest is another important consideration. The maximum effect of the program would be expected shortly afterwards, with gradually diminishing effects in the following days or weeks (Watts & McGuire, 1964). An immediate posttest should catch the maximum effect but it would not show anything about its persistence, while a delayed posttest might miss much of the initial effect. An ideal design, found in a few of the studies, would include both early and later posttests to show both initial effects of the program and how long they lasted over time.

3. Research Design

Some studies gave posttests only, and they thus could not provide any evidence of attitude changes, except through retrospective reports, which are known to be often fallible. Other studies used pretests and posttests, but for various reasons, they gave them to different samples. This is an accepted research design, but in it, the comparability of the samples is crucial in discussing pre-post differences, and the design only allows analysis of aggregate differences; it precludes any analysis of *changes* in views by particular individuals or groups. A repeated-measurement, or panel, design is ideal for showing changes in individuals or groups and analyzing possible causal factors related to the degree of change. However, a repeated-measurement design also introduces the question of respondents' possible sensitization by the pretest so that they then respond differently to the media program. Ideally, this should be guarded against by including an additional group of respondents who were not pretested, as was done in several studies.

4. *Method of Data Collection*

Face-to-face interviews, telephone interviews, and written questionnaires all have their own advantages and limitations in data collection (Backstrom & Hursh-Cesar, 1981). Because of time pressures, face-to-face interviews were not used in any of the American studies discussed here. Telephone interviews can be designed to allow fairly free expression of attitudes and beliefs, but in these studies, the investigators used almost entirely multiple-choice questions and the interviews were quite stringently limited in length. The written questionnaires in these studies also used mostly multiple-choice questions, which limit free expression, and which may suggest ideas that respondents would not generate by themselves. However, most of the written questionnaires were longer and allowed a fuller coverage of topics than the telephone interviews.

5. *Locale and Sample*

A nationwide probability sample is ideal in allowing generalization of research findings to the entire population. However, the way a nationwide telephone sample is chosen determines how representative it is of the total population; and in the reports analyzed here, information on sample selection is insufficient to determine representativeness. Studies with probability samples of a city or community also allow generalization to their underlying populations, though not to the whole nation. Results of the many studies using specialized local samples—most often, college students—may or may not generalize to a broader population, but there can be no automatic presumption that they do. However, such studies can be valuable for their intensive study of particular variables or for data collection and analysis that is more comprehensive than in commercial public-opinion studies.

The size of the sample is also an important factor, because a sample of several hundred cases imparts stability to the resulting data. The demographic makeup of the sample is another consideration affecting the generalizability of findings. Most studies of *The Day After* included only adults or only college students, though a few also questioned children or teenagers; and it is quite possible that these groups had differing reactions to the film. In any sample, it is important to know how many viewed the film and to investigate whether their responses differed from those of nonviewers.

6. Dependent Variables Studied

The various studies of *The Day After* investigated a wide variety of beliefs, attitudes, and behavioral intentions. Even when the same conceptual variable was under study, measurement methods often varied enough to make comparison of results difficult. A crucial consideration here is the relation of the variables studied to the content and message of the film. Many studies included quite a range of variables that would not be expected to be influenced at all strongly by the film, as discussed subsequently.

In addition, an explicit theoretical orientation is very helpful in determining what variables to study. The studies varied widely in the extent, clarity, and specific content of their theoretical orientations.[2]

III. THE EARLY INSTANT-ANALYSIS REPORTS

There were six survey studies, the results of which were cited and discussed by the popular media in the week following the showing of *The Day After*. Table I summarizes the information available about them, though in two cases I have not been able to obtain any information beyond the skimpy media descriptions. (Note: After their initial mention, the studies are generally cited in this article by their identifying numbers, as shown in Tables I and II, enclosed in parentheses.)

Several of these studies employed quite large national samples (from 900 to 1900 respondents) and aimed at being representative. However, only one (6) definitely used a pre–post panel design, as is necessary in order to show changes in the views of any given group of respondents. The others used posttest-only designs or separate pre and post samples.

A. Topics

All of the topics that the available reports indicated were covered in these studies are listed in Table I. Four quite conventionally focused on program content and related public opinion issues, with an occasional question about the program's value (e.g., public service versus propaganda). However, the coverage of the ABC study (1), and to a lesser extent that of the J. Walter Thompson (JWT) study (4), was unique in focusing mainly on the reputation of the network, the program, and the program's advertisers.

---

[2] All of the foregoing considerations in analyzing the studies, plus other characteristics, are included in synoptic form in Tables I-III.

TABLE I

Early Instant-Analysis Studies

Study feature	1	2	3	4	5	6
Source	ABC (undated); see also Lometti & Feig (1984)	Abt Associates (see "Fallout From," 1983)	W. C. Adams et al. (1984) (November 21, 1983 press release)	J. Walter Thompson (1983); Kaatz (1984)	Warner Abex QUBE cable TV network (in McFadden, 1983; Kaatz, 1984)	Washington Post (Sussman, 1983)
Method	Telephone interview	Unknown	Telephone interview (95% response)	Telephone interview	Interactive television	Telephone interview
Research design	Post only	Pre-post (perhaps different samples)	Separate pre and post samples	Post only	Pre(?)-post (possibly different samples)	Pre-post (panel)
Timing	1–2 days after	Unknown	1–90 minutes before 1–45 minutes after	1 day after	Immediately after *Viewpoint*	13–17 days before; 1 day after
Locale and population	National (probability)	Possibly national	National (probability)	National	6 cities in Midwest, Texas, and Pennsylvania	National
Sample size and features	1921 (including 109 children and 179 teenagers) (viewers = 53%)	Viewers (N unknown)	510 before (all intended viewers), 418 after (all viewers), adults	205 adults (viewers = 49%)	5500 viewers	1505 before; 850 after (viewers = ?%)
Dependent variables with pre-post scores (with significance where stated)[a]	Demographic characteristics of viewers Amount of program watched How heard about program What heard about program beforehand	Nuclear war not likely by year 2000 (32–35%) Personal survival in nuclear war (7–5%) U.S. doing all it can to avoid nuclear war (37–41%) Approval of U.S.	U.S. defense spending is too much (39–37%) Support bilateral nuclear freeze (76–79%) Support unilateral U.S. nuclear disarmament (12–11%) Likelihood of	Demographic characteristics of viewers Reasons for viewing or not viewing Evaluation of program Reactions to program beforehand Attitude toward	Film was public service or propaganda Is there hope of avoiding nuclear war? Support for nuclear arms control or buildup (postfilm changes: 12% now	Nuclear war would be worse than shown Likelihood of nuclear war (35–33%) Approval of nuclear freeze (83–85%) Approval of Reagan's performance as

	defense policies (54-58%)	nuclear war (45-47%)	program advertisers	support arms control, 6% now support arms buildup)	President (63-65%)
Reasons for not viewing	Preference for Reagan over Mondale (49-53%)	Personal survival in nuclear war (12-14%)		Worry about nuclear war a lot (26-88%)	Reagan's handling of foreign affairs is increasing chances of war (57-43%)
Evaluation of program		Efficacy to influence war or peace (63-68%)			Reagan's plans for building nuclear weapons are too little (24-15%)
Reasons for evaluation		Nuclear war would be more likely if Reagan, rather than Mondale, was President (36-27%)*			Is nuclear freeze or nuclear arms development a better policy?
Appropriateness for children		Film will be (was) politically fair (40-63%)**			Should children have been allowed to watch the film?
Recall of network showing program					Was the film worthwhile?
Attitudes toward ABC and television for showing film					
Attitude toward rebroadcasting film					
Conditions of watching film and discussing it					
Attitudes toward and memory for program advertisers					
Whether watched *Viewpoint* (after film)					
Reactions to *Viewpoint*					
Other comparisons	Viewers vs nonviewers**	Men vs women[b] Other demographic differences**	Viewers vs nonviewers**		Viewers vs nonviewers[b] Men vs women[b]

[a] *d* for significant variables ~ .2–.25.
[b] Large differences, but significance not reported.
*$p < .01$.
**$p < .001$.

Was the Movie "Political"?

The ABC study (1) did not ask a single question about attitudes on nuclear issues related to the program's content. However, it concluded, in a statement widely reported in the news media, that "the overwhelming majority of *The Day After* viewers did not evaluate it as a political film (97%)" (ABC, undated, p. 8). The way that ABC researchers arrived at this conclusion, without asking any questions about political issues of the film's message, is striking. They obtained the percentage figure from answers to the following questions: "What was your overall reaction to *The Day After*... did you think this program was...excellent, very good, good, fair, or poor?" "Why do you feel that way?" The following kinds of responses to the follow-up question were tabulated.

Statements	Percentage of positive responses
General presentation (e.g., good acting, well produced)	48
Increased awareness of nuclear war/the tragedy of war	27
Thought provoking	11
Made a statement/had an important message	6
Other	8

Of the 6% who said the program had a message, 3% responded in "general terms"; 1% made pronuclear comments and 2% made antinuclear comments, and the latter 3% were the ones who were said to evaluate the film as political in character. Thus, by avoiding asking about its message, ABC concluded that *The Day After* was nonpolitical. In order to maintain that viewpoint, they asked no questions about attitude change as a result of the program, except as concerned attitudes toward the network and the advertisers.

From this analysis, it is clear that despite publicity to the contrary, the data from the ABC study do not support a conclusion that the film had no political message or that it had no effect on viewers' attitudes.

B. Evaluations of *The Day After*

The six early instant-analysis studies agreed that viewers generally felt favorable toward the program. In the *Washington Post* survey (6), 85% said it was a worthwhile film. In the QUBE Network study (5), 63% of viewers said it was a public service, versus 22% who labeled it as propaganda; while in W. C. Adams *et al.*'s study (3), 63% called it politically fair versus 20% who considered it propaganda. Among ABC respondents, 77% evaluated the program as good to excellent (1), while 54% of JWT respondents rated it as "better than most shows on TV" and 39% more said it was "average" (4). Similarly, there was majority agreement that children under the age of 13 should have been allowed to watch the film [59% yes to 29% no (6)]. ABC found over 10 times as many viewers feeling more favorable toward the network for showing the film as those who felt less favorable; and 75-80% of viewers stated that the film should be shown again and that it should be shown in other countries (1).

C. Nuclear Beliefs and Attitudes

Before discussing *changes* in viewers' beliefs and attitudes, a brief survey of general public views on nuclear issues will be useful. As of November, 1983, about 87% of the public said there was hope of avoiding nuclear war (5). However, the number who said that a nuclear war was likely varied from about 33% (6) to 45% (3) to a higher figure (2), depending upon whether the question asked about the next few years, about the next 10 years, or about a longer time period. The number of people who thought they had a chance of living through a nuclear war varied from 5% (2) to 14% (3)—again, depending slightly on the wording of the question. About 80% of viewers said the effects of nuclear war would be worse than shown in *The Day After* (6), and following the film as many as 88% of viewers said they worry about nuclear war a lot (5). Perhaps surprisingly, about two thirds of program viewers felt that there *were* some things they could do to influence war or peace (3).

Concerning policies for dealing with the threat of war, a very high figure of about 80% of the public favored a bilateral nuclear freeze (3, 6), leaving little room for an increase in approval of that approach. When a nuclear freeze option was pitted against continued development of nuclear weapons, however, 67% chose nuclear freeze as the better policy for avoiding war, while 26% chose continued nuclear weapons development (6). In the Midwest and in Texas, with a nonrepresentative sample, a similar question pitting nuclear arms control against "strength through nuclear arms buildup" found a 61% to 35% margin for arms control (5). On the other hand, barely over 10% of respondents favored the more extreme policy of unilateral U.S. nuclear disarmament (3). When asked their opinion about U.S. defense policies in general, about 55% of the public expressed approval (2). However, in the same sample, only about 40% thought the United States was doing all it could to avoid nuclear war (2). In another study (3), the plurality of respondents (nearly 40%) declared that U.S. defense spending was too high.

D. Attitudes toward Reagan

When questions were posed concerning President Reagan, there was majority approval for his performance as president (6) and as a candidate in opposition to Walter Mondale (2). However, views on his specific defense policies were less favorable. About twice as many viewers thought nuclear war would be more likely with Reagan as president than with Mondale (3). A plurality of over 40% said Reagan was going too far in his plans to build more nuclear weapons, as compared with only about 20% who thought he was not going far enough (6). A plurality of over 40% declared that the way Reagan was handling foreign affairs was increasing the chances for war (6).

E. Public Opinion Changes following *The Day After*

The changes in public beliefs and attitudes following the broadcast of *The Day After* are the central interest of this article. Unfortunately, most of these early studies were not well designed to measure such changes, the widespread publicity that their conclusions of "little effect" received notwithstanding. Only the *Washington Post* study's design and pretest time schedule were adequate for the measurement of anticipatory attitude change resulting from the preprogram buildup of attention to nuclear issues (6). The ABC and JWT studies (1, 4) used a posttest-only design and did not purport to study pre-post differences. Two of the studies (2, 5), as reported in the press, apparently only asked four or five questions; the timing of their pretests was not reported and may have been so late as to already have been influenced by all the preprogram publicity and controversy. The latter is definitely true of W. C. Adams *et al.*'s study (3), which gave its pretest to intended viewers of the program in the $1\frac{1}{2}$ hours before the broadcast began, so that its supposedly unexposed pretest group had already been influenced by all of the preceding media concentration on nuclear issues (Oskamp *et al.*, 1985).

Of the four studies reporting pre-post differences, the Abt study (2) had a maximum difference on its five items of only 4%—a difference too small to be significant unless the sample was very large. However, each of the other three studies had two items out of the four to eight questions they asked that showed pre-post changes that appeared significant, though only one actually reported significance (3).

Clearly, the most dramatic change was in the QUBE Network study (5), in which the percentage of viewers who stated that they worry about nuclear war a lot increased from 26 to 88%. An alternative answer to the same item, putting war "out of my mind," decreased from 58 to 10%. These responses were obtained 1 day after the film's showing, however, and the study did not investigate whether such changes in worry and suppression of thoughts were merely temporary or whether they were longer lasting. Another item with a smaller change, though large enough to be significant with a sample size of 5500, showed 12% of viewers changing in the direction of now supporting nuclear arms control, while 6% changed toward supporting a nuclear arms buildup (5). In W. C. Adams *et al.*'s study (3), there was a large increase in those thinking the film was politically fair from pretest to posttest.

The other substantial changes were on items concerning Reagan and showed that, in general, his public standing was not hurt by the film. Following the program, there was a 9% decrease in the number of people saying nuclear war would be more likely with Reagan as president than with Mondale as president, though still nearly twice as many thought it was more likely under Reagan (3). Similarly, there was a 14% decrease in those saying Reagan's handling of foreign affairs was increasing chances for war, though that was still slightly the most frequent response (6). In the same sample, however, there was a 9% decrease in those saying Reagan was not going far enough in his plans for building more nuclear weapons, and a 9% increase in those saying his plans were about right, though still a plurality opposed them (6). Thus, though there was considerable opposition to Reagan's policies, there seemed to be at least a trace of the "rally-round-the-flag" phenomenon of increased support for the president that has been found in various episodes involving national emergency situations (Mueller, 1973).

In summary, these early instant-analysis polls did show a number of changes in public views after the screening of *The Day After*, though none of them asked respondents about specific consequences of nuclear war, which was the central topic of the film. The most notable change was increased worry about nuclear war. There also appeared to be some increase in support for arms control, but a clearer effect was increased favorability toward some of President Reagan's policies, despite continuing opposition by large portions of the public. On a number of items, public views before the film were so high (e.g., approval of a bilateral nuclear freeze) or so low (e.g., belief in the chances of one's personal survival in a nuclear war) that there was little room for change toward a more extreme position due to having viewed it.

IV. THE MORE COMPREHENSIVE STUDIES

In contrast to the instant-analysis studies that were conducted and reported within a very few days, academic survey studies tend to be more thorough and more comprehensive, both in their data collection and statistical analysis, as well as in being less fully staffed; as a result, they are much slower to be completed and reported. The remaining reports, summarized in this section, studied the question of *The Day After*'s effects with a wide variety of theoretical viewpoints, research designs, and measurement techniques. Listed in Tables II and III, in alphabetical order, are all of the studies for which I was able to obtain reports. Omitted from the tables, but listed as references, are the following four studies, for which I have been unable to obtain reports: (13), Fenwick (1984); (15), Funderburk, Karns, & Walker (1984); (27), Smith (1984); (28), Thomas et al. (1984).

Study Characteristics

With a few exceptions, the summarized studies were conducted with specialized local samples rather than with representative local or national samples, which may make their findings less broadly generalizable. However, many of them compensate for that limitation by adopting a more intensive and careful approach to data collection and analysis. Most gave written questionnaires to college students, though a few used telephone interviews (7, 10, 12) or face-to-face interviews (17). Others ranged widely, from laboratory experiments (8) to surveys of high school and elementary school children (26) and from unrepresentative collections of adults (16, 25) to representative samples of adults in a community (7, 10, 12, 18, 24) or a nation (17). Almost all of them had relatively large groups of participants, the survey studies ranging from 87 respondents (21) to more than 1000 (9, 14, 17).

Most of these studies gave pretests and posttests to the same panel of respondents, but a majority also intentionally included posttest-only groups to check on the possibility of different media effects for respondents who were or were not sensitized to the program by pretesting. Six studies gave delayed posttests, as well, to investigate the persistence of belief and attitude changes (16, 18, 23-26). The timing of pretest measures was most often 2-6 days before the broadcast, but it ranged from only minutes beforehand (8, 25) through 1-2 weeks beforehand (14, 18, 22-24) to 4-10 weeks prior (9, 20). Initial posttests were mostly given 1-5 days after the broadcast (7, 9, 14, 17, 18, 20, 21, 23, 25, 26, 29) or up to 2 weeks afterward (10-12, 19, 22, 24, 30), rather than minutes after the program finished (8). Delayed posttest data were gathered about 3 weeks (23, 24), 6-8 weeks (26), or 3-5 months (16, 18, 25) after the broadcast.

In the studies conducted in the United States, the percentage of respondents who had watched *The Day After* ranged from 51% in Fresno, California (7) to 96% in Lawrence, Kansas (26)—the main site of the film's action—with a median of 69% or more. (Because some of the studies reported the percentage who watched the *whole* program, the actual number of viewers—of some portion of the program—was probably slightly higher than these numbers indicate.) These data from academic studies indicate very high viewership levels, even higher than the Nielsen ratings and ABC's (1) nationwide probability sample figure of 53%. Thus, it seems that college students were even more attracted to the program than were older viewers. This is demonstrated in these summary data by the fact that the community-resident samples were all at or below the median level of 69% viewership. Omitting these samples, and also eliminating the personally involved Lawrence, Kansas samples, the median level of viewership for the college students in these research reports was 75% or more. Another factor in these high viewership levels was probably sensitization and increased awareness of the program caused by the pretest in these predominantly panel designs. However, one of the two studies that reported posttest-only viewership figures (10) found that 63% of its sample of Boston residents watched the program—a figure still well above the national average, despite the absence of any pretest sensitization—and the other posttest-only study in Fresno (7) had a viewership figure very similar to the national average.

As is shown in Table III, all of the studies (except 7) investigated some aspects of belief or attitude change; however, the measures that each used, the issues with which they were concerned, and the nature of their findings were highly varied. Twelve studies also obtained some measures of respondents' actions, behavioral intentions, or commitment to taking actions related in some way to the nuclear arms race (8, 9, 11, 14, 16, 18, 19, 21, 23, 24, 29, 30).

The variables that were studied as shown in Table III have been reclassified from the authors' original terminology into categories that are listed in as consistent a manner as possible. Thus, for instance, several specific items might be lumped together under "consequences of nuclear war" or "attitudes about defense issues." When the resulting listing was composed of a single item or scale, or when there was one central item among a group in the same category, the table shows mean pretest and *initial* posttest values for that item or scale, together with significance levels if they were stated in the research report. Where significance figures were not given, the superscript *a* is used to indicate a large difference, which probably would be significant within the given sample size. Mean scores often were not reported, but significant main effects and interactions (indicated by superscript *b*) may still be shown, arbitrarily limited to the .05 level of significance or beyond. The effect sizes shown in Table III, estimated as previously described, were computed by approximation from the data given for the smallest and largest of the significant findings reported in each study. Thus, they give a rough idea of the size or strength of the significant relationships that were found.

V. FINDINGS OF THE COMPREHENSIVE STUDIES

The major findings of the comprehensive studies, and of the preceding early studies where relevant, are summarized in this section. In reporting the findings of the studies quantitatively, the phrase "large or significant differences"

TABLE II

Design Characteristics of the More Comprehensive Studies

	Study number		
Study feature	7	8	9
Source	R. C. Adams & Webber (1984)	Baumann et al. (1984)	Brown (1984)
Method	Telephone interview (20 items) (response > 58%)	Written questionnaire (9 items + others)	Written questionnaire (22 items + scales)
Research design	Post only	Experiment (randomized) Separate pre and post samples in Experiment 1	Pre–post (panel)
Timing	1–3 days after	30 minutes before 1–30 minutes after (in Experiment 1) Experiment 2 was after film aired	1 month before 1–3 days after
Locale and population	Fresno and Clovis, California residents (probability)	Texas college students (previous nonviewers in Experiment 2)	5 middle Atlantic colleges
Sample size and features	230 after (viewers = 51%)	41 in Experiment 1 (saw film, read, or took pretest only); 116 in Experiment 2 (saw film or other movie, half with expectancy of being upset)	268 panel 359 post only 379 pre only (viewers = 79%)
Statistical techniques	Discriminant analysis, χ^2, Cramer's V	F, t	t
Theory or concepts	Viewer characteristics; "gender gap" in reactions to the program	Media images and expectancies	Attitudes toward violence

Study number			
10	11	12	14
Cross & Saxe (1984)	Ehrlichman & Kobasa (1984)	Feldman & Sigelman (1985)	French & Van Hoorn (1988)
Telephone interview (6 items) (response unknown)	Written questionnaire (48 items + scales)	Telephone interview (>34 items) (response = 66%)	Written questionnaire (19 items); Identical telephone interview with adults (response unknown)
Post only (retrospective reports)	Quasi experiment Pre-post (panel) and post only	Quasi experiment Pre-post (panel) and post only and pre only	Pre-post (panel)
1-10 days after	2-6 days before 1-12 days after	2-6 days before 1-10 days after	2-13 days before 1-3 days after
Boston residents (probability)	7 colleges in New York City	Lexington, Kentucky residents (probability)	4 colleges and 4 high schools in central California Adults in same communities
435 after (viewers = 63%)	252 panel 289 post only 159 pre only (viewers = 73%)	496 panel 426 post only 200 pre only (viewers = ?%)	867 panel (students) 372 other students 126 telephone (adults) (viewers = 77-90% among students)
F	Factor analysis, t	Factor analysis, multiple R, t, Z, discriminant analysis	Test for difference of correlated proportions
Media effects on adults	Worry vs denial; personal stress resistance	Media effects on adults' attitudes, beliefs, salience of nuclear issues, and emotional involvement; perceived realism; viewer knowledge	Media effects on attitudes toward nuclear war; inattention and denial

TABLE II *(continued)*

Study feature	Study number 16	Study number 17	Study number 18
Source	L. M. Goodman (1984)	Gunter & Wober (1988)	Gutierres *et al.* (1984)
Method	Written questionnaire (26 items)	Face-to-face interview (plus telephone recontact) (>27 items) (response unknown)	Written 31-item questionnaire with home contact (response = 67%); Postfilm phone contact for pretest group
Research design	Quasi experiment Pre-post (panel) and post only and pre only and delayed post	Pre-post (panel)	Quasi experiment Separate pre, post, and delayed post samples
Timing	Unknown Delayed: 4-5 months after	2-3 days before 1-2 days after	13 days before 1 day after Delayed: about 3 months after
Locale and population	New Jersey volunteers (white citizens, age 15-65) Delayed: college students and professors	Great Britain adults (age ≥ 15) (national quota sample)	Lawrence, Kansas; Tempe, Arizona; Austin, Texas (probability)
Sample size and features	124 panel 98 post only 135 pre only ? delayed post (different subjects) (viewers = ?%)	864 panel 155 pre only (viewers = 47%)	130 post only 143 pre only 148 delayed post (Lawrence viewers = 93%; other viewers = 69%)
Statistical techniques	Sandler A test, t, rho	Partial r, CR	F
Theory or concepts	Attitudes toward nuclear war	Impact of television on risk perception and nuclear beliefs; locus of control	Risk perception; availability; emotional salience; recency; vividness

Study number			
19	20	21	22
Kulman & Akamatsu (1984)	Mayton (1984)	McClenney & Allbright (1985) (first study)	Nelson & Slem (1984)
Written questionnaire (52 items)	Written questionnaire (34 items)	Written questionnaire (42 items)	Written questionnaire (22 items)
Pre-post (panel)	Pre-post (panel)	Quasi experiment Pre-post (panel) and post only (only posttests analyzed)	Pre-post (panel)
2-6 days before 1-2 weeks after	10 weeks before 1-5 days after	2-6 days before 1-5 days after	5-11 days before 9-11 days after
Ohio college students	Idaho college students (urged to watch)	Connecticut college students	California college students
537 panel 222 post only 274 pre only (viewers > 66%)	106 panel 72 pre only (viewers = 78%)	~43 panel ~44 post only (viewers = ?%)	>289 panel <81 pre only (viewers > 64%)
Factor analysis, t	Factor analysis, t	Factor analysis, path analysis	r, t, multiple R
Media effects on adolescents; cognitive reality of nuclear war; lifestyle and planning; nuclear illusions	Media effects on adolescents	Theory of reasoned action; beliefs and attitudes about a nuclear freeze; subjective norms; behavioral intentions; sense of control; personal responsibility; denial	Attitude and belief consistency; media effects on adolescents

TABLE II *(continued)*

Study feature	23	24	25
Source	Oskamp et al. (1985)	Pavelchak & Schofield (1984)	Reser & Wallace (1985); Reser (1984)
Method	Written questionnaire (62 items)	Written questionnaire (>24 items) (response = 19%)	Written questionnaire (post and delayed returned by mail) (~55 items) (response = 60%, 53%, and 33%)
Research design	Quasi experiment Pre-post (panel) and post only and pre only and delayed post	Quasi experiment Pre-post (panel) and pre only Separate delayed post (panel)	Quasi experiment Pre-post (panel) and post only and pre only and delayed post
Timing	2-10 days before 1-5 days after Delayed: 16 days after	1-14 days before >1 week after Delayed: >3 weeks after	1-30 minutes before 1 day after Delayed: 3 months after
Locale and population	California college students (urged to watch) California adult professionals	Pittsburgh residents (stratified, probability)	Townsville, Australia cinemagoers (including children) (representative)
Sample size and features	298 panel >65 post only <244 pre only 98 delayed post (viewers = 86%) 56 adult professionals (viewers = 72%)	~120 1-week panel 82 pre only ~59 3-week panel (viewers = 61%)	239 panel 62 post only 130 pre only (80 delayed post subgroup) (viewers = 100%)
Statistical techniques	Item analysis, r, F, t, trend analysis	Item analysis, r, F	F, t, Wilcoxon matched-pairs, eta
Theory or concepts	Media effects on adolescents and adults; comparison with other studies	Media effects; availability; concreteness; dimensions of affect; attitudes and behavior; efficacy	Impact of film on attitudes; fear arousal, anxiety, defense and denial; imageability and behavior change

Study number: heading over columns 23, 24, 25.

	Study number	
26	29	30
Schadler, Miranda, & Day (1984)	Wolf, Gregory, & Stephan (1984)	Zolik et al. (1984)
Written questionnaire (>21 items)	Written questionnaire (~45 items)	Written questionnaire (77 items)
Quasi experiment Pre-post (panel) and post only and delayed post	Quasi experiment Pre-post (panel) and post only	Pre-post (panel)
2–6 days before 1 day after Delayed: 6–8 weeks after	2–3 days before 1–2 days after	4–6 days before 8–10 days after
Lawrence, Kansas elementary and high school students	New Mexico college students	Chicago college students
? panel ? post only 455 delayed post (viewers = 96%)	176 panel 106 post only (viewers = ~67%)	166 panel (viewers = ?%)
r; no significance tests	Factor analysis, r, multiple R, t	Not stated (probably t and difference between proportions)
Media effects on children	Protection motivation theory (about effects of fear-arousing communication)	Media effects on beliefs, attitudes, and possible behaviors

TABLE III

Dependent Variables and Findings of the More Comprehensive Studies

Study number	7	8	9
Dependent variables, pre–post scores, and significance (where stated)	Reactions to film Reasons for watching or not watching Likelihood of nuclear war Favor home bomb shelter Favor more government spending on civil defense Attitude toward Reagan toughness with Soviet Attitude toward Reagan foreign relations	Worry and fear about nuclear war (Exp. 2**) Consequences of nuclear war[+] (Exp. 2, less) Likelihood of nuclear war Likelihood of limited nuclear war Consideration of survival (Exp. 1: 1.9–3.1)** Behavioral intentions to prevent nuclear war	Attitudes toward violence[I] Thoughts about nuclear war Likelihood of nuclear war Attitudes toward government leaders Efficacy to prevent nuclear war Attitudes toward defense[a] Behavioral intentions re antiwar actions[a]
Effect sizes of significant findings	$d \sim .2-.7$ (for sex differences)	$d \sim .9$ (Exp. 1) $d \sim 5$ (Exp. 2)	$d \sim .23$ (for women)
Other comparisons	Viewers vs nonviewers (*on likelihood; *on bomb shelters; *on civil defense; *on Reagan toughness; *on Reagan foreign relations; *on education; *on religious affiliation; ***on reasons for watching or not) Men vs women (*on reactions to film; *on bomb shelters)	Expectancy of being upset (Exp. 2[I])	Men vs women[I]

10	11	12	14
Thoughts about nuclear war***	Reactions to film	Thoughts about nuclear war (50–48%)**	Thoughts about nuclear war (36–46%)***
Likelihood of nuclear war***	Anticipations about film (more negative than reactions***)	Importance of defense policy (96–96%)	Likelihood of nuclear war (71–68%)
Personal survival***	Thoughts about nuclear war	Knowledge about nuclear war (65–69%)	Likelihood of own death from nuclear war (67–68%)
Efficacy to prevent nuclear war*	Likelihood of nuclear war	Consequences of nuclear war (.12–.08)*	Likelihood of limited nuclear war (12–14%)
Attitude toward government policy	Consequences of nuclear war	Likelihood of nuclear war (35–34%)	Efficacy to prevent nuclear war (57–58%)
Upset by thoughts of nuclear war***	Personal survival	Personal survival (19–15%)	Willing to countenance nuclear war (10–9%)
	Preference not to survive (55–71%)***	Emotions about defense (.54–.52)**	Nuclear war can be prevented (91–90%)
	Attitude toward world leaders	Attitudes toward defense issues (27–18%)**	Value of arms control (73–79%)**
	Efficacy to prevent nuclear war	Attitude toward arms control (.83–.85)	Favor government spending on civil defense (32–36%)*
	Past actions to prevent nuclear war	Attitudes toward Reagan policies (53–58%)	Have discussed nuclear war with family and friends (87–95%)***
	Behavioral intentions to prevent nuclear war[1]		Behavioral intention to contact elected officials re nuclear war (37–43%)
			Behavioral intention to contact news media re nuclear war (19–22%)
Can't be computed	$d \sim .4–.65$	$d \sim .06–.2$	$d \sim .15–.3$
Interviewer effects**	Men vs women (***on preference not to survive)	Pretesting effects	Viewers vs nonviewers (+ on thoughts; + on countenancing nuclear war; + on behavioral intentions)
Viewers vs nonviewers***	Viewiers vs nonviewers (*on behavioral intentions)	Sample mortality	
		Viewers vs nonviewers	
		Effects of media exposure re nuclear war**	Men vs women (+ on value of arms control; + on favor civil defense spending)
		Effects of panel*	
		Effects of personal discussion of film**	Younger vs older (+ on thoughts)
		Perceived realism**	
		Demographic effects (education[1], age +)	SES differences (+ on efficacy to prevent nuclear war)

TABLE III (*continued*)

Study number	16	17	18
Dependent variables, pre–post scores, and significance (where stated)	Attitude toward nuclear war (7.2–11.4)** Thoughts about nuclear war (10–28%) + Likelihood of nuclear war (84–92%) + Consequences of nuclear war (59–70%) + Preference not to survive (48–56%) + Attitudes toward nuclear war issues Would not use nuclear arms to aid an ally (70–60%) + Behavioral intentions to prevent nuclear war (54–62%)	Worry about nuclear war (71–67%) Likelihood of nuclear war (26–29%) Personal survival (14–12%) Risk of nuclear attack (40–39%) Favor British nuclear disarmament (27–26%) Likelihood of limited nuclear war (46–45%) Likely causes of nuclear war Beliefs about other nuclear war issues Worry about nuclear energy Risk from nuclear energy	Fear of nuclear war Likelihood of nuclear war + Likelihood of limited nuclear war Consequences of nuclear war [I] Personal survival [I] Consideration of personal survival [I] Efficacy to prevent nuclear war Personal responsibility to prevent nuclear war Antinuclear activities Beliefs about nuclear arms policies Attitudes about nuclear arms policies Attitude about nuclear energy Risk of nuclear arms accident or terrorism Risk of nuclear energy accident
Effect sizes of significant findings	$d \sim .33$	$d \sim .16–.8$	$d < .2$ (for interaction)
Other comparisons	Men vs women (+ on attitude toward nuclear war) Consistency of responses Persistence of antinuclear attitudes	Viewers vs nonviewers (**on worry; **on likelihood; **on survival; *on risk; + on causes; + on beliefs) Internal vs external locus of control ([I] on worry; [I] on survival; [I] on disarmament; [I] on beliefs)	Viewers vs nonviewers [I]

19	20	21	22
Reactions to film	Reactions to film	Attitude toward a	Anxiety about nuclear
Worry about nuclear	Thoughts and worry	nuclear freeze	war (1.98–2.15)***
war (29.0–30.3)*	about nuclear war	Belief about usefulness	Likelihood of nuclear
Likelihood of nuclear	Likelihood of nuclear	of signing petitions	war (2.58–2.58)
war (14.8–14.8)	war	Belief about usefulness	Consequences of
Likelihood of limited	Consequences of	of joining a nuclear	nuclear war
nuclear war* (2.3–2.1)	nuclear war (1.6–3.0)	freeze group	(3.21–3.36)**
Consequences of	Attitudes toward		Attitude toward arms
nuclear war	nuclear war issues		control (2.92–2.90)
(11.8–11.1)**	Efficacy to prevent		Attitude toward nuclear
Personal survival	nuclear war		superiority (2.10–2.09)
(2.4–2.2)**	Civil defense effectiveness		Belief about Soviet
Attitudes toward	(9.6–9.9)		arms control inten-
nuclear issues	Favor nuclear escalation		tions (2.10–2.24)***
(15.2–14.8)*	(6.8–6.0)		Belief about Soviet
Efficacy to prevent	Favor first strike		military goals
nuclear war	(2.8–2.1)*		(2.30–2.31)
Actions re nuclear war	Favor nuclear retaliation		
(1.5–1.6)*	(14.6–14.4)		
Denial of nuclear issues	Patriotism and surviva-		
(13.6–13.7)	bility (6.3–6.2)		
Knowledge about	Attitude change toward		
nuclear war	nuclear freeze +		
Future concern about	Attitude change toward		
nuclear war	deterrence		
(29.4–30.7)*			
$d \sim .2-.3$	$d \sim .5$	Can't be computed	$d \sim .5$
Viewers vs nonviewers (*on denial; **on consequences; ***on actions; *on attitudes)	Viewers vs nonviewers	Effects of thoughts about nuclear war and efficacy to prevent nuclear war on attitudes and beliefs about a nuclear freeze* Effect of efficacy to prevent nuclear war on viewing/nonviewing film* Effect of subjective norm on behavioral intentions* Pretesting effects	Viewers vs nonviewers Men vs women (***on nuclear war anxiety; ***on consequences; *on likelihood; *on attitudes) Consistency of various attitudes and beliefs about nuclear war

TABLE III (*continued*)

Study number	23	24	25
Dependent variables, pre–post scores, and significance (where stated)	Reactions to film Thoughts and worry about nuclear war (3.26–3.68)** Likelihood of nuclear war (0.00–0.07) Likelihood of limited nuclear war (2.73–2.37) Consequences of nuclear war (0.03–0.29)*** Personal survival (29.4–21.5)** Civil defense effectiveness (2.49–2.12)** Beliefs about nuclear war issues Attitudes about defense issues Efficacy to prevent nuclear war (1.67–1.62) Efficacy to survive nuclear war (1.41–1.53)** Nuclear war information learned Attitude changes Behavioral intentions to prevent nuclear war [I] Behavioral intentions to survive nuclear war Behavioral commitments re nuclear issues [I]	Thoughts about nuclear war (2.05–3.60)** Likelihood of nuclear war (47–52%)* Personal survival (2.41–2.18)** Desire to survive (3.37–2.91)** Efficacy to prevent nuclear war (4.35–4.02)* Arousal of affect re nuclear war (4.17–3.48)** Attitudes toward antinuclear war actions [I] Subjective norms re antinuclear war actions Behavioral intentions re antinuclear war actions (2.75–3.18)*	Reactions to film Thoughts about nuclear war (2.97–2.70)* (increased) Likelihood of nuclear war (2.75–2.67) Consequences of nuclear war (3.51–3.23)** (increased) Personal survival (1.77–1.79) Concern for future of world (1.59–1.57) Attitude toward nuclear weapons (3.25–3.81)* (decreased) Attitudes toward other nuclear war issues Personal locus of control (3.85–3.63)* (decreased) Imageability of nuclear war is most important world problem (48–49%)
Effect sizes of significant findings	$d \sim .33–.45$	$d \sim .35–.5$	$d \sim .45–.6$
Other comparisons	Viewers vs nonviewers [I] Men vs women*** Demographic differences (*on learning; *on attitude change) Pretesting effects Persistence of attitude changes*** Students vs adult professionals +	Viewers vs nonviewers (*on thoughts; [I] on survival; [I] on behavioral intentions) Persistence ([I] on thoughts; [I] on survival; [I] on attitudes; [I] on behavioral intentions)	Persistence of attitude changes (*on likelihood; *on nuclear weapons; *on world leaders) Men vs women* Age differences [I] Other demographic differences [I]

+ Large difference but significance not reported. [I] Significant interaction reported. *$p < .05$. **$p < .01$. ***$p < .001$.

26	29	30
Reactions to film	General effect*	Reactions to film
Worry about nuclear war	Likelihood of nuclear war	Distress about nuclear war*
Consequences of nuclear war	Personal survival	Attempt not to think about nuclear war (?-62%)
Knowledge about nuclear war	Consequences of nuclear war	Likelihood of nuclear war (?-56%)
Knowledge about film events	Efficacy to prevent nuclear war	Likelihood of limited nuclear war (65-55%)[a]
Learning from film	Beliefs about nuclear war issues	Likelihood of escaping (26-17%)*
	Attitudes about nuclear war issues*	Personal survival*
	Antinuclear activities	Desire to survive*
	Behavioral intentions to prevent nuclear war**	Attitude on nuclear issues*
		Attitude toward U.S. nuclear weapons (53-48%)*
		Trust in government
		Civil defense effectiveness*
		U.S. civil defense preparedness (26-?%)*
		USSR civil defense preparedness (42-?%)*
		Belief about USSR military goals (?-80%)
		Behavioral intentions on nuclear issues
		Behavioral intentions if 1 hour warning
		Nuclear war information learned
No significance tests	$d \sim .3$	Can't be computed
Girls vs boys[a]	Viewers vs nonviewers (**on behavioral intentions)	Men vs women ([a] on USSR military goals; [a] on U.S. nuclear weapons; [a] on U.S. civil defense)
Age differences[a]	Prediction of behavioral intentions***	

(or effects) is occasionally used—necessitated by the fact that some papers did not state significance and others reported it only sporadically.

A. Viewer Characteristics

Who chose to watch *The Day After*? Were viewers systematically different from nonviewers? These issues are logically prior to, though perhaps less interesting than, questions about the effects of the program, and they were discussed in a number of reports. In general, the results seem to show a mild degree of selective viewing.

1. Demographic Variables

The ABC nationwide study (1) found that viewers were more likely to be male (as did Study 23) and less likely to be separated, divorced, or widowed. Substantially more viewers than nonviewers were in the 18-49 age range, and fewer were 50 or older (1, 4), indicating that older people tended to avoid the program. Viewers were socioeconomically better off than nonviewers, more of them had attended college (1, 4), and more had incomes over $30,000 and subscribed to cable or pay television (1). Among college students, there were significant but weak tendencies ($r < .2$) for more viewers to be U.S. citizens, white, farther along in college, veterans, and employed at least part-time (23); for viewers to have more self-reported knowledge about nuclear war (19); and for more nonviewers to be religious fundamentalists, believing in miracles and the coming of Armageddon (29).

2. Attitudes and Beliefs

Given the enormous audience for *The Day After*, it is clear that many people from every background and viewpoint watched it. But the research findings demonstrate that, on the average, viewers were slightly less favorable to nuclear armaments than nonviewers prior to their watching the program. In a national sample, 86% of viewers supported a nuclear freeze compared with 80% of nonviewers (6). Among representative samples of Pittsburgh and Boston residents and among California college students, viewers were higher than nonviewers on thoughts and worry about nuclear war (24, 10, 14), but some studies with college students failed to find such a difference (19, 20, 22). Similarly, concerning the likelihood of nuclear war, some studies found viewers to give higher likelihood estimates (7, 10), but others did not (20, 29). In one study, fewer viewers than nonviewers said there were causes worth fighting a nuclear war for (14).

In Great Britain, *The Day After* was telecast on Saturday, December 10, 1983. There was far less hoopla than in the United States, yet a surprisingly high 47% of the adult population viewed it. Perhaps more so than in the United

States, there was mild but consistent evidence of selectivity in who chose to watch. In a nationwide quota sample, about 10% more viewers than nonviewers were worried about the possibility of a nuclear war, thought one was likely in the next 10 years, felt that having nuclear weapons increased the risk of being attacked, thought that America might start a nuclear war, preferred surrender to suffering a nuclear attack, and felt that Britain did not need nuclear weapons as protection from a Soviet attack (17).

3. Viewers of the Viewpoint *Panel Discussion*

The audience for the *Viewpoint* program that immediately followed *The Day After* in the United States was also a huge one for a public affairs program; over two thirds of *The Day After* viewers remained tuned in for the beginning of the panel discussion. Though a Fresno study (7) found that many more women than men watched the *Viewpoint* program, a nationwide study found no differences between *Viewpoint* viewers and nonviewers on age, gender, education, or party identification, as well as no differences on attitudes toward defense or nuclear issues (3). The only significant difference uncovered was that viewers of the panel discussion were twice as likely as nonviewers to express feelings of political efficacy (i.e., that they had some possibility of influencing war or peace).

B. Reactions to *The Day After*

1. *Detailed Analysis of Reactions to the Movie*

Earlier in this chapter, the overall evaluations of *The Day After* reported in the instant-analysis studies were summarized. In addition to those data, seven studies reported viewer reactions in more detail (4, 11, 19, 20, 25, 26, 30). In a free-response format, 15% or more of adult viewers volunteered each of the following reactions: frightened, disturbed, it was realistic, informative, realized the possibility of nuclear war, and destruction not as bad as expected. By contrast, much smaller percentages said it was unrealistic, or they could not believe it; and in response to a direct question, only 4% said they were offended by anything in the film (4).

Among college viewers, the most thorough study of reactions (11) found frequent endorsement of the following reactions during the 2 weeks following the broadcast: informative (77%), I was upset (72%), I felt the need to talk about it (69%), and I have not been able to get the movie out of my head, even now (41%). This same study investigated expected reactions to the film beforehand and found empirical evidence that it did not live up to viewers' expectations, as many commentators had suggested. On a scale of negative affect, these New York college students' anticipated reactions were significantly more severe than the actual reactions they reported after seeing the program. Similarly, before the broadcast, 28% said that they expected that watching it would disrupt their routine on the next day, whereas afterward only 16% said that it had done so (11).

College students in Idaho rated the film as quite unpleasant but also fairly useful, effective, and wise (20). Among Chicago college students, 82% rated it as realistic and many considered it upsetting (30). In another study (19), Ohio college students rated it as somewhat frightening and more than somewhat realistic. However, schoolchildren in Lawrence, Kansas, remembering the film 6-8 weeks later, said that they were neither terribly frightened nor impressed by it (26). From fifth-grade students through high school seniors, only 18-23% said they were frightened or upset "quite a bit" or "a lot," whereas 50-59% said "not at all" or "not much." Similarly, 29-33% said they had seen quite a few or a lot of movies on television that were more frightening or more upsetting than *The Day After*, and only among elementary school respondents did a majority say they had not seen many as upsetting. Only 30-44% of these Lawrence children rated the film as good or great, whereas 17-24% rated it below the scale midpoint. Because these were delayed posttests 6-8 weeks after the film was broadcast, however, it is quite possible that the immediate reactions were stronger and more favorable.

An Australian study that investigated the impact of *The Day After* when it was shown in a movie theater (25) found considerably stronger viewer reactions than the delayed responses of the Lawrence children—more like the aforementioned responses of the New York college students (11). One day later, the Australian viewers said the film made the threat of nuclear war seem more real and easy to imagine; they rated the film as quite disturbing and frightening, and moderately depressing; and 74% said they felt the need to discuss it with others. Observations of their reactions in the theater supported these ratings. Similarly, many open-ended responses of California college students emphasized their shock and horror while viewing the program (23).

2. Reactions to the Viewpoint *Panel Discussion*

The *Viewpoint* program evidently maintained audience interest; its average audience of about 50 million viewers was five times larger than usual for that time slot (Kaatz, 1984; Schofield & Pavelchak, 1985). The only study investigating viewer reactions to it was ABC's (1), which asked how much it helped to clarify the issues raised in *The Day After*. Among its viewers, 22% said "a lot," 46% said "a little," and 30% said "not at all"—not a terribly strong endorsement.

C. Effects of *The Day After* on Information Learned

Only five studies investigated informational learning from *The Day After* (12, 19, 23, 26, 30), and only one used items tapping specific knowledge (26). On six items about occurrences in the film, Lawrence, Kansas school children were found to have learned an average of four to five of them, with older students learning more than grade-schoolers (26). This events score did not correlate with self-reported learning, which showed a negative relationship to age. Among high school seniors, 29% said they learned "a lot" or "quite a bit," compared to 40% who reported learning "not much" or "a little"; for ninth graders, the corresponding figures were 43% and 30%; and for fifth and sixth graders, 56% reported learning "much," versus 17% who reported learning "not much" or "a little" (26). Thus, older children displayed more information but attributed less of their nuclear knowledge to the film.

Somewhat similarly, among college students, graduates and upperclass students reported learning less central information from the film than freshmen and sophomores; men reported learning less than women (23). One college study found no change in self-reported knowledge about nuclear war after the broadcast among either viewers or nonviewers (19), but half of Chicago college students reported learning that some of their beliefs about nuclear war were wrong (30).

Among representative adults in the community, the most thoroughly analyzed study found self-reported knowledge about nuclear war not to have been significantly influenced by watching *The Day After*, or the *Viewpoint* panel discussion, or by discussing them with someone afterwards (12). However, self-reported knowledge *was* positively influenced by the number of television or newspaper stories about nuclear war that the respondent had seen in the preceding week. Here, then, is some empirical evidence that all the media publicity about *The Day After* had a significant impact in this area.

D. Effects on Attitudes and Beliefs

In this category of finding, we come to the central question addressed by most commentators and researchers: What were *The Day After*'s effects on people's relevant political beliefs and attitudes? Most investigators expected to find significant changes in these areas, though there is very little past research that is directly relevant. Two previous studies of films about nuclear war have shown increases in viewers' anxieties about such wars, decreases in their desires to survive a nuclear war, and several changes in relevant attitudes and beliefs (Granberg & Faye, 1972; Zweigenhaft, 1984). A very wide variety of belief and attitude issues were investigated in the studies of *The Day After*, and they are considered here in a series of subclassifications.

1. Effects of the Viewpoint Panel and Other Communications

Though most studies did not consider the *Viewpoint* panel discussion separately from *The Day After*, there was one paper that painstakingly differentiated the effects of these and other communication variables [Feldman & Sigelman (1985) (12)]. This was accomplished by a complex multiple regression approach that determined the *independent* effects of the film, the panel discussion, exposure to media coverage of *The Day After* and nuclear issues, and personal discussions about these topics. There may be a substantial amount of "noise" or error in the complex estimation procedure for determining these independent effects, but when significant findings are obtained, they give considerable confidence that the source(s) of the obtained communication effects have been correctly pinpointed. Thus, the results of this study are presented in detail where they bear on particular dependent variables.

2. Thoughts, Worry, and Fear about Nuclear War

This was one of the two most often studied effects of the film (together with likelihood of nuclear war), and it was clearly the one most often found to have been influenced. It was measured in 18 studies, of which 12 reported large or significant increases in thoughts or worry (5, 8, 10, 12, 14, 16, 19, 22–25, 30) and only 6 did not (9, 11, 17, 18, 20, 26). Of the latter group, two did not state results for this item or items (20, 26), one reported a nonsignificant tendency toward an increase (9), and one that asked how much respondents feared a nuclear war may have encountered a ceiling effect due to the wording of the item (18). Another study may possibly have missed some anticipatory changes in frequency of thoughts about nuclear war due to the timing of the pretest, which was conducted relatively close to the time of broadcast (11), though others with about the same timing did show increased thoughts and worry (e.g., 12, 19). In the British study (17), there was actually a slight, nonsignificant decrease in worry about nuclear war after seeing *The Day After*, but the wording of the item specified a war involving Britain, which may have been less affected by seeing a film about nuclear destruction in Kansas. One other study found some significant changes in general affect (i.e., anxiety, depression, etc.) after viewing *The Day After* (29).

In general, there is strong evidence that many viewers experienced an increase in thoughts, fear, or worry about nuclear war after seeing the film. In addition, on this and several other variables, some studies that carefully analyzed nonviewers' responses showed that *nonviewers* increased their thoughts or anxiety as well (23, 24). Because such changes could not have been due to their having viewed the film itself, they clearly demonstrate the occurrence of anticipatory attitude change due to the preceding media publicity and resulting personal discussions of nuclear war issues. On the variable of frequency of thoughts about nuclear war, Feldman and Sigelman (12) demonstrated three independent effects: that of the film itself, of exposure to media coverage of the film, and of nonviewers' personal discussions of it with someone else.

3. Emotions Concerning Nuclear War

Related to the category of thoughts and worry, but somewhat different in tone, were questions about attitudes or emotions regarding nuclear war. Such questions, using a variety of wording, were only asked in five studies (10, 12, 16, 19, 24), perhaps because other researchers assumed that *everyone* would be negative or opposed to nuclear war in responding. Nevertheless, in all five studies in which respondents were asked, they displayed highly significant changes in negative emotions. Kulman and Akamatsu (19) showed increases in a factorially derived scale called "future concern," which included negative emotions about nuclear attack, concern about nuclear war in making plans for particular future actions such as marriage and raising children, and worry about nuclear war in general. Similarly, L. M. Goodman (16) found increases in negative "attitudes toward nuclear war" with a scale of 10 miscellaneous items, which included questions concerning attitudes about defense and nuclear issues as well as attitudes toward war and destruction. Cross and Saxe (10) found retrospective increases in reports of being upset by thoughts about nuclear war. Feldman and Sigelman (12) studied three factorially derived dimensions of emotions about "this country's defense against nuclear war"—anger, worry, and satisfaction—and found significant changes only in increased worry. Their detailed breakdown of the sources of this effect showed that both the film and the *Viewpoint* panel discussion contributed significantly to "worry," but that exposure to media coverage of the film and personal discussions about it did not.

Pavelchak and Schofield (24) found a rather different effect of the film on feelings about nuclear war. They did not observe significant changes in levels of fear or anxiety, but they did find *decreased* emotional arousal due to an increase in hopelessness. This may be a delayed effect of the film because their measurements were taken more than 1 week and more than 3 weeks afterward, and it rather resembles the significant delayed changes in pessimism about nuclear war found by Oskamp et al. (23). Another somewhat similar delayed effect was displayed on an item about "concern for the kind of world in which your children will live" asked by Reser and Wallace (25). In this study, Australian theatergoers showed very high concern on this item both minutes before seeing *The Day After* and 1 day following. However, by 3 months later, their level of concern had dropped off significantly.

It is interesting that all but one of these studies that asked about changes in emotions concerning nuclear war were done with adults in the community, and only one was with college students (19). This difference in the questions asked of the two groups may reflect the impression of researchers that college students were already maximally opposed to nuclear war before seeing the film and thus could not change further.

4. Perceived Likelihood of Nuclear War

This was the other most often studied dependent variable, though various studies often asked the question in different words and about different periods of time, and hence the absolute levels of the mean scores for different studies are often noncomparable. Of 21 studies that asked about it, only 4 reported large or significant increases in likelihood as a result of seeing the film (10, 16, 18, 24). None of them were huge changes, though in some cases they represented increases from very high levels [e.g., from 84 to 92% likelihood (16)]. However, it is striking that all four studies were done with samples of adults in the community, and only one of the pre-post studies conducted in the United States with community samples failed to find this effect (12), whereas none of the many studies with college students showed significant increases in their estimates of the likelihood of nuclear war. Because young people's estimates on this dimension have historically been higher than the general U.S. population's (L. A. Goodman, Mack, Beardslee, & Snow, 1983; Plous, 1984), this lack of changes for college students may be at least partially due to a ceiling effect in measurement.

5. Perceived Likelihood of a Nuclear War Remaining Limited in Scope

This related item involving likelihood estimates was only asked in seven studies (8, 14, 17-19, 23, 30). Three U.S. studies found no change in estimates (8, 14, 18), and a British study (17) found no change in agreement that a nuclear war in Europe would not necessarily lead to a nuclear attack on America. However, two studies with college students found large or significant decreases in the likelihood of a limited nuclear war (19, 30), and the remaining study reported a nearly significant decrease that became significant by the time of a delayed posttest 2 weeks later (23). Thus, there is some indication of changes on this item for college samples, but none for adult or foreign samples.

6. Perceived Consequences of Nuclear War

This category is probably the topic most closely related to the content of *The Day After*, and accordingly it was included in 13 studies. However, strangely, it was considered in only 1 of the instant-analysis studies (6), and in 2 studies (6, 26), it was asked in a way that precluded analysis of changes due to having viewed the movie. Many different types of consequences and wordings of the questions are subsumed here, and one or more of these variables were found to show large or significant changes in 8 of the 11 pertinent studies (8, 12, 16, 18, 19, 22, 23, 25).

Of the five studies that used a scale of several items regarding disastrous consequences of a nuclear war, four showed significant increases in seriousness after the film (12, 19, 22, 23), and the fifth had a nonsignificant trend in the same direction (20). Typically, the individual items that showed significant effects were rather specific catastrophic predictions about a postwar world. For instance, they included more deaths (22, 23), fewer survivors (12, 19, 23), inadequate medical care (12, 23), the respondent's own death (19, 23), insufficient food and shelter (12), social chaos (23), extent of destruction (19), and nuclear war devastating Australia [reported in an Australian study (25)]. By contrast, a more global type of item about extinction of civilization and human and animal life, though it increased in one study (16), typically did not show significant changes (11, 22, 23) and correlated very little with more specific consequences (22). The only exceptions to this pattern were one unspecified item, which showed no change (29), and an item about the percentage of survivors of a nuclear war, which showed no change in one study (18) and which, in an experimental study, actually yielded a higher estimate from people who had just viewed *The Day After* than from ones who had just seen the movie, *Missing* (8).

Feldman and Sigelman (12) found that the only experience that significantly increased their scale of consequences was viewing the movie itself, but not watching *Viewpoint* or being exposed to media coverage or personal discussions of nuclear war. However, in Gutierres et al.'s study (18), some selective viewing of *The Day After* was demonstrated in that, even before the film, viewers scored near the maximum on an item about physical destruction, whereas nonviewers generally increased their scores afterward, presumably due to media exposure or personal discussions. The two studies that did not investigate changes both reported large percentages of respondents agreeing that the effects of a real-life nuclear war would be worse than those shown in the movie (6, 26).

7. Expectations Regarding Personal Survival

Another important dependent variable that was frequently studied was chances of one's own personal survival or death in a nuclear war (2, 3, 10-12, 17-19, 23-25, 29, 30). In nearly half of these studies, there was a significant drop in survival estimates following *The Day After* (10, 18, 19, 23, 24, 30). In most of the other studies, survival estimates were so low to start with (from 7 to 19%) that a significant decrease was difficult to achieve, but small decreases were observed.

Other aspects of survival were also studied. Amount of consideration given to personal survival increased after *The Day After* in one sample (8) and increased in one of three cities in another study (18). Belief in the possibility that some actions could help a person survive a nuclear war increased (23), but behavioral intentions to take war-survival actions did not (23). In fact, preference *not* to survive a nuclear war went up by a large or significant amount after the movie (11, 16, 24, 30). Though this effect was only measured in four studies, it was one of the most dramatic results of *The Day After*, and it occurred for nonviewers as well as for viewers because of all the movie publicity (11).

8. Perceived Efficacy to Prevent Nuclear War

Another frequently asked personally oriented question was whether individuals could in any way help to prevent a nuclear war. In the 11 studies that measured this (3, 9, 10, 11, 14, 18, 19, 20, 23, 24, 29) only 2 found significance—both reporting lower efficacy after the film for some or all viewers (10, 24). One other study showed a nonsignificant decrease (23), but another found a nonsignificant increase (3). The remaining studies either found no change in efficacy (9, 11, 14, 18, 29) or did not report data for that item (19, 20).

9. Behavioral Intentions to Prevent Nuclear War

Despite these pessimistic findings concerning efficacy, the picture regarding behavioral intentions was generally positive in the 10 studies that assessed them (8, 9, 11, 14, 16, 18, 23, 24, 29, 30). Two studies found significant increases following *The Day After* (24, 29), two found a substantial trend in the same direction (14, 16), and posttest respondents in another study said they were more likely to participate in antiwar activities (9). In addition, five studies reported large or significant interactions, with viewers changing more than nonviewers on behavioral intentions and/or commitment (11, 14, 23, 24, 29). Thus, only two studies in this group displayed nonsignificant findings (8, 18), and one did not report its findings (30).

10. Involvement in Activities to Prevent Nuclear War

A final category related to efficacy and behavioral intentions is actual antiwar activities. This variable might be seen as the ultimate behavioral criterion of *The Day After*'s effects, but it would not have had much time to change in most studies. Nevertheless, it was investigated in four studies (11, 18, 19, 29) and was reported to have already increased significantly in one (19). In addition, reports of past discussions about nuclear war issues with families and friends increased in a fifth study (14).

11. Attitudes and Beliefs about Nuclear Issues

Changes in this category of effects were expected by many researchers to be a logical result of viewing *The Day After*, and so 19 studies asked about a wide variety of such attitudes and beliefs (2, 3, 5-7, 12, 14, 16-25, 29, 30).

In general, tests of these effects showed quite limited changes, with only a few significant main effects or interactions.

Before examining changes on these variables, here are some overall pretest findings. In an Australian study, nearly 50% of respondents ranked nuclear war as the most important world problem (25). In the United States, over 85% of people said there was hope of avoiding a nuclear war (5, 14, 16). Yet, only about 40% of U.S. respondents thought the United States was doing all it could to avoid nuclear war (2). About 90% of respondents favored an arms control agreement with the Soviet Union (12), and over 80% supported a bilateral nuclear freeze (3, 6, 12, 22), though this support dropped to 40% when the question specified that such a freeze would maintain Soviet superiority in land-based ICBMs (22). On the other hand, there was also substantial support for nuclear strength as a deterrent to international aggression. Only about 10% of U.S. respondents favored unilateral U.S. nuclear disarmament (3), and in England only about 25% of respondents favored unilateral British nuclear disarmament (17).

Perhaps partially because of the high support for arms control in several studies (5, 12, 22, 23, 25), only four reports showed large or significant changes on this variable following the film (5, 12, 14, 30). In the QUBE Network television study (5), 12% of respondents changed toward support for arms control after seeing the movie, whereas 6% changed toward favoring an arms buildup —a finding that demonstrates the possibility of contrary or offsetting effects of the film. Feldman and Sigelman (12) found that increases in support for arms control and a nuclear freeze among their Kentucky adults were due entirely to exposure to media coverage of nuclear issues rather than to the film per se. Similarly, of five other studies investigating support for a bilateral nuclear freeze (3, 6, 19, 20, 21), one did not measure changes in support (21) and four reported slight increases, only one of which was significant (19), whereas another study without a significance test found 66% of respondents reporting that they had changed toward more support for a nuclear freeze (20).

The possibility of contradictory changes among different viewers is emphasized again by the latter study (20) in which 41% of respondents reported changing toward more support for deterrence through military strength. Based on these figures, some viewers must have increased in favorability toward *both* nuclear deterrence and a nuclear freeze, which are ordinarily considered to be opposing policies. Other findings on support for nuclear strength showed a significant drop in support for a nuclear first strike (20) and for developing more U.S. nuclear weapons (30), but only slight nonsignificant decreases in favorability to nuclear escalation or to survivability as a goal (20), and no change in support for nuclear superiority (22). In England, airing of *The Day After* produced no changes in favorability either toward British nuclear weapons or toward British readiness to surrender rather than suffer nuclear destruction (17). However, in Australia, theatergoers came away from the film with a significantly decreased feeling that it was important for the United States and Europe to have nuclear weapons for protection against attack (25).

Beliefs in the desirability of civil defense and/or its effectiveness to reduce nuclear casualties decreased significantly following the movie in two studies (23, 30) but increased slightly in two others (14, 20). Feelings of safety stemming from local nuclear weapons also changed nonsignificantly in opposite directions in two studies (16, 17), as did willingness to use nuclear weapons in retaliation (16, 20). Other variables that showed no changes were attitudes and subjective norms toward antinuclear activities and protestors (24, 25).

Beliefs about Soviet policies and intentions displayed only a single significant change—an increase in belief that Soviet arms control intentions are genuine (22). However, items about Soviet military goals (22, 30), Soviet government policies, and the similarity of the U.S. and Soviet people's opinions on nuclear issues were relatively unaffected by the film (18).

Also unchanged by *The Day After* were viewers' estimates of the risks of terrorist use of nuclear weapons (17, 18), of nuclear weapons accidents (17, 18), of the likelihood of nonnuclear conflicts escalating (23), and of the likelihood of arms control agreements and other nuclear war events (29). It should be emphasized that there is no clear connection between the content of *The Day After* and many of these beliefs and attitudes, so there is no logical reason to expect many of them to be changed by the film.

12. Attitudes and Beliefs about U.S. Defense Policies

This category, closely akin to the preceding one, was investigated by nine studies (2, 3, 7, 9, 10, 12, 20, 23, 30) with somewhat mixed results. Almost every respondent agreed, both before and after the film, that U.S. defense policy was an important matter (12). There was a significant increase in those saying we should try hard to get along with Russia, but it was entirely traceable to media coverage of nuclear issues rather than to the film per se (12). As was mentioned earlier, both the movie and the *Viewpoint* panel discussion contributed significantly to making viewers more worried about our defense policies (12). Though viewers in another study (10) were significantly more convinced than nonviewers that U.S. policy was increasing the threat of war, that difference was an indication of selective viewing, as viewers did not increase on this item following the film.

In general, seeing *The Day After* did not produce any decrease in approval for U.S. defense policies (2). However, following the movie, a majority of viewers reported that they were now more likely to consider nonmilitary options for dealing with international conflict (9), similar to the increased support for a nuclear freeze (20) that was reported previously. There was also a significant decrease in respondents' beliefs in U.S. (as well as Soviet) civil defense preparedness (30). In one study (23), there was no change in attitudes about recent use of U.S. troops in Grenada (a topic unrelated to the film's content), but there was a marginally significant change toward favoring a decrease in the number of U.S. nuclear weapons (more closely related to the film). Another study found a significant decrease in support for U.S. nuclear weapons (30).

On the topic of U.S. defense spending, one national study reported no change (3), whereas a community sample showed a significant change in opposition to lower spending on the part of poorly educated respondents, which was traceable to the effect of the movie (12). However, a study with college students found a change toward favoring lower spending, which remained significant at a delayed posttest 2 weeks later (23). These last two findings are not as contradictory as they appear, for Feldman and Sigelman (12) have demonstrated, on the topic of defense spending, that there was a very large interaction effect between the film and the education level of the audience, such that individuals who were college-educated or above increased in their opposition to defense spending, whereas the less education viewers had, the more they favored increased defense spending. This again demonstrates the fact that *The Day After* had very different effects on different types of viewers.

13. Attitudes toward World Leaders

The five comprehensive studies that investigated this area (7, 9, 11, 12, 25) have little to add to the findings of the instant-analysis studies. One of them did not measure change (7) and three (9, 11, 25) found no change after the film in people's confidence in world leaders to prevent war. The fifth, like some of the instant-analysis studies, found a slight nonsignificant tendency toward greater support for President Reagan's policies (12). However, as with the topic of defense spending, there was a significant interaction with education level, such that better educated viewers changed more toward opposition to Reagan's policies, whereas less educated viewers changed toward supporting them.

14. Other Beliefs and Attitudes

Finally, a few other attitudes, some of them further removed from the content of *The Day After*, showed a mixed pattern of findings. There were no changes for attitudes and emotions toward nuclear energy (17, 18) or for beliefs about risks from nuclear energy (17, 18). However, a scale of attitudes toward interpersonal violence showed a significant decrease for women viewers but not for men (9). In an Australian study, an item measuring an internal locus of personal control decreased significantly after the film was seen (25).

E. Differential Effects of *The Day After*, the *Viewpoint* Panel Discussion, and Other Communications

As has been mentioned, several studies found evidence that nonviewers as well as viewers of *The Day After* changed on various items from before to after the film's showing (11, 12, 18, 23, 24). This is clear evidence of the powerful effects of media publicity and controversy that accompanied the film. However, it is quite possible that these media forces might produce different kinds of changes than those stemming from the film itself. For instance, past communication research has demonstrated that televised commentaries after documentary or political programs can have "coda effects" that modify the preceding program's impact (Robinson, 1976; Paletz & Vinegar, 1977). It was probably the hope of Secretary of State Schultz and several of the panelists on the *Viewpoint* program to do just that by presenting ideas and arguments that would counter the expected public opinion effect of the film they were discussing. Most studies of *The Day After* were not designed to split up the stimulus "package" and differentiate the film's effects from those of the *Viewpoint* panel discussion or of other publicity and communication. However, the Feldman and Sigelman study (12) was imaginatively designed to do just that, and it succeeded in finding many differential effects of the movie itself and what it called the movie's "by-products." These findings may or may not generalize to other samples, but because they come from a representative group of adults in one city (Lexington, Kentucky), there is a possibility that they may apply more broadly as indicators of the American public's response to the various stimuli surrounding the film.

1. The Viewpoint *Panel Discussion*

Feldman and Sigelman's (12) findings show that independently of the film and other publicity, the *Viewpoint* panel had its own effects on two dependent variables: (1) watching it increased respondents' negative emotions of worry about U.S. defense against nuclear war—the same direction of effect, but not as strong an effect, as that of the movie itself on viewers' worries—and, (2) the panel discussion made respondents less favorable to national defense budget increases. Thus, as Feldman and Sigelman point out, the panel's effects were opposite to the administration's hopes that Secretary of State Schultz and the former cabinet officials appearing as panelists would be able to reassure viewers about U.S. nuclear defenses and maintain public support for heavy defense spending.

2. *Exposure to Media Coverage of Nuclear War*

Another key communication dimension was operationalized as the number of television or newspaper stories about nuclear war that the respondent had seen during the preceding week (12). Of course, a large proportion of these stories were stimulated by the showing of *The Day After*, but independently of the effects of the movie itself, seeing a number of these stories changed respondents' views on four dependent variables. Logically enough, it increased respondents' self-rated knowledge about nuclear war (and was the only significant influence on that variable). Second, it increased the frequency of their thoughts about nuclear war (as did the movie itself, and personal discussions about the movie). Third, it increased respondents' scores on two attitude items: favorability to trying hard to get along with the Soviet Union, and favorability to arms control steps, including a nuclear freeze. (On both of these items, media exposure was the only significant influence.)

3. *Personal Discussion about the Movie*

This communication factor was examined as an independent variable only in regard to nonviewers of the movie, and it was found to have a significant effect on only one dependent variable (12). It increased the number of thoughts about nuclear war (as did the movie itself and exposure to media stories about nuclear war).

4. *Perceived Realism of the Movie*

This factor, defined as saying that the movie gave an accurate picture of the results of nuclear war, was conceptualized as possibly having an effect on respondents' attitudes over and above that of just seeing the movie (12). In fact, it significantly affected only one variable—it had a negative impact on favorability to U.S. defense spending, whereas viewers who thought the movie was unrealistic became more favorable to defense spending.

5. *The Movie's Own Separate Effects*

Feldman and Sigelman (12) considered the movie's separate effects, independent of its "by-products," in combination with the educational level of individual viewers because they found that it sometimes had quite different effects on viewers of different educational levels. Altogether, of 14 dependent variables, they found the movie affected 5 significantly.

First, seeing the film had a very large effect on increasing the frequency of respondents' thoughts about nuclear war. This effect held for all educational levels, but it was greater for the least educated viewers. Second, the movie increased viewers' negative emotions of worry about U.S. defense against nuclear war. Again, this effect was largest for the least educated viewers, and it diminished to nothing and then reversed for college-educated and postgraduate viewers (a likely implication being that they were already quite worried before seeing the film). Third, in the area of nuclear war consequences, seeing the movie strongly decreased viewers' beliefs that there would be adequate shelters, medical care, and food available after a nuclear war.

The movie was the only factor that affected this dependent variable, and it had nearly equal effects on viewers at all educational levels.

A fourth effect of seeing the movie, among those viewers who felt it was unrealistic, was to increase support for U.S. defense spending (an outcome that partially frustrated the hopes and anticipations of antinuclear activists). However, this effect interacted very strongly with educational level, such that viewers with less than a high school education became much more favorable toward defense spending and high school graduates became very slightly more favorable, whereas college-educated and postgraduate viewers became much more *negative* toward defense spending. Finally, the same interaction pattern was found on the attitudinal variable of approval of Reagan's handling of foreign policy. There, the least educated viewers became a bit more favorable, high school graduates became a bit more unfavorable, and college-educated and postgraduate viewers became much more unfavorable.

One very great benefit of this differential analysis of effects by Feldman and Sigelman (12) is in demonstrating that the same stimulus (the film) can have markedly different and even opposing effects on different viewers. A corollary of this point is that some of the various researchers' findings in which the movie seemed to have no particular effect may have been the result of contrary and offsetting effects on different groups of viewers. For instance, in the Australian study (25), respondents who were opposed to nuclear arms changed in the direction of estimating greater likelihood for a nuclear war, whereas viewers favorable to nuclear weapons changed slightly in the opposite direction after seeing the film. Because most studies of *The Day After* did not analyze their data for such individual differences, Feldman and Sigelman's study (12) is one of the very few that shed light on that possibility. In their study, half of the dependent variables showed at least tendencies toward differential effects for different educational groups, and of course other differential effects might possibly occur for other classificatory variables, such as political viewpoints, gender, or age. In turn, these differential effects may help to explain the occasionally conflicting findings of various studies of *The Day After* done with different demographic groups of respondents.

F. Persistence of Attitude and Belief Changes

If it is granted that *The Day After* and its communication by-products did produce many immediate changes in people's attitudes and beliefs, then the persistence of those changes becomes a very important question, for if they remained relatively long and strong, then the impact of the film would be more impressive.

Among the studies summarized here, six gave delayed posttests to investigate the persistence of initial change (16, 18, 23–26), but two of these have not presented data that are analyzable for this purpose. One reported only the final posttest data, so that changes cannot be measured (26). Another merely summarized verbally that, 4–5 months later, scores for various samples on a scale of nuclear attitudes were higher than those obtained before the film (16), which may show general societal trends rather than (or in addition to) the effects of the film itself. However, the other four studies give some useful specific evidence.

Gutierres *et al.*'s study (18) with residents of three cities reported four significant items, of which three showed initial pre–post changes. Three months later, in an independent but comparable sample, all three items displayed delayed changes that had not decayed appreciably. Pavelchak and Schofield's (24) study with Pittsburgh residents reported on eight significant variables at the 1-week posttest. At the delayed 3-week posttest, with a comparable pre–post panel of respondents, five of those variables showed persisting or even increased changes, while the other three displayed a dropoff. Oskamp *et al.*'s study (23) with California college students used a three-wave panel and found 11 of 20 variables to show significant changes 2 days after the film. Two weeks later, eight of these variables were still significantly different from the pretest, and one additional item showed a significant delayed change. Finally, in Reser and Wallace's Australian study (25), four items were reported to have significant changes 1 day after the film. Three months later, in a three-wave panel, two of the initial changes remained strong and three other items became significant, whereas the other two items had reverted since the immediate posttest.

By classifying the foregoing four studies' items according to their content, we can see which types of variables were most likely to display long-lasting changes. I will refer here mainly to the time span of persisting changes, though of course there are many other differences among these studies that could account for differences in persistence.

1. Thoughts or worry: greater increase at 2 weeks (23), but drop off at 3 weeks and 3 months (24, 25)

2. Emotions regarding nuclear war: The immediate decrease in arousal (increased hopelessness) remained at 3 weeks (24), but the initial high level of concern for one's children's world diminished at 3 months (25)

3. Likelihood of nuclear war: An immediate increase remained at 3 weeks (24), but a stable initial level dropped off at 3 months (25)

4. Likelihood of nuclear war remaining limited: Decrease remained at 2 weeks (23)

5. Drastic consequences of nuclear war: Four of five variables remained at 2 weeks (23), and two different items remained at 3 months (18, 25)

6. Chances of personal survival: Initial increase dropped off slightly at 2 weeks (23), became even greater at 3 weeks (24), and remained at 3 months (18)

7. Consideration regarding personal survival: Initial increase remained at 3 months (18)

8. Desire to survive: Initial decrease remained at 3 weeks (24)

9. Efficacy to prevent nuclear war: Initial decrease became a significant one at 2 weeks (23) and remained at 3 weeks (24)

10. Behavioral intentions to prevent nuclear war: The initial increase for viewers dropped off at 3 weeks (24)

11. Nuclear attitudes and beliefs: One of two initial belief changes remained at 2 weeks (23); initially favorable attitudes toward antinuclear activity decreased for nonviewers at 3 weeks (24); decreased belief in the importance of U.S. and European nuclear weapons remained at 3 months (25)

12. Defense attitudes and beliefs: Initial opposition to U.S. defense budget increases remained at 2 weeks (23)

13. Attitudes toward leaders: Initial level of faith in leaders dropped off at 3 months (25)

14. Miscellaneous: The initial drop in belief in personal control had almost recovered in 3 months (25).

In summary, nearly two thirds of the initial changes in attitudes and beliefs following *The Day After* remained significant on a delayed posttest weeks or months later—a rather striking degree of persistence.

G. Postmovie Differences between Viewers and Nonviewers

As has been mentioned, there were several studies that found *both* viewers and nonviewers changing significantly following the movie on from one to many items (11, 12, 17, 23, 24). In contrast, there were two other studies, both with college students, which analyzed pre-post changes separately for viewers and nonviewers and found no changes for nonviewers on any of a total of 14 dimensions (19, 22). A third study with students found no changes on two dimensions for that small group of nonviewers who had not discussed the film with anyone (14).

However, the most common pattern of change scores was for viewers to change somewhat more than nonviewers on various items, and quite often, significantly more. This pattern was found, for instance, in viewers' (a) increasing thoughts and worry about nuclear war (10, 12, 14, 19, 22, 23); (b) increasing ratings of the likelihood of a nuclear war (10) or the unlikelihood of a limited nuclear war (23); (c) increasing estimates of the devastating consequences of a nuclear war [12, 19, 22, 23—though in one study (18) in which viewers' estimates were already high, nonviewers' estimates increased more]; (d) decreased expectations of their personal survival (10, 23, 24); and (e) increased behavioral intentions to help prevent a nuclear war (14, 23, 24). The same differential pattern of change was also shown in viewers'

(a) increased support for a nuclear freeze and opposition to nuclear deterrence (6, 19); (b) decreased approval of a nuclear first strike (20); (c) increased belief that Soviet arms control intentions are genuine (22); and at the same time, (d) increased support for U.S. defense spending (12). Only on three unspecified items measuring general affect and some aspect of nuclear war attitudes were nonviewers reported to have changed more than viewers (29).

A different, but very interesting, pattern of differential change was reported following *The Day After*'s showing on nationwide television in Great Britain (17). There, both viewers and nonviewers had relatively small and similar mean changes on a variety of items. However, viewers were shown to have significantly lower pre-post correlations than nonviewers on four key items about nuclear war. Because the mean scores were relatively stable, this indicates that viewers changed more than nonviewers *in both directions* on these items (e.g., toward both higher and lower estimates of personal survival). This finding is reminiscent of and highly consistent with Feldman and Sigelman's (12) finding that different educational-level groups changed in opposite directions on the same item.

A final aspect of postmovie differences between viewers and nonviewers was the occurrence of large posttest differences in studies that did not measure or report pre-post change scores. Because premovie scores were not measured in these studies, posttest differences could be due to people with different characteristics selectively viewing or not viewing *The Day After*. However, the large size of some of the differences and their consistency with the aforementioned change scores makes it more likely that they largely reflect genuine effects of the movie. Among adult professional psychologists and engineers, 53% of viewers and only 18% of nonviewers said they were very worried about the possibility of a nuclear war after seeing the film (23). In the area of antinuclear behavioral intentions, one study found intentions were held by 53% of viewers and only 37% of nonviewers (11), while another study found viewers significantly higher than nonviewers on six out of eight different antinuclear behavioral intention measures (29). A similar variable, where respondents made actual behavioral commitments to obtaining more antinuclear information, was more than twice as common among viewers as among nonviewers (23). Likewise, self-reports of knowledge about nuclear war and of actual activities relevant to nuclear war were significantly more frequent among viewers than nonviewers (19). On another item related to nuclear information, 59% of viewers said children under age 13 should have been allowed to watch the program, compared to only 28% of nonviewers (6). Finally, one study showed differences between viewers and nonviewers in their sense of control regarding nuclear war (21), and another found significant differences (in logical directions) on five belief and attitude items and two demographic characteristics—education and religious affiliation (7).

H. Demographic Comparisons

1. Men versus Women

The demographic groups most often studied in relation to *The Day After*'s effects were men and women. Several of the studies that analyzed demographic variables pointed out major gender differences in attitudes at the pretest, before exposure to the movie. For instance, women generally expected to experience more upset and emotional reactions to the film, and afterwards they reported having done so (11). On specific attitudinal variables, women were more opposed to nuclear war and more anxious about it than men (16, 22), gave higher estimates of its likelihood (22, 25) and its consequences (22), were lower in their beliefs about the need for U.S. nuclear superiority (22), were more opposed to heavy defense spending (3), and saw more value in arms control talks (14).

Given these preexisting differences between men and women, some of the reported postmovie gender differences may simply reflect prior viewpoints rather than, or in addition to, the specific effects of the movie. Examples include women's greater favorability to home bomb shelters (7), self-reported increases in emotional distress and unhappiness after the film (23), posttest self-reports of increased approval of nonmilitary options in international conflict, increased opposition to spending for nuclear weapons, and increased behavioral intentions to help prevent nuclear war (9), and girls' (higher than boys') reports of having learned a good deal from the film (26).

However, there were a number of studies that measured the size of men's and women's pre-post *change scores* and found significant differences that were clearly reactions to the film and the publicity surrounding it. In the Australian study (25), changes by women accounted for most of the pre-post significant findings, such as increased thoughts about nuclear war. In the United States, college women were higher than men in the central information they learned from the film (23), and they decreased in their estimates of the likelihood of nuclear war, while men increased (23). Women decreased far more than men in their desire to survive a nuclear war (11). And in separate studies, they increased more not only in the belief that Soviet arms control intentions were genuine (22), but also in the belief that the Soviet goal is world domination (30). Women also increased more in skepticism about U.S. civil defense preparedness (30), favorability to U.S. civil defense spending (14), and opposition to U.S. nuclear weapons (30), while men increased to the women's initial high level in recognizing the value of arms control talks (14). Finally, after the film, women decreased significantly in favorable attitudes toward interpersonal violence, whereas men did not (9).

2. Other Demographic Factors

As with gender differences, some other demographic categories showed substantial premovie differences in attitudes and beliefs. For instance, on the issue of defense spending, college-educated respondents were less favorable than non-college-educated respondents, 17- to 29-year-old respondents were less favorable than over-30s, and Democrats were less favorable than Republicans (3). However, none of these demographic groups was found to differ from its opposite category in the amount of pre-post *changes* on six different attitude items (3). Similarly, among high school students, feelings of efficacy to help prevent nuclear war were positively linked to socioeconomic status (SES) level, but again no differential pre-post changes were noted (14).

Only a few studies took the trouble to investigate demographic factors related to postmovie changes. As described earlier, Feldman and Sigelman (12) found educational level to be a potent interacting variable that influenced the movie's effect on some relevant attitudes. Viewers younger than 21 increased most in frequency of thought about nuclear war (14). In Australia, the younger age categories (up to 17, and 18-25) were found to be particularly susceptible to the movie's effects (25).

Other scattered findings showed that respondents without children increased in their estimates of the likelihood of nuclear war after seeing the movie, whereas respondents with children decreased (25). Respondents' degree of religiousness was also related to decreases in their rating of the likelihood of nuclear war, but positively related to increases in their estimation of its consequences (23). Protestant and Catholic viewers reported more increases than other religious categories in emotional distress and unhappiness after the film, and college freshmen and sophomores reported learning more central information about the film than did the more senior students and graduate students (23).

I. Additional Substantive Issues

Several studies investigated other substantive research issues. In one, the expectancy of being upset by the film was experimentally manipulated before college students who had not previously seen *The Day After* were shown it or another film, *Missing* (8). This expectancy was found to interact cumulatively with seeing *The Day After* to produce greater worry about nuclear war and greater consideration of surviving a nuclear attack, but it did not affect ratings of likelihood or consequences of a nuclear war or behavioral intentions to help prevent one.

Another personal characteristic, locus of control, was studied in conjunction with the film's effects in the English study (17), and it was found to interact with the film on several dependent variables. After seeing the film, viewers with an external orientation (i.e., a feeling of lack of control over events in their lives) decreased in their amount of worry about a nuclear war, whereas viewers with an internal orientation decreased in their expectations of personal survival in a nuclear war. Locus of control also showed complex interactions affecting attitudes and beliefs about disarmament.

Two studies investigated aspects of consistency of attitudes and beliefs about nuclear war (16, 22). Nelson and Slem (22) found, on premovie scores for both men and women, that attitude toward arms control correlated significantly with beliefs about the need for nuclear superiority, the consequences and the likelihood of a nuclear war, the genuineness of Soviet arms control intentions, and the degree of anxiety about a nuclear war. However, Goodman (16) found that the after-movie rank-order positions of 10 antinuclear attitude scale items showed no significant relationship to their before-movie scores, indicating quite different amounts of change.

Wolf *et al.* (29) tested Rogers's (1983) protection motivation theory about the effects of fear-arousing communication and found that behavioral intentions to engage in antinuclear activity could be predicted fairly well, for both movie viewers and nonviewers, from measures of their affect and cognitions about nuclear war, and particularly from their beliefs about the efficacy of their actions. McClenney and Allbright (21) tested Fishbein and Ajzen's (1975) theory of reasoned action and found support for the hypothesized relationship of subjective norms to behavioral intentions regarding nuclear issues, as well as for other relationships not included in the theory.

J. Research Artifacts

1. Sensitization from Pretesting

A final important issue for several studies was the possibility of research artifacts affecting the data. Of these, the question of whether pretesting sensitized respondents to the issues involved was the most crucial because a majority of the studies involved pre-post panel designs in which exposure to the pretest might possibly affect later responses. Fortunately, results of all of the relevant studies agree that there was practically no evidence of pretesting sensitization affecting postmovie responses. This held true for college respondents (11, 21, 23) and also, most importantly, in a careful and large-scale study involving telephone interviews with random community samples, where a posttest-only group differed hardly at all from the posttest data of the pre-post panel sample (12).

2. Sample Mortality

Selective attrition from the panel of respondents was only investigated by a few studies, and by only one of those done with college students (11). In many of the college-student studies, it seems possible that differential attrition of different types of respondents did occur, but there was very little evidence of it in the larger-scale community surveys (12, 25, 29).

3. Interviewer Effects

A final possible artifact, the occurrence of response bias due to interviewer characteristics or behavior, was applicable only to the interview studies and was checked on by only one (10). That study used inexperienced undergraduate students as interviewers, and it did find significant interviewer effects for several of its dependent variables. However, further analysis showed that they were accounted for by only one or two of the 21 interviewers, so they apparently had little overall effect on the data of the study. It is likely that the large-scale studies that used more experienced interviewers would have had even less of a threat from this source.

VI. DISCUSSION

A. Summary of Findings

The Day After had a huge viewing audience in every sector of the populace, and there was apparently only a mild degree of selective viewing by certain types of people—probably very little among college students, who were even more likely to watch it than the rest of the population. Most viewers found the program disturbing but informative, although for many people, it did not live up to their anticipations. Women and younger or more inexperienced viewers said they learned more from it than did men and older viewers, but people's knowledge about nuclear war issues was also positively influenced by the upsurge of newspaper and television coverage of nuclear war topics stimulated by the showing of *The Day After*.

Though the widely publicized instant-analysis studies were reported as finding almost no effects of *The Day After* on public attitudes and beliefs, practically every study that asked about them did find some significant effects. These effects varied in strength with the sample of people, the timing of contacts, the research design involved, and—most importantly of all—the relevance of the questions asked in relation to the message of the film.

Increased thoughts, worry, or fear about nuclear war was one of the most prominent effects, and it was found in a large majority of studies that investigated it. A closely related variable—increased negative emotions about nuclear war—was also significant in most studies that considered it.

The other topic most closely related to the content of *The Day After* was the consequences of nuclear war. Significant increases in respondents' ratings of the seriousness of various consequences were found in most of the studies that investigated them. Expectations about the chances of one's own personal survival also decreased in many studies, though they were often very low to begin with.

Increases in the estimated likelihood of nuclear war were only found in a few studies, primarily those with adults in the community. Judgments about the likelihood of a nuclear war remaining limited in scope were not affected for adults, but they were sometimes decreased for college students. Many studies asked about respondents' efficacy to prevent wars, and though this usually was not affected, it sometimes decreased following the film. However, behavioral intentions to try to help prevent wars were found to increase after the movie in most studies, particularly among its viewers.

A wide variety of other attitudes and beliefs about nuclear war were investigated in many studies, and in most instances they were not found to change. For example, greater support for arms control, which was widely expected to result from the film, was found only to a small degree in a few studies. Findings on this and other variables often demonstrated the occurrence of contrary and offsetting changes among different sectors of the public. Beliefs about U.S. defense policies and attitudes toward world leaders also showed mixed results, with different respondent groups changing in different directions. Other beliefs that generally showed little change included the effectiveness of civil defense, beliefs about Russian policies and goals, and the risks of nuclear terrorism or accidents. However, the movie was not about these topics, and so there was no logical reason to expect that they would change.

Importantly, the most frequent kinds of changes were found not only for viewers of the film, but also for nonviewers in several studies, though viewers often changed a bit more. This pattern makes it clear that much of the movie's impact came through the widespread publicity, controversy, and discussion that it engendered. When these factors were studied differentially, it was found that the *Viewpoint* panel discussions added to viewers' worries and doubts about U.S. defense policies and budget increases. The widespread media coverage of nuclear war issues stemming from *The Day After* increased respondents' self-reported knowledge, their frequency of thoughts about nuclear war, and their favorability toward arms control steps. Personal discussions about the movie by nonviewers increased their thoughts about nuclear war, just as watching the movie did for viewers. Viewers also became more convinced of the disastrous consequences of a nuclear war. Three other effects of the movie, all of which interacted with viewers' educational level, involved the amount of worry about U.S. defenses against nuclear war, the support for defense spending, and the degree of approval of Reagan's handling of foreign policy. In all three cases, poorly educated viewers changed toward a higher score on these topics, whereas college-educated or postgraduate viewers changed in a negative direction. These offsetting changes may help to explain why some studies found few or weak overall effects of the film.

Several studies that gave delayed posttests to investigate the persistence of belief and attitude changes found that a substantial majority of the significant initial changes remained significant for weeks or months afterward—an impressive indication of the power of the movie and its accompanying publicity and discussion.

In studies that examined demographic factors before the movie was shown, women frequently were found to be more opposed to nuclear war and more anxious about it than men and to display other related attitudinal differences. Following the broadcast, several studies found greater changes by women on various relevant dimensions. Other demographic factors were occasionally found to be related to attitudes or change scores, but in general, the studies summarized in this chapter did not emphasize an individual-difference approach to their data. The several studies that considered possible research artifacts that might have affected the data generally concluded that neither pretest sensitization of respondents, sample attrition, nor interviewer effects posed any major threats to the validity of the findings.

B. Limitations and Implications of the Research Reports

With all of these findings concerning the effects of *The Day After*, then, why did the early instant-analysis studies report that the movie had practically no effect on public attitudes? Partly, it was a matter of selective media reporting of their results, for they did find a number of large and/or significant effects, but those were not emphasized in the press accounts. Another factor, particularly in W. C. Adams *et al*.'s study (3), was the timing of the pretest, only an hour before the program, when much of the public had already undergone anticipatory attitude and belief changes as a result of all the publicity and controversy about nuclear war issues that preceded the airing of the film; thus, the study missed all of those changes. Also, the fact that the film had differing and often offsetting effects on different groups of people contributed to some of the research conclusions that it had little overall effect. Finally, a crucial reason for the absence of reported changes in several studies was that they did not ask the right questions. Two did not ask about attitudes or beliefs concerning nuclear issues at all (1, 4), and others focused largely on attitude topics that were important but that the film did not address, such as the cause of nuclear wars, how best to prevent them, the desirability of a nuclear freeze, or the merits of the Reagan administration's policies. Communication research findings have shown that media effects are usually confined to issues that are the specific focus of a program (Kaid, Towers, & Myers,

1981; Robinson, 1976), and several of the present studies have reached similar conclusions (12, 17, 24; Fiske, 1985; Schofield & Pavelchak, 1985).

Thus, important implications for future media research of this sort include these two points: Ask the right questions (ones that are relevant to the message), and analyze individual differences in responses to the communication. The findings of several studies discussed here are consistent with much past research on attitude polarization in indicating that the same message can produce changes in opposite directions for people who start at different points on an attitude continuum. However, none of these studies—except possibly Feldman and Sigelman (12)—gave any thorough attention to individual differences as a factor mediating attitude changes.

Among the later reports on *The Day After* that were done in academic settings, there were also differences in the comprehensiveness and care of the research, as well as in the relevance of the research questions to the program's content. In general, it seems that the studies that reported weaker effects were apt to have a limited number of variables, variables that were not relevant to the program, or less complete data analyses. Another factor that probably contributed to less dramatic findings was that all the preceding publicity for the program had raised people's expectations of it to such a pitch that its actual content, although impressive, was judged by many as anticlimactic and somewhat disappointing (11). However, the fact that most attitude and belief changes that were significant persisted for a period of weeks or months is further evidence of the film's impact.

The size of the effects that were significant is another important consideration. The estimated figures given in Table III show that, though the power of these effects was sometimes small, a majority of them reached a d-index figure of .3 or more, and several were in the .5 to .8 range. In comparison with metaanalysis studies in the literature, these are very respectable levels (Glass et al., 1981).

Who changed most as a result of the film? Unfortunately, no studies made careful analyses of individual differences, and few looked at demographic differences in much detail. However, there is suggestive evidence that younger viewers and those who were less experienced and less politically involved were more influenced by the film (14, 23, 25). [W. C. Adams's contrary conclusion about the lack of age differences (3) may be a result of the timing of the pretest, which caused anticipatory attitude changes to be ignored.] Certainly, much past research on attitude formation and persuasion processes indicates that young people are apt to have less information, less rigid attitudes, and greater susceptibility to influence than most adults (see, e.g., Himmelweit, Oppenheim, & Vince, 1958). A surprising number of the college viewers in these studies indicated that they knew little or had thought little about nuclear war and related defense issues, and the ones who indicated they had learned the most from the movie were frequently the ones who said they were most moved to take actions to prevent a future war (Schofield & Pavelchak, 1985).

A particularly important question is whether changes in attitudes and beliefs will be carried over into people's everyday behavior. Because these studies were nonobservational, the closest approximation to behavioral change that could be studied was in behavioral intentions or commitment statements about future actions to help prevent nuclear wars. It is interesting and important that this category of changes was significant in most of the studies that investigated it. However, past research findings on the effects of fear-arousing communications clearly indicate that if high levels of behavioral change are the goal, it is necessary to give specific, detailed recommendations of actions that people can take that will be effective in reducing their fear (see, e.g., Leventhal, 1970). Thus, with behavioral change as the goal, one would design a film with different content from *The Day After*. In addition to arousing fear by showing the disastrous consequences of nuclear war, one would want to point out specific ways available to viewers in which they can help to reduce the threat of war (Reser & Wallace, 1985).

To the extent that *The Day After* did produce changes in viewers' attitudes, beliefs, and behavior, it probably accomplished it by means of two cognitive processes: by making specific ideas about nuclear war more salient (that is, more readily available in viewers' thoughts), and by making the abstract concept of nuclear war concrete and personal. Topics and ideas that are more cognitively available are more apt to be used in people's everyday decisions and actions (Tversky & Kahneman, 1974), and images of nuclear war that are concrete have been found to be more likely to lead to antinuclear political action (Fiske, Pratto, & Pavelchak, 1983). It appears that such images in *The Day After* have moved many viewers to new attitudes and to contemplate taking relevant new actions (Fiske, 1985).

In considering the size of media effects, it is well to keep in mind that corporations often spend millions of dollars for advertising just to increase their market share of a product by 1 or 2%. If, similarly, only 1% of the viewers of *The Day After* changed their attitudes and actions afterwards, that would still be *one million* people who were affected—enough to have a potent impact on current affairs, if they actually acted on their beliefs.

C. Conclusion: A Media Event

As described earlier, *The Day After* was a unique media event. It not only had a huge audience and unprecedented publicity, but it also marked the first time that issues concerning nuclear war had been presented to a broad U.S. public in network television entertainment. Thus, it may represent a never-to-be-repeated phenomenon, because later shows of a similar sort, like the

British movie *Threads*, will not be "firsts" and consequently will not get the same all-encompassing media publicity. Certainly it had most of the key characteristics—a huge audience, high credibility, and a clear thematic approach—that have been described as explanations for the power of network news programs to help shape the public's political agenda (Feldman & Sigelman, 1985; Robinson, 1976).

What did the program accomplish? The studies summarized here show that it did have at least short-term powerful effects on citizens' beliefs, attitudes, and behavioral intentions, and that all of its accompanying by-products in media and personal communication noticeably affected many persons—even people who did not see it. In addition, it generated a variety of public and semipublic behaviors relevant to preventing war, which have been summarized by Schofield and Pavelchak (1985). Perhaps the most striking example is that 50,000 people called a toll-free number within the next week to follow up on television ads about getting information to help lessen the chances of war ("Fallout From," 1983).

Thus, a major part of *The Day After*'s importance stems from the tremendous public attention that it won. As Comstock (1984) put it,

> The publicity, the controversy, the news coverage, the promotion—all these made *The Day After* a media event for which the experiencing of the film itself was unnecessary and irrelevant. The most likely effect of *The Day After* was...its success in television's own terms—the capturing briefly on a scale unprecedented a few decades ago of public attention.

ACKNOWLEDGMENTS

This article was prepared during a sabbatical leave at the University of New South Wales in Sydney, Australia. Grateful thanks for their many kindnesses are extended to my hosts and colleagues there: Keith Llewellyn, Laurence Brown, Joseph Forgas, and John Taplin. I am also grateful to my Claremont Graduate School collaborators in our original research on *The Day After*: Jeanne King, Shawn Burn, Alison Konrad, John Pollard, and Michael White, and to Vera Dunwoody-Miller, Lynn Macbride, Anita Kantak, and Aaron Cohen, who also assisted in that effort.

Most of all, I am indebted to the many researchers who sent me preprints of their still-unpublished studies. Their names appear in the tables, and their papers are listed in the references to this article.

REFERENCES

ABC, Inc., Social Research Unit. (undated). *The social impact of "The Day After": A summary of research findings*. Unpublished paper. New York: Author.

Adams, R. C., & Webber, G. M. (1984). The audience for, and male vs. female reactions to, The Day After. *Journalism Quarterly*, **61**, 812–816.

Adams, W. C., Smith, D. J., Salzman, A., Crossen, R., Hieber, S., Naccarato, T., Valenzuela, R., Vantine, W., & Weisbroth, N. (1984, May). *Before and after "The Day After": A nationwide survey of a movie's political impact.* Paper presented at the meeting of the International Communication Association, San Francisco.

Attanasio, P. (1983, December 5). Big bang, little box. *New Republic,* pp. 13-14.

An audience of 100 million. (1983, December 5). *U.S. News and World Report,* p. 52.

Backstrom, C. H., & Hursh-Cesar, G. (1981). *Survey research* (2nd ed.). New York: Wiley.

Baumann, D. J., Bettor, L. L., Curtis, S. M., Heller, L. S., Lamb, N. F., Ritter, B. E., Roberts, C. M., Wessels, D. G., & Wiebe, A. (1984, August). *The Day After: An experimental investigation of media impact.* Paper presented at the annual meeting of the American Psychological Association, Toronto.

Brown, J. M. (1984, August). *Attitudes toward violence and the film "The Day After."* Paper presented at the annual meeting of the American Psychological Association, Toronto.

Cialdini, R. B., & Petty, R. E. (1981). Anticipatory opinion effects. In R. E. Petty, T. M. Ostrom, & T. C. Brock (Eds.), *Cognitive responses in persuasion.* Hillsdale, NJ: Erlbaum.

Comstock, G. (1984). The Day After—Influence?... Perhaps not much: Some communications principles. *Television and Children,* **7**(1), 40-42.

Cooper, H. M. (1984). *The integrative research review: A systematic approach.* Beverly Hills, CA: Sage.

Cross, T. P., & Saxe, L. (1984, August). *The Day After: Report of a survey of effects of viewing and beliefs about nuclear war.* Paper presented at the annual meeting of the American Psychological Association, Toronto.

Ehrlichman, H., & Kobasa, S. C. O. (1984, August). *Thoughts and feelings about nuclear war among college students.* Paper presented at the annual meeting of the American Psychological Association, Toronto.

Fallout from a TV attack: After all the hype, *The Day After* raised more questions than it answered. (1983, December 5). *Time,* pp. 38-40.

Farber, S. (1983, November 13). How a nuclear holocaust was staged for TV. *New York Times,* pp. H1, H34.

Feldman, S., & Sigelman, L. (1985). The political impact of prime-time television: "The Day After." *Journal of Politics,* **47**, 556-578.

Fenwick, R. (1984, May). *Did "The Day After" have any effect?* Roundtable session at the meeting of the American Association for Public Opinion Research, Delavan, WI.

Fishbein, M., & Ajzen, I. (1975). *Belief, attitude, intention, and behavior: An introduction to theory and research.* Reading, MA: Addison-Wesley.

Fiske, S. T. (1985). Adult beliefs, feelings, and actions regarding nuclear war: Evidence from surveys and experiments. In *Proceedings of the Symposium on Medical Implications of Nuclear War.* Washington, DC: Institute of Medicine, National Academy of Sciences.

Fiske, S. T., Pratto, F., & Pavelchak, M. A. (1983). Citizens' images of nuclear war: Content and consequences. *Journal of Social Issues,* **39**(1), 41-65.

French, P. L., & Van Hoorn, J. (1988). Half a nation saw nuclear war and nobody blinked? A reassessment of the impact of *The Day After* in terms of theoretical chains of causality. *International Journal of Mental Health,* in press.

Funderburk, C., Karns, D., & Walker, J. L. (1984, May). *Did "The Day After" have any effect?* Roundtable session at the meeting of the American Association for Public Opinion Research, Delavan, WI.

Glass, G., McGaw, B., & Smith, M. (1981). *Meta-analysis in social research.* Beverly Hills, CA: Sage.

Goodman, L. A., Mack, J. E., Beardslee, W. R., & Snow, R. M. (1983). The threat of nuclear war and the nuclear arms race: Adolescent experience and perceptions. *Political Psychology,* **4**, 501-530.

Goodman, L. M. (1984, August). *Attitudes to nuclear war: Before and after "The Day After."* Paper presented at the annual meeting of the American Psychological Association, Toronto.

Granberg, D., & Faye, N. (1972). Sensitizing people by making the abstract concrete. *American Journal of Orthopsychiatry*, **42**, 811-815.

Gunter, B., & Wober, M. (1988). The impact of *"The Day After"* on public beliefs about nuclear war: A British study. *Public Opinion Quarterly*, in press.

Gutierres, S. E., McCullough, G. W., Marney-Hay, R., Petty, R., Baumann, D. J., & Trost, M. (1984, August). *Impact of "The Day After" on those closest to it*. Paper presented at the annual meeting of the American Psychological Association, Toronto.

A hard look/The impact of a nuclear war film. (1983, November 13). *San Francisco Sunday Examiner and Chronicle*, pp. A1, A6.

Himmelweit, H. T., Oppenheim, A. N., & Vince, P. (1958). *Television and the child*. London: Oxford University Press.

J. Walter Thompson U.S.A., Media Resources and Research. (1983, December). *The Day After: A gamble that paid off*. Unpublished paper. New York: Author.

Kaatz, R. B. (1984). The Day After: A gamble that paid off—An advertiser's assessment. *Television and Children*, **7**(1), 37-39.

Kaid, L. L., Towers, W. M., & Myers, S. L. (1981). Television docudrama and political cynicism: A study of *Washington: Behind Closed Doors. Social Science Quarterly*, **62**, 161-168.

Katz, E., & Feldman, J. J. (1962). The debates in light of research: A survey of surveys. In S. Kraus (Ed.), *The great debates: Kennedy vs. Nixon* (pp. 173-223). Bloomington: Indiana University Press.

Knap, T. (1983, November 22). *"Day After"* impact slight, poll finds. *Pittsburgh Press*, A, p. 12.

Kulman, I. R., & Akamatsu, T. J. (1984, August). *The effects of television on large scale attitude change: Viewing "The Day After."* Paper presented at the annual meeting of the American Psychological Association, Toronto.

Leventhal, H. (1970). Findings and theory in the study of fear communications. In L. Berkowitz (Ed.), *Advances in experimental social psychology* (Vol. 5, pp. 119-186). New York: Academic Press.

Lewis, A. (1983, November 26). The question after. *New York Times*, p. 19.

Lometti, G., & Feig, E. (1984). The Day After—Caring about children: The role of audience research. *Television and Children*, **7**(1), 32-36.

Malcolm, A. (1983, November 18). Scenes from *"Day After"* haunt Kansas town. *St. Petersburg Times*, A, pp. 1, 4.

Mayton, D. M., II. (1984, August). *The Day After: A quasi-experimental study of its impact*. Paper presented at the annual meeting of the American Psychological Association, Toronto.

McClenney, J. T., & Allbright, L. (1985, August). *Psychological responses to the threat of nuclear war: Structural modeling of the relationships between attitudes and behavior*. Paper presented at the annual meeting of the American Psychological Association, Los Angeles.

McFadden, R. (1983, November 22). TV atom war spurs vast discussion. *New York Times*, p. 11.

Mermigas, D. (1983, November 21). Controversy lingers a "day after"; Falwell vows ad boycott. *Advertising Age*, pp. 1, 68.

Meyer, N. (1983, November 19-25). Bringing the unwatchable to TV. *TV Guide*, pp. 6-12.

Mueller, J. E. (1973). *War, presidents and public opinion*. New York: Wiley.

Nelson, L. L., & Slem, C. M. (1984, August). *Attitudes about arms control and effects of "The Day After."* Paper presented at the annual meeting of the American Psychological Association, Toronto.

The nightmare comes home: ABC's movie *The Day After* stirs a storm of nuclear debate. (1983, October 24). *Time*, pp. 84-86.

Oskamp, S., King, J. C., Burn, S. M., Konrad, A. M., Pollard, J. A., & White, M. A. (1985). The media and nuclear war: Fallout from TV's *"The Day After."* In S. Oskamp (Ed.), *Applied social psychology annual: Vol. 6. International conflict and national public policy issues*. Beverly Hills, CA: Sage.

Paletz, D. L., & Vinegar, R. J. (1977). Presidents on television: Effects of instant analysis. *Public Opinion Quarterly*, **41**, 488-499.

Pavelchak, M. A., & Schofield, J. W. (1984, August). *The Day After: Before and after*. Paper presented at the annual meeting of the American Psychological Association, Toronto.

Plous, S. (1984). *Psychological and strategic barriers in present attempts at nuclear disarmament: A new proposal*. Unpublished manuscript, Stanford University, Department of Psychology, Palo Alto, CA.

Reser, J. P. (1984, October). *Thinking the unthinkable: Impact of the film "The Day After" on the imageability of a nuclear holocaust*. Paper presented at the meeting of the New Zealand Psychological Society, Palmerston North.

Reser, J. P., & Wallace, N. (1985). *Do film images mediate attitude change? Impact of the film "The Day After" on an Australian audience*. Unpublished manuscript, James Cook University, Townsville, Queensland, Australia.

Robinson, M. J. (1976). Public affairs television and the growth of political malaise: The case of "The Selling of the Pentagon." *American Political Science Review*, **70**, 409-432.

Rogers, R. W. (1983). Cognitive and physiological processes in fear appeals and attitude change: A revised theory of protection motivation. In J. T. Cacioppo & R. E. Petty (Eds.), *Social psychophysiology*. New York: Guilford.

Schadler, M., Miranda, J., & Day, M. C. (1984, August). *Young persons view "The Day After."* Paper presented at the annual meeting of the American Psychological Association, Toronto.

Schofield, J., & Pavelchak, M. (1985). *The Day After*: The impact of a media event. *American Psychologist*, **40**, 542-548.

Sears, D. O., & Chaffee, S. H. (1979). Uses and effects of the 1976 debates: An overview of empirical studies. In S. Kraus (Ed.), *The great debates: Carter vs. Ford* (pp. 223-261). Bloomington: Indiana University Press.

Shales, T. (1983, November 18). Must viewing for the nation: Devastating images of horror. *Washington Post*, p. C1.

Sigelman, L., & Sigelman, C. K. (1984). Judgments of the Carter-Reagan debate: The eyes of the beholders. *Public Opinion Quarterly*, **48**, 624-628.

Singer, D. (1984). *The Day After*, catalyst for communication: A psychologist's perspective. *Television and Children*, **7**(1), 27-29.

Smith, D. D. (1984, May). *Cognitive psychology, information processing & "The Day After."* Paper presented at the meeting of the American Association for Public Opinion Research, Delavan, WI.

Sussman, B. (1983, December 5). "Day After" didn't hurt Reagan. *Washington Post National Weekly Edition*, p. 12.

Thomas, J. G., Zolik, E. S., Bartee, R. L., Watkins, P. L., Jason, L. A., Nicholas, J. E., & Perloff, L. S. (1984, August). *Impact of "The Day After" on residents at ground zero*. Paper presented at the annual meeting of the American Psychological Association, Toronto.

Turco, R. P., Toon, O. B., Ackerman, T. P., Pollack, J. B., & Sagan, C. (1983). Nuclear winter: Global consequences of multiple nuclear explosions. *Science*, **222**, 1283-1292.

Tversky, A., & Kahneman, D. (1974). Judgment under uncertainty: Heuristics and biases. *Science*, **185**, 1124-1131.

TV's nuclear nightmare. (1983, November 21). *Newsweek*, pp. 66-72.

Watts, W. A., & McGuire, W. J. (1964). Persistence of attitude change and retention of inducing message content. *Journal of Abnormal and Social Psychology*, **68**, 233-241.

Wolf, S., Gregory, W. L., & Stephan, W. G. (1984, August). *Protection motivation theory: The effects on behavioral intentions of "The Day After"*. Paper presented at the annual meeting of the American Psychological Association, Toronto.

Zolik, E. S., Thomas, J. G., Watkins, P. L., Bartee, R. L., Nicholas, J. E., Perloff, L. S., & Jason, L. A. (1984, August). *"The Day After": Consciousness raising for survival?* Paper presented at the annual meeting of the American Psychological Association, Toronto.

Zweigenhaft, R. L. (1984). What do Americans know about nuclear weapons? *Bulletin of the Atomic Scientists*, **40**(2), 48-50.

Index

A

Aaron, Henry, 279
ABC, 87, 88, 89, 293
Abel, G. G., 170
Abelson, R. P., 72
Acceptance of Interpersonal Violence (AIV), 182, 184, 185, 187, 191, 197
Acceptance of Women as Managers Scale (AWMS), 184
Action
  short- and long-term, 70
  versus violence, 121
Activating, networks of knowledge, 72
Active viewing, 111–114
Adams, W., 210, 345
Adler, R., 210
Adversarial Sexual Beliefs (ASB), 182, 185
Advertisement, 145
  and political campaigns, 208
  three types of, 134
Afrikaner, 17
  opposition to television, 2–3
Age
  changes in, distribution, 4, 8
  and price guidelines, 92
  violence in successively older groups, 25–26, 41–43
Agenda
  building, 80
  setting, 78, 79, 245–248, 262, 270–271
Ageton, S. S., 188, 189
Aggravated assault, 14
Aggregated data, hypotheses tested through, 45
Aggression
  attitudes of, 175–177
  laboratory, 187–188
  legitimizing, 190
  in naturalistic settings, 188–193

Air crash stories, 87–88
Airline Passengers Association, 89, 90
Airline Stewardesses Association, 90
Alcohol consumption, changes in, 5, 11
Alder, C., 190
Amish, and television, 16
Amount of invested mental effort (AIME), 112
Analysis
  cultivation, 239–240
  individual-level, 217
  instant, of *The Day After*, 301–307
  limits of content, 220–226
  refraction, 273–276
  time-series, 249–253
  units of, 256
Anderson, D. R., 120, 123, 130
Animation, 125
Antisocial behavior
  against women, 163
  environmental influences on, 163
  from thought patterns to, 185–194
Arabs and Jews, 94
Arousal theory, 150
Arrest rates, change in, 42, 43
Artificiality
  of attentiveness, 216
  of context, 216
  of stimuli, 215
Asch, Solomon, 248
Assimilation, 72
Associated Press (AP), 64
Attention
  artificially high levels of, 216
  auditory, 127–129
  gender differences in, 122
  model of, 117–118
  recruit and maintain, 119
Attitudes
  about U.S. defense policies, 332–333

353

aggressive, 175–177
beyond, 236–240
change versus creation of, 216
ideological, 174–177
measurement of, 218
nuclear beliefs and, 305, 322–323, 330–332, 336–338
psychological, 76
rape, 187, 194
social and media, 195
toward Reagan, 306
toward world leaders, 333
versus beliefs and behavior, 217
Attitudes Toward Wife Abuse, 197
Attitudes Toward Women Scale (ATWS), 184, 197
Audiences
active, 241
attracting largest, 63
direct influence on, 79
gap between journalists and, 62
sexual violence and arousal in, 169–172
size of, 120
Auditory
attention, 127–129
and visual attributes, 106
Availability, of sexually explicit media, 168

B

Bachen, C. M., 237
Bagdikian, B., 210
Ball-Rokeach, S. J., 210, 231
Bandura, A., 165
Barnett, A., 44
Barriers
to information flow, 61
removal of information, 62
Batman, 132
"The Battle of the Britain," 214
Baxter, R. L., 168
Becker, L., 78, 236, 237, 248
Behavior, attitudes versus belief and, 217
Behavioral response, complexity of, 234
Beliefs
about U.S. defense policies, 332–333
attitudes versus behavior and, 217
nuclear, and attitudes, 305, 322–323, 330–332, 336–338
Belson, W. A., 51

Beniger, James, 261
Bennett, L., 70, 73, 91, 94
Bentley, P. M., 196
Berelson, B., 208, 217, 218, 226, 242
Bishop, G. F., 210, 238
Block, Eva, 265
Blockade, 92
Blumler, Jay, 82, 241, 243
Bobo dolls, 215
Boezio, S. L., 194
Born Innocent, 162
Boundaries, blurring of, 257
Brice, P., 194
Briere, J., 163, 168, 178, 180
British Broadcasting System (BBC), 68, 83
Brody, Richard, 276
Brown, J. R., 243
Brownmiller, S., 165
Bryant, J., 210
Buchanan, Patrick, 82
Bullet theory, 231–232
Burke, Kenneth, 69
Burt, M. R., 187, 194
Byrnes, J. E., 248

C

Calder, B. J., 24
Calvert, S. L., 124
Canada, 29, 30
capital punishment in, 11
compared to South Africa and United States, 17–18
homicide rates in, 3
sexually explicit media in, 168–169
television and homicide in, 5–8
television programs in United States and, 18
Cantor, M. G., 210
Capital punishment, changes in, 5, 11–12
Capsulization, 96
Captain Kangaroo, 149
Carter. *See* President Carter
Cartoons, violence in, 104
Case population, South Africa, 16–17
CASTLE, 222
Causal
inference from field stories, 228
relationship between television and violence, 47

CBS, 88, 89
Ceiling-effect phenomenon, 252
Ceniti, J., 179
Central archive, lack of, 225
Chaffee, Steven, 209, 236, 260
Characters, 70
Check, J. V. P., 171, 180, 188
Children
  animation for, 125
  comprehension of gender connotations by, 135-136
  comprehension of television form for, 129-141
  comprehension of television syntax by, 130
  developmental changes in, 114-115
  developmental differences in, 132
  instant replay for, 131
  language forms on television for, 109-110
  schemas for, 112
  segmental cues for, 130-131
  selection of content for, 143-145
  separators and boundary markers for, 132
  television programs for, 108-109
  understanding media syntax by, 132
Children and Social Television Learning. See CASTLE
Civil unrest, changes in, 12
Clarke, Peter, 236, 237, 244
Coding, simplistic, schemes, 225
Cognition, and learning, 236-238
Cognitive
  goal-directed, activity, 113
  operations on television material, 111-112
  processing, 126
  shift in, functioning, 115
  skills as domain specific, 115
Coleman, James, 256
Collins, A., 112
Collins, W. A., 123
Combs, J., 87
Commission on the Freedom of the Press, 65
Commission on Obscenity and Pornography (1970), 160
Commission on Pornography (1986), 160
Communication
  complexity of, 233-234, 255
  effects, 213-235, 253-254, 277-278
  environment, 234
  flow, 232, 272-273

  freedom, 95
  research, 208, 210, 235-253
  social problems orientation of, 278-279
  symbolic, 239
  unintentional, 240
  word-of-mouth, 76
Communication and Persuasion (Hovland et al.), 208
Communication Research, 236
Competing interest groups, 88
Complexity
  of behavioral response, 234
  of stimuli, 215
Comprehension, 73
  children's, of gender connotations, 135-136
  of television form, 129-141
  of content and formal features, 141-147
  news, research, 83-95
  of television syntax by children, 130
Comprehensive studies, on *The Day After*, 307-322
Comstock, G., 210, 212, 256
Conceptual processing, 113
Conflict
  over Vietnam War, 12
  social, narrows knowledge gap, 77
  stories, 99
Connections, hypothesized, 185-187
Connotations
  gender, of television form, 133-136
  reality versus fiction, 136
Constraints
  of convenience, 227-228
  on news story production, 65
Content
  complexity of communications, 233, 255
  conceptualizing, 145-146
  formal features and comprehension of, 141-147
  form differs from, 106, 120, 121
  informative qualities of form and, 123-124
  limits of, analysis, 220-226
  media, as social indicators, 261
  parallel, analysis, 209-213
  selection of central, 143-145
Content analysis, 133-134
  computerized, 225
  distraction of adversarial, 224
  limits of, 220-226

as methodological ghetto, 223
parallel, 209-213, 253-280
"Content Analysis" (Janowitz), 207
Context, artificiality of, 216
Convenience, constraints of, 227-228
Convergent findings, lack of, 224
Cook, T. D., 24
Coombs, S. L., 210
Cooper, E., 215
Corne, S., 180
Cox, Archibald, 80
Cree Indians, 50
Crime, pornography and, 162
Criminal acts, frequency of television viewing and, 22
Critical school, 240
Criticism, in news stories, 89, 90
Cultivation analysis, 239-240
Cultural
  climate, 164
  indicators, 264-270
  influences reinforce sexual violence, 164
Cultural Indicators (Melischek et al.), 264
Curran, J., 210

D

D'Alessio, D., 168
Data collection, method of, 300
Davis, D., 210
The Day After
  conditions of broadcasting, 295-296
  demographic comparisons on, 340-341
  evaluations of, 304
  instant-analysis reports on, 301-307
  making of, 293-294
  more comprehensive studies on, 307-309
  as "political" movie, 304
  public opinion changes after, 306-307
  quantitative analysis of, 298
  reactions to, 323-324, 338-339
  research reports on, 298-301
DC-10 crash, 87, 89, 98
Deciding What's News (Gans), 210
Decoding, of new information, 72, 73
Deep processing, 72, 73
Defense policies, attitudes and beliefs about, 332-333
De Fleur, M. L., 76, 84, 231
Del Rosario, M. L., 24

Demare, D., 168, 180, 183
Demographic
  comparisons on *The Day After*, 340-341
  variables on *The Day After*, 322
Dependent variable
  broader definition of, 239
  and *The Day After*, 301
Dependent variables, narrowly defined, 231
DeRiemer, C. D., 168
Desensitization, 184
Deutsch, K. W., 259
Developmental
  changes in children, 114-115
  changes and media experience, 139-140
  differences in children, 132
DeWeese, L. C., 259
Diagnosis, of homicide, 19-20
Dialogue, 107
Differential effects, 241
Diffusion, media characteristics and, 167-169
Diversion, 242
Domain specific, 115, 139
Donohue, G. A., 77, 85
Dramatist theory, 69-71
Dramatization, 99
Dr. Who, 138

E

Economic
  changes in, conditions, 4, 9
  prosperity and violence, 46
  public knowledge of, system, 60
Edelman, M., 70, 73, 91, 94
Education, 77
Educational daytime programs, 108, 110
Effects
  accumulation of, over time, 239
  beyond direct, 241-249
  of communication, 213-235
  contingent, 244
  of *The Day After* on attitudes and beliefs, 325-333
  definition of communications, 253-254, 277-278
  differential, 241, 334-336
  indirect, model, 162, 163-165
  interviewer, 343
  lost in measurement noise, 228-231
  a movie's separate, 335-336

short-term media, 276
of television forms, 141
time frame of, 234
of *Viewpoint*, 326
The Effects of Mass Communication (Kraus and Davis), 210
The Effects of Television Advertising (Adler et al.), 210
Efron, Edith, 224
The Emergence of American Political Issues (McCombs and Shaw), 246
England, 29, 30. *See also* Great Britain
Entman, R. M., 210
Environment
  communications, 234
  influences of, on antisocial behavior, 163
  research in natural, 255
  social, 60, 61
  surveillance of, 242
Erbring, L., 246
Eron, L. D., 51, 52, 194
Error
  measurement, 219
  Type II statistical, 220
Ettema, J. S., 252
Experimental research
  on form and social behavior, 148-151
  limits of, 214-217
  on sexually violent media, 161, 181-185
Experiments on Mass Communication (Hovland et al.), 208
Exploration, 114
Exposure
  frequency of, to sexually explicit media, 168-169
  interacts with other influences, 181
  media, to thought patterns, 180-185
  to media coverage of nuclear war, 334
  sexual responsiveness and media, 178-179
External control population
  Canada as, 17
  United States as, 17
Eyal, C. H., 270

F

Falsifiable hypotheses, 44
  need to test, 23
  See also Hypotheses

Falwell, Jerry, 295, 298
Fat Albert and the Cosby Kids, 145
Fazio, R. H., 186
Feature-signal hypothesis, 124-125
Federal Aviation Administration (FAA), 88, 89
Field research, limits of, 226-231
Finland, 29, 30, 49
Firearms, availability of, 5, 13-15
Firestone, J. M., 259
Fischer, C., 130
Fischer, P., 194
Fisher, W. A., 184, 185
Fishman, M., 65
Five principles, of communications effects, 233-235
Focusing operations, 110
Force, 174, 191
Formal features
  of audience size, 120
  and comprehension of content, 141-147
  roles of, 126
  of visual attention, 118-120
Forms
  child and adult, 121
  differ from content, 106, 120, 121
  effects of television, 141
  language, on children's television, 109-110
  as processing aids, 142-146
  television, 106-111, 116-117
  and social behavior, 147-151
Freedman, J. L., 187
Functional theory, 241
Funkhouser, G., 84
The Future of Political Science (Lasswell), 207

G

Galvanic skin response (GSR), 127
Gamson, W. A., 212, 271
Gans, H. J., 63, 64, 65, 210, 271
Gender
  connotations, 133-136, 135-136
  differences in attention, 122
  homicide rates and, 29
  violence and, 40, 41
The General Inquirer, 223, 225, 259
Gerbner, G., 223, 239, 240, 259, 260, 274

Gitlin, T., 210
Glass, G., 298
Goffman, Erving, 66
Goldenberg, E. N., 246
Graber, D., 81, 85, 212, 247, 272
Graber, Doris, 74
Granzberg, G., 50
The Great American Values Test (Ball-Rokeach et al.), 210
Great Britain
  obscene films in, 169
  See also England
Greenberg, B. S., 168, 210, 222, 223
Greenfield, Meg, 261
"Greenfield Index," 261
Grenier, G., 184, 185
Gross, N. C., 249
Group membership, 76, 77
Gurevitch, M., 210, 241
Gutierres, S. E., 337

H

Hall, E. R., 194
Hardt, Hanno, 206, 208
Hearold, S., 187
Heath, L., 24
Hennigan, K. M., 24
Herzog, H., 241
High-tech search, 87
Himmelweit, H. T., 210
Historical correlation, inferences from, 229
Holsti, O. R., 223
Homicide
  diagnosis of, 19-20
  as intraracial, 19, 28
  and physical aggressiveness, 20, 26
  television and, 5-8, 23
Homicide rates, 7
  per 100,000 population, 37, 41
  1955 television sets and, 35, 36
  changes in, 3
  of exposed population, 26
  by gender, 29
  measured by two methods, 25, 32
  by population of city, 38, 39, 40
  by race, 28, 37, 39-40, 46
  and television, 6, 15, 20-22, 27, 30, 34
  and urban distribution, 10
  by weapon, 14, 16

Homicide victimization, trends in, 18-19
Hostility Toward Women (HTW), 191, 192
Hovland, C. I., 208
Howard, J. A., 194
How Voters Decide (Himmelweit et al.), 210
Huesmann, L. R., 52, 194
Hughes, H. M., 226
Human frailty and endurance, 88
Human interest stories, 99
Huston, A. C., 124, 125, 128
Hypotheses
  tested through aggregated data, 45
  three major, 25-29
  See also Falsifiable hypotheses

I

Ideological
  attitudes, 174-177
  bias in news, 68
Individual differences, 174-175
  among rapists, 171-172
Inference
  central problem of, 223
  from historical correlation, 229
  problematic causal, from field studies, 228
Information
  age of, 60
  barriers to, flow, 61
  contradicting schemas, 74
  decoding of new, 72
  diffusion of, 249-250, 260
  effects of *The Day After* on, 325
  gap theory, 251-253
  journalism in, age, 63-66
  manipulating release of, 65
  "nonlinear" method of presenting, 103
  in previous eras, 61
  processing theory, 71-75
  removal of, barriers, 62
  strategic rituals to gather, 64
  television as, medium, 60
  transmitting, 76
  two kinds of, getting, 114, 116
  See also Public knowledge
Informative qualities, of form and content, 123-124
Ingelfinger, F. J., 2
Initial decoding, of new information, 72

Index

Instant replay, 131
Interest
  level of, 77
  model of, 117-118
Interest groups, competing, 88
Interpretation, of communication, 233-234
Intraracial phenomenon, homicide as, 19
Iran-Contra affair, 82
Israel, 29, 31, 49
Iyengar, S., 74, 75

J

Jahoda, M., 215
Janis, I., 208
Janowitz, Morris, 207, 208, 223, 225, 257, 261
Jessor, R., 195
Jessor, S. L., 195
Jews and Arabs, 94
Johnson, P., 259
Johnson. *See* President Johnson
Journalism
  in the information age, 63-66
  "user friendly," 95-100
  See also Journalists
Journalists
  gap between, and audiences, 62
  ideological bias among, 68
  lack of self-analysis by, 65
  as libertarians, 95
  and norms of public service, 64
  responsibility of, to inform, 95-96
  See also Journalism
Joy, L. A., 2, 50
Jury studies, 196
J. Walter Thompson (JWT), 301

K

Katz, E., 208, 241
Kelley, H. H., 208
Kennedy, Ted, 92
Kennedy assassination, 76
Kibbutz, 49
Kimball, M. M., 2, 50
Kinder, D. R., 74, 75
Kirby, M., 168
Klapper, J. T., 209

Klein, R., 194
Kleitman, D. J., 44
Kline, Jerry, 236, 237, 244, 252
Knowledge
  gap hypothesis, 77-78
  preexisting, 77
  See also Public knowledge
Koss, M. P., 180
Kraus, S., 210
Krippendorff, K., 223
Krull, R., 127
Kruttschnitt, C., 52
Kuhn, Thomas, 209

L

Landini, A., 168
Lane, R. E., 212
Lang, G. E., 80, 273
Lang, K., 80, 273
Language, forms on children's television, 109-110
The Language of Politics (Lasswell), 207
Larsen, O. N., 76, 84
Larson, R. C., 44
Lasswell, Harold, 207, 223, 257, 261
Lazarsfeld, Paul, 208, 241
Leaflets, 76
Learning
  cognition and, 236-238
  differences, 77
  from television, 105
  as participatory, 113
  as receptive, 113
  story themes and, 87-95
  two types of, 71
Leary, A., 136
Lepper, M. R., 73
Leslie, L., 168
Libertarianism, 95
Lichter, L. S., 210
Lichter, S. R., 210
Life on Television (Greenberg), 210, 223
Likelihood of Sexual Harassment (LSH), 197
Limitations
  in news production, 65
  of research reports on *The Day After*, 345-347
  of social construction of reality, 69

Linz, D., 183
Lippmann, W., 239
Lips, H., 168
Literature, on television and aggression, 48–53
Literature, Popular Culture and Society (Lowenthal), 264–265
"Little people," troubles of, 88, 89
Locale and sample, 300
Lorch, E. P., 120, 124
Love, G., 168
Lowenthal, Leo, 264–265
Lowry, D. T., 168
Lumsdaine, A. A., 208
Luxury commodity, television as, 45

M

MacArthur Day Parade, 274
McCombs, M. E., 78, 84, 236, 245, 246, 247, 270
McDowell, C. N., 132
McGaw, B., 298
McGovern, George, 80
McGuire, W. J., 195
MacKuen, M. B., 210, 270
McLeod, J., 78, 248
McLeod, J. M., 228, 236
McQuail, D., 82, 239, 243
Macrolevel analyses, 119
Malamuth, N. M.
  on exposure to sexual violence, 170, 171, 179, 180, 183
  on indirect-effects model, 163
  on likelihood of rape, 197
  on sexual aggression, 174, 178, 190–191
  on thought patterns and aggressive behavior, 187, 188
Manitoba, 50
Mannheim, Karl, 259, 261
Markoff, J., 223, 225
Marolla, J., 194
Marx, Karl, 261
Mass Communication and Society (Curran et al.), 210
The Mass Media Election (Patterson), 210
Mayberry, D., 132
"May Day Slogans in Soviet Russia," 221
Measurement
  attitude, 218

error, 219
  small effects lost in, noise, 228–231
  time-series, 256
Media
  availability of sexually explicit, 168
  characteristics and diffusion, 167–169
  content as social indicators, 261
  The Day After as, event, 347–348
  developmental changes and, experience, 139–140
  exposure to, coverage of nuclear war, 334
  exposure and sexual responsiveness, 178–179
  exposure to thought patterns, 180–185
  "messages," 161
  nonsexual, violence, 194–195
  predictions on *The Day After*, 294–295
  sexually violent, 161, 162, 167, 168–179
  short-term, effects, 276
  verdicts on *The Day After*, 296–297
Media Agenda-Setting in a Presidential Election (Weaver et al.), 210, 246
The Media Elite (Lichter et al.), 210
The Media Monopoly (Bagdikian), 210
Media Power Politics (Paletz and Entman), 210
Megatrends (Naisbitt), 259
Melischek, G., 264
Memory, 71, 73
Mental effort
  expenditure of, 112
  stimulating, 142–143
Merton, Robert, 241
"Messages," media, 161
Microlevel analyses, 119
Milavsky, J. R., 48, 51, 52, 210
Milgram, Stanley, 248
Miller, A. H., 246
Model
  of attention and interest, 117–118
  indirect-effects, 163–165
  input-output, 262
  multimethod, 254–255
Moral Majority, 295
More Than News (MacKuen and Coombs), 210
Motivational criteria, 126
Mr. Rogers' Neighborhood, 104, 110
MTV, 168
Muckraking, 88, 89
Mullins, L. E., 248

Index

Multimethod models, 254-255
"Multitel," 2, 50
Musarewa. *See* President Musarewa

N

Naisbitt, J., 225, 259
Narrative
  structure, 70, 81
  theory, 69-71
National Broadcasting Company (NBC), 48, 49, 88, 89, 162
Natural environment, research in, 255
Natural variation, 228
NBC. *See* National Broadcasting Company
The Netherlands, 50
Newcomb, H., 210
Newcomb, M. D., 196
News
  applications for, research, 100
  bias, 68
  comprehension, 83-95
  constraints on, story production, 65
  criticism in, stories, 89, 90
  current research on, 77-83
  design of future, research, 99
  diffusion studies, 76
  factors affecting flow of, 76
  ideological bias in, 68
  lack of self-analysis in, 65
  learning from, 77
  limitations in, production, 65
  narrative, 69-71, 81
  objective, 64
  organizations, 63-65
  recall of, 86-87, 90-95
  relevance of, stories, 99
  social construction of reality theorists on, 66-69
  stories, 70
  three theories of, 66-75
  tradition and ritual in, 64
Newsflow
  early, research, 75-77
  research findings on, 84-85
Newspaper reading, 242
The News Twisters (Efron), 224
New York Times, 80
Nicaragua, 93
Nimmo, D. D., 87

Nixon. *See* President Nixon
Noelle-Neumann, E., 79, 84, 247, 248-249
Norway House, 50
"Notel," 2, 23
Nuclear issues, attitudes and beliefs about, 330-332
Nuclear war
  emotions concerning, 326-328
  exposure to media coverage of, 334
  perceptions regarding, 328-330
  prevention of, 330

O

"Objective reality," 66
Objects, 70
Obscenity and Pornography, Commission on, 160
Olien, C. N., 77, 85
Orientations, toward social world, 75
Over the Wire and on TV (Robinson and Sheehan), 210, 222

P

Paisley, W. J., 210
Paletz, D. L., 210
Palmer, E. L., 132
Parallel content analysis, 209-213, 253-280
  models of, 266-267
  as research strategy, 257-264
Parsons, Talcott, 233
Participation, stimulating, 143
Participatory learning, 113
Passive viewing, 111-114
Patterson, T., 210
Peabody Picture Vocabulary Test, 139
The People's Choice (Lazarsfeld et al.), 208
Peplau, L. A., 187
Perceptions
  of *The Day After*, 335
  regarding nuclear war, 328-330
Perceptually salient features, 107, 119
Perceptual processing, 113
Personal, identity and relationships, 242
Personal Influence (Katz and Lazarsfeld), 208
Perspective, single "true," 68
Perspectives on Media Effects (Bryant and Zillmann), 210

PG-rated film, rape in, 161
Photographs, limitations of, 97
Physical aggression
  and homicide, 20, 26
  literature on television and, 48–53
  rates of, 2
  See also Sexual aggression
Piaget, 146
Plot, 70
Poland, 29, 49
Political
  advertising and, campaigns, 208
  cognition, 271–272
  public knowledge of, system, 60, 61
Political Communication (Chaffee), 260
Politics and the Professors (Aaron), 279
Population distribution, of aggression, 21
Pornography
  Commission on, 160
  and crime, 162
Preliminary Report (Weber), 206
President Carter, 90, 91, 92, 93
The Presidential Debates (Bishop et al.), 210, 238
Presidential popularity, 276–280
President Johnson, 277
President Musarewa, 91
President Nixon, 80, 277
President Reagan, 82
  attitudes toward, 306
Press, sociology of, 206
Prime-Time Television (Cantor), 210
Processing
  forms as, aids, 142–146
  perceptual versus conceptual, 113
Processing the News (Graber), 247, 272
Promotional communicators, 65
Props, 70
Protest, 92
Pryor, J. B., 196
Psychological attitudes, 76
Public
  journalists and norms of, 64
  opinion after *The Day After*, 306–307
Public Broadcasting System (PBS), 107
Public Communication Campaigns (Rice and Paisley), 210
Public ignorance
  journalists and, 62–63
  and technology, 61
  See also Public knowledge

Public knowledge
  distribution of, 61
  of political and economic system, 60, 61
  technology and, 61
  See also Information; Knowledge; Public ignorance

Q

Quebec separatist movement, 12
Quinsey, V. L., 170

R

Race, homicide rates and, 28, 37, 39–40, 46
Rapaczynski, W. S., 50
Rape, 171–172
  attitudes of three groups, 194
  condoning attitude, 187
  date, 189
  imitation, 162
  index, 170
  likelihood of, 197
  in PG-rated film, 161
  positive versus negative, portrayals, 181, 182
  tumescence, index, 191, 192
  two theories on, 172–174
Rape Myth Acceptance (RMA), 182, 183, 184, 185, 187
Rapists, convicted, 194
Ratings game, 64
Reagan. See President Reagan
Reality cues, understanding of, 137–139
Receiver barriers, 62
Receptive learning, 113
Redundant prediction, 191
Reeves, B., 228
Reflective features, 107
Refraction analysis, 273–276
Regions, of United States, 27, 31, 34, 35
Reisen, E., 183
Relevance, of news stories, 99
Reliability, in diagnosis of homicide, 19–20
Remembering, 73
Representation, of knowledge, 72
Research
  applications for news, 100
  artifacts, 342
  bias, 68

calls for pragmatic, 259
current, on news, 77-83
on *The Day After*, 298-301
design, 299
design and data collection, 83-86
experimental, on sexually violent media, 161, 181-185
limits, 214-220, 226-231
longitudinal, 195-196
models of communications, 235-253
in natural environments, 255
new, perspectives, 253-257
news comprehension, 83-95
on newsflow, 75-77, 84-85
on news organizations, 63-65
origin of communications, 208
parallel content analysis as strategy of, 257-264
recommendation of future, 99-100
social problems orientation of communications, 235, 278-279
themes of communication, 210
uses and gratifications, 82-83
Rice, M. L., 146
Rice, R. E., 210
Ritual, in news gathering, 64
Roberts, D. F., 237
Robinson, M., 210, 222
Rogers, E. M., 249, 253, 345
Rolandelli, D. R., 128
Rosengren, Karl Erik, 261
Ross, L., 73
Rothenberg, M. B., 1
Rothman, S., 210
Runtz, M., 180
Ryan, B., 249

S

Sagan, Carl, 296
Salomon, G., 71, 112, 130
Sanday, P. R., 174
Sandinistas, 93
Saturday morning programs, 108
Saturday Night Massacre, 80
Schemas, 72, 73, 75
activation of, 93
affecting, 79
for children, 112
information contradicting, 74
learning of new, 78
most accessible, 75
utility of research on, 99-100
Schiller, D., 64
Scholarly interest, failure to stimulate, 222-223
Scholastic Aptitude Test (SAT), 228
Schrank, R. C., 72
Schreibman, F., 210
Schudson, M., 64
Scripts, 72, 75
Scully, D., 194
Search, 114
Sears, D. O., 187
Segmental cues, 130-131
Self-ratings, 175-177
Selvin, H., 220
Semantic network, 71, 77
Separators and boundary markers, 132
Sesame Street, 105, 107, 110, 124, 125, 151
Setting, 70
Sexual aggression
Ageton on, 189
arousal to, 172-178
availability of, in media, 168
as "positive," 165-166
three classes of, 190-191
See also Physical aggression
Sexual arousal
to aggression, 172-178
sexual aggression as, 165-166
and sexually violent media, 167, 169-179
"Sexual Attitude Survey," 182
Sexual harassment, and wife beating, 196-197
Sexual responses, 175-177
Sexual violence
experimental research on media's, 161
frequency of exposure to, in media, 168-169
indirect effect of, in media, 162
mass media and, 170-171
in media and arousal, 169-179
and nonsexual violence, 167
two routes to, 164
Shapiro, G., 223
Shaw, D., 78, 84, 245, 246, 247, 248, 270
Shaw, E. F., 248
Sheehan, M. A., 210, 222
Sheffield, F. D., 208
Shultz, George, 296
Singer, Jerome, 237
Singer, J. L., 50

Singer, D. G., 50
Singletary, M. W., 168
Sirica, John, 81
Situation defining forms, 70
Smith, M., 298
Smith, R., 130
Soap operas, 168
Social
  behavior, 147–151
  conflicts and knowledge gap, 77
  construction of reality, 66–69
  orientations toward, world, 75
  position, 76
  problems orientation, 235, 278–279
  public knowledge of, environment, 60, 61
"Social and Behavior Science Research Analysis," 161
Sociology, of the press, 206
Somers, A. R., 1
Somoza, 93
Source barriers, 62
South Africa
  as case population, 16–17
  compared to Canada and United States, 17–18
  homicide rates in, 3–4
  television and homicide in, 5–8
  without television, 2–3
Soviet Communist Party, 221
Spinner, B., 183
Spiral of silence, 79, 247, 248–249
Stage, 70
Star, S. A., 226
Star Wars, 105
Stimulating
  mental effort, 142–143
  participation, 143
  scholarly interest, 222–223
Stimuli
  artificiality of, 215
  complexity of, 215
  manipulation of, 113
  package of, 298–299
Stimulus-sampling model, 125–127
Stone, P. J., 220, 225, 259
Stories
  air crash, 87–88
  criticism in news, 89, 90
  dramatization of news, 99
  human interest or conflict, 99
  in human societies, 70

importance and relevance of, 99
innovative, 73
learning and themes of, 87–95
recall of news, 86–87
similar, separated, 98
structure of, 96–99
ten, 87
tightly-constructed, 97
viewer responses to content of, 88–90
Strategic rituals, 64
Structure, of stories, 96–99
Survey research, limits of, 217–220
Symbolic
  communication, 239
  interactionists, 66
Syntax, of television form, 129–133

T

Technology
  information and new, 60
  and public ignorance, 61
Television
  aggression and homicide, 5–8, 20–22, 23
  Amish and, 16
  animation in, 125
  auditory and visual attributes of, 106
  changes in, ownership, 4
  children's comprehension of, form, 129–141
  cognitive operations on, material, 111–112
  exposure to, 2, 25
  forms, 106–111, 116–117, 141, 147–151
  gender connotations of, 133–136
  as information medium, 60
  instant replay for children's, 130–131
  language forms on children's, 108–110
  learning from, 71, 105
  literature on aggression and, 48–53
  as luxury commodity, 45
  in metropolitan and nonmetropolitan areas, 28, 32, 35, 37
  in nine census regions of United States, 27
  "nonlinear" method of, 103
  ownership of, in 1955, 25
  ownership and homicide rates, 6, 15, 27, 30, 34, 35, 36
  programming in Canada and United States, 18
  separators and boundary markers in, 132

shortcomings of, 60
syntactic functions of, form, 129-133
viewing as active or passive, 114
Television and Aggression (Milavsky et al.), 210
Television and Human Behavior (Comstock), 210
Television Network News (Adams and Schreibman), 210
Themes
 of communication research, 211
 of competing interest groups, 88
 contrasting or conflicting, 97-98
 explicitly verbalized, 97
 of human frailty and endurance, 88
 of muckraking, 88
 story, and learning, 87-95
 stress single and clear, 96
 of troubles of "little people," 88, 89
 used in air crash stories, 87-88
Theories
 relating form and social behavior, 147-148
 three, on news, 66-75
 two, on rape, 172-174
Theories of Mass Communication (De Fleur and Ball-Rokeach), 231
Thought patterns
 to antisocial behavior, 185-194
 media exposure to, 180-185
Tichenor, P. J., 77, 85, 251, 252
Time frames
 of effects, 234
 short, 216
Time-series analysis, 249-253, 256, 270-271
Timing
 and *The Day After*, 299
 of television ownership and homicide, 27, 30, 34, 36
Tradition, in news gathering, 64
Truck driver's strike, 91-92
Tuchman, G., 64
TV Guide, 224
TV: The Most Popular Art (Newcomb), 210
Two-step flow theory, 250-251
Type II statistical error, 220

U

Uniform Crime Reports, 28, 29
Union meeting, 92-93

United States, 29, 30
 capital punishment in, 11
 compared to Canada and South Africa, 17-18
 East South Central region of, 31
 as external control population, 17-18
 homicide in, 3, 28
 Middle Atlantic region of, 31
 television and homicide in, 5-8
 television in nine census regions of, 27
 television programs in Canada and, 18
 urbanization in, 4
"Unitel," 2, 50
University of Glasgow, 68
Urbanization
 changes in, 4, 8-9
 homicide rates and, 10, 28, 32, 35, 37-40, 44
Uses and gratifications research, 82-83, 241-244

V

Vallone, R. P., 73
Vanderbilt Television News Archives, 225
Van der Voort, T. H. A., 195
Variable, news comprehension, 86
Variables, affecting flow of news, 76
Verbal formal features, 146
Vietnam War
 conflict over, 12
 legitimizing aggression in, 190
Viewer
 active versus passive, 111
 characteristics, 322-323
 descriptions of story content, 88-90
 difference between nonviewer and, 338-339
 "literate," of television, 130
 recall of political news, 90-95
 of *Viewpoint*, 323, 324
Viewer's Guides, 295
Viewpoint, 296, 298
 differential effects of, panel, 334-336
 effects of, 326
 viewers of, 323, 324
Vigilantes, 165
Violence
 action versus, 121
 in cartoons, 104

definition of, 121
differing baseline rates of, 25
economic prosperity and, 46
and gender, 40, 41
nonsexual media, 194–195
sexual and nonsexual, 167
in successively older age groups, 25–26, 41–43
Visual
formal features of, attention, 118–120
superiority, 128
Vlietstra, A. G., 115
Voting (Berelson *et al.*), 208, 217, 218

W

Wales, 30
"War of the Worlds" (Wells), 136
Washington, D.C., 92
Washington Post, 80, 304
Watergate crisis, 80, 81
Watt, J. H., 127
Weapon, homicide and assault rates by, 14, 16
Weaver, D. L., 210, 246
Weber, Max, 205–207, 261, 277
Weber, R. P., 259, 269
Weitman, S. R., 223
Wells, Orson, 136

Wharton, J. D., 24
The Whole World is Watching (Gitlin), 210
Wiesel, Elie, 296
Wife beating, sexual harassment and, 196–197
The Wizard of Oz, 138
Wolf, S., 342
Women
acceptance of violence against, 182
antisocial behavior against, 163
arousal and disgust of, 173
Woodall, W. G., 73
Woollacott, J., 210
World leaders, attitudes toward, 333
World Politics and Personal Insecurity (Lasswell), 207
Wright, J. C., 115, 124, 125, 128, 132

X

X-rated film, 161, 184

Z

Zabrack, M. L., 2, 50
Zanna, M. P., 186
Zillmann, D., 210
Zimbabwe-Rhodesia, 90–91
Zucker, H. G., 270